Peter Giacomini was born and brought up in rural northern Italy and entered the luxury hotel restaurant profession as a trainee waiter at age fifteen. He became a senior executive with Marriott International with whom he worked for thirty-two years. He is now a public speaker and consultant to the hospitality sector. Peter lives in the sunny south of Portugal.

Peter Giacomini

"Peter has written a fascinating book which details the ups and downs of life and in particular how vital attitude and passion are in becoming successful, no matter what obstacles are put in your way. Peter's courage, expertise and success are known around the world. Peter never underestimated what he could accomplish. This book will inspire you and teach you how to achieve more success than you ever imagined." - *Lee Cockerell, Executive Vice President, Walt Disney World ® Resort (Retired) and author of Creating Magic, The Customer Rules, Time Management Magic and Career Magic.*

Marianne Dojones
Enjoy!

If you want to return. . . .
3513 Quebec St. NW
D.C. 20016
202-363-5250

To Janet, Emily and Paul

Without your unconditional love my life, and therefore this story, would more likely have followed a path to perdition rather than one to success. Never once did you refuse to leave our home, your school and your friends to embark on new adventures in distant lands where foreign tongues, contradictory cultures and religions anything but Christian ruled. Your unflinching support gave me the strength to do better every day and your love remains the fuel which propels me to be the person that I am. For all this I am forever grateful. I love you. - PG

THE
CARDBOARD
SUITCASE

Peter Giacomini

ISBN : 978-1721704002

Peter Giacomini

The Cardboard Suitcase

CONTENTS

Peter Giacomini

FOREWORD

It is said that within every person there is a book waiting to get out. This is undoubtedly true but in reality very few life stories ever escape the realms of the individual's mind and find their way into print. It takes a great deal of time and energy to transform ideas and experiences into a manuscript and the writer must possess the firm conviction that what he has to say will not only be of interest to readers but will capture their imagination and deliver a compelling read.

The Cardboard Suitcase is biographical but it's also a romantic adventure presented with energy and purpose. My story spans six decades, four continents, a host of countries, people of all shades and dozens of the world's finest luxury hotels. It's an epic tale of a lad born into poverty in northern Italy but who cherished a dream to wait on the rich and famous in the splendour of grand hotel restaurants and whose eventual rise in the industry far exceeded even his wildest ambition.

Of course, without the many characters who touched my life, be it briefly or more deeply, and brought to it their experiences and influences there'd be no story to tell. So my thanks go to every single person mentioned in these pages, however grand and meaningful their contribution or however fleeting. All are part of the whole, they are real people in real places and all the events which I describe actually occurred. However, I have chosen to alter the names of some individuals (and of locations pertaining to them) in order to protect their integrity.

And my profound thanks go to fellow author Joseph Tom Riach, my rewriter and editor in chief, without whose outstanding ability and months of relentless dedication my text would not have seen the light of day.

PROLOGUE

Friday July 30th, 1943

The war was still raging. But the day was hot and sunny and the sweet aroma of dry hay wafted on the air of the tiny village of just one hundred and fifty souls which huddled at the foot of the Alps on the western side of Lake Orta in Northern Italy.

The walls of the 1902 vintage house were scarred with the stains of humidity which had soaked through over the years and, in a second floor bedroom, a woman was giving birth. She was assisted in her labour by the village midwife, her mother and two other local women who were well practiced in the art of delivering babies as they had gone through that very exercise themselves many times over. Between them they soon coaxed into the world a tiny boy child ...

And so I was born!

Chapter 1

A WAITER IN THE MAKING

At the time of my birth my father was still serving in Mussolini's decimated army and did not know that his boy was on his way into this world until forty days after I was born. But on the 8th of September of that year the fascist regime collapsed and my dad trekked two weary days back home to find this delightful surprise.

The civil war went on for another two years until the Allied army removed the last German soldier from Italy. These were difficult times as the retreating Germans, helped by the still many loyal fascists, were taking men away from their homes for deportation to labour camps in Germany. It was common for all the men in the village to run to some improvised hiding place or take off to some remote village across the valley that did not have roads on which the German army could take their trucks and motorized vehicles.

Finally the war ended. Yet life was bleak, the destruction was everywhere; factories without roofs, churches with huge craters where once the altar stood and houses with walls barely standing as a result of the air raids which had, for three long years, been a daily event. Like the rest of the families in the village, mine was poor and the war had made them even poorer.

It was difficult for the villagers to put food on the table and it was only thanks to the American help that the children could enjoy the nourishment provided by condensed milk. Along with polenta it was the staple food and its sticky sweetness stayed with you for days. I can still taste it now! And so myself, my older sister Anna, my mother, my father and my grandmother eked out our existence in the old house. My father and mother were doing what could be done to make ends meet and to provide a meal for the family each day.

My grandfather had died in 1940 from alcoholic poisoning as he had spent most of his adult life in a drunken stupor. For the last twenty-two years of his life he had turned the house into a restaurant of which he was both manager and chef.

The fact that he was his own boss gave him the license to down a huge quantity of wine every day then release his drunken rage by flinging regular volleys of pots, pans and any other kitchen ware which came to hand at those around him. My mother was the waitress and nearest person to him so she suffered a great deal. In the last decade of his sad life he would spend the nights roaming around the house with all his kitchen knives under his arm, out of his mind chasing an imaginary enemy he wanted to find and kill. My grandmother, my mother and my father were totally fear stricken.

When my grandfather died the restaurant was immediately closed. A paltry stash of just 500 liras was found, a miserable sum even in 1940, being all there was to show for a lifetime of toil and his years as a restaurant owner. Plus there was a cow in the byre, a pig in the pig-sty, some rabbits and scrawny chickens and a few fields where my mother could grow some potatoes, beans, carrots and anything else God would provide.

I grew, as children tend to, free of the worries my mum and dad were experiencing and enjoyed happy times with the other village boys and girls at the kindergarten school run by the local nuns.

It was during my kindergarten years that I came close to death for the first time. It was at the hands of my father and I still have the scar on the side of my left eye to prove it. I enjoyed helping him to cut and chop wood in the back yard which was the home of the pig-sty, the chicken coop and the rabbit hutch. In that area there was also stored a pile of wood to dry in the summer sun. After cutting the logs they were chopped into smaller pieces so that they would fit inside the stove. On this day, while my dad was chopping one of those logs with a long handled axe and with me watching nearby, one of the pieces flew off and caught me full in the face. I was felled like a tree and thrown to the ground, my face a bloodied mess and I in shock, trembling like a leaf in the wind.

My father rushed to me, picked me up and took me down to the kitchen where my mother, fearing for my life, applied cotton wool over my eye and kept it pressed there until the blood stopped running. Half an inch (1.25 cm) to the left and that huge splinter would have hit my temple and it would have been the end of me.

SCHOOL DAYS

At age six, elementary school started and it was a fun thing to do. The classes were held inside just one room with five grades being taught by the one teacher, juggling materials, books and the personalities of each child. I was fortunate to be a quick learner – and smart. I soon realised that being in the good grace of the teacher was a distinct advantage. This would give me a front seat in the classroom and, in winter, a warm seat near the wood burning stove. My teacher, Signorina Carla Carne, was a single woman in her early forties. In today's day and age she would be considered somewhat unusual as, because of her strong Christian conviction, she had never dated a man.

She was almost certainly a virgin as she displayed those behavioural traits not uncommon in the character of deeply religious and pious people who live a life of restraint. These apparent frustrations led her to harshly discipline some children, particularly those of non church-going, outspoken, politically left-wing inclined parents. For an infraction for which I would receive but a ten minutes 'standing-face-to-wall-in-corner' punishment, Giuseppe, his sister Licia, Pulcino and Gigi would be brought to the front of the class, near the wood burning stove, to be slapped open-handed by her in the face continuously for as long as ten minutes. By the time these poor children were sent back to their seats their faces were red and carried all the marks of Signorina Carne's frustrated fingers. I often cried even more than some of the recipients of the beatings as cruelty is something I could never accept, not to people nor to animals. Today of course, the pendulum as regards punishing school children has swung so far to the other side that, if a teacher even looks sternly at a pupil, he or she might be removed from their post.

Also, when elementary school began, and every winter thereafter, mother had a preventive measure for the colds, coughs and sneezes which the family was sure to suffer from in a house with no heating other than in the kitchen. Her potent concoction was made with six of our chickens' eggs washed, dipped in lemon juice and turned over daily until all the shells dissolved in the juice. The eggs were then carefully removed and their skin punctured to separate the yolk from the white. The whites were put aside to make omelettes while the yolk was put back into the lemon juice and given a good beating. A bottle of egg flavoured marsala wine plus a fair amount of sugar was added and beaten some more until the sugar was completely dissolved.

The mixture was put into used wine bottles and placed in the cold cellar to rest for about a week. Then it was ready for consumption. I was given a shot of the medicine, knocked back in one mouthful, every morning before going to school. Nowadays, were a mother to administer such a home made elixir to her children she might well be jailed for child abuse but in those days it was good and it worked well, keeping us healthy and free from horrible winter colds.

The years passed and the economics were not getting better.

MY FATHER

My father was a very nice man with almost no education and no profession. He would do anything and everything that was legal and moral to be able to feed and clothe us. He worked as a woodcutter in the forest, helped the local masons and worked in factories in the nearest town, a 7.5 miles (12 km) journey he made by push bike in the warmer months of the year and in winter riding the local bus. To catch the bus he had to walk 2 miles (3.2 km) down the hill. When finally the bus came it was usually full so he and other village men would ride on the roof. During the winter when he could not work as a woodcutter or as a helper to the masons, he would set traps in the back yard in the hope of catching sparrows to eat for lunch with some polenta. If you have ever eaten sparrows you will know how bitter they are.

Other than being a loving father who made all sort of sacrifices for us he had a gentle soul, kind and slow to anger. He was also the artist in the family. He could read music, played the trumpet in the municipal band and the mandolin in a dance quintet. But his musical pursuits had to be discarded when he married my mother. Had he continued to play in the bands, it would have meant that every Sunday during the day he would be gone with his fellow musicians to play at some village or other where the patron saint day was being celebrated. In the evening, in the same village, there would be a dance in the workmen's club and his quintet would be asked to play for the dancers. He loved my mother and under no circumstances would he spend the Sundays away from her.

He loved to talk to me in the years to come about music. His favourite piece was Verdi's Va Pensiero from the opera Nabucco. On one occasion his band was required to play that very piece in a competition. While they played very well, at the right tempo and all, another band was given the award. This was due to the fact that the band in which he played was known to be more socialist and not a supporter of the fascist regime which was running the country at the time. He also loved his mandolin and the Neapolitan romantic songs. Some years later I bought him a second-hand mandolin on his birthday but, much to my disappointment, he could no longer remember how to play it. His gift to me is the passion for music I inherited and, albeit with limited talent, I love to sing his favourite aria and think of him.

The fact that we had a cow, a pig and some other domestic animals to sustain us in addition to the fields where to grow some vegetables made us somehow one of the better off families in the village. Oh yes, there were families who had more material things than us, however, the majority had less and we kind of got by somewhere in the middle. But there was little money for essentials, let alone cash to spend on luxuries. In winter it snowed and we fabricated by hand and with a lot of ingenuity, our sleighs to play with in the snow.

Every one of us in the family had one pair of shoes. They were a kind of low boot with a heavy rubber sole, the kind that today you would use to hike on a trail. They were standard throughout the village. Some of my friends even had to share a pair of shoes with their brothers, so we had nothing to complain about. The only problem was that snow burns the leather and the shoes would not last long if we were outside more than was necessary. My father therefore would ensure that we stayed indoors as much as he could. The shoes were a big deal to him. In spring, summer and autumn we would try to play soccer but it was a repeat of the snow scenario with my father coming to drag me inside. Kicking the ball would reduce the life of my one and only pair of boots.

The years passed and my grandmother died. She had been in very bad health and, among other illnesses, she had suffered from arteriosclerosis. This made her extremely violent at times. I vividly remember her attacking my mother, throwing kitchen utensils and other household items at her.

AFTER GRANDMA

With her gone the four of us continued with life, doing what we could to have a reasonable existence. My sister was five years older than I and loved to feel responsible for me; this included administering discipline. Naturally, this part of her caring did not go down well with me and caused a lot of fights. I screamed and kicked her as she tried to take care of me during those early years of my life. During one of those fights I kicked her in the shin and called her a cow. Poor me! My mother heard my profanity and very quickly got hold of a bean stick, chased me down the five steps leading to the locked front gate and whacked me several times on my shins. This kind of mean name calling never happened again.

Christmas presents consisted of a basket with some wrapped candy, an orange, two tangerines and maybe a pair of hand-made socks my mother had knitted during the long winter nights. Invariably there were two or three pieces of charcoal. This signified that Santa was not entirely happy with our behaviour and was our reminder to be better behaved the coming year. But when the following Christmas arrived the coals would still be there. The nativity scene was always set up in the kitchen. Our Christmas tree was a solitary branch of a pine tree. You see we did not own the forest so we could not cut down a tree, a branch had to be enough.

One day my father announced that he was going to work in a foundry manufacturing water taps, hard and unhealthy work. To this day I believe that if you wish to give a health and safety inspector a heart attack all you need do is walk him through one of those factories. The job consisted of working a furnace used to melt down brass. My dad had to reach into the furnace with a long ladle and retrieve the volcanic lava-like, hot melted brass and pour it into moulds held by other men and women. There was no protection from the heat, the smoke and from all the poisonous gasses emanating from the flames and the melting brass.

When my father told us he had found steady work in a factory we were all delighted. I immediately proceeded to give him a list of things I expected him to buy for me from his new found 'wealth'. It included a racing bike, football boots, a real football and the kit of my favourite team; plus all and every object my youthful imagination believed was due to me for all the years of privation I had endured. Well you have guessed correctly, I never got any of them.

Work at the foundry, which eventually caused my father's death, did marginally improve our family situation. His regular take-home pay of about 66 US dollars per month helped to boost our meagre diet. We now enjoyed the added 'luxury' of salt cured anchovies twice a week for lunch and dinners of salt cured merluzzo (cod). The fish was soaked over-night in water to remove the salt and then pan fried in butter and olive oil with garlic and onions. All were eaten with polenta, the traditional corn flour porridge.

I shall never forget when my mum started buying meat at the butcher shop that opened only on Saturday evenings. Of course it was a cheap cut but because of the training she had received from my drunken grandfather she was able to cut out four very thin steaks to be eaten on Saturday night for dinner accompanied with our home-grown vegetables. The rest of the meat would be boiled on Sunday morning and eaten at lunch time with pickled fruits.

The leftovers were for dinner after my dad's return from his Sunday afternoon card game, in winter, or his 'boccie' game in summer, at the workmen's club. My father never in his life ate a meal in a restaurant. Apart from the fact that he felt that the restaurants were charging too much, he couldn't afford it anyway. Sometimes, during his card or 'boccie' game he would feel peckish. Rather than order a sandwich at the bar where he was he would carry a roll and salted anchovies with him to snack on until he came home to his dinner of the left-over boiled meat. But oh the joy and luxury of now having meat to eat on weekends.

A BIKE ARRIVES

A few years passed and then one Christmas morning, lo and behold ... there it was under the pine tree branch, a brand new bike! But after the initial rush of excitement, I looked at it more closely and wanted to die. It was a woman's bike. Worse still it was as green as a frog and with a handle bar so old fashioned that I almost fainted looking at it. My father had the perfect explanation; it was a woman's bike so that both my sister and I could learn to ride it. Had it been a boy's bike my sister could not have ridden it as, in that era, girls did not wear trousers and it was considered most improper for women to raise a leg as required in mounting a man's bike with the cross bar.

My father in all his life only ever possessed a black push bike, no motorcycle and certainly not a car. This meant that his knowledge as to the 'necessities' of a young boy growing up were somewhat limited. He failed to realise that my boy's pride was hurt and that the girl's bike really ate into my young masculinity. How could I let my friends see me riding it? My choices were very limited though.

Either I put aside my pride and take the bike out on the street and start giving myself riding lessons or I would not ride it at all. So I learned a lesson in humility and took the bike out and slowly, very slowly, I learned how to ride it. Strangely enough my sister never learned to ride the bike anyway. That was fine with me because I did not have to share the bike with her. In the event, having the girl's bike didn't turn out too badly after all.

I continually rode the 'frog' (as I had christened it) for quite some time until, one Sunday afternoon, I crashed down a hill and bent part of the already ugly handle bar. Fortunately I was not hurt but my father thought it necessary to take the bike away from me. You see, in his mind I had crashed because I was showing off to the other boys and girls who did not have bikes; that I considered myself better than them and had an affluent father who could buy me a green girls' bike. It was probably one of the lowest points in my entire life. I felt impotent against my father's power and need to teach me a lesson.

And then a radio came into the house, great excitement. It was of German make, a Magnadyne model. I doubt the brand exists now. It was put on a wall shelf in the kitchen. We could only hear the news each evening but on Tuesday nights there was a variety programme my father liked to listen to. The programme started at 9.00 pm, the same hour as our bed-time. A compromise was arrived at whereby we were allowed to stay up until 10.00 pm ... provided we listened to the radio in the dark. My father's reasoning and discipline had a certain logic to it. If electricity was to be consumed by the new radio which he had sacrificed so much to acquire, then power used for lighting had to be saved in order to compensate. It was that or no radio. There was no argument from any member of the family.

And so we were happy. My sister and I were growing up and my parents were growing older.

School went on for me, rather well, but my sister stopped at grade four of elementary education. This meant that at the age of ten she had finished her formal schooling. Like most young girls in the village she started to work doing anything that came along that her limited physical strength would allow her to do. This work included working at drying hay and carrying it to the stable where it was stored to feed the cow during winter months. I, on the other hand, went at age nine part-time to 'university' every evening from 5.00 pm to 8.00 pm, five days a week, and on Thursdays from 7.30 am to 7.00 pm. The name of the university was the 'university of hard knocks'!

THE WATER TAP FACTORY

My 'university' education consisted of learning how to make water taps. The 'professor' was the owner of the factory. He screamed, swore, humiliated and physically kicked and punched us young boys all day long. Any problems with child labour? No, not in those days. While the law was very specific that no one under the age of fifteen was supposed to work, it was common practice that all of us, boys and girls, would go to work full time at age eleven after we had completed the fifth year of elementary education. I was to be no exception. It would have been shameful for me to go on to three more years of formal education. At least that is what my father said to my mother when she begged him to let me go into town and attend school there.

Oh yes, he did have a valid argument. For me to catch the bus to town I would have had to walk for 2 miles (3.2 km) down the hill in the morning and back up the hill in the evening. My dad felt that, with the snow and all, it would have been too much for a young boy my age to endure. Yet I ended up doing exactly that as my 'university' moved to the town where I would have had to catch the bus. So I walked that road up hill and down every day until I was fifteen years old.

During these years I learned that attending Mass every Sunday, being a good altar boy and being nice to the local priest had its advantages, besides the drinking of the communion wine before the priest arrived! The priest was also the brother of my teacher. I already had an 'in' with her and being an altar boy from seven to fourteen years of age meant that I could get access to the regulation football, a pair of skis and, since he had the only car in the village, once in a while he took us boys on short trips in his 'giardinetta'. It was a small five door FIAT with a brown wood body. Today when I look back at those days it amazes me how congenial it all was.

In the years following the end of the war many men from our area, both single and married, had to emigrate to other countries around the world in order to find work and support their families. As we had a quarry in the village many were masons to trade and stone workers, so they could earn well abroad and send badly needed money back home. The disadvantage however, of this mass emigration of men folk was that young women were left with little opportunity to find a husband. This meant that the handful of young men still in the village were faced with the terrible responsibility of shepherding the entire female population from precocious adolescence into full fledged womanhood. Not unsurprisingly, a lot of illegitimate children were born in the process!

As for married women whose husbands had emigrated to Switzerland, Germany, France, England, Argentina and many other places, they too were missing the warmth and the touch of their men. There resulted many cases of domestic confusion and not knowing if babies born were prematurely or if they were conceived by some miraculous stork flying over the village.

TELEVISION AND WINE

By that time also television had arrived in the village at the workmen's club. A big set, black and white picture of course and with a huge antenna stuck in the yard. You can imagine what a novelty that was. On Thursday nights there was a programme hosted by an American-Italian called Mike Bongiorno. He had come to Italy along with the TV show's American format to find his fortune while most of our men were trying to find it somewhere else. But yes, it did work for him. He became rich and famous plus all of the girls in the country absolutely adored him. My sister even named our cat after him.

On Sunday afternoons there was a show presented by a Neapolitan singer and his band and another variety show which was a run-down on all the famous people who had arrived and departed from the different airports around the country during the past week. It was during these afternoon that I had my first experience with the effects of wine.

All the boys of the village of all ages would gather at the workmen's club after vespers to watch the two programmes. I was ten or eleven years old at the time. One of the older boys (now very old, still living in the village and seriously ill with liver cirrhosis) bought wine for all of us. To be at the club and being given straight wine to drink was illegal but, as always, nobody cared. During the show this older lad encouraged us to drink. By just the second glass my head was spinning and my stomach was telling me to get up and go outside to vomit. I did that and not only vomited the wine but apparently my entire innards too. I felt worse than horrible.

One of the irresponsible games that the older boys were playing was to buy us younger lads wine to see who would get drunk first. Then they'd laugh their heads off at the crazy things we would say and get up to. It was innocent enough but it did not do any good to the victims' well-being. I barely made it home that day and when my mother saw me she got quite a scare. When she reported to my father what had happened he immediately marched off to the guilty party's home and sought out his father for a serious tête-a-tête. I have no idea what was said but that boy never bought me wine at the club again.

Working as a waitress in my grandfather's restaurant had given my mother the experience of seeing people enjoying the service she was providing. From an early age she would talk to me about how it felt to be of service to people in that way. It was she who, contrary to the word of others, always maintained that to be a waiter in a luxurious hotel in Rome, Paris, London or New York was the best job in the world one could have. She would describe to me how it would feel to be dealing with kings, princesses, the rich and the famous even though her own experience of being waitress in my grandfather's restaurant had hardly taken her to such dizzy heights. No matter, she had imagination. With that she would carry us to all those places and more. She would describe them to me just as if we were there and living the experience.

Her enthusiasm was contagious to say the least. I easily saw myself as a famous waiter in black tuxedo and welcoming guests in a luxurious hotel in one of those cities she had never (with the exception of one week of honeymoon in Rome) seen. I felt I was walking on Persian rugs under Murano chandeliers, serving the emperor of Ethiopia, the president of Indonesia, the actor Clark Gable and all those other celebrities whose names I had only heard mentioned by city visitors to our village in summertime.

So the seed was planted and I knew what I wanted to become in life - a waiter in a luxurious hotel in Rome, Paris, London or New York!

Chapter 2

THE LITTLE WORLD OF CENTONARA

THE VILLAGE

Centonara barely merited the title of 'mountain village' as it is perched on the slopes between the lakeshore and the foot of the Alps at just 1,722 feet (525 m) above sea level. But a mountain village it is.

The four seasons were very clearly defined by mother nature and each in turn showed its beauty and presented its gifts. Spring time started as soon as the snow began to melt with snowdrops piercing through the remaining patches of the no longer pristine white carpeting. Primroses with their magnificent colours - some yellow, some white, some red, some purple – soon followed, turning the field into the most spectacular kaleidoscope of colour you could ever wish to see. The fruit trees were not to be left behind and they too covered themselves in seasonal dress. The apple trees with their white and pink blossoms; the prune trees also bedecked in white, pink and touches of red; the cherry trees wore white and dark pink. The grass in the meadows would not be short-changed and it turned to the richest green imaginable.

Summer was the time when every villager was out and about until after ten at night as it was warm and pleasant to be out of doors. It was the time to cut the hay. Men used scythes, women used sickles. It was dried in the sun. After a few days when it was ready, the women would climb with it up the rustic wooden ladder to the stable's upper floor where it was stored as winter feed to sustain the cows, sheep and goats through the long winter months. We, the children, all shed our winter woollies and hand-knitted long socks and wore shorts. School was out and we all enjoyed playing in the streets and in the fields.

One of the favourite games was to throw stones at the sleeping lizards with the aim to chop off their tails. Cruel as it was, the child who chopped off the highest number of tails was the winner and kingpin, at least until another kid beat his tally and dethroned him. Another cruel game was to catch dragon flies and attach a string to their tail and see if they could fly away. Cicadas and crickets were the musicians who would sing and play during the day while frogs and toads would take over at night.

As it started to get dark thousands and thousands of fireflies would light up the sky. We would catch them and put them in a glass jar, cover it with paper and pierce a few small holes in it with a sewing needle with the good intention to let air into it so they could breathe. When we finally went to sleep the jar would be placed on the bedside table and the fireflies would continue spreading their light while we fell asleep. Needless to say the poor creatures would die overnight and all that we could do was empty the jar, wash it out and get it ready for the following evening's inhabitants.

Autumn was no less present in our lives. School invariably started the first week of October. The long hand-knitted socks and long trousers would come out again and be worn until Easter; heavy jumpers and mittens would also become the norm. The trees would change their seasonal dress and all the leaves would turn to rich golden hues. The chestnut was the most majestic. By November they were loaded with prickly husks turning yellow, falling to the ground and opening, revealing their beautiful brown and shiny chestnuts which were collected and carried home. Some were eaten straight away, either roasted or boiled, and some were dried in the weak sun to be eaten during the winter months ahead. The prickly husks would be collected and burned while the leaves were dried in the woods and then carried to the stable to be used as bedding for our solitary cow.

Mushrooms were also growing in the woods further up the mountain and my father would trek for miles looking for them. I was too lazy to go with him and besides, I was incapable of distinguishing the edible from the deadly. The mushrooms he collected were pan fried in butter with garlic and parsley and made a delicious topping for polenta, our staple food. Trout fishing was also in season and my father went fishing every Sunday morning. Without fail he returned home with some lovely fresh trout. Some we would eat the very same day and some would be sold to those more affluent people who found it was much easier to buy them than go for miles up the steep river banks to fish for them.

By December it was winter. I do not remember a Christmas during my childhood without at least a foot of white snow on the ground. Snowmen were made. Snowball battles were staged. Hand-made sleighs would come out and the fun started. Christmas came and went. The three kings and also the befana (the good witch) who brought gifts to the children on January the 6th came and went too. The cast iron, wood-burning stove was lit by mother at 4.00 am each morning and would roar happily until our 9.00 pm bedtime; at which hour we all went to bed with a bottle of boiling water to take the frost out of the sheets before we could lie down on them.

Centonara was so beautiful!

It was almost beyond belief that, in a small village like that, so many things had happened and would continue to happen. I was too young to understand most of the goings-on and the involvements of the various families in them. It was only when I grew older that I could start to comprehend the intrigue and drama which intertwined the lives of the inhabitants and the tragedies that occurred and recurred year after year, passed from generation to generation almost as a birthright.

During the long winter nights it was customary for the families to get together at one or other of their homes, sit around the wood burning stove and eat roasted or boiled chestnuts. While the women knitted socks and cardigans they would exchange tales of witchcraft and who in the village had a bastard child and by whom. The men talked about the two world wars and the Italian war in Africa. One particular story related to the first world war was that a soldier came home on leave unexpectedly. He claimed to be cold and urged his wife to put more and more wood into the cast iron stove. Once the stove was red hot he became very romantic. He proceeded to undress his wife in the kitchen with the excuse that it was the only warm place in the house where they could enjoy an intimacy far too long missing in their lives. Once his wife was naked he lifted her and forced her on to the hot stove, holding her down until she died in ghastly pain!

Another soldier from the village had apparently returned to the regiment after a spell of leave and informed the man that it was rumoured that, while he was fighting the Austrians in the trenches, his wife in the village was having a wonderful time in his own bed with a much younger man. And this was the cause of the fury in this man which led him to murder her without even asking if the allegation was true or not.

OUR HOME

Our home was the last at the far western end of the village. It was old, relatively solid and by the standard of the times it had all one could wish for. It was mercifully humid and cold in summer as air conditioning was non-existent.

The house stood between the stone mulattiera (mules' road) which crossed the village to continue up the mountain to the next village and a walking path with a small brook running down to the river which, in turn, flowed to the lake. Where the front walls narrowed there were three steps to a green iron gate. Five more steps passed the gate before reaching a cement courtyard on which a small dirt strip served as a flower garden. A huge hydrangea bloomed there every summer sending exhilarating aromas throughout the house. There was also a wisteria growing up from the dirt which created an arch over the green gate and added its beautiful smell to the house.

At the other end of the yard stood a concrete table which, at the time of the restaurant, was used by diners in the summer months to set down drinks while chatting and smoking. Also there was the laundry wash basin where mum, once a month, would wash the bed sheets of the family after she had boiled them using ashes from the stove and the fireplace as detergent.

At that level there was also the kitchen. It was the heart of the house, where everything happened. In the centre of it there was the life of the house, which was the cast iron stove. To the right of the stove there was the rustic rectangular wooden table and four straw chairs, one for each member of the family. The table also had a drawer where mum kept the loose change for regular purchases at the shop, from the cheese man, the equine butcher and the regular butcher each week. I used to steal from her little metal box 200 liras (about 30 cents) every Sunday to go to the local bar to play table football. Fortunately for me I was never found out.

My father shaved every Wednesday and every Saturday evening. Strangely, after going to bed on those nights, I would invariably hear through the partition wall separating our rooms, my mother laughing until I would fall asleep. The next morning I would ask her why she was laughing and she would blush lightly and say, "Your father is a naughty boy and he was tickling me under my arms all evening." I thought that that was a childrens' game and that adults no longer played it.

Then a sewing machine was purchased for my sister. She was expected to learn how to make her own dresses and also working shirts for the men of the house. The machine was placed in the kitchen opposite the table on the other side of the stove. Some time after that my mother bought a three burner gas top to cook on in the summer months. This was a treat as she did not have to get up early in the morning to light it. The hunchback mayor was also the gas canister supplier and when gas was needed either my sister or I would run to tell him that we needed a new canister. Netto, more about him to come, would be summoned by the mayor and given the canister to be brought over to the house and connected.

Against the furthest wall in the kitchen there was the open fireplace. This was used only for making polenta and roasting chestnuts in the appropriate pan and iron skillets. A long chain hung above the burning wood with a large hook attached to hold the skillet or the pan, depending on what we were preparing. Also at the corner stood my grandfather's stove, still in place but only used twice a year. Once when the family came together to celebrate the patron saint day and then on the day the pig was slaughtered. The light in the kitchen came through the door and one window. The kitchen was the place in which, shortly after starting school at age six I had, for the second time in my life, a brush with death. This time I was entirely to blame and only my father's quick reaction saved my life.

SUGAR AND SPICE?

As a child my two favourite foods were sugar and, not spice, but salt. Whenever I could I would eat either of them by the handful. A craving for and eating of salt freely was considered a sign of wisdom. There is a famous Latin saying – 'sal sapientiae' – which refers to it. This, at least, was the excuse I gave for eating handfuls of salt when my parents chastised me. Eating sugar by the spoonful was, on the other hand, considered pure gluttony and absolutely unacceptable. So most of the time I had to satisfy my craving for sugar in secret when absolutely no one and I mean no one, especially my sister, Anna, could see me - as she would tell on me.

On this particular occasion my father, fortunately for me, had joined my mother, my sister and I for a cup of tea. My mother loved everything that was English as her aunt had spent thirty-six years living in London. Among other material things and habits she had brought back to the village when she returned was the custom of enjoying an afternoon cup of tea. Our afternoon tea was in no way comparable to what you would get in a fancy hotel in London. Ours consisted of three dry biscuits each and a cup of cheap black tea with some cold milk graciously provided by Oliva, our cow. Sugar was kept in a metal rectangular box and was taken directly from there to be put in the tea cups and stirred.

As we sat there my eyes settled on the metal box. My lust for its sweet contents gradually overcame me until, unable to resist the temptation, I reached over the table and with my two small hands grabbed hold of the large can. I lifted it up high and poured the sugar into my mouth as if I were drinking it. The reaction in my throat and mouth was immediate as the sugar filled my wind pipe and I could not breathe. My face quickly turned blue and it was only my father's natural reaction which saved my life. He got hold of my feet, turned me upside down, stuck two fingers down my throat and freed all the sugar from my mouth so I could breathe again. Had I died, is this what would be called a case of 'white death'?

A few years later the kitchen would also become the place where my friends, both boys and girls, would get together on Sunday afternoons in winter to practice dancing tangos, waltzes, the cha-cha-cha and the fashionable mambo. Music was provided by borrowed 78 rpm records played on my great aunt's manual turntable which she had carried all the way back from London in 1936.

The single light bulb in the kitchen hung from the ceiling as did four large hooks. Long poles were inserted into those hooks and once a year, when the pig was slaughtered, salami were hung there to dry before being put in terracotta jars with melted fat poured over them to act as a preservative. Two pancettas, today considered a specialty, would also be produced from the belly of the pig and hung along with the salami to dry for about forty days, depending on how cold and wet the winter was.

Every year I spent the morning of the pig slaughtering crying; but it really was quite a ceremony. On the Saturday night Bili, the pig butcher, would send to the house his huge case containing all the instruments used during the slaughter of the pig. There were also those used to make the salami, the lard, the pancetta and the black pudding (blood sausages). To me they looked terrifying. I envisioned the suffering which the poor pig my mother had so caringly tended for an entire year would have to go through before it died.

My father, three of his friends and Bili would normally be in the kitchen by 5.00 am. The day started with a generous shot of grappa (a powerful liquor that contains up to 120 US proof per volume) downed in one gulp before proceeding to the back yard and the pig-sty. One year my father spilled some of the grappa on the plate which served as a tray. Not wanting the liquor to go to waste he drank it straight from the plate but he swallowed it down the wrong pipe and we really thought that the one to die that morning would be him and not the pig!

Next, the pig was let out of the pig-sty and given some feed in the middle of the back yard. One of the men would sneak up behind it with a rope in his hands, make a loop around one of the rear legs, pull the rope with all his strength and the poor pig would fall. At that same moment the other three men and Bili would run to it, each of the men grabbing hold of a leg to hold it down. This was the most cruel moment of the day. Bili, without much of a fuss, would stick a wooden pole down the throat of the screaming animal and, with a very long fine knife, pierce into its heart hoping that the knife would get to it at the first attempt.

After those few tense moments the rest of the day was fun and by the time the day came to an end we had secured good food for the next year and most of the men helping the butcher would be well into a high level of intoxication provided by cheap wine.

COOL AND DARK

The pantry was really a small room under the stairway to the two floors above. It contained a concrete wash basin with cold running water. The dishes, the glasses, pots and pans were washed in a basin of water boiled on the stove, in winter, and on the gas burner in summer. It was a tedious job but had to be done.

The pantry also had two wooden shelves along the wall where all the kitchen equipment for daily use was stored. There was a space where the home-made salami jars were stored and the lard from the pig, cured under salt, was also kept there in a wooden barrel. Because that area was so humid there was a huge population of slugs which appeared every night. They would all disappear by the time we got up but left behind long streaks of silver slime that was quite disgusting to look at. We put down poison and salt hoping to kill them off.

The cellar, strangely enough, was a step up from the kitchen and, because it was dug out of the side of the hill, it was always cold and humid. Not having a refrigerator we kept all the perishable food there. The little brook flowing by the side of the house was slightly diverted and the water channeled through to the cellar. It was funneled into a cement basin in which a few bricks were laid. The home-made butter, the cow cheese and sometimes the purchased goat cheese would be set there to stay fresh.

This was also where my father made his wine from the only variety of grape growing in the area. This grape was called American grape and the wine nicknamed Americanin, which means the little American in the local dialect. It was a very acid wine and not really pleasant. It generally had to be drunk mixed with water. My sister and I were given some of this wine every evening. As we grew up the amount of water would be reduced and the measure of wine increased. By the time we were fourteen it was pure wine. As this was common practice in all the households it's small wonder that there were so many alcoholics in the village.

Once a year, on Saint Mary Magdalene day, mother would retreat to the cellar and emerge with the best mayonnaise ever which she'd prepared to top a delicate dish of veal and tuna fish sauce. What a delight.

Separated from the kitchen by a wall and a connecting door was the naturally well-lit dining room. This room had more light than the kitchen. Beside the connecting door from the kitchen it had its own door to the yard, two glass-paned windows at the side of the mulattiera road and another one on the yard side of the house. The room was only used twice per year for lunch and sometimes, on very special occasions, for an afternoon tea.

During the time my grandfather owned the restaurant it was the main dining room for the patrons as well as the place where the locals could meet to play cards on Saturday night and Sunday afternoon. Now it had two large wooden tables, six chairs made out of straw and one old china cabinet where the fancy porcelain dishes and the nicest glassware were kept. We treasured the tea cups and the real fine espresso cups my great aunt had brought back from London and rarely used them (some of these cups are still used by us on special occasions in our home in Arizona). This room also was the garage for my father's black road bike. The room was also the most humid apart from the cellar and the inside walls were in a dreadful state.

A HIGHER PLACE

Exiting the kitchen door, sharp to the right there was a huge wooden door and behind it the granite stairs with sixteen steps taking you to the upper floors. On the landing, a green wooden door led to the house's only toilet. The toilet consisted of a Turkish WC (the type one had to squat down upon) and one hand sink with running cold water. Because we did not have toilet paper there was no need to have a toilet paper holder. Instead we used to cut a newspaper into small squares and hang them on a nail stuck into the wall. When there was no newspaper, we used nothing.

There was no bathtub or shower in the house but, as no other house in the village had them either, none of the villagers bathed and we all smelled equally as bad!

My mother and sister were probably the cleanest women in the village. In order to achieve this they would carry a basin of boiling water up the sixteen steps to the bathroom, add cold water from the tap and do the best they could to clean up. My father and I, like all other men, only washed on Saturday night. The washing was done in the kitchen with a basin of boiling water with cold water added. We would strip to the waist and with a cloth wash our upper body and arm pits, then use the same water to wash our feet. No other part of the body was ever, and I mean ever, washed. Before going out for the evening we would smear our hair with gel and plaster it down to the head with a centre parting like Rudolph Valentino, the famous '20s Italian-American movie star. Boy, were we cool or what?

25

A small corridor with a wooden floor led out on to the veranda stretching the entire front length of the house. My sister and I shared the bedroom off the corridor. The room was small with two single, very high metal beds. The headboard on mine was painted with a hunting scene. My sister's was altogether more feminine, the headboard depicting a more peaceful scene of a river gently flowing into a mountain lake. There was a bedside table in which a night pot was stored as in the winter nights going out on to the corridor and to the toilet was out of the question. We had one chest of drawers where our clothes were kept plus a trunk by the window for extra storage. On the wall a print of the Sacred Heart was hanging along with a crucifix topped with a small olive branch which was renewed every year on Palm Sunday.

Off to the left, half way through the veranda was our parents' bedroom. This was slightly larger than our room. A high, wooden, king size bed carried the marks on the foot end of the frame made by a German soldier hitting it with his gun barrel while insisting that my mother turn in my father during one of their retreating marches toward the Austrian border. There were two bedside tables, a wardrobe with a full length mirrored door, a chest of drawers and a large straw armchair with two cushions on it.

The chest of drawers was off limit to me as stored there was my grandfather's unlicensed hand gun which my father had kept. It was a blessing the retreating German soldiers never found it. Had they done so that would have given them enough cause to burn down the house and the entire village!

Once, like all boys fascinated with firearms, I defied the prohibition and took the gun out to play with. I loaded a bullet but when the time came for me to remove the bullet from the case I could not do it. Fortunately I eventually succeeded and was able to replace the gun as I had found it. Had I not, then the consequences could have been drastic – being confined to the house, having my toys and games confiscated and the Sunday afternoon record playing sessions cancelled.

On the right end of the veranda the stair led to the solarium.

This was a large, open terrace-like space which, in the days of the restaurant, had been the summer dining room. It had a different use now as mother would store here chestnuts, walnuts, beans and all the other vegetable that could be left out in the air and didn't need to be stored in the cellar. It was also a general storage space. We used to love this area. As the name suggests, the sun shone on it from early morning to the end of the day.

Additionally it had a beautiful view of the lake below, the chain of mountains across the lake and Mottarone. This is the highest peak at 4,500 feet (1,492 m) and always the first mountain top around the lake to be covered with snow in winter. In the early fifties a ski resort was set up and it is still thriving today. In summer we would eat our Sunday lunch in the solarium, provided we helped mother to take the dishes up and down. As the sole waitress in the twenty-two years that the house was the Fioravanti Restaurant she had served all the meals up there, climbing those stairs up and down every day about a million times. So she had promised herself that she would never carry a plate up there ever again. By golly she kept her promise.

On the landing of the stairs a door connected to the newer part of the house built by my great aunt in 1936 upon her return to the village. The house was flanked by some small fields on which stood a walnut tree, a hazelnut tree and where vegetables were planted and grown every year.

In this house I spent, happily, the first fifteen years of my life.

THE VILLAGE CASTLE

Yes, the village had a castle … well kind of.

It was actually a house, but a rather beautiful one. It sat at the entrance of the village near the little church dedicated to the village patron-saint, Saint Mary Magdalene. This house contained several luxurious apartments which were rented to city families to enjoy summer holidays at the foot of the Alps and at the lake. The area attracted painters. They were often to be found by the waterside or in the foot-hills in the early morning or late evening.

They would lovingly paint water colour scenes of the lake, sunrises, sunsets, the rivers and the snow-capped mountain tops.

My favourite holidaying family were the Buonarottis; older father, mother and one unmarried daughter. I loved when they came because I was hired for the entire summer to go to them at eleven o'clock each morning. They'd send me to the village shop to fetch their shopping. I got paid for that work something like a quarter of a dollar a month and I was happy with that.

Then there was the mayor of the village, his live-in companion and his son Agostino from his abandoned wife. They lived in the bottom floor apartment. The mayor was a hunchbacked man. He was the scandal in the village. At that time living with a woman without being married to her was not an everyday affair and always got the gossip machine going.

He also ran the workmen's club and it was said that he watered down the wine and pocketed the profit. His son Agostino was a Marshal in the uniformed police in Milan and something of a local personality. He had fought as a volunteer in the Spanish Civil War of 1936 to 1939. That, and the fact that he drove a rather cute little FIAT Topolino black convertible, cemented his celebrity status.

It is hilarious to recall that the same mayor who had a live-in mistress would impose fines on holidaying girls from the city for wearing shorts. But he did. Not that it made any difference. The girls, mostly young and carefree, continued to cavort in the sunshine unaware that they were contravening any silly local law.

THE WORKMEN'S CLUB

This was the social centre of the village. It was open every day as the manager, who was also the mayor as you'll recall, had moved there from the castle where he used to live with his mistress and his son. The good point of this was that if you happened to run out of wine in the middle of your lunch, you could simply pop over to the club with an empty bottle and 100 liras and get a litre of his watered down wine.

Every evening a bunch of hardcore card players would meet there and play cards into the wee small hours of the morning, drinking several litres of the same wine. Then, according to a local tradition dating back many generations, they'd line up against the nearby wall and empty their bladders before going home to sleep. Because of this continuous practice it was advisable, particularly so in summer, to only get near the workmen's club after sunset. If you really had to go by that wall it was suggested that you held your breath, pinched your nose and ran past as fast as your legs would carry you.

Since the arrival of the first television in the village, Thursday night had become a very popular night. This because an American style show called 'Leave or Double It' was on. It was a quiz where participants were asked questions about a selected subject. A correct answer saw their money doubled and they could win up to 5 million liras. In those days this sum would buy a three bedroom apartment in Rome. But, when their answer was wrong they were eliminated and were out of the game.

The entire village attended each Thursday night, from the oldest to the youngest. My sister and I were allowed to go. Our entire week's budget was spent in that night by buying a lemonade and putting 50 liras towards the collection to pay for the TV. This amount was equal to about 12 cents of a US dollar, but it was money well spent. My sister would sit there mesmerized by the Italian-American host of the show, Mike Bongiorno.

Another highlight of village life was when, once a month, an apprentice barber (maybe sixteen years old) would come from a nearby village to cut the hair of all the men and boys. Because the barber was afraid of the dark his mother would accompany him. From about 6.00 pm to 10.00 pm he would busy himself making a complete mess of the heads of all the men and boys who were foolish enough to expose themselves to his untrained hands.

Once a year on the feast of Saint Mary Magdalene, the workmen's club would dress up for the occasion and bring in a band, normally a quintet from a nearby town, to play dance music.

The tango, waltz, samba and mazurka were the dances of the time and the occasion was lots of fun for everybody. The children were allowed to sit next to the band and watch them play while the young adults danced and the youths tried to impress whichever girl they most fancied. The older couples just danced and all had a great time.

I, as an altar boy, had been imbued with strong Catholic principles which implied that dancing was sinful. Each year I would not sleep on the night of the dance. I had this nightmare in which the devil transformed himself into a huge snake and took all of the people from the dance floor off to hell. My trepidation was only relieved once I saw all those people in the village on the following day and again going about their business as usual!

THE FUSOS

This was a family, still existing today who, because they were farmers, had probably the best life of us all. The family was composed of father Ernesto, his wife Angela, sons Gianni, Pietro and Dino and two sisters.

The family owned about thirty cows and a fair amount of land and also worked other people's land for which they did not pay any rent. They also owned woods and sold firewood to the other villagers. Their mule named Araz had been bought at a surplus equipment sale from the armed forces and was their locomotion machine, carrying all the supplies up the mountain to where the cows were. Araz was a funny animal and when I think of her I feel like laughing as I did when I was a child. As she walked past our house early in the morning she would leave behind a concert of farts one could hear a long distance away.

Pietro, the middle boy, was the working son. He did everything the patriarch asked of him and never took a day off. He was a very reliable son. He worked from sunrise to sunset minding the cows, cutting hay, working the fields, chopping down trees, bringing the wood home on a cart pulled by Araz and preparing the wood for sale. Pietro met a nice girl from a nearby village, got married and had two sons who, as of today, carry on doing exactly as their father had done. The only difference is that Araz died and is replaced by a tractor.

The oldest boy, Gianni, was, on the other hand, the black sheep of the family. He loved to drink and get drunk, prefering cards and boccie at the workmen's club to tending cows, working the fields or handling wood. Work was not his favourite past-time. He did however have one of the first motorcycles that came to the village. A red Parilla 125 cc!

One Monday morning on my way to school I bumped into him walking towards the village pushing the motorcycle. His face, hands and legs were covered in blood and he was so drunk that he could barely stand. It transpired that he had drunk himself stupid at the workmen's club the previous night, had left there at 1.00 am and had crashed his bike into a ditch. He had lain unconscious there all night until shortly before I met him staggering home. Such events were of course not uncommon in his life and he eventually died, victim of his incessant drunkeness and the cheap wine of the bars and workmen's club he frequented. He left behind a wife and two sons and, as the saying goes - "qualis pater talis filius" - like father like son! At least that is true of one son; the other has taken more from the hard working uncle.

LINA

Lina was a single woman reputed to have overactive hormones as she could not stay long without a male companion. Because of this she was the subject of the gossip of the 'well-to-do' women of the village who were 'more pious then thou' and therefore felt fit to judge her. She had first become the focus of such gossip when it was noticed that the cheese salesman, on his weekly visit to the village, spent an inordinate amount of time inside her house while the rest of the women waited impatiently for their turn ... to buy cheese!

When the cheese salesman stopped coming to the village she got more serious about her relationships. She took in a steady boyfriend named Maurizio who abandoned his wife in her favour. This despite his wife being much younger, more attractive and, by hearsay, a better lover than Lina. This Maurizio, according also to village gossip, was a child molester. He allegedly took advantage of a young cripple girl who was deformed from polio. There was never hard evidence (such as the girl falling pregnant) that anything illegal or immoral ever took place and Lina and Maurizio saw their lives through to old age together.

THE CAVALLIS

The patriarch Cavalli had passed away long before I came on the scene but his wife was still alive and remained so for many years. Once she told my mother something about me that I'd rather have kept secret and I got into real trouble as a result. I soon learned that in the village there were no sacred cows.

The son, Santo, was a good young man, conservative and well to do. He was the sacristan of the little village church of Saint Mary Magdalene. Once a year during the feast in honour of the patron saint, the 'nice people' of the village would bring home-made cakes, butter loaves, baskets of fruit, cow milk cheese and any other gift they though appropriate to the church and Santo would auction them off in support of the church upkeep fund.

He had served in the war in North Africa. By good fortune he was taken POW by the British and spared the El Alamein slaughter where so many Italians soldiers were killed. During the long winter nights while touring different homes and eating chestnuts with his village buddies, he told this war story :- As POWs, he and the other Italian prisoners were given the choice by their captors to either eat in the Italian kitchen three meals per day or in the British kitchen and eat five meals per day. Of course they chose the five meal regime until they realised that the five meals included 'elevenses' and a light supper which, even when added to the other three meals, could in no way match the spaghetti meals of the Italian kitchen. So they all reverted to choosing the Italian way!

Santo had a brother, Rico, who moved to the nearby city and

married. I don't remember him well. He also had two sisters, Roberta and Guglielmina. Roberta married a guy from a nearby village who owned a water tap factory and moved there. Guglielmina married one of the two carpenters of the village and had a son and lived in a nearby house happily ever after. Santo himself was by now getting on in age and had to find a wife. My parents were extremely good friends of Santo's family and therefore he asked my father if he would ask my mother to ask Olivia, a beautiful young woman, if he could date her. My mother arranged their very first rendez-vous and, sure enough, they got married and had two sons, Lorenzo and Roberto.

Santo had the most conservative motorcycle in the village, it was a Galletto by Guzzi. Everyone in the village laughed about this motorcycle but his reasoning for having it was sound ... he could ride the bike wearing his suit and not have oil spilled on his trousers. He also had the only wine press in the village and, as my father made his own wine every year, it was Santo's press which squeezed the last drops of wine from the residue of dad's grapes.

Santo is now 93 years old, still happily married to Olivia. Their sons are grown up men. Lorenzo, a very successful hotelier, is retired and living back in Italy in his wife Carolina's village. They have a daughter, a very successful lawyer in New York, and a son. Roberto lived twenty-nine years in the UK before returning to the village to be with his parents. He has his own apartment within their large house.

THE NUNS

The Cavallis' house was divided into two parts. Entering the main door there was first the convent of the nuns! There were several and they performed the most humble tasks in the village – such as being the kindergarten teachers, looking after the sick and elderly, helping the priest with the church activities and growing vegetables in their garden to donate to the less fortunate. It was common knowledge that during the war the mother superior had put herself in front of a German firing squad in an attempt to stop them executing a partisan.

As for her predecessor, before my time, she was reputedly tormented by Satan himself, chasing her around the convent, pushing her down stairs and beating her. My mother would say that she would show up with marks all over her face and hands which, because of her attire, were the only visible parts of her body. Whether this is true or not is impossible to confirm but she has been proposed for sanctification.

ORCO STRETTO

He was the owner of my first 'university'. That one of hard knocks where, at nine years of age, I started working making water taps. He was the bastard son of the mayor and his live-in mistress Gigliola. An extremely mean man, apt to lose his temper in seconds, he would scream, blaspheme, push and kick the boys working in his factory. I was one of the abused. My wages amounted to the equivalent of 5 cents an hour. He had purchased a police surplus 500 cc Guzzi motorcycle through his half brother the Marshall to which he attached a side-car, home-made of course. With that he would transport taps from the other factories to his in order to work them and return them. A year or so later he moved his factory 2 miles (3.2 km) away, next to the factory in which my father worked and, naturally, I went with him.

Years later when our daughter and son were still little, maybe seven or eight years old, he was retired, a widower and still living in the village. He had a grown up daughter, had taken up beekeeping and produced honey for sale. He was kind to our children and they nicknamed him 'Mr.Honey'. Amazing how age can mellow a man.

THE MIOLIS

They were also known as the Allemagnas in a derisory reference to a wealthy Milanese family who operated large factories producing ice cream and panettoni, the traditional Italian Christmas cake. They were one of the most colourful families in the village. Pietrone was the father and grossly overweight, his wife Gianinna was as slim as a broomstick. Ettore was the oldest son, Aurora the daughter, Ferno the third child and Sparto the fourth child; in total three boys and one girl.

Pietrone had no passion for work and remained unemployed as long as he could. He lived off all the odd jobs Gianinna would do and then the wages of his children when they became old enough to work. But he was a talented musician and every day at noon, while the rest of the villagers took lunch, he would pick up his trumpet and start playing to the delight of all. This, however, did not spare him being the butt of the standing joke which said that as they had nothing to eat due to Pietrone's laziness they would replace the lunch with good music.

The family all lived in a rented house consisting of one kitchen and one bedroom. There was no running water and the toilet was under the stair that led up to the living quarters of the house. They used chestnut leaves laid out on the floor on which to deposit their excrements and once every six months or so, they shoveled the waste into a wooden back basket and carried it to a field not far from our home. For several days afterwards we would have to endure the uncomfortable smell invading the entire village but mainly our home. The children however, turned out very different from the father regarding work ethic ... and bathrooms!

Aurora, the only daughter, was a very pretty girl and soon started dating a professional in the village, married him and moved into his house where she had a real bathroom with running water. Ettore, the older son, married too. He also moved to a house with running water. Both Ferno, the third child, and fourth child Sparto married and each built his own house - complete with running water. The sons, all of them together, opened a small factory and did quite well for themselves. This is a particular case which blasts the saying 'like father like son' to pieces.

Pietrone and Giannina loved to spend lots of time at the workmen's club. There they could drink wine and be in the company of others who enjoyed the same pastime. Once I was present when another woman asked Gianinna if she was not worried about her husband leaving the house on his own so often.

But she shot back her immediate response, "Don't worry, I always milk him before he leaves!"

THE REGGIOS

This family consisted of Fernando, his wife Rosetta and three daughters, Unice, Bruna and Luce. He had no profession nor formal education but possessed a tremendous sense of family and honour. The family worked the little land they had and also kept a cow, some chickens and rabbits. Fernando also worked with my father doing the same dirty and dangerous work in the foundry making water taps.

The oldest daughter Unice worked in the factory just like the rest of us and married the bus driver Andrea. He was an ordinary fellow, quite vulgar and uneducated. He built a house out of a cow shed he owned and they lived there in comparative happiness until his death at a fairly young age left Unice and their daughter behind.

Bruna, the second daughter, was full of hormones and literally could not keep hold of her panties. So much so that at the age of seventeen she gave birth to a boy conceived with the help of a man twenty years her senior. The man was a drunken weasel who saw an opportunity to get into a family with at least a house, a cow, some chickens and some rabbits and he did not hesitate to get her pregnant in order to avail himself of a better situation than the one in which he lived.

Unfortunately for him he did not take into consideration Fernando's firm character. When he learned of his daughter's condition he immediately expelled the weasel from his house never to be seen again. Today the boy born under those circumstances is a very successful doctor in a nearby town.

Luce, the third daughter, was no less endowed with active hormones than Bruna and had become an easy pastime for most of the boys in the village. Alas for the lads though she soon married and moved away, to reappear only once a year with her very jealous husband during the feast of Saint Mary Magdalene.

FRANCESCO GIACOMINI

This man was not a relative of mine as such but our lives became entwined under the strangest of circumstances. He was a widower, fairly well off with money, some decent land, a nice house and plenty of spare time on his hands. My aunt Clementina was my uncle Sasso's wife and while their son, Eros, was doing his military service, she ran away from my uncle and came to live with Francesco in my village. This raised eyebrows all around and started a barrage of gossip that never ended.

You see my cousin Eros was not really my cousin because he was not my uncle's son. Aunt Clementina was a beautiful and sexy young woman which made her well sought after and one day she found herself to be pregnant. An inquiry was launched in all the villages and towns around the lake to establish who the father was but the lovers my aunt had entertained numbered in the hundreds and no one would claim responsibility. There was one man among this lot who actually loved her and that was my uncle Sasso. He claimed that the child was his and married Clementina. Eros, upon terminating his military service, did not go to live with his 'father' but instead came to my village to live with his mother and Francesco. Aunt Clementina was very nice to me and whenever we ran into each other at the local shop she would buy me candies or chocolates. Sometime later my 'cousin' met a girl who lived in the nearest town, got married and moved there.

My uncle was not made for a solitary way of life and found himself a nice lady who also had been abandoned by her husband. She moved in with him. Several years passed and the torment of his broken heart had calmed down when, quite unexpectedly, Francesco died. Shortly afterwards my uncle's companion died too. Guess what happened next? Yes, Clementina showed up at his door. My uncle cried, took her into the house and held her as if she had never left, had never broken his heart. He told her that he had never stopped loving her and that every night since she left he had cried himself to sleep. Now he did not want anything else in life but to have her with him. This is real love.

I have often wondered when I think of this story, how many men could love with such devotion, passion and kindness to not only forgive her but to act as if she had never left nor caused him any pain or disgrace?

THE RUSCELLOS

This was a family that kept very much to itself. Piede was the village carpenter. His business was right in front of our house but I don't recall ever seeing him do any work for anyone in the village. His wife died when I was but an infant so I did not know her. The two daughters, Margherita and Giglia, both unmarried, moved to a nearby city and made their living as teachers in the local school as well as giving piano lessons. Uncle Buono was the widower who came back to retire and eventually die in the village after spending forty-five years in New York, specifically in Brooklyn, which was the area of N.Y. where most Italian immigrants had moved to. More about Mr.Buono later.

THE MACELLIS

This family had really not much except the old house in which they lived. Grandmother was a widow, who the village gossip leader had identified as 'the witch'. While she always wore only black clothes, there was never anything that could be seen to connect her to sorcery. She lived in the house with an unmarried daughter, Rina, who had four illegitimate children from four different unknown (to the villagers) men. Rumour had it that the first child was supposedly fathered by the parish priest ... but as so often that was just village gossip.

Netto was the name of the first born. He was by far the ugliest man in the village, tall, very slim with a golden heart and a foul mouth. He enjoyed the company of young women and Luce from the Reggio's family who I mentioned before was one of them. He bought the first Vespa scooter in the village and he would lend it to us younger kids to learn how to ride. A bit irresponsible maybe but in those days nobody was afraid of minor laws which were there to be ignored. Then he bought a car and, although always broke, he was by far the happiest man in the village. He sang, played cards, danced and enjoyed life. He never really enjoyed working so he did as little of it as possible. He never married and lived contentedly to old age never worrying about anything.

Marta was the second child and oldest daughter. She was a real beauty. There was not a single boy in the village who would not run after her. She had black hair, big black eyes and was slender with a shining skin that, in the nights of full moon, seemed to first absorb and then reflect back its light, making her look like a white angel. She, like all the young women in the village, was working in the sewing factory making pyjamas. The army set up a training camp nearby and young boys on conscript duty would be sent there for their boot camp for a period of six months. Here appeared this luscious Roman boy with film star looks, handsome Roman nose and Roman accent fit to sweep any village girl off her feet. Man he was handsome and naturally he got to pick the flower of the village. Marta it was.

In the factory where Marta worked alongside my sister, there were only women. Women who each had several children and knew all about pregnancy. Yet Marta managed to fool them all. She was expecting a child but concealed it so well, with her mother's help in strapping her tummy up tightly, that not one of the other women suspected. Every morning my sister walked with Marta to the factory. One morning her mother sent Marta's little sister to tell my sister that Marta would not be at work that day as she was not feeling too well. In reality, Marta had given birth to a little boy during the night, helped only by her mother.

At that time there was in a nearby village a caravan of gypsies and they had become friendly with Marta's mother. She arranged to sell Marta's baby to them for the equivalent of 50 US dollars. The gypsies came to and left the village in the early hours of the morning before anyone woke up or would see anything suspicious. Then they went to register the birth of the baby as if it were their own. But they couldn't produce a doctor's certificate when asked and the police were called. It was quickly established that they had bought the baby from Marta. The police Marshal personally knew everyone in the village and did not want to pursue this issue which would have ended with the imprisonment of Marta and her mother, and the little baby being put in an orphanage.

He chose instead to have the baby returned to the mother and for the gypsies to get their money back. The baby's good fortune in that respect was, quite literally, short lived. Marta and her mother slowly starved him to death and he was buried not long afterwards. A few years later Marta found a nice young man, got married and they lived many quiet and happy years together. After all there is somewhat of a happy ending to the tragedy.

Omino, this was his nickname, was the third child, also of unknown father and he worked with my father in the water tap factory. His unknown father must have been handsome as he also was good looking and, like his half-brother Netto, had a good heart. When his time came he married a beautiful girl who had, with her family, emigrated to the village from Sardinia. She was a real beauty as only Sardinian girls can be. That mixture of Italian and Arab beauty which totally mesmerizes all men who behold her. Unfortunately, while he really loved this girl, she cheated on him with a fat, ugly, married, father of three called Algero. Omino died of a broken heart at a very young age.

Augusta was the fourth and last of the children. She enjoyed an altogether less exotic life; no illegitimate children, no cheating husbands. She moved away from the village and returned only once for a very short visit during her mother's lifetime.

In addition to this family make up there was an aunt living with them called Ania. She was a middle-aged woman and it was a known fact that she never owned a pair of underwear in her life. She was always unkempt, wore rags and definitely never took a bath in all her years. Because of her shabby appearance and questionable personal hygiene she was sarcastically nicknamed Aniana, after a luxurious department store in Milan which could be compared to Macy's in the US or Harrods in London. Despite this she had a boyfriend.

His name was Luigino but he was known locally as Piuz, which means pig in the spoken village dialect. He suffered from scavenger/hoarder syndrome. It was impossible to walk through his house unimpeded. Piles of newspapers, all sorts of bottles, old books and you name it, Luigino had them all. His house was near a brook and because of all the junk it became infested with huge rats that bred there. One night while Luigino slept, one enormous rodent chewed at his big toe. It was only when he woke up the next morning that he realized that the entire nail was gone, eaten by a rat!

THE ROVIGOS

The Rovigos had a huge, centrally located house and were definitively the richest family in the village. Father, Fonsi, was a partner in the granite quarry, had a motorcycle and he was the first person in the village to use an electric shaver. In the year 1953 that was unquestionably luxury. He had three daughters, Alfa, Giasmina and Giuse. Alfa was the brightest of the three, at least it so appeared, for she became an administrative assistant to the owner of one of the many factories. One day a travelling salesman came from Athens to make a deal to export taps to Turkey and Greece. Sure enough, Alfa married him. They rebuilt a house in our village, had three sons and lived together until death did them part. The husband died in terrible pain from gout.

Giasmina, on the other hand, did not marry but that did not keep her from having an exciting life. First she started working for herself and did well as a sales rep for various cosmetic companies. Then, after her parents died, she lived alone in a house that her parents had bought near the church. The fact that the house was near the church was either a trick of destiny or some kind of unknown complicity on the part of Giasmina's parents many years before when they bought this house. Because it turned out there was a good looking young priest in the village and Giasmina, being single and full of passion, quickly got to know him outside of the confessional ... and into the sacristy, where they had their sexual encounters anytime the opportunity presented itself. Even this was not enough for her as she started another affair with Chiaro, much younger than either the priest or herself. He would visit her house every time he had a lot to drink and felt cold and lonely in the long winter nights.

Giasmina also liked X rated movies. As she was travelling all over the country for her work she had the opportunity to buy them in the cities she visited, there being no such risqué items available in our backwood village. She would invite special people over to her house to see those movies. Among the invitees there was, naturally, Chiaro and also my brother-in-law; he who would not miss any chance to screw around thinking that nobody, especially his wife, would know. Giasmina's life was short. She died in her early sixties of cancer. Many men, including the priest who led the funeral service, mourned her passing.

Her sister Alfa is still alive as of this writing. She lives in the house she and her late husband built and she receives regular visits from her sister Giuse who lives in Milan. Giuse was much younger and it seems that she was a quiet and reserved girl. She met a city boy, married and returned to the village only to visit with the older sisters.

THE PIANOS

The Pianos were a particularly interesting family, also distant cousins of my mother. There was Erasmo and his wife Antonia, then Giuseppe, then Licia, then Fiore, then Selva and lastly Veliero, the fifth born of a father who only started having children after he was fifty years old. He married Antonia, thirty-five years his junior when she was fifteen and he already fifty. How could this be? The answer is simple ... well kind of .....

Erasmo spent thirty years from age twenty in state prison for killing a butcher. He was what you would call a 'screwed up kid'. He liked to drink and party and, while drugs were not available in those days, alcohol was cheap and plentiful. He hatched a plan to earn some easy 'wine money' which involved luring the local butcher to one of the hilltop farms with the promise that the farmer there had a fine cow for sale. The butcher fell for his ruse and set off up the hill on the appointed day with enough cash in pocket to make the supposed deal. But Erasmo ambushed him in the forest and split his head open with an axe! He took the butcher's money and left him to die under some old oaks.

Erasmo was spotted by an old woman back in the village, trying to wash the blood from his clothes. He explained to her that he had chopped the head off a rooster for his dinner and got covered in blood in the process. The old woman believed him but the police who came to the village the next day did not. They arrested him and, after beating a confession out of him, put him in jail. He was then tried and sent to prison in Bari, a small town near Brindisi in the south of Italy. During his detention he escaped three times, was shot, captured, beaten and put in solitary confinement. But his spirit was not broken. While in prison he learned some skills such as nursing and shoe repairing which would come in handy when he returned home at fifty years of age with a fifteen year old bride.

How on earth did he meet a fifteen year old girl while in prison? Well, from his cell window he could see the house opposite and the young Antonia growing up there. He decided that when he became a free man he would marry her, take her back to the village, have many children and live happily ever after. So he did just that. When he was released from prison he crossed the street to her house. He told her father that he had watched his daughter over the years from his cell window, loved her with all his heart and asked him to give her to him in marriage.

He realised that, with his background, he would never find a wife back in his home village. His only chance lay in marrying a girl from the south where, when a man had served his sentence for a crime, he was accepted back into society (albeit with no right to vote nor hold public office). So he married Antonia and returned to the village with her at the beginning of 1940. By year end Giuseppe was born and in 1941 Licia. Within a few years Fiore, Selva and Veliero had arrived. Life was not easy for the large family, they did not own any land nor domestic animals. They at least had the old family home over their heads.

Erasmo was a sour man and did not get along with many people in the village. Stubborn and violent he would not hesitate to beat his wife and children at every opportunity. He lived by his own rules and despised society in all its aspects, being ruthlessly antagonistic to the rule of law and the church in particular. Vocal and foul mouthed, he extracted enormous pleasure in swearing loudly whenever the priest, his sister, the village teacher or a nun was within earshot. It was sad because this behaviour was also assumed by his children.

In order to make ends meet, Erasmo cut wood and opened a shoe repair shop at his home, employing the skill he had learned while in prison. This barely produced a life of comfort. While Giuseppe and Licia had to repeat two years in elementary school they still had to go at age eleven to work in the evenings in a water tap factory. Licia became friendly with a family from Milan who regularly visited the village on holiday and, as a result, the family took her to the city to work in their home. The fact that she moved to the city gave her a better status and the opportunity to learn a different way of life unknown to the rest of us.

Saro was her boyfriend from childhood. Eventually she came back to the village to marry him. They opened a small factory, were quickly successful and amassed a small fortune. Saro died at age forty. Licia never married again. It was quite unusual for a village girl to be alone at that age but she continued in the business, an independent lady and still making money.

Giuseppe and Fiore met two Belgian sisters who came to visit an uncle of theirs in the village. Both couples married and moved to Belgium where they still live today. Selva enjoyed a better childhood as times had changed by the time she was growing up and she could do more schooling. She married a nice young man from the nearby city and moved there. Veliero moved to New York where he is now a very successful chef in a leading restaurant. He has no intention to return home.

Erasmo eventually died in old age leaving Antonia, who had become totally blind by the time she was sixty, to live on alone for many more years.

THE RIALLOS

Brother and sister, Raffa and Zina lived together in a house inherited from their parents. Zina never married and was a sweet lady who liked children. Raffa, also never married and he too liked children and took a special shine to the Piano boys. At that time I did not understand that the reason he liked the boys was because he was a fully fledged paedophile! Like many other unpleasant things in the village this was never spoken about, particularly as it would have meant yet another scandal with the Piano family at its heart. After the murder case involving them no one had the stomach to face this issue so it was left dormant, never to be confronted. Raffa emigrated to France. He spoke the language and lived there many years working as a builder, saving enough money to live comfortably on for the rest of his days. He and his sister both died at an advanced age, together in the same house they were born in.

THE VIES

Biancaneve was the mother in the family and a lead gossip monger in the village. There was a son, Giovanni Pietro, and two daughters, Emanuela and Vergine. They lived in a nice house next to us. I never figured out how they could eat as there was no one earning any money in that household. One of the sisters had married a municipal traffic cop in the nearby town, the other had moved to a town across the mountain and had her own life.

Giovanni Pietro was two years older than myself and always wanted to be a priest. The local priest decided to help him to get into the seminary and so he enjoyed several years of education that none of us other children in the village had. He was about twenty years old when he discovered that his love for priesthood was only surpassed by his love for girls! So he gave up the seminary and turned civilian. He married, had a son and became the mayor of the village, a position that his son occupies today. The years of extra schooling that he received allowed him to secure a good job in the local hospital and for that he is still grateful to the priest who helped him as a lad.

Where was the father? I never met him because after the three children were born he was taken to a mental asylum never to be released again. As for Biancaneve, the mother, she carried on for many more years doing what she did best - constantly looking out of the kitchen window in search of tasty gossip to spread around the village.

THE BETULLES

The father was one of the men who emigrated to Switzerland after the second world war to find work and support his wife Evora, their two sons and daughter. Evora worked in a water tap factory. The oldest son, Aldo, never married and was very much a drinking, party animal. One particular Saturday night he was so drunk that on his way home from the bar he fell off his bike and lost the middle finger of his right hand cut off by the rear wheel. Eating was his other passion. Over the years he become so bloated that he suffered all kind of illnesses from diabetes to high blood pressure and, finally, the heart attack which killed him at a young age.

Algibra was the middle child. She, like so many, went to work very young in a factory. She started dating in her mid teens and when she was twenty she found herself pregnant by her steady boyfriend. Her father, thinking he was doing the right thing, had them married in a hurry. A daughter, Elda, was born but the marriage was destined to be a disaster. After just a few years they separated.

Attila was the young husband in question. He was mean, drunken and always ready to pick a fight with anyone who, in his estimation, had done him wrong. He lived alone in his dead parents' house, often using the pots and pans and the kitchen floor as his toilet as he would be too drunk to walk to the outside loo. He died alone from liver failure. Algibra had in the meantime grown to be a beautiful young woman and oft times in need of the touch of a man. She had little difficulty in engaging the companionship of the banker, the two leading businessmen in the village and ... my brother-in-law. He who was always agreeable to extra-marital passion and intrigue, the more so if the woman involved was a 'friend' of his wife. The fact that my sister and Algibra had grown up together and lived next door to each other had an aphrodisiac effect on him. Algibra died while still a young and attractive woman. She suffered terribly in her final years from diabetes, having had all her fingers and toes amputated.

Chiaro, the last child, had reached the grand height of 5 feet (1.5 m) tall by the time he reached twenty. That disqualified him from doing military service. He did not look at all like his father, a tall, well-built stone cutter with a six-pack mid riff that he would not hesitate to show off whenever he had the opportunity. Chiaro was a year older than me and a year ahead of me in school. He was a quite intelligent kid but, because his father and mother openly supported the communist party, he was not privileged at school. He did not get a seat near the stove in winter nor near the window in spring and autumn. He did, however, serve as an altar boy and that allowed him to play soccer with the regulation football, borrow the priest's skis and go on the regular outings in the priest's car. These jaunts invariably ended in a fight between the two of us which, in spite of my superior size, he always won through being stronger and meaner than me.

As time passed it emerged that Chiaro's mother, Evora, had started to flirt with the owner of the factory where she worked in the time prior to his birth. This could help her to get extra hours at work and more time off work. There was also the bonus privilege of being driven home, 2 miles (3.2 km) up the hill, every night after work. It was during one of these drives home that the car stopped half way up the hill - and Evora conceived Chiaro on the back seat of the tiny Topolino car. How could anybody have sex in such a small car? Well here is the explanation for Chiaro's size ... his real father was even shorter than him and only measured 4 feet 6 inches (1.35 m)! So without much effort he could manoeuvre his way quite comfortably in the little car.

As children are inevitably mean at school, we would call Chiaro names and tell him that he was the son of Curtin (meaning small) which was the nickname his real father had. He would respond that he had asked his mother and she had painfully described to him that the reason why he had not grown like his father and brother was because, while she was expecting him, she would be looking at the owner of the factory all day long and therefore he was born short. Isn't that a great story to tell her son?

THE LEGNAS

This was an old and very traditional family in one specific way. There was the father, Antonio, the mother Celia, one son Celio and a horse. Celio, like all people in the village, worked in a factory from a tender age. However he had a vision and that was to leave the village and open a bar in some other place. And so he did. After he had married a young woman from a town on the other side of the mountain, they opened a bar. Today his children still run a very successful restaurant on top of the same mountain which Celio had to cross every time he went to visit his fiancée.

The most interesting character in the family was the father. He used to run a small business selling home-grown vegetables, hay and wood. In order to transport these items either to the market or to the final consumer he used his horse and cart. This meant that he would leave early in the morning and travel as far as 25 or 30 miles (40 to 48 km) to deliver them. After dropping off the merchandise and getting paid in cash, as always was the case in those days, he would start the journey back home. Like most men in the village he loved wine with a passion. This lust caused him to stop at every watering hole, workmen's club and bar he passed on the road. By the time he had travelled about 10 miles (16 km) he was drunk out of his mind and unable to guide the horse back home.

To his good fortune the horse did not drink wine. It would simply take him back home, walk into the porch of the stable and stop. With his wife and child asleep in the house by this time, he would continue to sleep on the seat of the cart or would fall off and sleep on the dirt floor. Only the rising sun or his wife dragging him physically into the house would waken him. This man was also the only one to use his faithful horse to plough his fields rather than using a hoe like everyone else did. He lived to a ripe old age and never had to give up either his horse nor his wine as both of these things were what defined his whole existence.

THE DOLCIS

There were two families of two brothers living in a huge house in the centre of the village. One side of the house was occupied by Elere, his wife Liana and two daughters, Pietrina and Fiorina. To keep the village tradition going Elere was an alcoholic and was drunk as far back as I can remember. He was also the other shoe repair man. His house was right across from Piano's house, who of course was the other shoe repair man and ex-convict who hated him with a passion. This caused much shouting, exchanges of insults and confrontation, at the end of which Elere would go to the workmen's club and a much needed drink to calm his nerves. His wife Liana had a cow and some fields. She worked hard to produce food to feed the family as, between the shoe repair business and his drinking, Elere had no money to support them.

Pietrina married Grenco, a boy from a nearby village who was a passionate trout fisherman. He would walk for miles upstream to catch a few trout to eat fresh for dinner the very same day. They had two daughters who, like so many others, moved away from the village in search of a better and certainly more exciting life. Pietrina and Grenco still live there in the same house.

Fiorina was definitely the prettier of the two daughters. She was two years younger than myself. Had I stayed in the village and gone to work in a factory for the rest of my life, she was the girl I would have married. She eventually married Gigi, a boy who lived two doors down from her. A couple of years afterwards she fell ill with tuberculosis. Can you believe that tuberculosis still existed in Italy in the sixties? Fortunately she survived. She and Gigi never had children and, like her sister Pietrina, they still live in the village today.

The other brother Lazzaro, came back with his wife from a nearby town to the village to retire. Unlike Elere, Lazzaro was a sober man who had emigrated as a young man to Paris to work as a waiter. For many years he ran his own successful La Côtolette restaurant in Paris. Because of this he was somewhat more sophisticated than most of the villagers. He was a real gentleman respectful of his roots. He never looked down on the locals nor made anyone feel inferior.

THE POLLASTRIS

This family had a little bit of everything that can be wrong in a family. The father, Eligio, was an old man by the time I remember him and so was his wife Nagga.

They had four children, Rutto and Carlotta, Oriano and Viana. At the tender age of twelve, the youngest child Viana was given the opportunity to leave the village and go to work in Milan as a maid. She was employed by an elderly couple who treated her more like a daughter than their maid-servant. She went to school and eventually married a city boy and never returned home, so I never knew her. Rutto was the oldest of the children and, just to maintain continuity in the community, an alcoholic. When drunk he would bet on anything. One day he bet that he could eat brilliantine.

This was a concoction used in those days by the male population around the world to keep their hair slicked down and shiny. Amazingly he won the bet, knocking back a bottle of the horrible grease along with a litre of wine in about three minutes flat. Another time he bet that he could eat a post card. No matter how much he chewed it he could not swallow it and this time he had to buy a litre of wine for the fellow whom he bet against. He worked mainly as a wood cutter. My father once hired him to help chop some wood and he severed the nerve of his own left hand index finger while doing so. He too died fairly young from cirrhosis of the liver. He had never married and did not leave a child, at least not one that could be seen.

Oriano was the third child. While he did not drink as much as his brother, he still drank his fair share. He too was a wood cutter and liked the open air. At a tender age he had an affair with his older sister, Carlotta. From this relationship a child was born! His name was Concetto. Because he was very small he soon acquired the nickname of Pulcino, meaning he was a small chicken. This poor kid was not only the child of an incestuous relationship between brother and sister but he was a battered one too.

Everyone in the family, starting with his mother, would beat him every day with a stick or belt for any misdemeanour, real or imagined. The uncles and the uncle-father would take a swing at him too, especially when they came home after a night out and too much to drink. Pulcino was only two years younger than myself. He would come to school in winter wearing a pair of short pants. He did not have long trousers until he was about ten years old. The entire village knew what was going on in that house but nobody would interfere. Everyone pretended that it was normal and that all was well. Eventually he grew up and left the village, sometime after I had left. His mother later become a prostitute in Milan. Years later we learned that Pulcino had been in jail and shot dead by a guard while attempting to escape. Nobody heard or saw any member of this family ever again.

THE PUBLIC WASHHOUSE

As the majority of the households did not have running water, a gigantic, public wash basin was provided in the middle of the village. On a regular basis the women would take their laundry, bed sheets, knickers and all, to be washed in the cold running water coming from a brook high up in the mountains. Hands became red and painful after just a few minutes of performing this chore. Depending on the quantity and on what they were washing, some would bring along a bucket of boiling water from the house to help with the cleaning and stain removal. Dry cleaning was not an option around there in those days.

Because there would be about ten women all washing at the same time this was also the place where gossip flourished. New stories were fabricated, new affairs created and the one who told the hottest story and told it with most flair and salacious detail would be the one whose story stuck. While the damage done would usually be limited to the malignity of the gossip, there were times when things got out of hand. Then a shouting match would ensue, name calling and sometimes pushing and shoving. On one particularly heated occasion, a brawl erupted between two women which necessitated that the police be called. The fight was eventually stopped but not before one of the two lost a couple of teeth and the other had sustained a broken nose. As the police had been called the Marshal had no choice but to charge both women with public affray with intent to cause bodily harm.

One of the protagonists was Carlotta of the Pollastri family, the other was called Alesandra. By a bizarre twist she had moved from a city in order to enjoy the peace and tranquility of country life! The case eventually ended up in court and created quite a stir in the village as the last time anyone had seen the inside of a courthouse was when Erasmo was arrested for killing the butcher. The outcome though was predictable. The judge slapped the wrist of both women (figuratively speaking) and, in order to prevent future bloodshed at the public washhouse, decreed that they were never to be there together at the same time again.

MISTER BUONO

In 1948, when I was five years old an interesting thing happened in the village ... Sixty-eight year old Mr.Buono retired and returned to his native home after having lived in New York for 45 years. The American social security cheque which he received each month afforded him a comfortable, if not a luxurious, lifestyle. Mr.Buono was a colourful character. He spoke Italian with an American accent but could no longer speak the local dialect which everyone in the village spoke. To speak Italian was considered snobbish by the villagers as it was not the language of their culture and generally it was only the well schooled city folk who spoke it.

Quite naturally, having spent such a large part of his life in Brooklyn, Mr.Buono was more progressive in outlook than the village people. He was also full of stories about his life which he loved to share with us boys. We soon learned that during his life he had been a waiter, a watch repairer and a boxer among a long line of other things. We also learned that his life in America had not all been rosy. He had been married for a few years to an immigrant girl from the south of Italy and they had a boy. Sadly his boy had died at a very early age. While playing barefoot in the street the lad had stepped on a rusty nail and consequently died of a tetanus infection. His wife had also died while fairly young and he had not remarried. He decided that the pain of losing first his boy and then his beloved wife so shortly afterwards was too much to bear for him to give it a second try.

Soon after his arrival in the village, he started to enlarge the little shed that was in front of our house and where his brother was running a small carpentry shop. First he added a garage and then, to my father's dismay, a second floor which would reduce by a couple of yards (1.8 m) the sunshine into our front yard. After that he bought a car. It was fairly old and posh, silver and décapoté. The longest trip the car ever did was from the village to the nearest town 6 miles (10 km) away where his two nieces lived and worked. Most of his time was spent fiddling about on the car; trivial things like moving the license plate from the back left corner of the car to the centre as he wanted the car to appear as American as possible. That car was in his possession until he died. At which time the nieces sold the shed, the garage and the car and they never came back to the village again.

One of the stories Mr.Buono told which most appealed to us boys was that all the streets in America go downhill, no road went uphill, so it was easy to walk or drive! Another fascinating story was that everyone in America always wore hats, never would an American man go without a hat. So we all found some old hat belonging to our grandfathers and started walking around the village feeling very American but looking kind of peculiar for boys of our age. Then he decided that the road in front of his garage was not steep enough. One morning he started to dig up all the stones to produce an incline for the rain water to run off down the street and not form a huge puddle in front of his door. This action got the hunchbacked mayor absolutely mad. The battle that ensued was so vitriolic that, short of coming to a fist fight, every imaginable swear word and insult I had ever heard – and some new ones which I quickly added to my vocabulary – were exchanged. He eventually got to finish his road improvements but incurred a fine for doing work on municipal property without planning permission.

Such was life in Centonara. This was a village with only one hundred and fifty inhabitants and yet, as you have seen, it embraced every imaginable character and scenario (and a few more besides). From loving parents to abusive ones, from incest to murder, from trafficking of babies to paedophilia, from extremely committed and loyal husbands and wives to serial cheaters and drinkers of epic proportions. The two most obvious and prevalent traits being the incredible number of illegitimate children and the endemic rate of male alcoholism. I grew up in this ambience and so I considered it to be all quite normal!

MY RITE OF PASSAGE

In many cultures and religions around the world, at thirteen years of age boys cease to be boys and are inducted into manhood. This passage is sometimes enacted by ceremonies in churches or synagogues, some are done in tribal settings and all are followed by a feast which can be a one evening affair or one that lasts for days. But my rite of passage was neither religious nor cultural - it was simply sex! It is hard to believe that at thirteen years of age I had my first intimate experience with a woman; not just any woman but one in her mid fifties. Not only the ugliest woman in the village but most likely in all of the country.

It happened one hot summer afternoon outside the workmen's club where 'she' was washing some shirts for the mayor. 'She' you may have guessed, was Aniana, the one known not to own a pair of knickers and who never took a shower nor washed any part of her body for that matter. I spotted her there and curiosity got the better of me, thinking this is my opportunity to find out if she really does not have panties on. I sidled up to her and made little effort to disguise my attempts to see up her skirt. She definitely liked the thrill of playing around with a thirteen year old virgin boy. As I approached her, she gave me a cat-like look and invitingly made vague provocative gestures, pulling her legs apart enough to show her thighs in an unmistakable offer. This glimpse of her upper legs gave me the chill but also the excitement of something I had heard the older boys, and sometimes full grown men when the wine got the best of them, speak about.

All that talk referred to the pleasure that a woman, especially an experienced one like Aniana, could and would give to a man. After some short preambulatory and empty chat and my probing under her ragged skirt she informed me that she would have to go into the forest to get some wood for her boyfriend's house. Did I want to go and help her? I was totally aware of her aim and thought, wow is this really happening to me? Would I have to try something new today for the first time? I had always thought that my first encounter would be a romantic one. On the other hand I grew up in a very carnal society where most of the men would jump at any opportunity to have sex.

By that time there was no holding back. Excitement and fear were running through me and there was no stopping. It had to go to the end, whatever that would be. She got her wood cutting tools and off we marched to the forest. As soon as we got under cover of the trees and bushes Aniana started touching me. This made me shake as I had never been touched by any women in such a way. At the same time my excitement was increasing. It topped when she proceeded to lift her large gypsy like skirt and, pulling me over her, undid my short boyish trousers. Indeed she wore no panties! ... but by this time I couldn't care less ... and with all the vigour and scant knowledge of a thirteen year old I penetrated her! Wow ...

and ... whoosh! I passed from childhood to manhood in less than sixty seconds!

Now we had to return to the village and to her boyfriend's house. We gathered some wood, put it in her basket and trotted back. She went first and after a few minutes I followed. As soon as I left the forest a fear and panic overtook me. On one side I was afraid of going to hell when I died and on the other side I was afraid of something more terrestrial. I started to wonder if I had caught some ghastly venereal disease.

I was, for sure, going to go to hell because my altar boy mentality was very concerned with heaven, purgatory and hell. I was trying to justify to myself that I had been a good boy, went to catechism, was confirmed at age five, did the holy communion and always went to confession, in addition to knowing all the Mass in Latin. As I could not tell the priest, even in the secrecy of confession, that I had sex with Aniana there was no other solution but to die, go to hell and get it over with. However, maybe just maybe, our Lord would be forgiving and just send me to purgatory. According to the priest that was no rose garden either, but it would have an end and I'd go on to heaven. As I write, I am still waiting to find out!

The fear of having caught VD was terrifying. I could not imagine having to tell my parents that I had some unknown problem in the lower part of my body without having to tell them where on earth that came from. The shame of having to say that I had sex with Aniana was even more scary to me than the eternal fire of hell. That part ended well as I did not get any illness. What did not go so well was that one of the nosey neighbours had been watching from her balcony what Aniana and I were doing by the wash basin. To the last minute detail she related it to my mother who was waiting for me with a bean stick as I arrived home. Without saying a word she struck me on my legs repeatedly with all the strength she had but multiplied a hundred times by the anger she had built up in her and for the shame I made her feel.

Little did I know that seven long years would pass before I would have another intimate encounter with a woman. By that time I would be twenty years old.

MY FINAL TWO YEARS OF VILLAGE LIFE

For the next two years my life continued as before - work at the water tap factory, being the good altar boy and drinking the priest's wine on Sunday mornings. Then, at fourteen years of age on the occasion of the celebration of the village patron saint day, I had my first experience of what was to become my life passion. To be a waiter!

On that day I had been asked to man a soft drinks bar set up inside the workmen's club by the most entrepreneurial of the Mioli brothers. The deal was that he bought the drinks from the hunchbacked mayor at a reduced price and I sold them for 10 liras each more than the club price. Between the discounted purchase price and the inflated sale price he made a good profit and he let me keep the extra 10 liras per drink. It was a good deal for both of us. Not only did I get to do what I always wanted to do but he was free to go dancing and chatting up girls for the evening. What a win-win situation. When the patron saint day ended so did the thrill to be behind a bar to serve customers.

Then, at fifteen years of age, my life truly changed. It was really extraordinary how it all happened. My 'university' (the water tap factory) had, among a plethora of other failings, no toilets. This meant that all the workers, men, women, young and old had to go outside to a nearby cave with a running stream to use as a toilet. Not a very private arrangement as you can imagine but at least the running water washed away whatever you left behind and it had a semblance of cleanliness.

One day on my way to the cave I bumped into an older gentleman who had worked at the Savoy Hotel in London for many years and was therefore a kind of celebrity around the nearby villages. As we exchanged greetings he told me that on top of the mountain a newly opened little hotel was looking for a young man to work there for the summer season. He recommended that I go up there and try to get hired.

In the evening I told my parents of my encounter. My mother, being the passionate one about service, was thrilled with the prospect of me changing from water tap factory labourer to a hotel worker. My father, with his customary suspicion of the unknown, was more difficult to convince. But next day I was on my way up the mountain for an interview - and I got the job!

Wow, that was great. Now I was fifteen, I could work legally and pay contributions for medical and old age pension. I was over the moon with happiness and full of enthusiasm. I got myself three waiter jackets, two pairs of black trousers, two white bow ties and some strange white shirts with just a front and no sleeves, and started work. Boy was I a lucky kid!

While all my friends were still making water taps, wearing mucky overalls and suffering bruised and damaged hands, I was wearing a pair of slick black trousers, a spotless white jacket, a bow tie and a pair of shining, real street shoes. That I worked from 6.00 am to midnight or one in the morning every day of the week, with no day off, bothered me not in the slightest. My morale and determination were high. I wanted to be a waiter, travel the world and work in Rome, Paris, London and, as one of my distant relatives had done, New York! This was an incredible feeling for a fifteen year old boy, the world was at my feet, it was like ripe fruit hanging on a tree and all I had to do was to pick it. This was 1958 and the Platters were singing 'Only You'. Of course I did not understand English but that did not matter. It felt good. So good that I wanted more.

One evening I was serving a table of nine guests. I must have pleased them as one gentleman asked me at the completion of their dinner what I would be doing when the hotel closed at the end of the summer season. I told him that my desire was to continue in the hotel trade. At that point he gave me his card and I realised then that, once more, God had been good to me. It transpired that he and his fellow diners were executives from the world renowned Bettoja Hotel chain in Rome. He told me that in spring he would send me a letter telling me when I could go to Rome to take up employment as an assistant waiter in one of their five world class hotels in the city. I doubt that anyone in the world could have been more happy than myself that night.

But the summer came to an end and the hotel closed its doors in September. I was jobless and sad. While working during breakfast, lunch, afternoon tea, dinner and at the bar afterwards was hard graft it sure beat being unemployed and with little prospect of getting the job in a luxury hotel which I really wanted. I could have gone to work as a barista in one of the town bars making expresso all day and night and serving an occasional drink before lunch and dinner, but that was not what I wanted. I wanted to be a waiter in Rome, Paris, London or New York! But, rather than stay home and do nothing, I chose to return to making water taps. Just in case I had not made enough of them since I was nine.

In the event the hotel executive from Rome kept his promise. Lo and behold a letter arrived in February informing me that I was expected to be in the city the following week to start work in a luxury hotel. I was as happy as a pig in shit. Next day the priest, who had the only car in the village, took me and my mother to a shop across the lake which sold hotel staff outfits. With my savings from the summer hotel work and the little I had been able to put aside from my time in the factory, I renewed my wardrobe ... three new white jackets, two new pairs of black pants, two more white bow-ties and three more front only shirts.

I also bought for myself a companion - A cardboard suitcase!

Chapter 3

THREE COINS IN A FOUNTAIN

In the case I packed all my working clothes, an extra pair of trousers, two shirts, four pairs of socks and some underwear. I wore the only jacket I possessed. In my pocket I had 50 US dollars and in my heart unbounded enthusiasm and passion. On Saturday February 13th of 1959, Don Ricardo the good priest, took me to the train station to catch the train to Milan. It was an emotional departure. Tears flowed and the one who cried most was my father. Then my sister, almost hysterical, would not let go of me. The most under control, as always, was my mother. Once more she, the strong pillar of the family, knew what was best for me. While her hugs said it all, she did not shed a single tear, just a wave and blessed me as the train pulled away.

In Milan I was picked up by some of the family members who came to spend the summer at our house and was given a place to sleep for the night. Early the next morning I was taken to the station and on to the train which took me to Rome about 500 miles (800 km) from my home. As the train rolled south I sat back with mixed feelings of joy and trepidation. At that point I knew very well that there was no return. For no reason other than it took such an effort on the part of my mother and I to convince my father to let me go to start a life by myself at the age of fifteen and in circumstances totally foreign to him. While being a waiter was to my mother the best job on earth, to my father it was something that a poor boy from our village with just an elementary education could not achieve. Working in Rome, Paris, London and maybe even New York was beyond reach. Additionally, far too many villagers had bet that I would run home by the latest the very next day as soon as I realised that I could no longer hear the village church bell sound the Ave Maria. I definitely had to prove them all wrong!

Up to that day I had barely ever been out of the village. The furthest I had been was to a town less than 6 miles (9.5 km) away. Now, gazing from the train window, I was seeing the names of cities I had only read about at elementary school. Piacenza, Parma, Bologna, Florence, all seemed to pop out of my geography books. It was hard to take in that these places really existed. By late afternoon the train arrived in Rome. I collected my cardboard suitcase and walked out of the station to the line of waiting taxis. When I asked the driver to take me to the Massimo d'Azzeglio hotel a smirk came to his lips. The hotel was just 200 yards (180 m) from the station but the driver saw the opportunity to make some quick money out of this innocent village boy. He drove me around the block a couple of times before depositing me at the front door of the hotel and charging me 400 liras (about 66 cents) for the privilege.

I dropped my suitcase in the employee accommodation in the attic of the hotel and went out to familiarise myself with the city which would become my home for the next three years. Walking around the block one of the first things I noticed was the fairly large number of women of all ages going back and forth. Some swinging their hand bags, some talking to every man passing by and some discreetly lifting their skirt to show a flash of thigh. I was not quite sure what they were doing, what they were saying to the men and most of all why would they lift their skirts to show people their thighs? I had never seen anything like it as in my village there was none of that. I wondered if I would ever get to understand these Roman girls.

Word had been left for me that I should meet the gentleman who had given me his card over dinner in the hotel in which I had worked during the summer, at the staff entrance the next morning at 9.00 am. I hardly slept that night. I was very excited to be in Rome, in a five star hotel and really going to work the next morning. Also I was scared, fearful that I might fall short of the expectation of my future superiors and be sent back home with my tail between my legs. In the morning I put on my best clothes and went to meet the gentleman. He told me that the plans had changed and that I would be assigned to the best hotel of the group, the Mediterraneo Hotel, just across the street. We crossed the road and he introduced me to the restaurant manager. He was a very tall man whose name was Mr.Cappelli, which means Mr.Hats in English. After taking a good look at me he sternly said, "Young man, you come from a little village and you do not even know how to walk on a carpet. I will put you in the kitchen washing glasses, dishes, pots, pans and floors and only when you are ready will I take you into the restaurant to be an assistant waiter." This little setback did not discourage me. If anything it made my determination to be a waiter someday much stronger. There was nothing, nothing in the world that would make me back down.

Washing glasses was not too bad and scraping the floor was bearable but washing pots and pans was sheer torture. Each of them had to be washed in almost boiling water with harsh detergent and bare hands. Even if they existed (doubtful) rubber gloves were off limits. So here I was with my hands in boiling water all day long and, being the 'new kid on the block', all the dirtiest jobs being assigned to me by the chief dish washer. That was part of the training. It was intended to make me tough. In other words I had to 'pay my dues' in the hardest jobs in the hotel before going into the restaurant. Working in the restaurant, no matter how hard it was going to be, would feel like a walk in the park after coming through the rigours of the dish room.

The first month finished and so did my 50 dollars. I wrote to my parents asking if they could send me some money to see me through to the end of the month. This request created a crisis in the family. My father in his usual conservative and restricted mind wanted to send me the money to buy the train ticket to return home. My mother was telling him that all beginnings are difficult. She persuaded him to speak to our distant cousin who had worked in New York and could convince him that this type of things can happen and to have faith in me. Thankfully some money did come and I resolved to ensure that I never had to ask for money again. In the first place I knew that my parents didn't have much and in the second place it would have meant that I had failed.

I was also sharing a bedroom with an older dishwasher who had been doing it for many years and knew all the tricks in the book about washing up. He kindly shared many of his professional secrets with me, the novice. Nonetheless there was many a night I cried myself to sleep but I was not going to give up whatever was the price I had to pay. At meal times the head chef and his crew, all men as no woman was allowed to work in a hotel kitchen in those days, would sit at a round table in the middle of the kitchen and eat the best food available. The assistant cooks would eat food of a slightly lesser quality at a separate table. The dish washers sat in the dish washing area eating what the rest of the hotel staff ate; normally a slice of provolone cheese and a tomato. With the exception of the head chef though, we were all equals when it came to the wine.

We each drank a quarter litre of poor quality white wine from the vineyards in the hills surrounding Rome. Because of his stature the head chef could drink a bottle of the best wine at lunch and at dinner, plus he would drink wine throughout the time the restaurant was open and the kitchen was preparing and serving food. At the end of each day he would leave work in quite a jolly condition and looked more like he was coming home from a party than returning from work.

Between meals and when the restaurant was closed I would sneak into the restaurant and walk on the thick Persian rug as I had been told that I had to learn that skill before I could become an assistant waiter. Six weary dish-washing months later the big day came. Mr.Hats revealed to me that he had been watching me teach myself to walk on the rug and he was taking me upstairs to work in the restaurant. I quickly shed my dishwasher uniform and put on my new black trousers, white jacket, white bow-tie and white shirt front, sparkling clean city shoes and I was in.

My first job was to be an assistant to the wine steward. This entailed pushing a drinks trolley from table to table from which the wine steward mixed cocktails. While he took the orders for the wines and water to accompany the meal, I would go to the cellar to fetch them. I was not allowed yet to serve the guests. In today's hotel and restaurant world this is unheard of but back then it was the norm.

A few months passed and I was eventually promoted to food assistant waiter. This was a step in the right direction. I was just sixteen years old and the youngest of the assistant waiters. Some of them were ready to go to military service and the oldest one was thirty years old and married with a child. How he and his family could survive on his insubstantial wage I do not know but he seemed to manage and was always cheerful. Definitely a case of ignorance is bliss. I was just happy to be doing what I had come to Rome to do even if the earnings were meagre, the hours long and the work itself very physical.

It consisted of fetching the food up from the kitchen one floor below the restaurant, then walking the length of a long corridor to bring it to the waiter who would then serve the diners. There was an elevator but it was broken most of the time. When that was the case I had a forty step flight of stairs to negotiate up and down all day and at full speed. Whenever the elevator broke down one of us assistant waiters had to go to the elevator room and hit the elevator trip switch with a broom stick to get the elevator going again.

Shortly after I was also assigned to be the breakfast assistant waiter. This was a job of more responsibility. Every morning, without fail, I had to start work at 7.00 am as guests would come to the dining room and expect to be served. There was a little plus to this extra sacrifice. The old cook who was preparing eggs, bacon, sausages, porridge and the like for breakfast took a liking to me. Not having enjoyed much of a grandpa myself I affectionately called him Grandpa - or maybe I did so because he was also in charge of preparing the staff luncheons and dinners! He knew that what he was allowed to serve us was falling short of the daily recommended quantity and quality of food which a sixteen year old growing lad required. So to compensate for that he would fry or boil two eggs, grill bacon and make toast just for me. I loved that. Even more so because I could pour myself a large glass of black coffee and lace it with some brandy nicked from the bottle used to make thousand island dressing for the shrimp cocktail. Thinking back to that time, I am not at all sure that having a generous serving of black coffee and brandy for breakfast is what my mother would have given me.

YOUNG LOVE

The elevator being frequently broken down provided me with the great benefit of having to pass through the telephone switchboard room in order to reach the elevator control room ... and Tonella Carlino worked in the telephone switchboard room. She was a black haired, black eyed beauty from Calabria with gleaming white teeth and a smile that never ended. Like me she was just sixteen years old. She was living with her parents, an older sister and brother and a baby brother in an apartment just a bus ride away from the hotel. Her father turned out to be the hotel carpenter so he was keeping an eye on her. Also he was a pure Calabrese man, this meant that you did not fool around with his daughter.

There were days when the elevator would work fine and therefore didn't require the broom handle treatment. That meant I did not see Tonella. This made me kind of sad as I really liked her. But the day came soon enough when the elevator stopped working again. Tonella was alone in the telephone room when I marched through it on my way to the motor room. I did not want to miss the opportunity to ask her out as I had seen some looks in her eyes which made my young mind think that maybe, just maybe, if I asked her out that she would agree.

The challenge was how and where to meet as her time was well controlled by her Calabrese father. But Tonella invented changes of shifts and some such excuse and we were able to meet for a few minutes during my afternoon break and her starting the late afternoon shift. There was a bar nearby that had a juke-box and we would listen to just three songs, as that already cost 100 liras. One of the songs we loved to listen to was the song from the movie Peyton Place. This was how I envisioned real love to be.

As time passed I was able to save enough money to buy a camera. I went around Rome taking pictures to send home to my family who would immediately rush round to the neighbours to show me off. Some months later I had saved enough money to buy a second hand bicycle. Only having ridden the bicycle in my village I found it hard to do so in Rome. There were lots of cars and in true Roman tradition, the drivers were crazy. They had no time nor respect for a young boy on a bike taking up 'their space' on 'their roads'. One day, while making my way to the Villa Borghese Gardens where I had found some other cyclists, I cycled on the fashionable Roman Via Veneto, not realising that push bikes were not allowed. A policeman caught up with me and made me turn back. Shortly after that I thought it best to sell the bike and continue to walk around or take the bus.

My dating with Tonella was going well. By now we were able to go to the movies in the afternoons and, when our days off coincided, we would take the train to the beach or go walking in the woods outside of the city. Many of our walks were now to the Gardens of Villa Borghese where there was a small lake, more like a pond, in which the temple of Aesculapius, the Roman god of healing and medicine stood. The god of healing and medicine part was not very romantic but the little row boats which could be rented for 50 liras an hour sure were. We got into the habit of renting one of those boats. I enjoyed being the macho man who rowed his beloved woman back and forth, back and forth on this small pond called a lake!

After a strenuous hour of rowing we sat on the wooden benches placed around the lake. We watched the elegant black-necked swans swimming peacefully around the calm waters under the huge poplars and rare fruit trees and surrounded by passion flowers, antique tulips and roses proudly showing a thousand shades of colour. And there were etrog, an Aramaic word for delicious, which were nothing else than citrus fruits brought into Rome from Israel many, many years before. It was in this idyllic setting that, on October 16th of 1959 Tonella and I first kissed. Why would I remember so well the date? There is an old Italian saying many times used in romantic song that goes something like this "il primo amore non si scorda mai" (one never forgets his first love). The kiss was sweet, her lips were soft, our mutual innocence was total. We were kind of embarrassed and yet it felt so good. I knew there and then that she ought to be my woman for life.

As we were eyes-closed, savouring the moment, I felt someone tap me on my shoulder. I did not look up to see who it was as I was almost in a trance. It still felt as if the whole world had stopped. I was light as a feather and was flying high in the sky, above the clouds with Tonella in my arms in an embrace which I never wanted to end. But the tapping on my shoulder continued and it soon brought me back to earth. When I opened one eye to look, there before me in his proud uniform stood a carabiniere (a uniform policeman).

His appearance there killed stone dead the romanticism and the magic Tonella and I had been sharing in the previous few minutes. In those days, the carabinieri were still respected and feared. He informed us that we had kissed in public, an act against the 'morale publica' (public morals). Therefore he was going to fine us 600 liras (about 1 dollar at that time). However, he said that he did not wish us to have our record stained for committing such a scandalous act in public, so he would write on the fine receipt that he had caught me jay-walking. Very generous of him to do so.

What he did not know was that at that time I had made up my mind that I was going to ask Tonella's father permission to marry her. A few days later I went to her apartment, met the family – the mother, older sister, brothers and the baby (crawling and farting under the table) - and, at sixteen, arranged to get engaged to be married. It was agreed that I would go at age nineteen to do the then mandatory military service for two years and after that we would get married. With that settled we took the bus and went to work. On the bus we were just so happy and coy, like two white doves in love. Really it felt good until I went to work and then it hit me like a ton of bricks. I had made a commitment to marry Tonella with her father, a man who would easily kill me or have someone break my legs. At least that is what we in the north of the country where I was born and had lived up to a few months before thought about southern Italian fathers. Crikes, I had to get out of this! But how was I going to do that without broken bones or maybe even getting killed? Mother of course, she'd know what to do ... again.

That same evening I wrote her a letter telling her what I had done but that I wanted to get out. I continued my letter by suggesting that she and my father write me a letter stating that, because I was under age, they were prohibiting me from getting engaged until I was at least twenty-one years old. They did write me that letter and then worried themselves sick until they heard back from me. When I received that 'Dear John' letter I showed it to Tonella who, not surprisingly, broke down in tears. But she did understand and would pass on the news of my parents' prohibition to her father. He did not take it lightly. He would not accept my parents decision until he had his wife and a midwife perform a check up on Tonella to verify that she was still a virgin. Examination completed, virginity confirmed, I was free to go with my body intact. My parents and I could sleep peacefully again.

Tonella and I were still very much in love and we continued our secret dating whenever we could manage it. I kept a photograph of her and it is still somewhere in a box at home in Arizona. After I left Rome I never saw her again but I thought of her for a long time ... until I fell in love again about three years later.

THE YEAR OF 1960

The year of 1960 saw many changes in my life. It was a year which taught me many lessons. By spring time I had been working for a little over twelve months at the Mediterraneo hotel. I felt that I now knew a lot and needed to experience something different, something more extravagant than a five star hotel. In June one of the waiters working in the hotel was caught fiddling the tips and was asked to leave. He did so and went to work in a Russian night club on the outskirts of Rome called, naturally, Samovar. What else could a Russian night club be called? As a bit of vengeance towards the hotel he took with him a couple of the hotel boys. I was one of them.

Working at the Samovar was completely illegal for me as the law required that I must be eighteen. I was more than a year short of that. In summer the club was open air. It boasted an elevated dance floor with the tables placed around it, some of them in the open enabling the guests to see the stars above and some under beautiful pergolas on a higher level. The romantic atmosphere was further enhanced by two bands which played alternately. The night club life was certainly new to me and intriguing too. I encountered many fascinating personalities; world famous movie stars such as Brigitte Bardot (now quite old and a champion of animal rights), Claudia Cardinale (now seventy-seven), Marcello Mastroianni (who suffered from pancreatic cancer and died in Paris in 1996) and Sofia Loren ... she born in 1934, still alive today and looking every bit the great lady she always was.

The most colourful regular guest was the exiled King Farouk of Egypt. His Majesty would visit two or three times per week and he was always the last one to leave in the morning. He was a heavy set man, round faced and had a pointed beard at the end of his chin. In a chauffeur driven black Rolls Royce he would normally show up at about midnight. He obviously had the money to indulge himself in an extravagant life style.

There were three things that he absolutely loved - French champagne, Russian caviar and ... women! He was always accompanied by five of the most beautiful ladies one could imagine. Contrary to the idea that royalty need be pompous, distant and would only shake your hand if wearing a pair of fine gloves, a la Queen Elizabeth of the United Kingdom, King Farouk was jovial, constantly laughing, never complaining and extremely generous with his tipping. This year was also the year of the Olympic Games in Rome and the city was crowded with people from all over the world. The congestion in the streets was really chaotic. In the midst of all this I decided to leave the club and go back to the five star hotels.

I got myself a job as an assistant waiter at the Michelangelo Hotel, at the side of Saint Peter's square. What a mistake that was. It was a terribly run business and by September I was fired along with many other workers as the season was coming to an end. With my dose of humility I went back to see Mr.Hats at the Mediterraneo Hotel. Either because I had made a good impression on him while working there or simply because he was a generous and kind man, he gave me my old job back.

But after only three months or so of working there I got itchy feet again. There were eight assistant waiters working at the hotel and we all decided that it was time for us to go abroad. This to learn other languages, live other cultures and meet new people, especially girls! We had heard that foreign girls, especially those in northern Europe, were more prone to fall for the charms of young Italian boys.

The procedure to find a job abroad in those days was a bit cumbersome. You had to find where good hotels were and write a letter (preferably in the language of the country) introducing yourself and offering them your services. The labour market in Europe for hotel workers was good at that time.

While French men were the elite of the kitchens all over Europe and the Germans were the most in demand for reception work we, the Italians, were the most wanted to work in the restaurants of the famous hotels all over Europe. Within two months all eight of us had secured work in different countries throughout the continent and all planned to leave the hotel in spring. This news of course could not be kept secret. Management found out about our intentions pretty damned quick.

One morning as we all showed up to work we were met at the entrance of the hotel, given our pink slips and told to clear out our lockers and go away. Eight new assistant waiters were already working in our place. What really was sad was the fact that, in those days to be a restaurant manager in Italy, it was a requirement to be fluent in French and English as a minimum; better still if you had a good command of German and Spanish too. The fact that we were fired because we wanted to go out of the country to learn those languages in order to come back one day and be better employees was beyond my understanding.

It was early March of 1961 and, since my job offer was in Switzerland and would not start until Easter which was in late April, I had about two months to kill. I could do nothing or find myself another job in Rome and turn down the Swiss offer. So I started going from hotel to hotel and immediately received an offer from the Grand Hotel. Mr.Hats yet again helped out by giving me a glowing reference. Naturally he disclosed to the hotel the reason for my dismissal and he made me promise that I would stay there for at least one year. I was five months short of my eighteenth birthday.

By now I was the complete city boy. I had learned how to walk on a carpeted floor and could tell anyone where to stick it in a perfect Roman accent! I had learned all the swear words and could use them with all the sophistication of a local. However I had yet to learn to do what every Roman man and boy does to show their appreciation of a beautiful young woman passing by. That is to pinch her behind!

Tonella was still in my thoughts but with less tenderness and longing in my heart. We would meet up occasionally in a bar in the afternoon to listen to some songs on the juke-boxes which had become very popular by then. One afternoon I happened to walk down Via Veneto behind her. She was holding on to the arm of a more mature man. I knew then it was all over. Fortunately a great embarrassment was avoided as they did not see me and I made sure to turn the next corner to avoid that possibility. After that I never saw or heard from her again. After all these years sometimes I still think of her. I wonder what she is doing and what would life have been like had I stuck to the original plan of marrying her.

LADIES OF THE NIGHT

As the time was passing and I continued to grow so were my male hormones. Naturally I was not the only one at the Grand Hotel to whom this was happening. All the other assistant waiters were the same age as me and experiencing the same thing. What could we do about it? 'Easy' girls were not too common as the more restricted southern Italian way of life became more prevalent the further one went toward the heel of the 'Italian boot'. So what could I and the other boys do? The solution we found was not original, it was called prostitutes. With our limited funds there were only two possible places to quell our passions.

One of these venues was the slums, called Mandrione, in the outskirts of the eternal city. Some evenings, after work, a bunch of us would get together on a tramcar heading for the slums and the 1,000 liras a throw (1.66 dollars) prostitutes. There, the girls would sit outside their doors displaying their merchandise as is done in Hamburg and Amsterdam, but in a less sophisticated manner. You simply chose your fancy and walked in. I can never forget one evening that I was lying in bed with one of these poor souls with her huge, black, pit-bull lying under it and her pimp standing outside the door, both ready to step into action in case there was trouble. A salubrious experience not and not one to be proud of.

The other venue was one of the most beautiful places in the world during the day but with an area which at night transformed into a meeting place for all the semi-retired and less in demand prostitutes. This was the Villa Borghese Gardens. Here these poor women sold their less attractive bodies for the same 1,000 liras, as if there was a price fixing mechanism in place with the slum women. There was a difference in the methodology in which the encounters took place here. While the shacks of the slums gave a little more privacy, here the action took place under the stars and the moon against a tree trunk. It was private enough as the trees were huge and the foliage made for a natural cover. Also it was clear that all of the men standing around were there for the same purpose so there was no risk to their anonymity. As for me, by that time my altar boy conscience was silenced and my fear of roasting in hell had totally disappeared.

Working at the Grand Hotel definitely added a feather to your cap in those days. Having this name on the resumé would open many doors in the city as well as in many other cities around the world, increasing the possibility of landing good jobs. There was, however, a price to pay for the privilege - the pay was one of the lowest in the city. The staff accommodation was just about okay with two boys per room but the common bathrooms and showers were not great. Being out of the hotel after twelve midnight meant you had to come in the main hotel entrance where the night concierge would take your name and report it to the personnel office the following morning. Too many such infringements was considered irresponsible behaviour and could result in you being fired.

While the learning was great, the teaching methods were primitives to say the least. No formal training was given to staff working in hotels in those days. The most common practice at the Grand was for the restaurant manager to come up behind an assistant waiter and, in full view of all the guests, kick him in the shins or punch him in the ribs. While the restaurant manager was the worst in this respect, the sous-chef in the kitchen was also mean. He ought to have been tried for cruelty. One common trick he would pull was to heat one end of a silver platter over the fire and then hand it hot end first to his unfortunate victim! He also kept at his side a metal bar about 2 feet (60 cm) long with which he would rap our knuckles just as we were reaching over the kitchen window to pick up the platters of food to take to the diners. Another trick of the cooks was to shower us at the restaurant entrance with handfuls of white flour when we were wearing black-tail formal uniform and then laugh their heads off as if this was the funniest thing they had seen in a long time.

I shall never forget for as long as I live the night that Harry Belafonte, the very famous Jamaican born American singer, was being honoured at the hotel by his recording company. A royal table (a large oval shaped one) with about fifty guests seated around it was set up in the middle of the ballroom. When the Grand had been a monastery the ballroom had been the chapel for the monks. It was built out of Carrara marble, with Murano crystal chandeliers and with four large affreschi (paintings) covering the entire ceiling. This artwork represented the four seasons. The ballroom was just stunning in its magnificence.

The elaborate menu consisted of a Russian caviar starter, a delicate fillet of sole fish course and a lemon champagne sorbet to cleanse the palate. This was followed by an individual heart of beef fillet Rossini with its medallion of rich French foie gras (goose liver paté) crowning it, then a tray of cheeses from the world and finally crepes suzettes (thin pancakes). These were prepared with caramelised sugar, orange juice and Grand Marnier liqueur (an orange based French delicacy) flamed at the table side with a Luis XIII cognac, the most expensive and considered the best cognac in the world. This cognac came in a Baccarat crystal bottle and if you were the last customer to drink from the bottle you got to keep it as a souvenir. The waiters and us assistants all wore a black livery of the eighteen hundreds, a white wig and white gloves.

The mean restaurant manager, wearing his impeccable white tuxedo, had given all of us a very specific order of service which we had to follow to the 'T'. We were to approach the table together and let each guest serve himself/herself the caviar with all the trimmings. We were assigned ten guests each. When our guests had helped themselves we were to step back three steps and hold the tray in our hand until he would give a nod. This meant we had to approach the table and offer a second helping. The tray on which the caviar was presented was a large, thick silver one. On top of it sat an ice-carved base with a battery powered light in it, a can of Beluga caviar weighing 5 pounds (2 kg), a silver bowl with quartered lemons, another with finally chopped onions and a silver caviar spoon. We were expected to stand still holding that enormous weight on our hand for a considerable time.

The young assistant waiter next to me couldn't sustain the

weight. Faced with the prospect of dropping the whole lot on the floor and getting sacked, he chose to set his tray down on a service stand just two steps away from him. No sooner had he done this than the mean restaurant manager walked up behind him and, without saying a word, kicked him in the shin with such brutal force that to this day I can hear the noise of his shoe hitting the bone. Fortunately for the rest of us the meal passed without any more beatings. A few years after I left Italy and started travelling and working around the world, a powerful union gained a hold in the hotels in the country and those abuses were not taken as a laughing matter anymore.

A GRAND CHOICE

The Grand Hotel was the hotel of choice in Rome in political and diplomatic circles. Foreign dignitaries, presidents, prime ministers, kings and queens would stay there while on official visits. Because of this status it was also the hotel which would provide outside catering at the various Roman villas in which some ministries were housed. Palazzo della Farnesina was the Ministry of Foreign affairs where many of these meals were delivered to. Her majesty Queen Elizabeth II was one of the most prominent dignitaries to be entertained there. Villa Madama also belonged to the Ministry of Foreign Affairs and was used for the same purpose. It was in this villa that Raffaello, one of the greatest Renaissance painters, was engaged to do major work. The story goes that one day while he was out for lunch Michelangelo paid him a visit. In order to let Raffaello know that he had been to visit him, Michelangelo in one corner of the loggia, on bare cement, painted an angel and left. Upon his return Raffaello immediately saw and recognised the brush strokes of the 'greatest of all' and, out of respect, left that corner untouched.

While the Excelsior Hotel was the preferred hotel of the 'movers and shakers' such as movie stars, opera singers, actors and the like the Grand had its share as well. At times actresses of great fame were invited by dignitaries and presidents to join them in the Royal Suite for cocktails, dinner or who knows what else? Well nobody really knew 'what else' because the room service waiters who would serve at those parties were, under penalty of being fired, sworn to secrecy.

There was one particular actress, very famous, who paid special visits to Asian presidents. Later on she was also known to have become the mistress of a French president. There was one occasion when 'everyone who was anyone' in the Hollywood world were there to celebrate the first anniversary of the movie Spartacus. This was in October of 1961. In addition to Kirk Douglas, Laurence Olivier, Peter Ustinov and all the cast, Elizabeth Taylor and her fourth husband Eddie Fisher were in attendance. The most vivid memory of this super luxurious party I have is the image of seeing Eddie Fisher, Elizabeth Taylor, Gina Lollobrigida and her husband Milko Skofic, a Yugoslavian doctor, sitting together enjoying each other's company. While Elizabeth Taylor was a very attractive women, Gina (known as 'La Lollo') overshadowed her beauty a thousand times over. At that time Gina was indeed the most beautiful woman in the world!

Among the powerful people frequenting the restaurant at the Grand there were remnants of the fascist regime. By then old men without political influence but with plenty time to reminisce about the 'good old days'. Also Arsenio Armatore, a super-rich old Neapolitan ship owner, businessman and politician was a regular guest, staying in the Royal suite when not occupied by foreign dignitaries. He always came accompanied by beautiful women. While this was the same habit as that of His Majesty King Farouk, Armatore was much more discrete. He would come with only one at a time. His usual routine was to have a romantic tête-a-tête lunch with Russian caviar and French champagne served. Then he would produce from his pocket an eighteen karat gold whisk and whip the champagne to remove all the natural bubbles which are the main characteristic of the wine.

In October that year the flagship of his fleet, the MS Arsenio Armatore, was hijacked off the Egyptian Coast by the PLO. One retired, wheelchair-bound, sixty-nine year old American was shot dead by the four hijackers who forced the ship's barber and a waiter to throw him overboard.

Weddings of the rich and famous were a weekly affair, political and social events were the norm and all in all it was a great experience for a boy of eighteen to work there.

At the Grand I reconnected with Renato, a cook six years older than myself who came from the opposite side of the lake to my home village and with whom I'd worked for a short time at the Michelangelo Hotel. We spoke the same dialect, had the same family values as our parents who were about the same age, and we enjoyed the same life style. Renato perfected me on how to play a card game that I had learned a few years earlier from our parish priest while an altar boy. The only problem was that I was naïve; he would cheat, win and I had to pay up all the time. Once in a dance hall I met a maid from the island of Sardinia. She was probably twelve years older than me and I introduced her to Renato. He promptly persuaded her not to go out with me anymore but to go out with him. Renato today is seventy-eight, semi-retired and divorced with two adult daughters, four grand-children and lives in St.Charles, MI. We are still close friends, visiting each other every time there is an opportunity.

By that time I had also started going to a trattoria (a typical Italian restaurant) for lunch on my day off whenever I spent it in the city. I went to the same trattoria, ate the same food and the bill came to the same 600 liras (1 dollar). I loved to start my meal with a plate of salt-cured anchovies and butter, the main course was a fillet of beef with a generous salad, the dessert was either a maritozzi (a bun-like soft pastry filled with whipped cream) or a cannoli (a tube-shaped shell of fried pastry filled with creamy ricotta cheese), a ristretto (a very short espresso coffee) and all washed down with a quarter of a litre of Frascati, (a dry white wine from the Roman hills of Frascati). Usually after this great lunch I would catch a matinée (afternoon show) at the nearby Volturno Theatre. For a mere 180 liras (33 cents) I could see a stage show of dancing girls in their skimpy outfits offering a generous view of their voluptuous bodies, some mediocre singers and a movie, in black and white of course. In the summer months it was more common for me to take a train ride in the morning to one of the beaches about 20 miles (32 km) out of the city. A very popular seaside resort at that time was the beach town of Ostia.

On one of my beach outings, following a lunch on the terrace restaurant with the customary quarter litre of Frascati, I decided to lie in the sun for a few minutes. I fell asleep belly down and with my back to the sun. I must have slept for quite some time. When I woke up, I felt very hot. It was now time to take the train back to the city. By the time I got to the main train station, I felt very hot indeed. Back in my room I took my shirt off and, to my horror, saw that my back was as red as embers. It was covered in water-filled, baggy blisters and causing me unbearable pain. I had no choice but to rush out to the emergency room at the nearest hospital where the young doctor on duty diagnosed me with third degree sun burn. He prescribed some cream to be generously splashed on my back and sent me on my merry way. It took many nights of sleeping lying on my belly before things got better. Eventually they did and I was back in top shape never to be burned by the hot Roman sun again.

It turned out that the mean restaurant manager at the Grand had some generosity in his heart after all. His good point was that, contrary to the behaviour of the management of the Mediterraneo who fired all their assistant waiters for wanting to better themselves, he annually chose the two best young men from his team and sent them to Baden-Baden in Germany to the Bellevue Hotel. During the sad marriage of Nazi Germany and Fascist Italy the son of the owner, now the managing director of the hotel, had worked at the Grand and forged a friendship with our mean manager. This friendship was based, as I would discover a few years later, on their mutual admiration and practice of the 'terror to young assistants' philosophy. In February of 1962 he told me and Romano, the second assistant chosen, that we would go to work in Germany starting in March. This was exhilarating news for me. The future, as I had dreamed it, was starting to take shape. Although I had envisioned that Paris would be my first move outside of Italy I was not about to turn down this great opportunity and gladly accepted to go. Preparations for my emigration were made and the passport needed obtained.

When anyone from the poorer south of Italy travelled on trains it was normal for them to carry their belongings in carton boxes wrapped with strings. This for a young man going to work in a foreign country and in a five star resort was inconceivable. So I discarded my faithful cardboard suitcase and bought myself two beautiful black leather ones. They had no wheels back then, you just filled them to the brim and carried them. As Romano, my friend and companion in the adventure, was from central Italy we decided that it would be a good idea to spend two weeks with our families before going on to Baden-Baden. It was also agreed that Romano would stop at my house for two days on the way north, meet my family and then move on. The last thing left for us to do was to visit the Trevi Fountain and toss in the traditional three coins which would ensure that destiny brought us back to Rome at some point in the future. With all that agreed and settled we left Rome for our villages full of enthusiasm and dreams of what life would bring us in the years to come.

And now I was back home, and ready to emigrate to Germany - or was I?

Back in 1958, and against my mother's best judgment, my sister Anna had started dating Tullio, a boy two years her junior and from a nearby village. While Tullio seemed a nice enough boy, hard-working and mature, my mother was more concerned about his mother's reputation as an 'easy lay'. This was well known in the communities around the lake as she had been besieged by boys clamouring for her sexual favours in her younger days. What concerned my mother was the old Latin saying 'tamquam matri tallis filius' (like mother like son) as it might apply to Tullio. Not for the first time, my mother's intuition would in due course be proved right. Tullio was the only son of his father but his mother's daughter and other son were children of affairs with two other men. Miriam, Tullio's sister, turned out to be promiscuous like her mother. This was known to her husband, a hard working and respected butcher, who forgave her and continued to live with her and their two boys. Be that as it may all was proceeding quietly at home and Tullio and my sister were madly in love and happy together.

BROKEN BONES AND SUMMER ROMANCES

As I was the village son who had taken up the challenge of going to Rome alone and had not slunk back with my tail between my legs as soon as the going got difficult, I found myself popular with the girls of the village, even ones older than myself. I was considered a 'prime pick' as it was perceived that I would be able to take a village girl away from factory work and poor housing to a higher standard of living. In the afternoon of March 19th, Saint Joseph's day, Tullio loaned me his Italian Vespa scooter to go for a run. I needed to be back before 9.30 pm as I had a date with Bruna arranged.

As I was returning to the village I clipped a kerb with the scooter and was thrown off and into a field. I struggled upright and put my right foot down. Fine for the first two steps but on the third step my tibia, the bone that goes from the ankle to the knee, totally snapped. It pierced the muscle of my shank sending pain shooting through all of my body as if a power drill had been driven into my leg. I staggered to a nearby walnut tree and propped myself against it. A short while later a girl from the village and her fiancé, riding also on a Vespa, came to my rescue. With their help I got on to the scooter and they took me to a doctor's home about half a mile (800 m) away. The doctor was out on an emergency call so his mother gave me coffee and I waited holding my broken right leg with both my hands. My family was informed and my sister and Tullio came to the doctor's home before he arrived back from his emergency call. When the doctor arrived he confirmed that my tibia was totally snapped as my foot was loose and going from one side to the other like the pendulum of a grandfather clock.

He told me that he would take me to the hospital in the city. "No way," I said, "I must be in Baden-Baden in two weeks." He laughed and replied, "Yes that's possible, but only if you go there with a plaster cast from your toes to your upper hip." I was devastated. He put me in his car and drove me to the hospital. Being a holiday the surgeon was not available, so the male nurse on duty gave me an injection of morphine to kill the pain and I was half asleep when my mother and father arrived at the hospital. It was not until the following day that the surgeon saw me and examined my leg. Because it was so swollen, setting my bone and putting a plaster on it was not possible for a few days. I was also sad as I thought of Bruna waiting for me and for me not to show up was really bad form.

About five days later I went home. Because my bedroom was on top of the sixteen step stairway I couldn't go up there so a bed was prepared for me in the kitchen. There I would sleep for the next three months. Lots of people came to see me. As I had no way to hide, I had to put up with even the ones I would have preferred not to see. One of the visitors I was particularly happy to see was Fiorina, without any doubt the prettiest girl in the village. On the other hand there was Girasole and her sister Pia who I did not like at all. What can you do? ... sometimes you have to take the good with the bad. The village was small and being polite to everyone and being liked was imperative for a peaceful co-existence.

A carpenter friend of my father made a pair of crutches for me. They were simply two poles with padding at the tops to serve as arm-pit rests. Thus 'armed' with my new crutches and with more determination than sense I, accompanied by two of my best friends Chiaro and Paolo, limped the half mile (800 m) up the very steep hill to join the other young boys and girls at the bar. Under a pergola of grapevines there was outdoor dancing every evening to the beat of the twist, rock 'n roll and slow dancing. This last dance looked and felt more as if the two dancers were lying on upright beds, swaying the upper part of their bodies, holding on tight to their partner and hardly moving their feet at all. It looked and felt just like a perpetual hug. No wonder this style of dancing was called 'il ballo del mattone' - the brick dance.

For the next three months I could not participate as my plastered leg would not allow me to stand on it and dance the night away. Fortunately, as summer came around, so too did the girls from the city for their well earned summer vacation. By then, with some strain, I could get on to the dance floor and dance all night. The twist was the new American dance. "Come on let's twist again!" shouted Chubby Checker from the juke-box and got everyone awake and bopping and putting a stop to the brick dance dream of floating on air with a beautiful girl in your arms. What a bummer.

Fulvia, a nice looking girl two years older than me, was my dream girl for the month she holidayed in the village. With black hair, big eyes and fair skin she just looked lovely. But at the end of her vacation she had to return home and I was very sad ... until ... Angela, also from the city, arrived. She was a different beauty. A sparkling blonde with an astounding figure, very outgoing yet mysterious too. She made me quickly forget Fulvia, the very religious and conservative beauty, who, for one month had my head spinning. After Angela left Giuseppina came to the village. She was a different kettle of fish altogether. A few years older, married and, while not necessarily a beauty, was a very liberated woman. She worked as a striptease dancer in a city night club but my adventure with her only lasted until one very hot evening in the middle of August when I donned a suit to go dancing. My dear mother confronted me as I was leaving the house saying, "So it's true, you are going around with that stripper?" So one more romance went down the drain. It was far more important for me to be at peace with my mother than to mess about with Giuseppina.

Towards the end of the summer the plot thickened when Paola returned to the village with her aunt and her grandmother. Her family had for many years rented a house in the village. Paola's family were from Milan and ran a toy shop. Paola was studying to be a nurse, a very prestigious profession at that time. She had short black hair, a beautiful face and a slim young body. Because the entire family belonged to the Alpine Club, they would go most weekends to the high Alps and hike for hours on end. This exercise kept her body strong and athletic, she looked healthy and fresh. Between the two of us something very beautiful happened, love blossomed! Paola and I become inseparable.

Her father was a decent man who would pedal his push bike the 60 miles (96 km) between Milan and the village every weekend to spend the time with his family. Ever since I remember he would never arrive in the village empty handed. He always brought me a toy from the shop as ours were all home made and looked a bit pathetic. He had little trouble in approving mine and Paola's romance but her mother had a different agenda. For her, a young woman like Paola had to have a husband of comparable status, someone with a degree. Also a man who would stay all of his, and consequently her, life near them. I on the other hand had only an elementary education, was from the village, from a family with no resources and was an assistant waiter. Although my family were morally good and I was now more of a city boy than a village one and determined to make it in life, all of the other minuses carried more weight with her.

Somewhere in a box there should still be a black and white photo which Paola gave me the morning she, her favourite aunt and her grandmother were leaving the village to return to the city. She kissed me 'goodbye' and slid me that photo. When she had left I looked at it, turned it over and she had written, "Ti voglio bene. Tre parole piene di comprensione, gratitudine e amore". (I love you. Three words full of understanding, gratitude and love).

Paola and I continued to write to each other for another two years.

Chapter 4

I LOVE PARIS

November 1962. My leg had regained the ability to support me and I could walk quickly and steadily. Ottavio, one of my friends from the Grand Hotel in Rome, had moved on to Paris working at the Grand Hotel there. He recommended me to the restaurant manager who promptly offered me a job as an assistant waiter. This hotel had opened in 1862. By European standards of the time it was very big with four hundred and seventy rooms. I was on top of the world. I could walk well again and had a job in Paris, wow! My life had taken the direction I wanted and I was so happy to get myself going again. I had to make the necessary arrangements for the trip to Paris. I did not speak French but that was only secondary to the fact that I was going to go from the Eternal City to the City of Lights. I was just a few months over nineteen years old. I was no longer making water taps and it looked like I was not going back to it either.

I arrived in Paris after an all-night train ride. Ottavio had made arrangements for me to share his room for a few days until I could find somewhere suitable for myself. After the luxury of the Grand in Rome the Grand in Paris was a big letdown - but that was not important. While in the early years of its life the Grand had been host to many famous people such as Tzar Nicholas and Tzarina Alexandra of Russia, there were no important nor famous people stayed at the hotel during the time I worked there. The guests were group after group of American tourists.

The restaurant was a very large room with a terrace spilling over the lobby of the hotel - and it was dirty. The walls were so dusty that you could write on them and one assistant waiter did indeed write on it the word 'Omo', the name of a popular washing detergent. At breakfast, lunch and dinner it was like serving an army as the many rooms would host about one thousand guests who had to be fed three time per day. The hotel had two entrances. The official postal address of 2, Rue Scribe under the porte-a-cocher led guests directly to the reception desk. The second, more discreet entrance at 12, Boulevard des Capucines was favoured by guests who did not wish to be seen checking into a hotel but which still led them and their paramours to the bar and to the restaurant.

The kitchens were a floor below the restaurant and I had to carry the food all the way up to the restaurant in record time to serve the multitudes. The general manager, Mr.Siebert, had white hair, a beautifully trimmed white moustache and always wore an impeccable Yves St.Laurent suit. When passing through the restaurant he would, in classic Gallic fashion, never greet anyone. Mr.Couturier (Mr.Taylor), the director of personnel, would have his meals every day in the restaurant wearing the same jacket and trousers. He would drink a litre of red wine with each meal. Because of that we nicknamed him Mr.Beaujolais.

In a very short time I was able to find a chambre de limonadier (a waiter's room) in a small hotel on Rue de Provence just a five minute walk from the hotel. This street was famous for having a large number of street walkers who were the principal users of 'chambres a la journee' (day rooms). My room was not very chic but not bad for a nineteen year old in Paris. It was long and narrow with one metal bed, a chair, a small wooden closet and a sink. The bathroom had to be shared with other guests who were mostly prostitutes. In the corner of the street there was a bar called Bar du Soleil. In the evening on my way from work, I would stop there and eat jambon de Bayonne (cured ham) in a long baguette (French bread) along with a demi-panache (a beer and lemonade). Right underneath my hotel there also was a restaurant called Chez Madame Violot with an affordable menu every day of the week.

The treatment we were receiving from the restaurant manager, contrary to what we had experienced in Rome, was excellent, polite and very fair. My day started at 6.30 am serving breakfast, followed by lunch service until about 3.00 pm, after which I rushed out to attend French lessons at the Alliance Française. Then I returned to work to serve dinner until about 10.30 pm. My day off was Friday. Every Friday night I would go dancing at the Alliance Française Club. It was a real bonanza to hook up with young people from all over the world, girls and boys, all about my age and sharing my same zest for life. Their dreams and mine were very much the same; their reasons for being there matched mine; we all wanted to learn French with the hope it would help us to a better future. So life was really looking up and things got even better when, after only four months, I was promoted to a waiter position.

The restaurant manager had taken a liking to me and promoted me quickly. Because he trusted me he installed me as the only foreign waiter and the youngest one to open the restaurant six mornings a week for breakfast. The usual waiters trusted with that mission were all French and had been working at the hotel for more years than my entire life. When there are more than one thousand guests coming to have breakfast in the restaurant the opening time cannot be delayed. Come hail or high water at 6.30 am I had to be there and open the restaurant.

Working all these long hours every day did not diminish my enthusiasm. If anything, it increased it. Discovering Paris for a twenty year old boy from Centonara was a reality beyond my wildest dream. Conquering Rome was already a great achievement but Paris was the pinnacle of success. The Champs-Elysees, the Eifel Tower, the Sacré Coeur during the day and Pigalle, the Moulin Rouge and the Lido during the night were no longer vague black and white photographs I had seen on old postcards – they were real! I could walk the streets and the markets of this beautiful city. I could go to eat soupe a l'oignon (onion soup) at Les Halles at 4.00 am. I could smoke Gauloises (full strength French cigarettes) and savour the aromas of freshly made coffee and warm croissants from the patisseries on my way to work each morning. The green public buses with their bells and open backs had become the trusted friends and companions who would take me around in the summer evenings while absorbing the sounds of a city that is always alive and never sleeps. Galleries La Fayette had no rivals in the world when it came to shopping. Even if I could not afford to buy anything there, just walking around it made me feel like a million dollars. At twenty years of age this was not just being alive, this was living life as if nothing else in the world mattered.

I had become an expert on Pigalle. I had loaned some money to a colleague, a boy a couple of years older than myself who also was a waiter at the Grand. I felt sorry for the guy as he had fallen head over heels in love with a prostitute whose base of operation was Place Blanche. After he had quit his job owing me money I decided I was going to find him and ask him for my money back. Knowing where his love would be walking the street, every night after work I walked up there in an attempt to find him. After spending some hours looking for him and finding no trace I would run down Rue Fontaine and go to bed. This lasted for several months until I decided that most likely I would never find him again and had to change strategy. I had his address in Nice and decided to write to his mother, a widow, telling her the whole story. She replied and said she was very sorry to hear about it. She told me that she would come to Paris to look for her son and she would definitely give me the money he owed me. This poor woman did exactly that. I felt so bad when she came to the hotel with tears of shame in her eyes and paid me back. Oh Paris, la Ville Lumiere, (the city of lights) how do I miss you even now at seventy-two years of age!

My social and amorous life also took a turn I did not expect. One afternoon, during the French class, I felt a light tap on my shoulder. In truth it felt more like a caress than a tap. When I turned I was confronted by this stunning Viking blonde with blue eyes and all-embracing smile. "Do you have an eraser, please?" This was my introduction to Anita Elberg, a goddess from Graenna in Sweden, a town at the edge of a lake famous for its sweets. Anita was in Paris to learn French. She was working as an au pair for an elderly aristocratic lady who lived in a magnificent apartment in the 8th municipality of Paris. This municipality, along with the 16th municipality, are considered the two best areas in which to live in

Paris. The au pair girls keep such older ladies company and in exchange they get a little money and a chambre de bonnes (maid's room) to live in. All of their meals are taken in the kitchen of the apartment, they would not normally be invited to eat with their employers. The maid's rooms are all located on the top floor of the building and are poorly furnished with typically just an iron bed, a chair, a small closet and maybe a hand sink. Very much like the waiters' rooms the toilet is outside and shared with other maids working in the same building. A proper bathroom with at least a shower did not exist either.

In spite of its meagre make up, Anita's room became a beautiful corner of paradise for me. There I learned what it meant to share the passion of a nubile, young woman. Anita taught me with patience and understanding how to love her and bring her to ecstasy, losing ourselves for hours at a time in loving that was so new to me and, to be frank, at the same time frightening too. During our intimate encounters the only chair in the room was placed near the bed to be used as a bedside table. On it we would place a lit candle, a bottle of whisky, two glasses, an ashtray and a pack of Parliament cigarettes. We were culturally very different. She was an open minded Swede brought up with the mentality that it was a normal thing to have sex with a virtual stranger. I, on the other hand, with my altar boy mentality, felt guilty and somewhat stressed and nervy in front of her statuesque body. Part of the challenge for me as a semi-virgin boy of twenty was the feeling that I had to 'perform' at all costs.

Our adventure lasted for a few months until the evening I decided to pay her an unannounced visit. As I climbed the six floors to her landing I heard a noise coming from her room. Cautiously I approached the door and looked through the key hole. What I saw was upsetting to say the least. The chair with the same items as before on it was placed near the bed. What I believed had become my place in bed was occupied by a handsome Moroccan boy. By the look and sounds of it he had a lot more experience than me. I thought it best to cut my losses and walked away as silently as I had arrived.

THE FAMILY UNITES

By now it was March of 1963 and I had been in Paris for four months. I had been promoted to waiter and had enjoyed a sensual relationship with a beautiful girl, and Swedish to boot. Things were going well ... too well. The evening came when I received a phone call from Centonara to tell me that my father had passed away that morning. The funeral was to take place in two days time. Needless to say how distressed I was. I got to the train station and booked a ticket on the first train leaving the Gare de Lyon the next morning. The train ride was nice, the views of the mountains and lakes I passed were fabulous and it could have been a beautiful trip had it not been for the sadness weighing heavily on my heart.

At ten in the evening I arrived at the station in Domodossola, a town 43 miles (70 km) from my home. Luckily I found a taxi which took me to Centonara but not until I gave the driver my story and the urgent reason I needed to get home that night. Either because of his kind heart or because of the fare he would earn, perhaps both, he eventually agreed to take me home. At the house, in spite of the wee hours, all my relatives were there waiting for me. My cousin Gianpaolo came with me to the bedroom where my father's stone cold body was at rest.

My dad was wearing the only suit he owned and he looked at peace, even with a smile on his lips. He looked almost happy to be dead. I kissed his forehead and a chill shot through me. It felt like I had kissed a frozen piece of marble. I did not know what to expect as I kissed him and I did not know that death was so cold. In those days, at least in the village, a funeral home did not exist. When someone died the person who would wash and dress the deceased was Erasmo. Yes, the same man who had spent thirty years in prison for the murder of the butcher. Because the deceased was only washed and dressed, the facial expression remained the same as when they died. If they died struggling it looked so, if they died at peace then they looked that way too. My dad looked serene.

As I had arrived, the uncertainty of me making it home on time for the funeral had gone and every member of the family was able to relax a little. After a glass of marsala wine we all retired until early next morning. While it was indeed sad there was also an expression of relief on my mother's face who, by that time, was almost totally blind. Morning came quickly enough but I was awake from about four anyway. By 7.00 am the casket had arrived and we transferred my dad's body into it. The top was not put on so as to give the family members and his many friends the opportunity to have a final sight of a man who had meant so much in their lives.

As 10.00 am approached, six of his friends who had requested the honour of being the pall bearers, brought the sealed casket out and laid it on a table in the centre of the front yard. Everyone came, the whole village was there; his friends from youth, the friends from the marching band and those from the dance quintet. In those days the popularity of a person in life was measured by the number of people who attended their funeral. Going by the number of people who came to say goodbye to my dad, he was indeed a very popular and well loved man. Soon the priest was through with the blessings and the procession set off for the mile (1.6 km) march up the winding road to the parish church. Of the six pall bearers, four would hoist the casket over their shoulders while the other two would serve as reliefs for when the others tired from the weight and the exertion of the steep climb.

The procession formed somewhat like this : At the head was the cross bearer with two altar boys holding large candles. After that came the priest and the altar boys carrying the holy water and the incense burner, then the casket carried on the shoulders of the pall bearers, then my mother holding my arm to her left and that of my sister Anna to her right and with her fiancé Tullio to her right. Then behind us the relatives and closest friends followed by everyone else.

As the procession started up the steep and winding road to the parish church my mind worked its way back as far as I could remember. It probably kicked in at about five years of age and all of my father's life from there on came back to me in the minutest detail. The good, the bad and the ugly of our family life reappeared. It was like I was reliving it all again. Such as the time I had behaved badly and my father and mother wrote a letter to the director of the local boys' reformatory asking that I be sent there to learn manners, of course it was never sent ... And the time when one of his friends cut the nerve of his left hand index finger with an axe while cutting wood and my dad took his shirt off to bandage the finger ... And the time at the workmen's club when I had been cheeky to him in front of the other men and he jumped over the table, grabbed me by the shoulder and walked me home to be grounded for the next two months.

But even than he had been a gentle man, he did not hit me nor shout at me. So I not only learned not to misbehave, he taught me a great lesson in self-control ... And the time he returned home from the hospital in Milan where his younger brother Bernardo (the only boy in the family who had never smoked a cigarette in his life) was dying from lung cancer. My dad shared with us the news that his beloved brother only had days to live, all the while fighting back the tears from his eyes, and yet smilingly recounting the blessings of having had such a wonderful brother.

Now we were reaching the church. The casket was set down in the central aisle and the priest started the Mass. In his elaborate eulogy about my father's virtues he mentioned that he particularly enjoyed playing cards or boccie with my dad as he was not a blasphemous man but a gentle soul who would not hurt anyone, not even when he was losing at the game they were playing. The church service was a sober, yet special and comforting ceremony very much as he would have wished his last goodbye to be.

About one hour later the pall bearers hoisted him on their shoulders again and walked back down the hill the four hundred or so yards (0.35 km) to the cemetery. The grave-digger there was, strangely enough, the same man who had cut his finger all those years before while helping my dad to cut wood. He had prepared the grave where my father was laid to rest for the next thirteen years. After that time his bones would be placed in a small box and put to his final resting place in an alcove of the cemetery. This is how an honest, gentle and kind man and father had lived and died at the age of fifty-three! One week later I returned to Paris leaving my mother and my sister to fend for themselves in the same village and same house that they knew so well.

BACK TO THE CITY OF LIGHT

My life back in the city of light quickly resumed its fast pace. Work was great, the classes at the Aliance Française were going well and soon, to help me to forget Anita, I got myself a new girlfriend. Aicha was a pretty Tunisian girl four years my senior, with long black hair and enormous black eyes. She had a delightful smile showing a perfect line of white teeth highlighted by her almost olive black skin. Her beauty was remarkable. She was the daughter of an officer in the French armed forces and had grown up in France. This made her a north African jewel but with the open mind of a twenty-four year old French woman. We enjoyed going to dances, eating in small restaurants and walking along the Seine under the stars and the moon at night. She was extremely sensual and had no hang-ups in teaching me what she believed I needed to know to be a good lover.

By that time I had moved out of the small chambre de limonadier and into a more upmarket hotel on Rue Le Pelletier, a cross road of Boulevard des Italiens. While it was a nicer hotel the only inconvenience was that I had to share a bed with another fellow who worked with me at the Grand Hotel. We did not have any problem with that. Neither of us were gay. We liked only girls – and lots of them!

Not far from the hotel there was a Wimpy restaurant, an English version of McDonalds, which served hamburgers in a roll, a novelty in Paris in those days. When the food at the cafeteria was reduced to a 'vache qui rit' (laughing cow cheese) and a roll we would go instead for 'un repas dans un pain rond' (a meal in a round bread), such was the elegant title with which the humble hamburger had been christened.

A few more months went by and, one morning as I was doing the breakfast service, I encountered a problem. The bakery contractor failed to deliver the bread on time and the restaurant was full of guests. I was so upset that, when finally the bread arrived and I collected it from the security entrance, I made some unpleasant remarks about the inefficiency of the French bakery and the delivery service. Here I touched the nerves of Mr.Couturier (Mr.Taylor, the chief of personnel) who happened to overhear me. He immediately confronted me and fired me on the spot. Unfortunately for me the restaurant manager who liked and trusted me was on his day off and therefore unable to save me. I went to Couturier's office, collected my papers and the little money the hotel owed me and was sent on my way. I was out of work and did not know what to do.

However, I soon got fixed up with a job at the Atlantic Hotel in Hamburg but it would not start until October. In the meantime, I decided to pay a visit to the owner of the Restaurant Valle d'Isere off the Champs-Elysees. I had met this gentleman five years earlier in the summer of 1958 when I started my hotel work at the Hotel Boletus near my village. He had told me to look him up any time I came to Paris. I was pleasantly surprised to find that, not only did he remember me, but he made me feel like a long lost friend. We sat at the bar and, in good Parisian style, sipped a couple of glasses of top quality champagne. We talked about all the things that had happened since we first met five years earlier and I was only fifteen years of age.

I found it remarkable that a man of his status would sit there with a twenty year old immigrant and share so many personal and professional anecdotes. He told me that his wife had died shortly after they had returned to Paris from their 1958 trip to Italy and he shared with me the fact that his son had no interest in following in his foot-steps in managing the restaurant. Only after about three hours of conversation did we come to talk about the fact that I was unemployed.

While he could not offer me a job in his restaurant he did

recommend that I speak to a friend of his who owned the largest pizza restaurant chain in all of France. I did speak to his friend and I started work in one of his pizza restaurants the very same day - but it felt odd. It might sound snobbish to say so but I was just so absorbed by what my mother had told me for all those years; that to be a waiter in a luxurious hotel in Rome, Paris, London or New York was the best job in the world.

Here I was serving pizzas and, even if it was in Paris, it was something of a let-down. Not just for me but also a kind of betrayal to my mum and her dream of me serving kings and queens seated atop of a Carrara marble floor and under Murano chandeliers. So I packed that in after only a week and went to the Italian embassy to sign for my exemption from mandatory military service (the law granted exemption from military duties to an only male child of a family as being the financial supporter of the family). Then I left Paris for home to take a rest before venturing to Hamburg in Germany.

Chapter 5

A HAMBURG SAUSAGE

October 1963

Armed with my two black leather suitcases I stepped on to the train which would let me off nineteen hours later in Hamburg. I arrived there at 4.00 am and took a taxi to the Atlantic Hotel. I told the doorman, in French, that I was the new assistant waiter. He could not understand French but, with customary German efficiency, he summoned the concierge. The concierge told me that if I were a new employee I had to carry the two cases around the hotel and enter through the employee's entrance. As it was early in the morning the human resources office was not open. The guard on duty showed me the large clock hanging on the wall and managed to tell me to leave my two cases there and come back at 9.00 am to speak to the human resources director.

Even with the long train ride behind me, excitement got the better of me. I walked around the half asleep city for the next four hours admiring the beautiful buildings, the churches and the river which, at that time of the year, appeared to be already almost frozen over. Then, as nine o'clock approached, I returned to the hotel to meet the human resources director. We could hardly communicate but with a mixture of French, English, German, Italian and sign language I was told that I could not start work at the hotel until I had found a room somewhere. He had several addresses of apartments within walking distance of the hotel where the owners would lease to young immigrants coming to work at the hotel. He gave me a city map and off I scurried.

The first two apartments I visited had no rooms available. I was by now starting to feel the body ache and effects of my long train ride, the lack of sleep and my four hour trek around the city. I really needed to find a place to put my head on a pillow and go to sleep for a few hours. Then, at the last address on my list, my ring of the door bell was answered by a sausage looking lady. Somehow I managed not to laugh and made my request for accommodation understood. Or maybe she was simply used to the fact that a young man of foreign origin ringing her bell inevitably wanted a room in which to sleep. Either way she ushered me into the apartment and led me to a small room with a bed. She showed me a common toilet at the end of the corridor but no shower. We agreed on the price and I paid her a week in advance. In the best sign language I could muster I told her that I was going to the Atlantic Hotel to get my two suitcases and would then return to the apartment. I was feeling good. In just a few hours I had already secured work and a place to live. What could possibly go wrong?

When I returned to the apartment with my suitcases I confidently rang the bell. The sausage looking lady opened the door, looked first at me and then at the two suitcases. Suddenly she became the devil possessed, screamed something in German and slammed the door in my face! Perplexed, I sat on the stone steps outside the door trying to think what I had possibly done that could have triggered such a reaction on her part.

At this time I also started to question my wisdom in coming to Germany and if learning German was, after all, so important for my career. I also began to dwell on all the horrendous war stories I had heard as a child. Such as the time the German soldiers were hitting the foot of my parents' bed with the butts of their guns. I recalled the execution of the three hundred and thirty-five civilians at the Ardeatine Caves in reprisal for a partisan attack and, for the first time in my life, I hated the Germans and Germany.

I was still pondering these thoughts and contemplating my next move when the apartment door opened again and the sausage looking lady came out. She eyed me up and down and then, with a half smile on her crooked mouth, she beckoned me to follow her. She guided me to the end of the corridor and opened the door to a room which had two beds. She scribbled a number on a scrap of paper which I deduced was the new price to rent one of these beds.

I understood that she would rent the second bed in the room to someone else. By now I was ready to grab her by the neck and choke her. However, I was too tired to do that and chose instead to go to sleep considering myself lucky that finally I could put my head down.

I do not know how long I slept. It seemed to be forever, until I woke up and needed to go to toilet. This was the next shock. German toilet bowls were not the same as in Italy or France. The German version had a kind of a double bottom and you couldn't see the water but you could see all the excrement. Only when you flushed the toilet did it all mysteriously disappear. Once again German ingenuity at work. While it is kind of unpleasant to see all that you are leaving behind, there is an advantage to this since there is no possibility of splashing water on the lower parts of your body and it was much more comfortable than any kind of toilet I had sat on in the past. As I went to the sink to wash my hands I had another surprise. Turning on the hot water provoked a loud bang in the corner of the bathroom. It took me a few seconds to figure out that this was caused by the ignition of the gas boiler. I was ready to return to sleep and so I did.

An hour or two later I heard the door opening and people speaking in low voices, then the door closed again. I was not too concerned about my personal safety and, since the German marks I had were stashed away in the underwear I had kept on, I did not pay any attention when I heard someone settling in the next bed. The previous day the human resources director had told me to report to him the next morning at 10.00 am as I was supposed to work in the grill of the hotel for lunch and dinner. When I arrived at the hotel I would be assigned a locker and a uniform. Since showering every morning was not common practice even in a clean and organized country like Germany, I woke up at 9.00 am. At that time the guy sleeping in the other bed also woke up and we introduced each other.

He was from a town not too far from my village in Italy and he too was going to work at the Atlantic Hotel in the grill room. He too had to report at 10.00 am to the human resources director. Additionally I found out that he was gay but he assured me I had nothing to worry about as he was going steady and that his boyfriend was a very jealous man who practiced boxing. That was kind of good news. We got ourselves ready and walked the few blocks to the hotel where the human resources director had already organized the lockers. He told us that we could also shower in the same area. I guessed this last offer was more for his benefit than ours seeing that we had not showered for the last who knows how many hours. Our uniforms were also ready, sparkling clean and ironed with a touch of starch on the short white jacket just to make it stand out. The black trousers were our own as were the shirt and the white bow-tie. Off he marched us to the grill room to meet with the ober kellner (the head waiter) who would only speak German to us although we soon found out he spoke perfect English, French, Italian and Spanish.

Our first job assignment was to polish by hand all the silverware that had to be used for lunch. This was done by rubbing each fork on a wine cork drenched with silver polish. The spoons and the handles of the knives were cleaned the same way. We were then assigned to two chef de rang (waiters) as their assistants. As the lunch service started we found out that the kitchen was one floor below the restaurant. We had to dive down a narrow, thirty step flight of stairs to fetch the food to be brought up to the restaurant for service to the guests. Once again I started to question my wisdom in having come here to work and again, was the German language really that important?

As the days were going by I felt more and more unhappy. By the third day I was just plain miserable. Then I was told that I was being moved from the grill room to the banquet department. At first I kind of welcomed the news but this work was no walk in the park either. By the seventh day I had made up my mind to leave Hamburg. I resolved to go south to Baden-Baden, the town where I was supposed to have gone to work directly from Rome had I not had the scooter accident. Romano, my friend from the Grand Hotel in Rome, was still working in Baden-Baden. The following morning I went back to the hotel and returned the locker and the white jacket. Then I went straight to the train station, bought a ticket on the next train and headed south. Yes I was going south but I was not going home, that was out of the question. Next stop, Baden-Baden!

NOT BAD IN BADEN-BADEN

At this time of year Baden-Baden, a thermal spa town often the play-ground of the rich and famous as well as the elderly and sick, was semi-dormant. Romano, my original intended travelling companion had made the trip there and had worked at the Bellevue Hotel for the summer as planned. In the autumn when it closed for winter, he had moved over to the Brenner's Park Hotel, considered to be the most elegant and top of the line hotel in town. With Romano's help I got a job at the Europaeischer Hof Hotel which stood right across the street from the casino where millionaires from all over the world would come to play and lose enormous amounts of money.

I was fortunate to be given accommodation on the fourth floor of the hotel. The furnishings consisted of three single beds, a small table, three chairs and a communal wardrobe. The toilet was outside in the corridor and for use of all the staff. The showers were in the basement and not very much in demand, but nevertheless available for those who wanted to use them. When I entered the room I found out that I was the only occupant. I chose the bed furthest from the other two, near the window and in the larger, more comfortable area of the room.

As my knowledge of German was non-existent I was hired as an assistant waiter. While I had been a waiter at the Grand Hotel in Paris this situation suited me fine. It was normal to be given the job as assistant as part of the process of learning German. With French under my belt, some basic knowledge of self-taught English and German in the making, I felt good and on my way to achieving my goal of becoming a fully fledged waiter in luxury hotels around the world. With all the enthusiasm and will to succeed powering on at full throttle I embarked on this new venture with greater confidence than had been the case at the less benign and more threatening Atlantic Hotel in Hamburg. Having a room and bed in the hotel also made life much easier.

I was assigned to assist a fairly young waiter, happy to work with an Italian assistant who did not yet speak his language but who had an obvious desire to learn. The kitchen and the restaurant were on the same floor. What a change from the Atlantic Hotel grill room with its narrow and steep steps down to the kitchen. For the first time we were to work with trays to carry the food rather than the typical silver platters and their heavy silver covers. Uniforms were also provided and laundered, a real plus. In keeping with good German style, they were always clean and crisply ironed. Two young German assistant waiters soon joined me in my room. This too was very welcome as we got along extremely well and watched out for each other.

While the food in the cafeteria was typically German with a lot of sausages, cheeses, soups and dark bread it was very pleasant and sufficient. Once in a while I would buy a fillet steak, onions and olive oil and sauté them in the room for the three of us, washed down of course with generous quantities of great German beer supplied by my new friends. At the hotel there were two other Italian assistant waiters, Giuliano, from the island of Sardinia and Luca Lucchese from Northern Italy. These two guys could not have been more different from each other. Giuliano was conservative and came from a low middle class family. He was serious about his work and very thrifty with his money.

Luca Lucchese, on the other hand, was born into a family with loads of money. As he had worked in London he spoke English and dressed like an Englishman, impeccable in three piece suit or a sports jacket, trousers, shirt and tie combination that made him look the perfect gentleman. His family owned a factory and at that time business in Italy was starting to thrive, increasing their wealth considerably. For Luca this family situation was partly a blessing but mostly a curse. His father sent him money every month but he spent it in drinking his way to alcoholism. Every morning during breakfast service at 7.00 am, while Giuliano and I would steal a cup of coffee and maybe a croissant, Luca would be at the other end of the corridor with the German assistant waiters drinking beer.

Every evening after work he would go to dine in a restaurant as he felt it was his due to have one meal a day outside the hotel. A restaurant named Wiener Wald was one of his favourites and there he'd eat wiener schnitzel, roast pork, roast ribs and rack of deer and wash it down with large quantities of beer. At midnight he would head for the bierstube (beer bar) to continue his feast. In the small hours of the morning he would return to crash out in his room for a couple of hours before reporting for breakfast service at 7.00 am. This life style soon turned that twenty-two year old, rich and spoiled boy into a toothless alcoholic with a dreadful, pock-marked complexion and a quite disgusting young man to behold.

Cristina was the executive secretary to Herr Mueller, the general manager. Perfectly by-lingual in German and Spanish, her family had left Germany in 1938 as the Nazis started to make life hard for the Jewish people. They took refuge in Buenos Aires where she was born in 1943. There they started a successful textile business which provided them with a comfortable life. Brunette, rich and classy, Cristina had a pretty face which made my heart beat faster when I saw her for the first time. We dated for a while and during the Easter week-end of 1964 we took the train to Hinterzarten, a beautiful village in the Black Forest. We checked in at the elegant and not inexpensive Adler Hotel with its traditional wood burning fire place in the lobby.

We enjoyed a superb dinner of roasted saddle of deer, apple strudel and a kirshwasser (cherry brandy) to complete the meal. It was all so romantic and exciting. Having been born in Buenos Aires, Cristina was elegant and sophisticated and wanted her boyfriend to be the same. As smoking a pipe was considered elegant and sophisticated at the time, I started to smoke a pipe! I was ever so happy. We would go to the casino to dance during the carnival season, go for walks when our time off coincided, just sit at a café sipping coffee during the day and enjoy a wine or Schnaps in the evening. I was in love again after Tonella in Rome three years earlier. Her boss, Herr Mueller was not too happy that his protegée would go out with an immigrant boy. He had other plans for her. He also was an alcoholic. One freezing winter night while driving home drunk as a skunk he stopped for a pee. He got out of the car and fell into a ditch where he fell asleep. Next morning he was found dead, frozen hard as a board.

By this time I had spent six months in Germany, taken private classes and I could manage a conversation in German. I decided to take up an offer from the Bellevue Hotel for the summer season. This hotel stood in the middle of beautiful gardens where very tall trees provided shade from the summer sun. I started as assistant to the head barman but soon reverted back to the restaurant where I was promoted to waiter. This after all was my goal. Now I was a waiter in Germany as well as having been one in Paris. One of the nicest features of this hotel was that, every afternoon, tea was served in the gardens. It made for a nice change from the typical routine of working three meals a day in the restaurant.

Being a waiter, I now had an assistant who would go to the kitchen to fetch the food while I mingled among the tables assigned to me. Life was not so hard anymore, pretty good actually. With Herr Mueller dead, Cristina moved on to Marbella in Spain for the summer to work as executive secretary in a resort there. We communicated by mail in letters which were a mixture of German, Spanish and anything else we thought we could communicate in.

Nearby the hotel was the public swimming pool. Every free afternoon I and all the other guys would go there. There was, however, one small problem ... I couldn't swim! That made me feel a bit inferior to my friends who were all good swimmers. I decided that I had to learn to swim before they found out my weakness. I had heard that the best way to learn was to just jump in the water and hope for the best. So I gathered all the courage I had, went to the deep end of the pool, held my breath and dived in head first.

Miraculously I came back up and, paddling doggy style, reached the side of the pool. Now, confident in my newly acquired ability, I practiced and practiced until I became a proficient swimmer.

Summer was advancing and I had two more tasks facing me. I had to find a job for when the season ended and my sister, Anna, was going to get married on October the 4th of that year. As in the past I started sending my resumé to a variety of important hotels. My plan to stay in Germany for two years to learn German meant I had another year to go. I was now a waiter so I applied for such a position in the classier hotels in the country. I did not want to go back to Hamburg. Berlin was my best bet as Mario with whom I had worked at the Grand Hotel in Rome was working there at the Notlih.

We considered ourselves to be cousins and refered to each other in those terms. He was the older of three children with a widowed mother whose husband had died of a war related sickness. We had become as family and as of today we still communicate often via Skype. He was just a couple of weeks younger than me but, having been born and brought up in Rome, was more street savvy than I was. He was extremely good looking with dark hair, a Roman nose and was a trained swimmer who always surrounded himself with beautiful girls. He had a cheerful personality and lived life to the extreme, always ready to dance and party. Unlike all of the others, he never drank any alcohol. This was very much the exception from the rest of the group which, including myself, had by that time taken to drinking more than was really good for us.

I applied to the Berlin Notlih and was offered a job as waiter at the then night club on the roof garden on the thirteenth floor of the hotel. I arranged to start there on the 25th of October.

The second task of convincing the owner of the Bellevue Hotel to release me on September the 30th for my sister's wedding rather than on October the 31st when the hotel closed for winter was a bit more problematic. But after some negotiation he finally agreed and I arrived home in time to be the best man at the wedding.

MY SISTER'S BIG DAY

The day of the wedding was a wonderful one. As the guests arrived at the house around 11.00 am, the equivalent of French pastries, wine and spumante were served. Then we all gathered in the front yard waiting for mid day when the bride would be ready to walk the mile (1.6 km) up the road to the parish church. There Don Antonio, the priest, would officiate the marriage and the High Mass. As my father had already passed away I was to act on his behalf and give my sister away as well as being the best man.

The procession from the house to the church has a protocol : First comes the bride in her white gown holding on to my right arm; then the bridegroom with his mother holding on to his right arm; then came my mother and the bridegroom's father; then the bridegroom's sister, her husband and younger brother; and then the uncles and aunties and all the friends followed. At the church I left my sister at the altar and moved to the other side to play the best man role. The priest had just arrived at the parish and this was his first wedding. Because he wanted to impress the congregation he had planned a High Mass with the few ladies who made up the choir singing in accompaniment. It was a nice and an emotional ceremony. Little did we know that for my sister that was the day that would signal the start of her health problems.

After the ceremony a banquet for about fifty guests was arranged at a restaurant in Gozzano, the bridegroom's village. We all sat down to a six course meal which went off without any serious malfunction, unusual for an Italian village restaurant! By 5.00 pm most of the guests had reached their limits of sobriety and it was time for us to accompany the happy couple to the nearby town where they would spend their wedding night before catching the train to Rome and then on to Venice for their honeymoon.

My mother and I returned home somewhat apprehensive as to whether we had done the right thing in allowing this marriage to go through. It would not be long before we realised that it was indeed a mistake on our part not to have stopped it when we had the opportunity. But now it was too late and my beloved sister

Anna was married to a man who turned out to be a sick tyrant. This is why Anna's wedding day was the day that the illness started which would eventually kill her at the age of fifty-nine.

For the next two weeks I helped my mother to adjust to life without her daughter. When the honeymoon was over, the newly-weds came home and a new routine started. My sister continued to work in the same factory where she had been working for the last sixteen years since the age of ten. Her newly acquired husband was working in a tap factory of which the owner had the same family name, Giacomini, as ours. But he was not (as far as we know) related to us. Because my sister and my brother-in-law were both working my mother helped out doing a lot of the chores at my sister's house. Things such as washing the clothes, preparing the meals, washing up and also sharing lunch with the still happy couple. It quickly became evident that my moody and tyrannical brother-in-law did not appreciate what my mother was doing for them. He often wore a long face and rarely spoke during the meals. The omens were not good.

Chapter 6

WHERE EAST MEETS WEST

Towards the end of October the time came for me to pack my two cases and head for Berlin. I got on to the train which would take me to the then divided Berlin, crossing the also still divided Germany. The train I took at the station in Arona was a modern one with an electric locomotive pulling the carriages and going at high speed. It covered the 492 miles (793 km) to Erfurt, the first town inside East Germany, in eight hours. There the electric locomotive was detached from the train in order to pull the next train returning west. We were then hooked up to an old steam locomotive which took us the 187 miles (301 km) to Berlin. This leg of the journey took another eight hours, the same time as the west German 'modern electric' leg had taken for a journey over twice as long.

Finally the train pulled into the Zoologischer Garten station in West Berlin. I had a ticket for the Friedrichstrasse station as the person I bought it from in Arona had no idea which station was which and decided it would be better if I had a ticket for the last one. As I was standing in the train corridor looking out of the window Mario came running alongside and shouting for me to, "Get off, get off now!" I grabbed my two suitcases from the racks and barely made it off the train before the doors were shut and it moved away again in the direction of East Berlin.

True to his reputation Mario had come to pick me up accompanied by two girls, his girlfriend Gisela and Erika (who would become my girlfriend for the next few months). He also had purchased an old Ford Taurus which proved quite useful during the time the two of us lived together like family in Berlin. We headed back to the one bedroom, toilet, small kitchen and living room with sofa apartment where he lived on the ground floor at Fasanen Strasse 40. It was near the Kaiser-Wilhelm Memorial

Church on the Kurfuerstendamm. At that time he was sharing his bedroom with another Roman assistant waiter who was also working at the Notlih but who was due to leave Berlin within days to return home to Rome. This arrangement had me sleeping on the couch in the living room for the next days before I could move into the second bed in Mario's room. After such a long and tiring trip I was ready to collapse. We dismissed the two girls and went to sleep.

The next morning I walked to the Notlih to the human resources office to let them know I had arrived and could start work anytime. I was told to return the same day at 4.00 pm, which I did. I got a locker, was fitted for a uniform and started work at 6.00 pm. My outfit consisted of a brand new green short jacket, a pair of blue trousers and a blue bow-tie. The uniforms would also be cleaned and maintained by the hotel. I had to supply and care for my own shirts. As my German was already quite good I was immediately assigned a station. I was given a key to the cash register and a crash training course on how to use it. Guests started to arrive and I had no option but plunge straight in to my new task.

As in the past I had to learn by doing rather than by formal training. What the heck, you might as well do it, learn quickly and move on. It was the first time that I had to write out the guest bills, take their payments, return the correct change, close the cash at the end of the evening and make sure that the money I turned in matched what I had punched in on the cash register. Any shortage would be found out by the night auditor and collected from my pocket the next day. A surplus was frowned on too as that meant that I had probably short-changed a diner who had not checked their change but, most likely, would come back the next day to claim it. Keep in mind too that I was working with my own money as float. The hotel only supplied change for me at the start of the shift. This meant no risk of financial loss for the hotel, only to me.

The management team of the restaurant was composed of a restaurant manager, three assistant managers and we, the waiters. We soon allocated appropriate nicknames. The restaurant manager became l'alleato (the allied, meaning Hitler as an ally of Mussolini). One of the assistants had a weight problem so he became il pezzo grosso (the big piece). The second assistant became l'aguzzino (the jailer) as he was in charge of discipline and punishment. The last of the assistants had the middle finger of his right hand cut off at the second phalanx. Because he was in charge of sorting out change for us and would count the coins with the stump of his finger he became capitan uncino (captain hook).

We also learned, in conjunction with the assistant barman, how to get free drinks from the bar, sell them to the customers and split the profit between us. Fortunately none of us ever got caught as that would have meant not only a dismissal but most likely a removal of our work permit and being barred from working in Germany ever again. All in all it would have meant deportation, not a good outcome if your goal is to become a waiter in luxurious hotels all over the world.

By November, prompted by Mario, I had purchased an old FIAT 600 with holes in the floor and rust all over. I possessed no driver's license and winter was upon us. I had to keep the car on the street under tons of snow until I learned to drive and got a license. Mario suggested that we should park the car under a nearby bridge where at least it would not be covered with snow and ice for the next few months. It seemed a good idea and so we did that. I then signed up for driving lessons. The driving instructor was a tall man who, during the war, had been a tank driver. He drove his VW Karmann-Ghia the same way he used to drive tanks. He was also short tempered, had no time for anything that was not German and harboured a special dislike for Italians and Jews. He was in his fifties and had a much younger wife, just thirty-six years of age and a young son. The driving school and his apartment were on the ground floor of the same building.

While he had a particular dislike of me, his wife had quite other ideas. She saw that I was young, polite and, like most Italians, charming and out for a good time. We became very close until one day the young son came home unexpectedly to find me holding and kissing his mother in a way that even a nine year old boy would question as appropriate.

After that I only saw her once when one day I was passing by the apartment and, curious as to the outcome of our last messy union, I stopped by. Of course I first made sure that her husband had left for an hour long lesson with a student and would not be back for at least that time. Unbeknowns to me, Cristina, my last love from Baden-Baden, was in the kitchen and heard our conversation. She did not reveal herself at the time but, when I met up with her a few days later in a café near the Kurfuerstendamm, she told me that she had overheard the chat as she had been visiting her cousin. Yes, the wife of the instructor was her cousin and as a consequence also a Jewish woman. After that I saw Cristina only once in Hamburg and I never saw the instructor's wife again.

WELL WORTH A VISIT

"Berlin ist eine Reise wert!" ... Berlin is well worth a visit! And better yet to live there for a whole year if you are twenty-one years old. With the four sections of the city occupied by the USA, UK and France in the West and the Soviet Union in the East, plus the German life style and culture, the city was a melting pot of people, customs, restaurants, clubs and languages. At that time also the immigrants, mainly from other European countries, were flocking there. Apart from the ones who came to work, learn German and move on in a couple of years there were fortune hunters, mafiosi, would be actors, artists, sculptors, petty thieves, con men, street painters, prostitutes and pimps roaming around town all day and all night long.

Finding an authentic Italian restaurant was just as easy as finding an authentic French restaurant, an English tea shop or an American hamburger joint. Night clubs were plentiful to suit every life style. I personally liked a Spanish, gypsy-like night club where all the waiters stopped serving your dinner when the time to go on stage to dance flamenco came. Others prefered strip joints and some frequented gay bars and pubs. The choice was huge. German bier stube (beer bars) were naturally everywhere. There was no reason to sleep at all unless you wanted life to pass you by and miss all the fun.

It was quite common for all the young people working in the West section to go to the Soviet side which was much cheaper whenever they had the opportunity. It was easy to reach, either by car or by metro through what was known as Checkpoint Charlie, the crossing point through the wall controlled by the Americans on one side and the Soviets on the other. While East and West Germany both used the Deutschmark as the currency, the west mark was worth three East German marks on the black market. The only problem was exchanging the money on the black market. As you entered East Berlin the VOPOS (East German Police) made you empty your pockets and write down how much West German marks you were carrying. If they were satisfied with your answer you then proceeded to the exchange window where you turned in your western marks and received eastern marks one for one.

This was an unfair exchange. However, had you been found with East German currency on your person you would be immediately arrested and given the choice, without trial, to either spend two years in an East German prison or go to Cuba to cut sugar cane for Fidel Castro. As none of the choices were to my liking I preferred to do things legally and exchange my money the official way. Even so, every so often the VOPOS would pull someone into a small room, make him or her take off all their clothing and subject them to a full body cavity search to ascertain that no money was hidden somewhere a bit harder to find than in your pockets.

One particularly brash Italian, a self-declared communist working with us at the Notlih was submitted to one of these searches. Fortunately for him this was one occasion on which he had not changed any money on the black market but the experience turned him politically so far to the right that he was never the same person again. I met up with this guy working in Bermuda several years later.

Once you finally made it to the Soviet side everything changed. It was another world altogether. The street lights were dim and the little traffic that there was consisted entirely of little Trabants, the only car produced in East Germany. There was an occasional Skoda, a Czech vehicle, or Soviet built car but these were few and restricted to the more affluent government or party officials. The wait for ordinary people to buy a car varied from five to fifteen years. The desolation and deprivation of the totalitarian system was very depressing. The shops had long lines of empty shelves and the restaurants had available, at best, only half of what the menu said they had to serve. Once I asked for chicken breast cordon bleu and it came without ham. When I asked the waiter why, he simply shrugged his shoulders and said, "We don't have any."

One of the most popular night spots was the Moscovie Café. A live band played dance music there every night of the week. It was quite sad really that, in order to get the attention of the prettiest girl in the room, all you had to do was to put on the table a pack of western cigarettes, Malboro being the most welcome. If you followed that move with a box of chocolates you were guaranteed that the girls would come over and ask you to dance. And if you were really well organized and had brought with you a pair of nylon stockings then the world, or at least the east Berlin part of it, was your oyster. Georgian brandy and Georgian sparkling wines which the Russians called champanski were the two most popular drinks. They were plentiful and reasonably cheap. Indeed you could have a nice evening dancing the night away for as little as 10 DM.

The East was also a dangerous place for the people who found themselves locked in there on the sad morning of August the 13th of 1961. That was the day when on awakening they found that a wall had been erected and that their city was now divided into two with no freedom of movement between them. While many east Berliners successfully made it to the west, as many as one hundred and twenty-five people are known to have died attempting escape at the Berlin wall. The twenty-seventh one to die was an eighteen year old brick layer called Peter Fechter. On August the 17th of

1962 he was shot by the VOPOS while trying to climb over the wall and left for hours to die, screaming for help that never came. Finally his dead body was picked up by the same heartless and cruel VOPOS who shot him.

While work was going quite well and I was happy to have achieved my goal to be a waiter - social life was even better. I was now dating Erika, going out to dance halls and especially to one that had a dancing waters show. And we spent many nights in our apartment together with Mario and Gisela in the other bed just a few metres away. By now I also had my first driver's license, proudly passing the driving test at my second attempt and being presented with a large plasticized document, valid for life and which I still have to this day. Actually it surprises me that Germany, the country of rules and discipline, would issue a document as important as a driver's license for life without at least testing the reflexes and vision of people over sixty.

At work an elderly lady was now in charge of the coatroom and assisted by her thirty-two year old daughter Christa. Christa was married to a policeman who always carried a gun with him and she had two small children, a boy and a girl. She was tall and beautiful and we became close. I was a frequent guest at their apartment and often invited to accompany them on family outings to the lake. Many a night the two of us, with her husband's blessings, would go to the theatre or cinema then top the evening off with a pizza and a bottle of sekt (German sparkling wine) consumed together in my newly rented room.

Yes, Mario and I had had a falling out. I had moved to a single room in a nearby apartment. The older couple who owned this apartment were very open to have me bring girlfriends home as long as we were quiet and did not disturb them or their neighbours. This affair with Christa was especially exciting when our encounters took place in her apartment and we were constantly on the look out for her husband's red VW bug appearing in the street. Several more adventures of that kind followed and certainly kept me busy for the rest of the time I spent in Berlin.

It was now 1965 and my second year in Germany was coming to an end. Soon I would leave. I have never returned there but it is on my bucket list as it must be a beautiful place now that it is all united.

My next country would be England!

Chapter 7

WHEREFORE ART THOU ROMEO?

As always, I had found myself a job. London had rejected me and I had to settle for a waiter's post in Manchester at the then Midland Hotel. This hotel belonged to the British Transport Authority which meant that I could travel free on trains throughout the country.

One cold autumn afternoon, after a few days spent at home with my mother, sister and her husband, I once again left my home village and headed for Paris and the Gare de Lyon. There I changed trains to travel to the ferry crossing port of Calais. My suitcases at this point had become considerably heavier to carry than the simple cardboard suitcase of seven years previously when I had first left home, as I had acquired a lot more clothing. At Calais I had to leave the comfort of the train and for the first time step on to the ferry which would cross the Channel to Dover in England. I had heard that the approach to the white cliffs there presented a stunning panorama and so it was. But the crossing was rough and I viewed the spectacle through the foggy eyes of a seasick landlubber. At least the fish benefited from the tasty croissant I had bought to sustain me on the crossing. At Dover a train was waiting for all passengers to be taken to London's Victoria Station. As I was travelling free of charge on British Rail I already had my ticket, sent to me in advance by the director of personnel at the Midland Hotel.

Renato was waiting for me at Victoria station. That's the same Renato the cook who was with me at the Michelangelo and Grand hotels in Rome. He, at that time, was working in an Italian restaurant in Soho as the cook. He invited me to dinner there and put me up in his apartment for the night. He found it hilarious when I used the common toilet outside the apartment in the corridor and I could not pull the chain. You see every country in

Europe has its own style of WC and to operate the English one you had to pull the chain with a sharp tug and let it go or it would not work. When I sheepishly told him of my problem he laughed and said, "Welcome to England! Now you will have to learn to do everything the opposite way from what you've been used to 'til now". He was right. Starting with the correct way to drive and walk in the street, as it is the opposite to continental Europe, to serving a meal in a restaurant where the customers are served and plates are cleared from the left side – even though this increases the risk of elbowing them in the face! He introduced me to Branca, his fiancée, a beautiful girl from Yugoslavia who was studying in England. They were madly in love and extremely happy.

My suitcases were kept by customs and I was informed by them that I should proceed to Manchester with just the clothes I had been wearing for the last three days. When I arrived in Manchester and went to the hotel, the director of personnel welcomed me with the news that he had received a call from the Customs Authority. He informed me that I had to return to London as they had finally figured out that the two suitcases were locked and therefore could not be inspected. So, back I went to London and to the Custom's office. There I opened the cases, they looked inside and told me to lock them, take them and go back to Manchester. You go figure these English.

At the hotel I was given three days to find a place to live but was temporarily put up in a small room. Renato had worked at the Midland a few years before and he gave me the address of an Italian family in the city where he had stayed. The house was located at 11 Hall Road just a short bus ride from the hotel. I rented the same ground floor room as Renato had lived in. The family comprised of the man of the house who worked in a lamp factory, his wife and two small children. It was made clear to me from the outset that their home was a family home and I had to live and conduct myself in the same manner as would be expected if living with my mother in my own family home. This boiled down to a prohibition of having girls visit the house. As I needed a place to stay and did not yet know that Manchester was an even better place than Berlin for social life, I agreed and took the room. I was earning 5 pounds sterling per week and the bus ride to work cost me 4 pence. With this money I had a comfortable and easy life.

The very first morning I walked into the restaurant to start serving breakfast I thought I was going to be sick, if not actually die, from the smell of smoked haddock boiled in milk. It is one of the most popular English breakfast dishes. I do not know if you have ever eaten it but it is (to me at any rate) a revolting dish. It smells disgusting, looks sickeningly pale and curls up at the edges as if ashamed of its own unappetising ugliness. After getting over that initial shock I summoned the strength and the courage to go into the dining room. There I met the maître.

He was a very distinguished English gentleman with beautifully coiffeured white hair and an equally elegant white moustache. Even at breakfast he wore an impeccable tail suit with a starched white shirt and an equally starched white bow tie (very much the Luciano Pavarotti look of some years later). I thought this kind of outfit a 'bit much' for breakfast but, then again, this was English elegance and style. His white moustaches gave me my second fit of the day. Too many hurtful memories of having known a maître with a white moustache flashed back to my mind. For a few seconds I was terrified that I had gone back in time and would start again getting kicked in the legs and punched in the ribs.

My fears were, however, unfounded as he turned out to be a really good person to work for. He was especially patient with us foreigners who had just 'got off the boat' and had yet to learn to speak English. Fortunately for me he spoke perfect German and when I did not understand his Queen's English he would communicate with me in that language. Keeping in mind what Renato had told me, I did everything the opposite way to which I was accustomed and it worked out fine. Serve the plate from the left, clear the plates from the left, do not elbow the guests on the face, if at all possible.

As on the continent the job required me to get up early and

work the breakfast shift. Then take a short break, work the three hour lunch shift, take an afternoon break and return for the dinner shift. The good thing was that there was one and a half days off per week. I quickly found a private teacher who would teach me English. Because the hotel was located behind the main train station many afternoons, when I did not have classes, I would go there and drink a cup of tea for 4 pence. On other free afternoons I would go to a small café called Le Macabre which was always packed with young people. All the tables were actual coffins and we sat around them drinking tea or coffee and having a good laugh.

The most interesting afternoon was my English class. My teacher was a single, tall and pretty woman, a few years my senior. Soon our lessons became more and more personalised to the point that we started going out to dinner-shows and dancing in a huge dance hall called The Mecca where two big bands played continuously. Because dancing in the mid nineteen-sixties was not as rocky and monkeying as is it today, we danced slow steps, blues, waltzes and the cha-cha-cha. This meant that we could dance without break for many hours without getting too tired. Soon my teacher invited me to her house to meet her mother, another real lady, and we enjoyed many wonderful cross cultural conversations. Social life in Manchester turned out to be even more lively than in Berlin.

I soon moved from the 'family household' to a room in a house owned by a Pakistani fellow. I was the only European guy there but that never bothered me. The kitchen and bathroom were common areas to be used by all and had to be cleaned after each use. In order to cook I had to put 10 pence in the gas meter and the same to take a shower. Life was good there, no rules except to not bother anyone. The only challenge I had was the different eating and cooking habits of the Pakistani boys. Opening the front door was a step into the unknown. While I would have welcomed the aroma of roast lamb or rabbit, smoked salmon or spaghetti with fresh tomato sauce and parmesan cheese, I was hit in the face with the heavy smell of curry; red curry, green curry, yellow curry, you name it they had it. But tolerating the smell of every curry known to man was a small price to pay in exchange for the freedom of movement I enjoyed without a 'mamma' reading me my rights every day.

One evening while at the Mecca with an Austrian friend, his eye fell on a stunning looking Spanish girl. She was from the Canary Islands and had long black hair, dark eyes as big as eggs, bronzed skin and legs that seemed to stretch forever. Her beauty would have inspired Michelangelo. At the same time I had found a nice girl standing alone by the wall waiting for an invite to dance. Without further ado I did just that. About an hour later we were on a bus taking us back to my room to continue a more personalised party. It lasted into the wee hours of the morning. A few hours later we woke up, me and my newly acquired friend on my single bed while my Austrian friend and this gypsy beauty were lying stark naked on the floor. Aah! the mindless madness of youth, never to be lived again ... but at that time just wonderful.

But all the social life, the individualised English lessons, the all night parties, the pleasant afternoons at Le Macabre sipping tea and the easiest job I ever had in my whole life did not make up for the miserable weather. It was the killer. During the four winter months I spent in Manchester I never saw the sun shining once. The sky was grey every day. The smog was heavy. The rain a constant torment. All quite intolerable for one who likes the sunshine, blue skies and, if at all possible, a sea vista.

Every morning to go to work and every evening to go back home I took a bus. Because it was so cold I had bought myself a warm winter hat, a long heavy woollen scarf, ski gloves and a winter coat. In all of the time that I went back and forth on that bus I'm sure that the conductor (the guy who in those days sold you your ticket) never once saw my face. With all that gear on covering my face and a foreign accent to boot, today I would probably be taken for a terrorist and arrested. I was very happy to be a waiter in a world class hotel but I had to make a decision. The choices were simple. One was to continue to live the unbeatable social life of the city while suffering the cruel punishment of the weather; the other was to move to Stratford-on-Avon and continue to be a waiter in a small sixty room hotel hardly known of in England let alone enjoying world renown.

IN THE SHADOW OF SHAKESPEARE

After a serious evaluation of the facts I chose to follow my heart and go to Stratford-on-Avon. This small town is as close as one could get to the Garden of Eden. Quiet and clean, with cobbled narrow roads. The river Avon flows through it with majestic black-neck swans drifting on the current as if they were dancing to the most beautiful music ever written. Rowing boats were going back and forth on the water, an altogether more romantic crossing than the walk over the bridge. All this beauty was surrounded by magnificently manicured English gardens with colourful flowers and trees of gigantic proportions aligned the streets. Ancient cottages clustered in the lanes and alleys, mediaeval churches and old pubs of character were everywhere. The jewel in the crown was the Royal Shakespeare theatre where Shakespeare's great plays are performed each night. This beautiful small provincial town is his birth place and his half wooden house is still there and on show to the visitors from all over the world who flock here. The cottage of his wife, Anne Hathaway, with its thatched roof and gorgeous garden is also a popular attraction.

Giuliano, who worked with me at the Berlin Notlih, was working in Stratford and had convinced me that life was good; no pollution, small town, quieter life but no less socially active. He was right. Shortly after I arrived I decided to take some driving lessons in order to get my license and to buy a car. Following the same practice I had done in Berlin, I bought a car before getting my British driving license. The car was a fourteen year old Morris Minor 803, green and, in the same tradition as my first car bought in Berlin, it featured holes in the floor. I soon discovered that it was necessary for me to always carry in the car a gallon of oil as the car used more oil than petrol. Every few miles I had to stop and top up the oil as it seemed to disappear down a black hole. It was somewhat strange that the car had passed the MOT test which is supposed to check such things but pass it had. In this day and age it would definitely not pass any test at all.

Since I already knew how to drive I did not need to take many practical lessons. I did, however, need to learn the theory and the hand signals which were still used in Britain. I also had to learn to drive on the left side of the road. After what I thought were enough lessons I presented myself for the test. I did very well on the theory part of it but failed miserably in the driving part. The examiner was concerned about my right turns and parking on the other side of the street. He failed me and told me to take more lessons and come back in a month's time. So he was shocked when he saw me getting into my own car and drive away. He called the police and they tracked me down to my hotel. But after showing them my German license they determined that I had not committed any crime and just told me to drive carefully.

At first I was given a room in a new building around the corner from where the other hotel staff members lived. I was on the ground floor and above me there lived a young Spanish couple, he a waiter and she a maid. They had the most animated fights I have ever heard. All the Spanish passion was put into them to the point that even the walls of the building were shaking. My English teacher from Manchester came to visit me for a weekend. It made for a nice change of routine. It felt good to be the tour guide to a person who surely knew more than me about Shakespeare, his work and his life in general. The weekend came to an end and she drove off home never to be seen or heard from again. This was not surprising to me as I was finding that friendships at all levels were being forged and dismantled at a supersonic speed. Such was life for me, a young free spirit, one day here, one day there and it seemed that there would never be a reason to stop and put down roots.

There was a coffee shop and a restaurant which myself and my friends used to frequent. The two were connected and the owners were even more connected, being an Italian gay couple who had come to England years earlier to work as waiters at the Savoy Hotel in London. The restaurant was called Giovanni after the one partner who ran it. It was a bit pricey for people at my financial level and I soon realised that it was only to be visited on special occasions such as celebrations, birthday dinners or when I wanted to impress a young lady. The coffee shop was called Gino after the other partner and, with tea at 4 pence a cup, a much more affordable proposition. Every afternoon it was 'de rigeur' for all the young people, English and foreigners, to go there and mingle, meet new people and make new friends. My friend Giuliano was there every afternoon too since he soon started dating a cousin of one of the owners. She was an Italian girl who had run away to England from a small town in northern Italy after a disappointing love affair. After about a year they got married and moved back to Italy, once more never to be heard from again.

Rosemary was definitely the prettiest girl in Stratford. She was blonde with a beautiful smile, blue eyes and a statuesque figure which would have stirred the blood of even the most reserved young man at the coffee shop. She also drove a two-seater Triumph sports car, green and with a fold-back roof. This girl had it all, the looks and a sports car but she also had a boyfriend. He was a young cook working in a local hotel who also had every afternoon free. This made it difficult to approach her but, as luck had it, one afternoon she showed up alone at the coffee shop and sat with our group of young foreigners.

She told us that she and her boyfriend had had a fight because he was very jealous and did not want her to speak with any other young men, especially the 'bloody foreigners' as she put it. One cup of tea led to another and before the afternoon was over I had a date with her for the same evening after work at 10.30 pm at the coffee shop. I walked to the coffee shop knowing that a ride in her Triumph would be more exciting by far than an oil burning chug-along in my delapidated Morris Minor. After a few cups of tea we decided to take a drive out of town and go to Warwick to walk by the banks of the river Avon, and so we did.

Under a sky with millions of stars and a full moon Rosemary's hair was shinier than the purest gold and her blue eyes were like a sea of turquoise water. It had been a long time since I had seen so much beauty and she was dating me. The image of her jealous boyfriend, however, kept niggling me. Not because of his body size or possible strength but because of his jealousy and because, being a cook, he had always an armoury of knives available to him. After walking for hours on end along the river banks and enjoying the starry sky we decide to drive back to Stratford.

As we were saying goodbye to each other a police car pulled up alongside. The constables seemed surprised to see us and asked what we were doing at that time of night still sitting in a car instead of being at home asleep. I thought best to keep my mouth shut and let Rosemary do the talking. The constables did not see any problem in our being in the parking lot but suggested that it would be safer if we were to call it a day, or better a night, and go home. So we did but not without arranging for another date the next night, same time, same place.

By the time that this was happening I had moved into a room inside the hotel with other members of the staff. Rosemary and I continued to see each other for some time and my new room had become our sanctuary. I decided to splash out and take her for dinner at Giovanni. Everything was fine until her ex-boyfriend showed up. He created a terrible scene in front of all the other diners. Much as I enjoyed Rosemary's company, her beauty, her sense of humour and her Triumph sports car, it was not worth the aggravation. Together we decided it was time to cool it off and go our separate ways. Shortly after that she appeared again at the coffee shop with her boyfriend. It seems that their little break from each other had a soothing effect on them and they were in love more than ever.

BY THE BANKS OF THE AVON

Work at the Swan's Nest Hotel was not very glamourous and I can only remember two customers as being special. One was Davy Jones, the late lead singer of the Monkees, an American group that was popular at the time. He came to the hotel accompanied by a 'groupy' who looked more like his poodle than a woman. They had dinner and breakfast in the dining room and I remember that his favourite breakfast food was a cluster of white South African grapes. He sure made a big ado about it.

The other customer who was constantly there for lunch and tea was Mr.Timothy Brown, Esquire. This gentleman had a beautiful silver Rolls Royce with the personal registration number 'TB'. He was a retired gentleman farmer and very wealthy; the last not least because he was so stingy. Every day at exactly 12.00 noon he would come into the restaurant, sit at the same table and order the cheapest dish on the menu. Then he'd eat it up as if there was no tomorrow and ask for a second helping which was free of charge. He drank only water and said that, while he loved sherry and wine, he could not afford any such luxury in his life. At about 2.00 pm he would walk out of the restaurant and sit on a bench in the beautiful hotel garden overlooking the river with its swans, rowing boats and weeping willows.

A long nap on the bench brought him to tea time at 5.00 pm. Here again he marched back into the bar area of the hotel where a real English afternoon tea was served daily. Eggs, cucumber and salmon sandwiches were his favourites; scones with Devon double cream and jam would follow. Miniature French pastries completed his afternoon gourmet undertaking. Two pots of tea later he had fed himself for the night. He claimed he could not eat dinner as it stopped him from sleeping and getting the rest he needed to get up next day and start all over again.

He was, however, an extremely clever man and good in his business. He lived the life of a miser who believed that he would live forever and was absolutely petrified that he would run out of money and have to live off the charity of others. He was also a very lonely man. He read all the newspapers which were around the hotel lobby and, I am sure, he never bought one for himself as that meant spending money. Poor Mr. Brown was found dead in his bed a few months later, apparently from a heart attack. He must have been happy to have died that way without having been sick as that would have necessitated medical treatment and incurring a cost he probably thought he could not afford.

Everything around me was moving at a rapid pace. Work, friendships, love, adventures. There were not enough hours in the day to accomplish all of the pleasurable things life had to offer.

Soon afterwards Mary appeared in my world. She was an Irish housekeeper at the Swan's Nest Hotel. While not as attractive as some of my previous girlfriends, she definitely was the most mature of them all. Our relationship was more of a caring one, mostly friendly and with not much passion. We shared mutual respect and personal appreciation perhaps because she, like myself, came from a poor family, had little formal education and had to work hard to make a living. Maybe this was the link that brought us close to each other in the way it did rather than the physical passion I had experienced in previous encounters.

One Sunday night, after work, Mary and I were sipping a cup of tea in her room overlooking the garden of the hotel. All of a sudden we saw two figures moving cautiously and advancing towards the hotel in short runs, hiding behind each tree as they advanced. Not knowing what to think of what we were seeing we just stared at the scene and at each other. As the two shadows reached the wall of the building they took out of a backpack some ropes and hooks and tossed them over the ledge of an open window and started climbing. Only at that moment did we comprehend what was happening. The window left open was the window of the general manager's office. The following day was pay day and, as we got paid in cash, the safe contained the total amount of money to pay the staff in addition to the entire week's takings for the hotel. As credit cards were not so popular in those days the amount of cash must have been quite considerable and the fact that the window was open was very confusing to us.

We decided that it was probably best to go down to the lobby and to alert the night porter, who also was an Irish fellow. When I got to him it was evident that he was as drunk as a skunk. His breath smelled of cheap whisky and even cheaper cigarettes. He could barely walk but grabbed a flashlight and, after falling down a couple of times and swearing like an old seaman, reached the back door which he noisily opened. To the two prospective thieves it was like an alarm bell. They dropped down to the ground and ran away as fast as their legs could carry them. The next morning when Mr.Wall, the general manager, came to the restaurant for his breakfast, I told him what we had seen the night before. He seemed to be more upset than pleased that we had foiled the attempted robbery in his office. Go and figure that one out because I sure never could.

Mary and I quickly came to the conclusion that we really were not interested in the same things in life. She wanted to get married and have children. She was already over thirty and, in those days, considered an old girl. I was just out to have a good time, eat well, drink better, meet as many girls as I could and I sure wasn't ready to settle down - at least not with Mary. We parted company but still met up to eat meals together in the small staff cafeteria and remained always civilized to one another.

Gino's coffee shop was always very interesting for the kind of people who came in every day for 4 pence cups of tea. One afternoon there was a new arrival. She was a girl from Rome who had come to England as an au pair looking after the children of well off families. Her main purpose was to learn English. We became good friends as we were all meeting there every afternoon and having fun singing Italian and French songs. The latter much to the dismay of the English hippies who also were regular customers of the coffee shop. One evening was this girl's birthday and, because I seemed to have been her best friend, I invited her to dinner at Giovanni's. We had a pretty nice evening and after dinner I drove her the 10 miles (16 km) to the magnificent house where she lived and worked. After dropping her off and saying goodbye I tried to turn the car to go back home but ended up in a field of mud and the car got stuck. By this time she had already gone into the house and she could not see that I was in trouble.

There were no mobile phones in those days so the only thing to do was walk back all the way to the hotel. It was already 1.00 am by then and I walked for three hours at a very fast pace to make it home by four. I also had a pair of low boots on, fashionable at the time, but by the time I had reached home I had blisters all over the soles of my feet. I collapsed on to my bed and fell straight asleep just to get up and go to work by seven to serve breakfast. When I told Giuliano what had happened the night before he suggested that we go back with his car, attach a rope to both cars and pull my one from the mud and back on to the asphalt road. This we did.

Also the hippies were becoming violent towards our group. One evening they were waiting outside the coffee shop for a couple of our fellows to leave. The hippies attacked them as they came out of the door but one of 'our guys' made it to his car and got a steel pipe he kept on the seat. He beat one of the hippies over the head with it, cracking his skull. The police arrived and they were all taken to the police station with the exception of the hippie with the cracked skull who was sent to the hospital. A short time later there was a trial. Amazingly enough the police had made the pipe disappear. They told the Italian fellow who had used it to say that he had only hit the hippie with his hand and that the hippie had cracked his head falling on the kerb. While the hippies were sentenced to community service for disturbing the peace and instigating a riot, he was cleared of any offence as it was found he had acted in self-defense. A few months later the policeman who had made the pipe disappear was kidnapped by the hippies and tied naked to a tree in the park as reprisal for his part in making the pipe disappear.

LONDON AT LAST?

Shortly after this incident, Guido Grilli, a fellow whom I had met in Baden-Baden and Romano Cardinale my friend from the Grand in Rome who would have been my companion on the German adventure a few years earlier, came to visit with me in Stratford. At that time both of them were working in Soho in London in an Italian Restaurant called La Capannina. They were making lots of money in tips and they convinced me to quit the Swan's Nest Hotel and join them. Lured by the money they were talking about and by the cars they were driving, I made the mistake of listening to them. One early morning about a week later I loaded my couple of suitcases into my battered Morris Minor and headed for London.

All my life I had worked in luxurious hotels. Now I found myself in a high volume restaurant serving spaghettis and pizza. What a shock to my system that was. Also I had to find a place to live. For the first few nights Guido Grilli and his wife were very kind and offered to share their bed with me. It was so arranged that Guido's wife would lie at one side of the bed, Guido in the middle and I on the other side. This arrangement worked fine, after all we were not in search of an orgy, just a place to lay down our tired bodies after a long day in a fast moving restaurant.

However, I was not convinced that the life of a waiter in an Italian restaurant, albeit in London, was what my mother had in mind for me. It was not what she had envisaged when she so emotionally told me, over and over, that being a top class waiter was the most beautiful profession a young man of my humble background could aspire to. The money was important and the Mini Cooper I would have bought was a nice car which I could never afford on a 5 pounds per week wage working in a first class hotel but the pizza place was not for me. Within one week I realised that I was letting down my mother's dream and I was letting myself down by being enticed by money and cars. These would come later anyway if I stayed with my original plan of working under crystal chandeliers and walking on the Persian rugs and Carrara marble floors of luxurious hotels.

To the disappointment of Guido and Romano, I left London to return to the English midlands. My first hope was that Mr.Wall at the Swan's Nest would still be looking for a replacement and would give me my job back. It was a surprise when he told me he did not want me back. He did allow me to sleep for a few days in the staff room I had occupied previously while I looked for employment and accommodation.

My search was short as I soon found a job in a very fancy

restaurant in Warwick called the Saxon Mill Restaurant. It still exists today although the style has changed from those days. The building was Tudor, traditional and very appealing. While this was not a hotel it did serve my purpose because it was a magnificent property. As the name suggests, this had been a mill. It was over a thousand years old and the paddled mill wheel still turned in the waters of the river.

On the ground floor level there was the bar with massive stone fireplace where guests in winter would enjoy a pre-dinner drink in front of the roaring log fire. The bar itself was the old mill counter and the barstools old flour containers. In wet and cold English evenings the warmth of the ambience would fill guests with a sense of well-being and imbue a total relaxation of body and mind. Naturally a couple of gin and tonics would also help as did the soft and soothing music of a piano and violin duo.

When the time for dinner came the guests were invited to climb a squeaky wooden spiral staircase to the restaurant where a tuxedo clad maître d'hotel would show them to their tables. We, the waiters, also dressed in evening jackets, would take care of their every possible whim from the moment they sat down until the moment they left. The service was complete but unobtrusive. The dining room was the old granary of the mill. Here too the floor was wood, the tables and chairs were rustic but stylish, the small windows with their glass panes were the originals, over one thousand years old. The guests really were the kings and queens at the Saxon Mill.

What made this restaurant so special were several touches I had never seen, not even at the Grand Hotel in Rome. One of the features was the wine cellar which boasted a reserve of fine French wine with many bottles as much as fifty years old and more. The only catch for the guests was that prices were exorbitant and, once a bottle was opened, they paid regardless of the condition of the wine. Buying these wines became a kind of a game for the very rich guests who would brag to their friends that after buying three bottles of impossible to drink wine they had finally got a drinkable and superb fifty year old wine. This game lasted for a while until a young and overly rich guest who dined every Sunday night with his lover, bought all the wines in the cellar and monopolized the game. This purchase was, besides being a power game, also an investment on his part as now he could sell these wines to his friends at triple his purchase price and under the same rules as the restaurant applied. Buy at your own risk!

Another of the interesting features was the table-side cooking and carving whereby dishes were cooked in front of the guest at the table on cooking burners. While I had heard a lot about this style of service I had never really done it before. It was exciting to prepare steak diane, steak au poivre, crepes suzettes and cherries jubilee along with crepes bresilienne in the dining room and to see the reaction of guests, especially the ladies, when these dishes were doused with brandy or rum and set alight. One lady was so shocked to see the fire that a scream was heard, much to the delight and the surprise of the ever so polished and polite English guests.

Carving of pheasants, ducks, chateaubriands and many other delicacies was also a great feature of the restaurant. Skill had to be learned quickly in order not to 'kill' a second time these poor beasts which had already been slaughtered once. The young and rather ill tempered Austrian chef would look at the carcasses of these birds when they were returned to the kitchen and raise havoc if, in his opinion, the carving job had not been done well.

The general manager of the restaurant was a retired British army brigadier general. While his experience as a restaurateur was limited he was shrewd enough to surround himself with the best available people. This kind of smart leadership was not common back in those days. The prevailing practice was for a manager who did not know the job to employ a dictatorial approach and institute a management by fear regime that would kill all creativity and turn all of the staff into numb robots. But the army training of this particular manager served him well. He practiced leadership from the front. Because of his uncommon style the working atmosphere at the Saxon Mill was fantastic. We all worked with joy, pleasure and pride to be part of such an excellent organization.

The dining room staff was composed of Italian, Spanish and one French waiter. Among these waiters there was an Italian gay who took pleasure in corrupting two of the young assistant waiters. He would pay them well and, according to him, teach them how to become real men. These sixteen year old boys of Italian descent could not use discretion. They would narrate, to the smallest detail, their encounters with this older and perverted individual; how much money he had paid them and for what services rendered. These stories were actually rather sordid and not at all edifying. It was sad to learn a few months after I had left the restaurant that one of these two boys had drowned in the river Avon during the regular afternoon swim.

Another handsome young Italian waiter, married and with two children, got hooked on horse race betting. He was losing every single pay cheque at the horse tracks. He would then go home to his young wife penniless and in a foul and violent temper. She desperately begged the restaurant manager to give her husband's weekly wage directly to her but, without a court order, he could not do that. The Spanish group of waiters at the restaurant were more unified than us Italians. The maître was a Spanish gentleman of solid Catholic background and worked to keep 'his people' in line with the faith. They had no gamblers and no perverted old men running after and corrupting young boys with money and gifts.

One of the Spanish guys owned a red, two seater Spitfire and true to the saying he really lived the Spanish pride. He sure believed himself to be God's gift to the world. Because he was really good looking, had a Spanish accent, a red Spitfire and maybe some other hidden qualities, he was always surrounded by gorgeous girls. He loved to parade them in front of everyone as trophies. While he was a success with the girls, he was not however loved by the chef who rated him as the worst carver he'd ever come across. In the eyes of the chef the Spaniard would kill a second time the ducks, pheasants and other meat assigned to him for carving table-side in the dining room. This meant that the chef would either come to the dining room and do the carving for him or he would send the fowl to the table already carved. Either of these two actions belittled the Spaniard and served to bring him down to earth a bit.

As for me, I had a wonderful life. My old, green Morris Minor was taking me anywhere I wished to go in spite of all the oil it burned and the holes in the floor. When I found that the paint was wearing I bought some green paint, sand paper and a brush and I proceeded to repaint it by hand myself. After some hard work it turned out rather well and I was proud of my achievement.

That summer I decided to challenge the English sun. In my mind it would be impossible for an Italian to get sun tanned in England. Boy was I wrong! One afternoon, along with some other guys, I went to the public swimming pool in Leamington Spa. There, after some vigorous swimming, I fell asleep in the sun just to wake up a few hours later with second degree burn. My back was red raw, hot and the skin was ready to burst open at any moment. Aloa vera gel was splashed all over me and after a few days I felt better again. It sure was a lesson and from that day I never trusted the sun again. If the English sun can burn me can you imagine what it would do to me anywhere else in the world?

THE START OF SOMETHING BIG

Another member of the restaurant staff was Josephine. One Sunday evening I was invited to a party in the staff quarters of another hotel. As at that time I did not have a girlfriend I invited Josephine. She readily accepted to go with me. Off we went in my old car the few miles to the hotel. The place was cool and the boys and girls working there had transformed the staff dining room into a real disco. Back in those days the dancing was more conducive to forging close relationships between a young woman and a young man. The only dance in fashion at the time that only had hand contact was the cha-cha-cha, all the rest were slow dancing, or the dance of the brick, as it was commonly known.

After a few gin and tonics and some very romantic music being played our senses were following the only natural road. That warm feeling of well-being created by dancing close to a pretty girl soon took over. By the time we left the party and drove back to the Saxon Mill we were totally in love, Josephine and I. I became Josephine's steady boyfriend and we were never apart. Where I was Josephine was, where Josephine was I was.

Soon after that I was invited to visit her family in the village of Hartford which is famous for a breed of cattle bearing the same name. I was so madly in love again that I easily enjoyed helping her father carry in the coal used in the fireplace. In those days terraced houses in England had very basic facilities and the coal fireplace in the living room was the only heating for the entire house. To me it felt so good to be needed even if only to carry coal in from the shed. Naturally, after an afternoon of this kind of work, a good clean up was needed. But there was only one bathroom in each house and water was expensive.

So, as I was the 'guest of honour' so to speak, I was always allowed to bathe first. Second would be Josephine and last would be her poor father. He washed in the same water, now ice cold and pretty dirty, as we had already bathed in. It seems that that was an acceptable practice common with any family in Britain at the time. At least they had a bathtub, unlike the house in which I was born and where our weekend wash down to just our upper body was done in the kitchen with an old cloth. Mind you, for the love of Josephine I would have bathed last if I were required to do so and in water already used by two other people. What won't you do for love?

And so time passed happily and rapidly. One of the young assistant waiters at the restaurant was always giving me hints about the reputation Josephine had created for herself around the restaurant. There were many ex-boyfriends who had forgotten that a gentleman has no memory and they were very graphic in their recounting of their affairs with her. They painted an image of the girl as an easy target and one to be quickly discarded after a short round of sex and games.

But, as the song 'When a man loves a woman' says, I would have none of that. For me Josephine was the perfect woman. After all, in my mind, she was going to be the mother of my children. How could she have done all those things the rumour mongers claimed? I was so blind to the truth that I decided to find ourselves jobs in Switzerland for the winter and go there together.

Chapter 8

NOT TONIGHT JOSEPHINE

Josephine and I started the routine of writing applications to hotels in winter resorts. Soon we both got an offer from the Victoria Hotel in Zermatt where I would work as a waiter and Josephine as a housekeeper. We were both thrilled at the prospect of going to Switzerland for a winter, high up in the Swiss Alps. The planning was exciting. The Automobile Association in England would give us a 'trip ticket' which was a detailed map indicating all the roads to follow, times of travelling, distances between cities and where to stop at on the way. Also places of interest to visit. What a GPS or Google search would quickly do today was a book almost as thick as an encyclopedia back then.

When the time came we loaded the Morris Minor and headed off to the coast to get the ferry to France. The trip was to be an adventure in itself. After driving from Warwick to Portsmouth we boarded the ferry which would deliver us to Le Havre, in France, eight and a half hours later. We had reserved a sleeping cabin with the intention of arriving at the other end rested and ready for the two hour drive to Paris. However, in my life I have never been very fond of water so it was no surprise that lying down on the ship for all those hours made me seasick. I spent the entire night running up and down the corridor to the public toilet.

When we arrived in Le Havre I was greener than a frog and felt like dying. The show had to go on. Josephine did not have a driving license. Sick or not, I had to drive. The other challenge was the driving on the right hand side of the road in a right hand drive car. The advantage of this set up was that I could drive the car very close to the edge of the road but the disadvantage was in overtaking. The road into Paris at that time of the morning is full of lorries carrying containers from the port to the city. The area is also heavily agricultural (near Rouen is duck country and home to the famous canard a la press delicacy) so at that time in the morning the roads were heavy with tractors and trailers. To overtake on the one lane road as it was then, was quite a challenge and highly dangerous. The alternative to not overtaking was to drive at snail pace behind these vehicle and double the journey time. So, with Josephine's help as look out, I risked our necks doing the overtaking. Then there were the roundabouts. With these I had the help of a fairly large sheet of paper stuck to the dashboard on which, in big letter, I had written 'Keep Right'!

A few hours later we finally arrived in Paris and found ourselves on Place de la Concorde. From there we could see the Champs-Elysees and the Arc de Triomphe. What a sight. The Arc was like a magnet and pulled us towards it. When we arrived at it we made a couple of circuits around it to take in all that beauty and then headed down Avenue Wagram to Place de Ternes. Following the road it makes a U-turn and brings you up to Rue de l'Etoile. Down Rue de l'Etoile to Rue de Montenotte, left to Rue Brey and there was the hotel we had selected.

The Wagram Arc de Triomphe Hotel was, like most hotels in Paris, one of the favourites for the renting of chambres a la journee which really meant renting rooms by the hour to prostitutes. But we did not have much money and the five star hotels were out of the question. I parked the car in the street below at the hotel entrance and, as an additional precaution against someone stealing my car, I had been advised to remove the spark plugs, so I did.

We visited all the sights possible in the time we had in Paris. The fact that I had lived there several years before and the location chosen made it easy to get around. The metro station was about 100 yards (90 m) from the hotel. As now, the metro was the quickest way to get around the city of light. Sacré Coeur, the Eiffel Tower, la Madeleine and Place Pigalle where life starts at midnight were all the places we enjoyed together. The city of light gets even more illuminated at that time of the year with all the buildings lit up for Christmas. Shopping at Galleries la Fayettes for us was not an option. That did not stop us from going in to see all the decorations and the displays of holiday goods. Nor did it stop us from eating in the bistros, drinking café crème at a street café, running and laughing along the bank of the river Seine and taking the bateaux mouches evening cruise with a glass of Moulin-a-Vent wine from Bourgogne.

This was a dream come true for me, twenty-four years old, running around Paris, holding hands with the woman I loved, it was more than I could handle. The happiness was pouring out of me like fresh water from a mountain spring. I had stopped the world and really nothing else mattered at the time. Alas, all good things come to an end, and one morning at 5.00 am we drove away; one more circuit around the Arc de Triomphe and down the Champs-Elysees to Place de la Concorde and out of Paris heading for Geneva. We planned to spend two nights there staying in the apartment of one of Josephine's cousin.

A DASH OF MUSTARD

Our trip ticket was directing us towards Troyes to the east and then southeast towards Dijon, the world mustard capital. The mustard originated in 1856 when Jean Naigeon of Dijon substituted 'verjuice', the acidic green juice of not yet quiet ripe grapes, for vinegar. Dijon is a city from the Neolithic period and continued to thrive through Roman times when it was called Divio. Dijon is one of the most picturesque cities I have seen. Its architectural styles are formed of many periods over the past millennium including Capetian, Gothic and Renaissance. One of the most interesting pieces of its architectures are the Burgundian polychrome roofs made of tiles glazed in terracotta, green, yellow and black and arranged in geometrical patterns. There are street markets selling cheeses, fruit and vegetables which are as charming as, and with vendors far less aggressive than, their counterparts in Paris.

We found a cosy bistro in a quite cul-de-sac and sat at a window table to watch the unhurried passers-by. Such a stop to enjoy some of the region's finest produce was de rigeur, it being impossible not to pass through without experiencing the classic and wonderful Burgundy cuisine and wine. Going native we started with a kir, the aperitif of Dijon. It was invented by Felix Kir, mayor of Dijon who was born in 1896 and lived 'til 1968. The original drink was made with Crème de Cassis and Aligote, a white inexpensive Burgundy wine. Today many version of it are found with the most elegant one being the kir royale made with a good champagne.

We then proceeded with six escargots (snails) in their shells. A perfect starter with the escargots cleaned and put back in the shell which is then stuffed with butter and herbs. Our main course just had to be boeuf bourguignonne accompanied by fresh vegetables and potatoes Anna. Our desserts were no less spectacular and all was washed down with a delicious bottle of Moulin-a-Vent. Before returning to the car we stopped in a side walk café for a café crème and then hit the road again.

The agricultural land driving into the heart of France was just magnificent, the soil rich and fertile. Lofty poplars lined the roads and, even in early December, the countryside was awash with regiments of flowers bedecked in the red, green, white and blue of Napoleon's army. Although the harvest had been completed a few months earlier, remnants of corn husk and symmetrical piles of wheat chaff littered the ground, apparently left to feed the birds. The grass on the side of the road was short and dark green, dormant and waiting for its coat of white snow to blanket it for its well-earned winter rest. The six hours that it should have taken us to make it to Grand Colombier, where we would start climbing the Jura mountains, were slipping away from us but we were not too concerned; arriving in Geneva before dark was our priority.

As we were approaching the town we could see in the distance the peaks covered with snow and, being the middle of the day, the sun shining on the white snow made for a breathtaking sight. Slowly we started the ascent, the road got steeper and more winding. As the climbing continued the temperature was dropping and by the time we reached the top of the mountain it was impossible to have windows open. The car did not have an interior heater and this not insignificant detail made the trip distinctly uncomfortable at this altitude. Then after a while it started to snow, reducing visibility to next to nil. By now we were driving downhill and the road was every bit as winding and steep as it had been on the way up and the snowfall even heavier. I turned on the windshield wipers. Guess what? ... they didn't work!

The snow was increasing in volume and intensity, I had to find a way to keep the windshield clear or risk ending our journey at the bottom of a ravine. Not an appealing prospect. My only option was to drive the car with my left hand while I stretched my right arm out of the window to operate the windshield wiper with my right hand. By this time it was also getting dark and I was scared. Negative thoughts started to build in my mind. What if the car breaks down completely? What if we suffer a puncture? What if I drive off the road and into oblivion? The situation proved the truth of the old saying that there are no atheists in the trenches, only in this case revised to state that there are no atheists on a winter snow storm night, in a clapped out Morris Minor with a broken windshield in the Jura Mountains!

I recalled all the prayers I had been taught as a child and which I believed I no longer needed as a grown man and invoked every one of them with a frantic and genuine religious fervour. After a few hours of praying and very slow driving the snow stopped just a few miles short of Geneva. All the way up to the top of the mountain and down to where we then were, I had driven the car in second gear. Now I could speed up and use the third and fourth gears – great - except that when I needed to go back to second gear I found to my dismay that the gear box was broken. I could only drive the car in first, third and fourth gear. Nonetheless we eventually reached Geneva and after a short search found Josephine's cousin's apartment.

A CHANGE OF HEART

Something had changed in Josephine's heart from the time we left the side walk café in Dijon and arrived in Geneva. She had grown suddenly distant. Her sweet smile had turned to a frown and her trade mark joyful laughter was absent from her beautiful and sensual lips. At the time I did not attach too much significance to this sudden change. I put it down to the stress which we had been subject to during the journey. The moment my head hit the pillow I passed out. I slept so soundly until the next morning that I did not hear Josephine's cousin returning to the apartment after her night shift working as a nurse at a local hospital. Sometime later I joined the two girls for breakfast. It was quickly clear that Josephine's humour had not improved. She remained distant and cold towards me as I had never seen her act before. As her cousin prepared to go to sleep we decided to go on a sight-seeing tour of Geneva.

It is a beautiful city and in keeping with the fine Swiss tradition of cleanliness it is spotless. No trash on the streets, no graffiti on the walls and everything freshly painted as if it had been done overnight just for us. It really was the first taste of how well the country and its people function. The French speaking cantons of Switzerland, as I found out later, are the easiest part of the country to live and to work in. The people just seem friendlier there than in the German or Italian speaking ones. Their proximity to France also makes their cuisine richer in taste and texture. Refined is probably the best adjective to describe it. Geneva is known as the 'City of Peace', possibly because the United Nations headquarters are based there. In addition to that there are about twenty international organizations based in the city and it hosts up to one hundred and sixty international consulates. For a city of just two hundred thousand inhabitants that is quite remarkable.

The major and most lucrative commercial activity remains the banking business. Millions and millions of dollars, euros, pounds sterling and just about every other currency pour in every day from all over the world for safe keeping in the strength of the Swiss Franc. The country makes a hefty profit on the taxes they levy on the foreign accounts. The depositors are happy and sleep well at night knowing that their money is being taken care of by the best bankers in the world. Watch making is another of the major activities. The Patek Philippe brand has been manufactured here since 1874 and it is still one of the world's most prestigious watches. A huge slice of the city budget is spent on maintaining

Geneva as one of the most cultured places in the world. On a per capita basis it invests more money in itself than any other place on earth.

Walking along Quai du Mont Blanc and admiring the fountain in the middle of the lake shooting water up to 90 feet (30 m) with the Mont Blanc back drop was a treat. Stopping at side walk cafés for a spiced hot wine before a cheese fondue lunch was another treat. In the afternoon we visited the museum of Natural History to admire the impressive displays of Hymenoptera, Coleoptera, Lepidoptera and Hemiptera art. By this time we had walked every possible corner of the city and our feet were claiming a well-deserved rest.

Josephine had remained silent for most of the day. A shade of sadness was showing in her eyes. It did not look good. I was trying to push away the thought that our love was about to end; that my dream to love forever only that woman was slowly dying. Going to Switzerland together and away from familiar faces and places was something we had agreed would be stimulating and strengthen our love. I was fighting the feeling of loss and refused to acknowledge the growing reality of our situation. That evening we dined with her cousin in the apartment. Josephine was cheerful throughout the evening. Perhaps because we were experiencing the Dole du Valais red wine for the first time things seemed easier, laughter came back and the spark in her eyes returned.

The next morning, alas, at breakfast I soon discovered that, without the Dole du Valais to assist, Josephine had relapsed to the sadness of the previous day and her eyes, once more, had turned morose and blank.

We spent the day walking to the parts of the city we had not visited the day before and to see some old churches. All faiths are found in Geneva from Russian Orthodox to Islam, Judaism, Hinduism and Lutheran. The two most prevalent and most represented are the Roman Catholic and the Protestant. Jean Calvin, the father of the Reform, was born in this city and from him and here came the Protestant faith. Visiting the Protestant St.Pierre cathedral was a special occasion for me. While I had never before been in a Protestant church, I prayed there to our Lord that the apparent impending loss of Josephine's love would not happen or at least it would be postponed for as long as possible. And, just in case my prayers were not heard because they were offered in a Protestant church, I convinced Josephine to accompany me to the Basilique Notre Dame de Geneve, the Catholic basilica, where I could pray to the Catholic God I had grown up with. I prayed in French, English, Italian, German and Latin just in case the Almighty favoured one language over another. Then I waited for the outcome.

Tired and cold we decided to turn in early that night and get up sharp the following day to restart our trip to Zermatt. During the evening I did not notice any change for the better in the depressive mood Josephine had displayed since leaving Dijon. I started to wonder about my visits to two of the most prominent churches in Geneva. All the prayers in different languages had apparently not done the job I was so hoping they would do. The night was long and sad. We were up by 5.00 am, wolfed down coffee and croissants for breakfast and were soon back in the car on our way to Zermatt and the beautiful Matterhorn, via Lausanne and Brig-Glis.

Now the car was still going well even with the broken windshield wiper and the non-functioning second gear. The view of the sun rising over the Lake of Geneva with the Alps surrounding it was really breathtaking. The white snow-capped mountains reflecting into the blue waters of the lake was like a picture postcard. The roads were lined with massive trees which had shed their leaves with the exception of the tall pines. This created the sensation of driving on a road to heaven. As we were getting closer to Brig-Glis my heart was sinking with a gloomy premonition of doom. Not only had the woman I loved turned stone cold towards me but the car was showing signs of terminal fatigue.

The plan was to go the 163 miles (263 km) to Brig, shelter the car there for the winter and then, at the end of the season, drive in it to my village. There my brother-in-law could use it to go up the mountains in pursuit of his favourite pastimes of mushroom picking and trout fishing. By huffing and puffing and at snail pace the car made it to Sion where, in front of the Garage des Alps gas station, it stopped and refused to go on. No matter how much I kindly spoke to it or kicked its tyres in frustration it just wouldn't move. I asked the garage owner how much he would pay me for it. Once his hysterical laughter had abated, he informed me that the car was worthless and he would not pay me a dime. I had put on four new winter tyres before leaving England and he said that they were the only things he could save. He did not tell me how much he would get from the sale of the car as scrap but he was kind enough to give us a ride to the train station.

There, loaded with our four suitcases, we took the train, first to Brig and from there up to Zermatt. At the exit of the train station I was sure we had arrived in heaven. This is the most picturesque village I have ever seen - as well as a very quiet one. Only the ambulance, the garbage removal and the medical vehicles are allowed to drive through it. Horse and buggies are the summer season taxis from the train station to the hotels, replaced in winter by horse pulled sleighs. What a heavenly place to spend four months during winter.

The hotel Victoria was just across the street from the train station and with a bit of a struggle we heaved our luggage there. At that time all the staff were arriving to prepare for the opening of the hotel a few days later. There was still no snow for the skiers to arrive to. Even so, the hotel was fully booked from the 15th of December and it had to function like clockwork. All the staff were housed on the fourth floor of the hotel, right under the roof. Josephine and I were assigned two rooms across the corridor from each other. Josephine was sharing with another young English woman called Pamela, I was assigned another Italian waiter as roommate. As all of the rooms were being populated by new and returning staff, we soon found a small United Nations was forming on the floor.

There were Germans, Austrians, English, Italians, Dutch, French,

Spaniards and even some Swiss on the team. These made for a nice mixture of young people from different cultures and backgrounds. Some were from upper middle class families and were there more for the experience and the opportunity to ski for low cost the slopes of the Matterhorn. Others, like myself, were there because they wanted to make a career in the hospitality business and working in Switzerland was a must name to put on your resumé. All of us, however, were also there because a Swiss winter ski resort is definitely an experience that all young people should partake of in their lifetime. At that time I was twenty-four years old and just the right age to do it justice!

After unpacking our cases and trying to find enough room in the small closet each room was fitted with, we were told to report to the staff cafeteria at 6.00 pm for dinner and a word of welcome from the general manager. We were all very excited about the dinner and about the word of welcome as hotel staff tended to look up to the general manager as the person who was just one step below the Almighty himself; and, depending on the hotel, he might even be sitting at his right side. What a disappointment when we entered the cafeteria and found out that the dinner consisted of two slices of dark bread, two slices of dry cheese and a cup of black tea. Even more disappointing were the words from our leader.

Rather than greet us with a hand shake and a smile, he stood there with a list of dos and don'ts as long as a country mile. In his stern native German he stipulated all the things that we, as staff of the Victoria Hotel, could or could not do. The things we could do were given to us in about thirty seconds flat. It took well over half an hour to recite to us all of the don'ts! Among the dos was that we had to work a minimum of twelve hours per day from 7.00 am to 3.00 pm with a break until 6.00 pm, and then serve dinner until at least 10.00 pm. Another of the dos was that we had to work six to seven days per week for the next four months.

Some of the don'ts were that we would not get any overtime payments; we were not allowed to be sick nor have the company of the opposite sex in our rooms; we were not allowed to stay out late at night (the night concierge would take the names of anyone coming in after midnight and report them to the general manager); we were not allowed to go skiing as there was a chance of getting injured and being unable to work; we were not allowed to go ice-skating. There were many other don'ts but some of us had already shut his voice out as we did not want to hear anymore.

Every winter in Zermatt a particular night spot would be the hot place to go, the in-place so to speak. The Swimming Pool Club had by repute been the hot spot the previous winter but we would have to wait until the 15th of December when all the bands and entertainment would start up to find out which one would become the place to go to be seen this year. While waiting for this to happen I took a four month membership at the Swimming Pool Club. In spite of being born at the foot of the Alps I never was a skier. Neither was I a good swimmer. I felt better however having something to do in the afternoons between 3.00 pm and 6.00 pm rather than go to sleep every day.

The entire team worked hard to get the rooms set up, the kitchen functioning, the dining room and room service ready and finally the bar. The management were all Germans or Swiss while the line employees were from all other European countries. The general manager was German and his wife, who had more to say about the running of the hotel then he did, was from Sweden. She was also in charge of the flowers and the decorations around the hotel. It was not an uncommon practice at the time in Switzerland that the wife of the general manager would be in charge of such details.

The kitchen chef was an old Swiss with a large moustache and a white beard; the front office manager was German; the maître d'hotel was a Swiss 'pied-noir', the name given to the Europeans, Christians or Jews, who had immigrated from Algeria and had become French citizens when the Algerian war of independence broke out in 1954. His name was, don't laugh, Herr Muff! Apart from being mean and ugly, he had the disgusting habit of continually picking his nose while standing at the kitchen to dining-room door watching that the table service was smooth and flawless. Not a nice practice for a five star hotel maître d'hotel. One evening he approached a family of five sitting at one of my tables with the intention of helping me to serve the main course. As he started to do so the father stood up, grabbed him by the arm and pulled him away and told him not to approach his table or his food until he had washed his hands. Naturally, all the guests witnessed this but he did not seem to comprehend the gravity of what had just transpired. He went back to the door to continue, unruffled, to stick his fingers up his nose.

I was selected to be the waiter in charge of room service for breakfast. This was a great challenge because all the guests would wake at the same time, order breakfast and, while waiting for it to arrive, get ready to take the first ski lift up the mountains. My assistant waiter was a young German, skinny as a bean pole, about a foot taller than myself. He was the permanent runner to deliver the breakfasts. The process was a simple one. The guest would ring my phone and I would answer. Because I did not know in which language the guest would speak to me and there wasn't a formal written procedure to follow, I decided that I would answer the phone in French. Then, once the guest started speaking in his or her favourite language, I would reply using the same one - provided I had enough knowledge of it. A long table to the right of the telephone was loaded with trays. I placed the written orders on them as appropriate and kept taking the next order.

The runner had to run up three floors, no elevator was allowed to be used. During a busy morning I would have the help of three or four assistants to speed up the service as time was really limited and the service had to be top notch. This was one of the most complicated services I had performed thus far in my entire career as a waiter in luxurious hotels.

It was now December the 24th, Christmas eve and the hotel was full. The festive dinner party was dragging on long past the normal dinner hour as the guests waited for midnight to come before going to church to celebrate Mass. Finally, a few minutes before midnight, the last guests left the restaurant and we all rushed to change clothes and join them in the pews. Walking to the church the sky was dark, a sliver of moon protruded from behind one lonely cloud and the heavens were a sea of stars. The roads were still free of snow. As we entered the Saint Mauritius church the scented aroma of burning candles was very pronounced and the flickering light emanating from them was soothing. A feeling of well-being engulfed me, I felt as if transported into a dream. This feeling did not last long. As the priest came to the altar I could hardly hear what he was saying as I was next to Josephine - yet we were miles apart.

No warmth was passing between us as it had done for many months in the past. The choir was singing Christmas hymns in German in beautiful harmony but which sounded to me like a goodbye melody. It was sad on the one hand and yet giving a sense of relief on the other at the thought that, while Josephine did not seem to love me anymore, she would find a more fulfilling love elsewhere. When the Mass ended we silently walked out of the church to find the snow falling, spreading flakes the size of coins. This was so beautiful that I stopped in the middle of the street and opened my arms and my mouth wide to take in as much of the cool feeling as I possibly could. The branches of the tall evergreen trees by the road side were already covered with fresh white snow and looked like gigantic Christmas trees. I knew Josephine did not love me anymore but I could not kill the love I felt for her. After a gluhwein in the first bar we came to, we all headed for the fourth floor of the hotel to sleep the few hours before going to work.

ALL WORK AND PLAY

Now the season was in full swing with the hotel full every day. The working day had been really a minimum of twelve to fourteen hours and the time was flying. I decided to do my best to get over Josephine and started going to the in place for this winter which turned out to be the bar of the hotel National, just a few doors away from the hotel where we worked and lived.

One evening I met a cute Swiss girl who was a sales girl in a boutique shop. Her name was Gisela and she came from Zurich. We danced and we had a pleasant evening with a bottle of what had become the staple wine of the group. At 2.00 am I walked her home and, behaving like a gentleman, I said goodnight to her at the door. She seemed to like that as she told me later that I was the first young man who, after having danced with her all evening, accompanied her home and didn't try to kiss her. Most of the guys and girls on the team had taken to going to the National to dance every night until 2.00 am and getting up to start work at 7.00 am. I wanted to perform well in my job and to be able to find work in an even more prestigious hotel come April when the winter season ended and the hotel closed. I decided to alternate my nights dancing with early to bed nights and that worked well; as did practicing sport at the swimming pool club in the afternoon. Most of the other guys were exhausted by just half way through the season.

My dating with Gisela was going well and we had found the most unlikely place to go to spend some loving time together after a night of dancing cheek to cheek. The night concierge, an Italian who worked both the winter and summer seasons at the Victoria, was very sympathetic with all the single fellows. At night he would leave the back door of the hotel open until after the National had closed so we could bring our dates in to spend the night. He had assigned to me a closet which had the remnant of a carpet stored in it. This was where we spent some time every night until my roommate started dating a girl on the team who was fortunate to have a single room. When this happened it was good for both of us as I now could take Gisela up to my room and be at peace for a night of tenderness.

It was during one of those evenings when Gisela had come back to my room that I discovered something that almost killed me. I had gone to the common bathroom to wash up and brush my teeth. On the way back to my room I had the silly idea to stop by Josephine's room to say goodnight to her. As always the door to her room was left open. I entered to find one of the Austrian cooks sitting on her bed gently kissing her face. Her roommate Pamela (who was in her own bed in the room) saw me just as I turned on my heels and left. Back at my room I locked the door behind me but Pamela had followed me and started pounding on the door and begging me to let her in. I could hardly do that with Gisela lying in my bed. Fortunately, after a short while, she gave up and returned to her room to find that Josephine and the cook were now fully in bed together. The following morning at breakfast Pamela told me she had wanted to see me as she was afraid I would do something stupid like try to commit suicide! My relationship with Josephine was now just one of friendship. She dated the cook and I dated Gisela. But whenever we met at the National we gladly shared a table as well as a bottle of wine.

The time to receive my first salary payment had come and to my surprise and disappointment I received only a half waiter's wage. I discovered that another German waiter had suffered in the same way, in both instances a clear breach of our contracts. When I conferred with the German lad he told me that he did not care how much he got paid as long as he earned enough money to buy his daily beer ration. I was not alright with that so I went to ask for a clarification from Mr.Muff, the maître d' hotel. He was not able to give an answer but passed on my concern to the general manager who forthwith called me to his office.

As Mr.Muff and I entered he motioned me to a low chair in front of his desk. I sat down and, as was my habit when I was nervous or upset, I took off my glasses and placed them on his desk. This sent him totally ballistic. Jumping off his chair he shouted, "Nimm deine Brille von meinem Schreibtisch!" ... which translates as, "Take your glasses off my desk!" Maybe he believed that he would intimidate me and that I would sheepishly leave his office after profoundly apologising for having inconvenienced him. But at that time in my life I was not afraid of him nor, for that matter, of anyone who would try to bully me. I knew we were in for a battle. Looking straight in his eyes I told him, calmly but firmly, that I had not been paid the correct wage for the position that I was contracted for. It came as no surprise to me that he replied that I was paid enough for an Italian and that I would earn far less in my own country than I was now being paid in the great country which Switzerland was. I quickly realised at that point that I had lost the battle and it was wiser to retreat and develop a new strategy.

Fortunately in Switzerland there is a governmental organisation that controls the amount of service charges collected by the hotels and sees that it is distributed to staff in a legal and contractually agreed manner. I contacted them and, after hearing my case, they asked me to continue working for the season. After the hotel closed in April they would carry out an inspection to find out if my claim was valid. Without sharing with anyone what I had done I put my best foot forward and carried on with my work just as they had suggested. Work for me then continued without any further major event or disruption.

A few day before New Year's Eve Mr.Muff informed us that on December the 31st we would work the whole day, no breaks. In the evening there would be a reveillon (gala dinner) with music and dancing until the early morning at which point we would reset the restaurant for breakfast. We would continue with the lunch service, take the usual short afternoon break and return to work for the usual dinner service. This we did and when this was over we had worked thirty-six hours straight! This was a normal part of working in a Swiss ski resort, considered at the time to be the cathedral of the hotel business.

The social life continued apace. Gisela and I had a fun time, dancing every second night and sharing many hours of bliss. Josephine was also having a great time and sported a different boyfriend almost every time she showed up at the National. I still felt great affection for her and truth to tell - I felt jealous.

In January of 1968 I received a letter from my mother and sister to tell me that Maria Ester, my sister's first baby was born. That brought joy to me and to my sister who had had a miscarriage in the past. My brother-in-law, with his constant bad attitude, was upset with my sister because he wanted a boy.

Slowly the season was coming to an end. Easter in 1968 was on April the 14th and on the 18th we wrapped up the hotel to close it down, the skiing season was over. By that time Gisela and I had said goodbye to each other. While we had enjoyed pleasant times together love was really far off, so there were no tears of sorrow, no promises to see each other again. It was more like 'thank you for the good time we shared and adios.'

RUBBING SHOULDERS WITH THE RICH AND FAMOUS

A group of us had decided to go to my village and spend a few days there before each one would go off to their respective new job and next life. Josephine, Pamela, Dafne and two other boys were part of the group. On my way down from Zermatt I stopped in Brig and bought myself a used FIAT 850 in blue with a red leather interior. It was quite a rise in stature from my two previous cars. This one was only two years old, had no holes in the floor and boasted the original factory paint job. What a luxury to arrive at the green gate of my house in a good car. I was very proud of myself and wanted my mother, sister and brother-in-law to be pleased for me. My sister was indeed pleased, my mother was worried sick and my brother-in-law was green with envy.

After finding a place for the other five friends to sleep we started to explore all the areas around the village. Up to the highest peak of the Mottarone mountain, around the beautiful scenery of Lake Maggiore and Lake Orta, eating pasta and pizza in real Italian restaurants and drinking the local Barbera wine. What a treat for a few days. After about a week of that life it was time to repack all the cases, load the car and take off for the next destination. While working in Zermatt we all had started to write to other city hotels to apply for jobs. As destiny had it Josephine and I had each found a job in Lausanne, she as a maid at the Palace Hotel, I as a waiter in one of the most prestigious hotels in the world - The Beau-Rivage Palace located on the shores of the lake.

One early morning we once again, as we had done before, found ourselves driving off together in my car to a new destination. We drove from my village to the Simplon Pass and back on to the same road we had driven a few months before on our way from Geneva to Zermatt. While I was doing everything possible to keep our relationship friendly and casual, just being next to her had an effect on me. My heart started beating faster. The more I looked at her the more I wanted to hold her and tell her that nothing had changed and, if anything, I loved her even more. Wisely though, I kept these feelings to myself as I had suffered a lot and did not want to start that all over again.

When we arrived in Lausanne I dropped Josephine off at the Palace Hotel which is in the higher part of the city and drove down to the the Beau-Rivage. We were both told that we would have to find a room before we could start work. When we met up in the late afternoon we followed up on some of the accommodation recommendations given to us by the respective human resources departments. I had been given an address at the top of the city and Josephine had been given the address of a convent run by nuns.

We both struck lucky and found rooms to move into that very afternoon. We returned to our hotels to pick up our luggage and to receive instructions regarding starting work on the following day. Then I dropped Josephine off at the nuns' convent and went up the hill to my new accommodation. Experience had taught me that part of my regular luggage should comprise of two sets of bed linen as none was ever provided. I made my bed up and I went to the corner coffee shop for a light dinner. Then I called it a night and went to sleep.

Josephine's room was within walking distance of her work. I had to drive about 2 miles (3.2 km) down the hill to reach the Beau-Rivage Palace. Next morning at the assigned time I reported to the human resource director who would introduce me to the maître d'hotel in the main dining room. This was a beautiful room with an equally stunning terrace with a magnificent view of the lake. All the new waiters had to start off working in the main restaurant of the hotel, it was a kind of initiation ceremony. Here we were informally evaluated by the maître d'hotel and closely watched by the maître of the Grill, the up-scale restaurant of the hotel. After working in the main dining-room for about a month I was told that I would be transferred to the Grill; much to the chagrin of the maître, who complained that the Grill was always taking away his best waiters. I was thrilled with the opportunity. Not only was the Grill where the best service was given and the best food was served, it was also where the best working hours were assigned. Quickly and without much fuss I changed my white jacket, black pants, and black bow tie for a green livery uniform with a green bow tie. As proud as a peacock the next day at 4.00 pm I walked into the Grill ready to put on my best performance.

The team of the Grill was small, only the maître, two assistant maîtres, five waiters and five assistant waiters. The working hours were from 4.00 pm when we were required to do the set-up of the room or from 6.00 pm when we only came in for the service. I had no breakfast nor lunch duties to perform. This was great as it gave me all the time to do whatever I felt like doing during the day. In the summer months that meant going to the beach and in the winter months I would rise late and spend the afternoon at the ice rink practicing the ice skating which I had taken up without much success in Zermatt.

The guests at the Grill were the elite from movies to royalty. One of the most frequent guests was Charlie Chaplin who resided in Corsier-sur-Vevey, not far from the hotel. His daughter Geraldine, one of his many children, was quite often with him. He was a real gentleman, never rude, never expecting more than he was purchasing and a great tipper. His eating habits were unsophisticated, his preference was the fish from the lake.

Geraldine also was a great guest. She never complained and enjoyed everything that was put in front of her. Food was not a main preoccupation in her life. At that time she was twenty-four years old and definitely full of life. She preferred fast motorcycles and the company of her many Greek friends, most of whom were the sons of Greek ship owners, who also lived in Switzerland. By that time she was already a celebrity in her own right having played the part of Tonya alongside Omar Sharif in the 1965 movie

Doctor Zhivago.

Another illustrious guest at the Grill was the Russian born American movie star Yul Brynner, best known then for his role of Ramses the Second in the 1956 movie The Ten Commandments. He was an enigmatic man and reserved in private despite his fame. He was a compulsive smoker with a cigarette permanently hanging from his lips. His favourite meal was a huge American T-bone steak with baked potatoes, sour cream and chives. His main requirement was that the steak was to be cooked directly on the charcoal of the grill making the outside of it burned black and the inside raw and bloody.

The former king of Spain, Juan Carlos, then only a prince and his father Juan de Borbon were eating in the Grill at least twice per week. They sat at the same table and were extremely refined eaters. Everything they ate was a top delicacy. From roast pigeon to filet of sole meunière, to stilton cheese marinated in Fonseca Port 1955 and souffles for dessert, everything had to be perfect. Just fit for a king as the expression goes. With their wine they were not any less sophisticated. Swiss wines were out of the question for them, only Château Lafitte 1955 vintage would do. All meals had an even more refined ending, a Cohiba Cuban cigar was the choice savoured with a Cognac Luis XIII. Two choices that only a few human being on this earth can afford. They were also extremely polite and generous which made serving them a very pleasant task.

One evening the general manager of the hotel, Mr.Schnyder, and his wife were entertaining the then Emperor of Ethiopia, Haile Salassie and it was my pleasure to attend to their needs. In his Swiss hotelier fashion, Mr.Schnyder wanted to impress his guests and asked that I prepare a pressed duck main course. Nowadays this dish is no longer served anywhere in the world except maybe at Maxim's restaurant in Paris. This is quite a difficult dish to prepare. First the ducks are slaughtered by strangling in order to save the blood inside the animals. The bird is then feathered and cut open when it is cold, so the blood will not run out. It is roasted in the oven and when ready is sent to the dining-room for the waiter to finish the process.

The waiter pours red wine and black pepper corns on a silver platter and slowly warms them on a table-top burner. The duck is carved and the thighs sent back to the chef who oven roasts them for a few more minutes. When the bird has been carved its carcasse is put inside the duck press, the wine and black pepper corns poured over it and pressed. The sliced duck is then placed on the silver platter on top of the table burner and the juice of the carcasse, red wine and pepper corn poured over it. It is then ready to be served. The Emperor was quite pleased with the fuss which was made around him and he seemed to have enjoyed the delicacy tremendously. But not so Mr.Schnyder. He told the maître to tell me that I made a horrible mess of the dish. However, this little setback was not going to stop me from enjoying my work.

The most colourful regular guest at the Grill was the Countess. She was a Texan born lady well advanced in years, probably over eighty and the widow of a Swiss count. Money was no object to her as she lived permanently in a suite at the Beau-Rivage Palace. Every night she appeared for dinner in a black, full length gown which had earned her the nickname of 'the witch'. As the Grill closed at midnight she would, as precise as a Swiss watch, walk in at exactly five minutes before the hour and sit at the same table. The first thing she ordered, and we always had it ready, was two finely chopped raw onions. While she devoured them she would, with lots of laughter, repeat the same refrain of 'An apple a day keeps the doctor away and an onion a day keeps everybody away' almost as if she were singing. And she was right. It was unpleasant to be near her, especially so when she talked directly in your face as she was prone to do.

There was also a Brazilian lady Mme.Ferreira, whose family had for generations owned plantations in her home country. She too resided at the hotel and every evening came for dinner, albeit at a more normal time than the Countess. Mme.Ferreira always ordered a whole chicken but only ate a small piece in order to leave the rest for us waiters to enjoy. Likewise, she would order half a bottle of the best wine, drink only half a glass and leave the rest for us. She was extremely polite, always thankful for the service she received and left enormous tips.

I had reached the zenith in my career. I was now twenty-five years old and I was a fully fledged waiter in one of the best hotels in the entire world. My mother was so proud of me and talked about my achievements with all the family and anyone else who was willing to listen. Life was also interesting on the social front. Because of its location Lausanne has the advantage that one can drive to France or Italy for lunch and be back in the late afternoon. I did this often. One of my favourite trips was to drive to Evian in France, just on the opposite side of the lake. I also enjoyed the 7.5 miles (12 km) drive through the Mont Blanc tunnel to Courmayeur in Italy to relax over a nice pasta lunch and Barolo wine. Then I'd leisurely retrace the two and a half hour drive taking in the magnificent Alpine views.

Josephine and I were not seeing much of each other so I was surprised when one morning she knocked on my door. She was very distressed and told me that the nuns had told her that she had to vacate her room. She said that she did not understand the reason and asked me if I could speak to the Mother Superior for her. As I still had a lot of feelings for her I decided that those mean nuns were being unkind to her. Driving to the convent she became silent and thoughtful as if something had triggered her uneasiness. Sure enough when we met with the Mother Superior the truth came out. The previous night Josephine had smuggled a young man into her room and the nuns had found out. This was of course a sin that could not be pardoned. The nuns had to call in the priest to reconsecrate the convent. Sex for the nuns, even if only by association, was out of the question. Just the thought of it would see them all sent to burn eternally in the furnace of hell.

Fortunately for Josephine a ground floor room had become vacant in the same building where I was lodged. That very afternoon she packed her two suitcases and I drove her to her new room. This for me was a blessing and a curse. On the one hand the thought of having her near me made me happy. On the other hand I was afraid of what I might see one day. The parking for my car was right outside her window and I had a bad predicament. For when returning from work I would look at her window and, if the light was on, I would go in to give her a goodnight kiss on the cheeks.

One evening as I entered the building I ran into a young man who occupied a room on the same floor as me coming from the direction of Josephine's room wearing only his underpants. My blood turned to ice. Fury was taking over my better judgement. I did not know if I should be really upset or just go to my room and pretend I had not seen anything. One side of me was saying to go to her room and beat her up. The other side of me was saying to go away and never, never look at her again. A third part of me could not stop loving her and was trying to find an excuse for her nymphomaniac behaviour.

Finally I decided to take this in a more rational way and went to her room, sat on her bed and looked at her. After staring at her beauty for what seemed like an eternity, I pulled myself together, kissed her on the cheek and walked away as if nothing had happened. I am not sure if she thought that I had not seen the skinny, semi-clad boy coming from her room or that I had just decided to ignore it.

By then I had mustered my resolve and decided to move away from her to another room in another building. That was the last time I saw her. Some years later I was told that she had returned to the Saxon Mill restaurant. She had married a young man who was an assistant cook while we were working there and he had progressed to the position of executive chef.

A PLACE NEAR HOME

By now it was the winter of 1968 and the itch for a new adventure was upon me. As always I had to find a new job before I could leave the one I had. The reports from my sister about my mother's health were not good. This was a major factor in influencing me to seek a job in the Italian speaking part of Switzerland where I would only be 43.5 miles (70 km) from home and able to visit there on my days off.

It did not take long to find a job at the Delta Hotel in Ascona. This was a golf resort of mediocre reputation but it was close to my home which, at the time, was my main consideration. At the end of March of 1969 I left the Beau-Rivage Palace to go to Ascona. This hotel had been closed for the winter and the process of reopening is always interesting. It is like Christmas all over again with the unwrapping of boxes of dishes, glasses and cutlery which have been stored away. It was always fun and the most important part was to get to know the team of which I would now be part for at least the next seven months.

I soon discovered that there were only two of us new on the team, all the other members worked there every summer and went to places like Davos, St.Moritz and Gstaad for the winter season. I also discovered that one of the waiters was the younger brother of the maître. This did not sound too good. The only other new guy on the team was Virgilio, an assistant waiter. As the waiters are paired off with their assistants it was only natural that the new assistant and I would be paired off. In addition to that we were given the area with most tables in the restaurant and the furthest away from the kitchen. We were also assigned to the same room which was good as at least one of us would always wake up on time to go to work for the 7.00 am start.

Virgilio and I soon discovered that all the other guys had created over the years their own little mafia-like group which was impossible to be part of. All of the toughest jobs were assigned to us as the maître wanted to treat his brother and the other waiters better than us. We did not mind however as it made us of more value to the hotel and not seen as being lazy like the rest of the team members were. The fact that Virgilio and I bonded in that way, shared the room and worked together as a team, created a friendship lasting to this days, some forty-six years on.

One particularly interesting individual at the hotel was its

German general manager. Herr Doenni was a man in his mid-thirties, short and skinny. This character never said hello to anyone working at the hotel and only if he really had to would he speak to a guest. Every morning, precise as a Swiss watch, he would come to the breakfast room. His breakfast of coffee with milk, toast, butter, marmalade and two, three minute boiled eggs in the shells, had to be on the table waiting for him.

The eggs could not be under or overcooked by a single second as he had mastered the ability to tell exactly what an egg boiled for three minutes looked and tasted like. For the rest of the day he would be locked up in his office. He only emerged for his lunch and then his dinner in the restaurant before going home for the day just to restart the same routine the next morning.

On my weekly day off, usually on a Tuesday, I had created my own routine. After finishing work on Monday night around 10.30 pm I would set off for home around the narrow and tourist-laden, lake-side road. By then I knew every pot hole, bump, bend and stone on the road. I had quickly got the time taken for the trip down to an hour and a half. I had also taken to loading the car with contraband cigarettes to take over the border to my brother-in-law whose circle of willing buyers would snap up the whole cargo in a matter of minutes. The modus operandi was to remove the front and back lights of the car, fill all the cavities with the cigarettes and then put the lights back in; not forgetting to wipe the rims of the lights to remove any finger marks which would signal to customs officers that the lights had been manipulated. The earnings were not massive but the thrill had no price!

On one of these trips back home I ran into Divina. She was the sister of the Italian-Turkish guy I mentioned earlier; he who had married a village girl, Alfa, and had built their home on top of the old carpenter's shop much to my father's dismay as it blocked the sun from shining into our home from the east. Divina was beautiful, really no joke. She was tall and had long hair down her back to just above her legs which, in turn, were so long as to be the envy of every Californian woman. Her skin was as white as milk, her teeth as white as pearls and her eyes were the replica of Cleopatra's. She was just the most desirable woman around and had a tremendously long line of suitors. I took a ticket and waited my turn, so to speak. The minor detail that she had become pregnant at seventeen and had a small daughter was not a big obstacle, her beauty would overcome that.

Her bedroom window was in front of my house. I could easily climb up the wall and sit there with her on the ledge, looking at the stars, the moon and fantasizing about what life would be like to be with her in Istanbul where she normally lived. She was also a Jehovah's Witness but that too did not present a barrier to me. My sister and my brother-in-law seemed to like her while my mother, wise as she was, did not particularly care for her. Naturally I disregarded my mother's advice and continued to see her whenever I came home.

One evening my brother-in-law, my sister, Divina and myself went for an evening out. When we returned home we sat in my sister's living room. It was there that Divina told us that her brother was keeping her prisoner in the house. She said that he would not give her any money, not even to go for an ice-cream with her daughter. The story seemed genuine. Her brother did not have the reputation of being a kind man therefore I believed it. After some cuddling Divina went back to her home to be with her daughter and get some sleep.

The next morning, as soon as the bank opened, I withdrew half a million liras (about 800 US dollars) which I gave to her that evening. One afternoon, not long after that, my brother-in-law drove her to Ascona to see me. Virgilio cleared out of the room and we spent the afternoon there together. I had never noticed before that her arms had a lots of contusions which looked like needle marks. Although I was already twenty-six years old and had by that time been exposed to a variety of girls and situations I had never seen anything like that. When I asked her about it she told me that she had to take medication for some kind of genetic disorder. She assured me that as long as she injected herself every day she was fine. I was naïve enough to believe it.

What I also did not grasp at the time was that my brother-in-law had other motives for bringing her to see me in Switzerland. A few weeks later it all fell into place when her brother asked me to go to his house one evening. I did so the very next week when I was home. He invited me to sit down and poured me a large glass of marsala wine. Once I had taken a few long sips, he revealed to me that Divina was a drug addict and would inject herself every day if she could find the product. He also knew that I had given her half a million liras and he gave it back to me on the spot. I took the money, digested his words and left ... but not before emptying the glass of marsala wine.

Then I put two and two together as it now became clear to me that my dear brother-in-law was her lover. They were using me as the excuse to have an afternoon and evening together in a hotel half way between the village and Ascona. I do not know if my sister ever found out and preferred to play stupid or simply did not have the will to throw him out; the latter was probably the real reason. After that I never saw Divina again. A few years later she married a fellow from Rome and shortly after that she died and is buried in the village cemetery. The official cause of her death was given as skin cancer. The real cause however, was drug overdose. The photo on her tombstone still shows a radiant and most beautiful woman who was overwhelmed by a battle she could not win.

At work the atmosphere was tense and unpleasant. It had reached the point that I was getting ill with duodenal ulcers. The kitchen chef, a good Swiss professional, appreciated the work Virgilio and I performed. He knew it to be streets ahead of what any of the mafia mob did. Because of this he took a particular liking to me. When he found out I had ulcers he prepared special meals for me every day. He fed me boiled rice, thinly cut and butter sautéed veal scallops and cream caramel for dessert. The rest of the mafia was furious and complained to the general manager who instructed the chef to stop giving me preferential treatment. The chef was brave enough though to tell him that I was the best waiter on the team and he was going to take care of me even if it meant that he would not be offered a return contract the next summer. This man had character. Most chefs would have folded and I would have lost the benefit of his healthy meals.

The summer was advancing and the time was coming when those of us who did not have winter jobs already arranged had to start writing away to various hotels to offer our services. Virgilio and I decided that Europe was getting too small and that the Bahamas or Bermuda were better places to go and explore. By August we were writing to every hotel we could find in those two countries in which we thought we would stand a chance of being hired.

The Bahamas were going through a kind of a rebellion at that time and so was Bermuda. Riots were common and eventually led to the assassination of Bermuda's Governor, Sir Richard Sharples and his aide-de-camp, Captain Hugh Sayers, on March the 10th, 1973. Bermuda is the oldest British colony and is well run. It has a good amount of self-determination and control over their internal affairs. The areas where Britain still has a major say are defense and finance.

The unrest and tensions were not however deterring Virgilio and I in our pursuit of employment on either of these supposed paradises we had heard so much about but which we had only ever seen on postcards or in the movies. Eventually Virgilio got an offer from the Princess Hotel in Hamilton, Bermuda as a bus boy, a new title unknown to us. Then I got an offer from the Castle Harbour Hotel in Tucker's Town, a few miles away from the capital.

By now the summer season was winding down as the German golfing fraternity had gone back to work leaving behind a bunch of retired guys and their equally retired wives. My visits home were continuing and I had to tell my mother that I was going far away this time, about 700 nautical miles (1,296 km) off the coast of the USA. Naturally she was a bit distressed and afraid that I would no longer visit her once a year as per our agreement. But after getting my assurance that I would continue to visit her she was at peace and believed that it was a good step in my career.

The end of October came and it was time to close down the hotel. As much as it is fun to open a hotel and all the boxes at the beginning of the season, it is fun too to close one down and pack things away. The more so when the work had not been such a great experience and knowing that, contrary to the rest of the team, I would not be reopening any of those boxes come the following spring.

November was a month to spend at home collecting mushrooms and chestnuts. The most fun was that, just as in childhood days, the old women of the village would come around to the house and repeat the same old stories of witchcraft and of devils; and the men likewise, repeating for the thousandth time the war stories that they had either lived or someone that they knew many moons ago had passed down to them. The ritual of roasting chestnuts on the open fire place was still as fascinating to me as it had been during my childhood days. They seemed to taste better than ever now that I was accompanying them with a glass of real good Italian red wine.

Chapter 9

THE BERMUDA TRIANGLE

My excitement was building every day as my departure date to Bermuda grew nearer. I wanted to make sure that I was properly equipped for the exotic island life - so I bought a beautiful new wool suit. I was told that the hotel would provide me with work jackets and bow ties and to bring only black pants and shirts. Then, after following the village tradition of going around to say goodbye to everyone from the mayor to the lowest and most humble citizen, I was ready to leave.

My brother-in-law drove me to the airport in Milan where I got on to a flight to London and thence to Bermuda. This was only my second time flying and I was still a bit nervous but I had to show that I was a man of the world and go without making a fuss. Virgilio had arrived in Bermuda a week before and was already settled at his work and in the dormitory provided by the Princess Hotel for their staff. Unbeknowns to me Rodolfo with whom I had worked at the Berlin Notlih was at the airport to welcome me with his VW Beetle. He took me straight to the hotel. I met the maître d'hotel and he assigned me a bed in the staff dormitory and told me to report to him next morning at 7.00 am. As my journey had been a long one I was ready to crash and so I did. My faithful wind up alarm clock that had accompanied me for so many years was put on my bedside table and, after unpacking the essentials, I passed out.

Next morning I showered and got ready then crossed the bridge from the staff house to the hotel. Right on time I was there in the dining room waiting for the maître d'hotel. As soon as he arrived he took me to the room service area. He told me that I would start off in room service for the winter and, in spring, I would move over to the restaurant. I met the other chaps there, one of whom was a young French guy called Joel. We got on well from the beginning.

Room service was a kind of starting point for all the new staff arrivals, a price to be paid. The working conditions were hard as the hotel had been built in stages. To bring food to the furthest off rooms in the golf club wing was quite an ordeal.

A trolley table with an alcohol heater inside it had to be set up and all the food placed on it. The table was taken by elevator to the appropriate floor and wheeled along an enclosed bridge to the club rooms. Once there the table had to be unloaded and dismantled to be taken up a fairly long stairwell before it was reset and you knocked on the guest room door - if you still had the strength to do so. To return the dirty dishes involved the same process but in reverse. One or two of these service during the evening and you were ready to close down and go home.

The next day I went to see Virgilio at the Princess and found out what the 'bus boy' job was. He had to put the bread and butter on the tables, fill the water glasses in front of the guests, set the salad plates in front of them and pass the dressing. That was it! He showed me their staff club; it was pure luxury with a bar fully stocked with all kinds of liquor, billiard tables, huge lounge chairs and background music. It was also a shock when he showed me the dormitory where they slept. It was a palace in comparison to what I had. He had already bought himself a Lambretta scooter and was well settled in. The biggest surprise was when I found that Alfredo Nussbaumer, a waiter with whom I had worked at the Beau-Rivage in Lausanne was working there too. The hotel world has indeed always been a small one.

Bermuda was paradise. Even today when I am asked which of the places I lived and worked in did I consider the most impressive I say, without hesitation, Zermatt and Bermuda. These two places have left their mark on me in totally different ways.

Zermatt, nestled at 5,274 feet (1,608 m) of altitude, commands a breathtaking view of the Matterhorn. This mountain, apart from being the third highest in the Alps, is very pointed with its tip slightly slanted towards the south. It stands alone against the mainly blue and cloudless sky. It appears to be a fortress placed there by some unknown gods to make the separation between Switzerland and Italy very prominent. It is common that, during the ski season, skiers who are staying in Zermatt ski to Cervinia in Italy for lunch and, vice-versa, skiers staying in Cervinia ski over to have lunch in Zermatt, then return home after lunch and before sunset. The village is also so postcard beautiful that it is impossible to describe. And what can one say about Bermuda? Just think of the Garden of Eden and you have the perfect image.

After a few months of work in the room service department spring arrived. As had been promised me, I was transferred to the restaurant. This was again a shock to me. I was used to the then European way of working and had to adjust to thinking and working in the USA way. The difference was extreme. In Europe when you reach the position of waiter you had to take care of four, or a maximum of five, tables during the breakfast, lunch and dinner service. In addition to that we also had an assistant who would go to the kitchen to fetch the food for the guests. In Bermuda I quickly learned that we were provided with huge trays which we loaded with the food in the kitchen and then carried into the restaurant to serve the guests.

This was back breaking work. It took about two months to get used to it. In addition to this heavy work, at the end of each meal we had to wash the cutlery assigned upon being transferred to the restaurant. There was, however, a big payback. The money was great. The base salary was abyssimal but the tips were huge. I was working at the far end of the restaurant and it was the area in which the groups and conventioneers had their meals. The service charge was included and we were paid that in full. I had never seen so much money in my life. They were American dollars and tax free. I really thought I was going to be rich in no time. What I did not consider was that, as you earn more, you change your lifestyle accordingly and so spend more. The nett result is therefore much the same as when you earn less and spend less.

I had also bought myself a moped. A new blue Peugeot, really nice. With this moped I had made myself mobile. I could go to the beach, to town, to the restaurants and to the cinema. Yes, there was one cinema theatre in Hamilton, the capital city.

As Easter came around the golf club opened its doors for business and some of us from the main restaurant were selected to work there. This was considered a positive move. The Golf Club was a more highly rated restaurant where only guests willing to pay higher prices would come. No groups or conventioneers were to be served their meals here. As we worked in pairs I was given an excellent German waiter, Volker Brant, as my partner. Volker is a great human being and we have kept in touch over the years. He and his wife Sheila love to visit the Algarve for a two week break every second year and we had dinner with them in our home in Praia da Luz as recently as two months ago. They always stay in the same aparthotel complex in Alvor. Volker and I got on immensely well from the very beginning.

Working in the club was a bit easier than in the main restaurant. In the club the restaurant was smaller and the walking distance to and from the kitchen shorter. We still had to wash the cutlery but by then I had discovered that the Portuguese dish washers could be employed to do it. They would gladly perform the chore for just a dollar thus saving us that tedium at the end of breakfast and dinner. The work day also was lighter. It started at 7.00 am with the breakfast and would finish around 11.00 am. Only on special occasions was there a lunch duty but that too could be contracted to a new waiter for 5 dollars.

The afternoons were free and I'd either sleep, go to town or head for the beach. At 6.00 pm I went back to work to serve dinner and finished by 10.00 pm. Most nights I then went out to town but, if not, I would stay in the cottage I shared with Danilo. He was another waiter from Florence who had been working at the Castle Harbour Hotel for a couple of years and knew the ropes.

Danilo was moody but a good guy and bit of an amateur photographer. He used his bedroom as his dark room where he developed his films. As a result the cottage smelled of chemicals but it was far superior to the dormitory the hotel offered even though my bedroom was actually the living room. He also was dating Malinda, the supervisor in the restaurant. Malinda was a very beautiful Bermudian woman who did not like local men. She was not married but had five children all conceived with the help of European or North American men. While her skin was dark and almost shiny her children's skins were an ivory off white and all five of them were just stunningly beautiful. I never met any of the fathers but, judging by the look of her children, those guys must have been really handsome.

Life was great. The team of waiters was international and a veritable league of nations; each individual displaying some typical national characteristics (not least language) as well as their own personal traits and idiosyncracies. While the majority were Italians there were also French, Germans, Austrians and Spaniards. In those days Asians were not immigrating to the islands. As the executive chef was French, all the guys working there were either French or Germans. What a great team of workers we had.

Friday has always been a very special day in my life as I was born on a Friday ... and Friday the 1st of May was to turn out to be very special indeed! It was my evening off. Dressed in my brick coloured trousers, double breasted blue jacket, brown shoes and polka-dot cravatte, I set off to have dinner at one of my regular haunts. It was the Little Venice restaurant which was owned and run by a family from Venice. It was the only Italian restaurant in Bermuda at the time.

After a delicious meal of ravioli bolognaise, breaded veal scallops and a rich tiramisu washed down with a half bottle of Valpolicella wine and rounded off with an espresso ristretto, I headed for the London Town discotheque. I chained my moped to a lamp post outside the Bermudiana Hotel where the disco was and went straight to the bar, sat on a stool and ordered a gin and tonic. I lit a Marlboro and looked around the room to see if there was any girl who tickled my fancy that evening. None caught my attention so I returned to my gin and tonic while keeping one eye on the door for new arrivals. That's when it all happened!

THE LIFE CHANGE LOVER

Two girls walked in, one more beautiful than the other. I was mesmerised! I followed them with my eyes to make sure I would not lose them or be too late to invite the prettier one to dance. The moment they sat at a table I jumped off the bar stool and I was there by their side. I was not going to be left out this time, not with a beautiful girl like this one. I was so nervous that I am not sure what I said to her but she easily figured out that I was inviting her to dance. Like a spring, she jumped up from the chair she was occupying and walked briskly towards the dance floor.

Back in the seventies the dancing was somewhat different. Yes there was rock 'n roll, the cha-cha-cha and the mambo but the most popular dances were slow and romantic. Dancing then meant you had to hold your partner fairly close to you and guide her with the tempo of the music. Moving thus together and getting to know her I soon found out that her name was Janet. She was English, lived in the YWCA in White Plains, New York and worked as a bank teller. I was flying. I was light on my feet and doubt if I have ever danced better in my life. I knew then and there that Janet was different from any girl who had ever been a part of my life before.

The evening was sheer bliss. Soon we were dancing cheek to cheek as if we had known each other for a lifetime. We danced and danced the evening away. The idea of taking a break from the dance floor never occurred to either of us. Janet's friend Mary was also having a great time, besieged by handsome looking fellows all eager to get to know her better. I learned that she and Janet had come to Bermuda on a one week vacation. They were on a tight budget, staying in a good but inexpensive hotel and saving their spending money for visits to the fashionable night spots like the London Town discotheque. The evening was going great but 'time flies when having fun' so it had to come to an end.

At 1.00 am the disco closed. Mary, getting the message that three is a crowd, walked back to the hotel while Janet and I took a stroll to the water front and looked at the enormous cruise ships anchored at the quay. After agreeing to meet the next morning to go to the beach together, I walked Janet back to her hotel and at the door I kissed her good night. I was on cloud nine!

I walked back to my chained moped and rode the few miles to my cottage. That night I could hardly sleep as I was thinking about Janet constantly. I was making plans, imagining what it would be like to take Janet home and tell my mother that this was the woman I was going to marry and give her grand-children by. Had I fallen in love at first sight or was all this just a dream from which I would wake up and return to reality? Alas, all too soon my alarm went off and I had to get up and go to work. The great thing was that only four hours remained before I'd see Janet again. That morning the guests got the best breakfast service that they ever received anywhere in the world. My partner Volker could not understand what had hit me. I was moving at supersonic speed and my smile stretched from ear to ear. I was the happiest waiter on the planet.

Eleven o'clock came round in a flash. I hurried home to change before rushing to pick up Janet from her hotel and take her to the Castle Harbour beach. I even went back to pick up Mary and took her to the beach too. We swam, we ran, we sat on the hot sand and Janet was looking prettier with every passing minute. She wore a white bikini and her white skin was slowly turning a light brown. She was a sight to be seen and treasured. The afternoon flew by and soon it was five o'clock. I had to take Janet and then Mary back to their hotel, rush home, change into my uniform and be at work by six o'clock.

I was surprised when Janet suggested that we should not arrange to meet again while she was on the island. She simply said that it was nice to have met me but she wanted to leave things as they were; if by chance we should meet again, then we should just take it from there. I was devastated but, having no choice in the matter, I had to go along with her wishes.

So Sunday was a sad day, I just could not get over it. Janet did not want to have anything to do with me ... or did she? It was not my habit to go to a dance club on a Sunday night. Normally I would simply finish work, go home and go to sleep. One of my colleagues however, convinced me to go with him to the Forty Thieves Club in search of companionship from a lonely tourist. Destiny played its trick on me that night. Who should be sitting at a table? - but Mary and Janet. They were accompanied by two handsome, dark haired and dark skinned Greek fellows who were part of the cruise ship Amerikanis. This ship cruised from New York to Bermuda weekly.

I was not quite sure if Janet was interested in seeing me or not. I kept out of her way but, while sitting at the bar, I kept an eye on her. I noticed that she was dancing with the Greek god but not cheek to cheek as she had been dancing with me. This was kind of reassuring to me. I was debating whether I should stay put at the bar and quietly sip my gin and tonic or be courageous and go ask her to dance. As I was not interested in picking a fight with some surly Greek boy I opted for the former. It was about 2.00 am, just as the club was about to close, that Janet shot a glance over to me, got up and headed for the ladies room. I could not miss this opportunity. Gingerly stepping down from my bar stool, I walked towards the gents, next door to the ladies. I sure did not want to go in as I did not want to miss Janet coming out, so I patiently waited outside the door. When she came out I said, "Hi, just wondering if you would like to go for a ride on my moped?" Fortunately she got the message and whole-heartedly agreed. I went to the bottom of the stairs to wait for her. She went back to the table and told Mary she had a terrible headache and was going back to the hotel. Mary understood what was going down and she played it very cool.

Down came Janet and hopped on the back seat of my moped. Off we went for a romantic ride around the island. Before I could get out of town however, the Greek fellow who was interested in her must have suspected something was going on because he immediately rushed down to his moped and started scouring the town in the hope of seeing Janet again some place. But I knew the town better than he did, managed to avoid him and smoothly took off towards the Pink Beach. It really is pink as the sand covering it is pure shells that over thousands and thousands of years have built up this unique beach, the only one like it in the world.

When we got there I chained up the moped. We took off our shoes. Then we walked hand in hand along the pink and still hot sand, looking at the moon and the stars and, once in a while walking in the water. We talked and talked and I believe we really said nothing. Just being together was a blessing. Suddenly it was 5.00 am. I took Janet back to her hotel without running into the Greek who, by this time, had given up the search and was surely asleep in his staff quarter on board the cruise ship.

Janet was to return to New York on the following Thursday so we had Monday, Tuesday and Wednesday to be together. We sure made the most of it. Every afternoon between 11.00 am and 6.00 pm we went to the beach and every evening after 10.00 pm we went for dinner and then on to dancing. These three days turned out to be magnificent. Nothing but happy moments, lots of laughing, lots of tender loving. But Thursday came around rather quickly and Janet had to go. She left without any promise or any hint that she would be interested in seeing me again. We did however agree to stay in touch and write to each other and she gave me her phone number at the YWCA.

From then on I spent every afternoon during my work break on the terrace of my cottage writing long and romantic letters. By September we knew that this was really serious, especially when Janet informed me that she was planning to come back to Bermuda for a week. The reason she gave me at the time was that she wanted to know if she was infatuated with the island or if she was in love with me. Sure enough she soon discovered that she was in love with me! While the hot pink sand might have helped, I was the raison d'etre for her return to the enchanting island.

This week we again spent in a state of inebriation born from the joy of sharing and dreaming together rather than from imbibing alcohol. November came and I decided I had to take a week off and go to New York to see her. The White Plains experience proved to be a repeat of our weeks in Bermuda such were our feelings. The difference was that, instead of sandy beaches and romantic night walks under a starry sky, there was the Radio City and Broadway shows, a visit to the Cloister, the many museums, the Rockefeller Center ice-rink and the Empire State Building. I also visited friends Sandy and Millie, who I had met when they were staying at the Castle Harbour as guests.

During this visit Janet told me that she had not been back to England to see her parents since she had come to the US over three years earlier. I in turn told her that I was going to see my mother and sister the following January. I proposed that, if she was to go back to visit her family, I would fly home via London and visit her there and also meet her parents. Janet agreed that it was a good idea. In the event Janet got home a few days before I was due to arrive. I guess this was done in order to prep her parents about this Italian fellow who would come and stay in their house for a few days. We also arranged that, toward the end of my vacation with my mum, Janet would come to my village to meet my family.

My flight to London turned out to be quite trying. While I was at the airport in Bermuda it was announced that, due to heavy snowfall in London, the aircraft destined to take me there was unable to take off from Heathrow airport. Then we were informed that we would be diverted to Boston and fly the next day to London. This was a blow, what to do? My only option was to go with the flow but, as Janet's parents did not have a telephone at home, I could not call her to tell her of the change of plans.

Janet's favourite aunt Margaret had come to visit Janet and was also staying at her parents' house. She went with Janet to meet me at the airport in the car Janet had rented especially for the occasion. When the Bermuda flight did not arrive and no information was given as to what had happened to the passengers booked on that flight, Janet assumed that I had changed my mind and that I did not after all want to see her nor meet her family. Her aunt suggested that, to drown their sorrows and disillusionment, they should forget me and go shopping. The plot was thickening here.

Eventually I arrived in London. After some inquiring I found which train I had to take to get to Bexleyheath Station which is on the other side of the city, some 60 miles (96 km) from the airport. Finally I got there and took a bus to the end of the street where Janet's parents lived. I was wearing shoes fit for Bermuda and here I was sliding around on the snow and ice of England with a winter gale blowing my head off. What one does for love!

ONE LONG MEAL

At the end of my struggle against cruel mother nature I arrived at 38 Clovelly Road and knocked on the door. After a few minutes the door opened and a white haired lady wearing an apron covered in flour stood there looking at me in an anything but friendly way. She was about to close the door in my face thinking that I was a door-to-door salesman trying to sell her something she didn't need when I asked her if Janet was at home.

At that the look on her face changed as if she had been hit by a ton of bricks. She ushered me in and explained how Janet had gone to the airport to meet me but I hadn't showed. So I explained my ordeal to her seated before their charcoal burning fire place with a cup of hot tea. A cup of tea is of course the remedy for all and every unfortunate situation, illness, disappointment and misadventure that can happen in life to an English person.

The white, flour-covered apron she was wearing was soon explained when, with my tea, she served me the freshly baked scones she had just taken out of the oven for me. She was a beautiful lady and from the moment she realised that I wasn't a dodgy salesman she treated me always with love and quickly became the president of my fan club. After recovering my strength with the scalding hot tea and the best ever scones with Devon double cream and jam, I was ready and anxious to see Janet.

I thought it would be better to change into my woollen suit which I had bought in Italy before going to Bermuda. In the year I had lived there I had worn it only once. Well, the weather was not exactly conducive for a woollen suit on the most beautiful island in the world. The conversation with Jane, this was her name, was easy and we talked freely about my feelings for her daughter. I told her about my aspirations in life and what I wanted for myself and eventually for my family.

After what seemed like an eternity, we heard Janet's hire car pull up in the street in front of the house. I thought best to hide behind the living-room door and surprise her. When Janet and her aunt entered the house her mother asked her where I was. Janet replied that I had changed my mind and had not come - and that was just fine with her. Her mother had a real hard time to keep from laughing aloud. When Janet came into the living room she got the shock of her life to find me there with a happy smile on my face stretching from ear to ear. The hug we gave each other must have lasted for ten minutes. When we eventually let go of each other there was a freshly brewed cup of tea and more freshly baked scones on the coffee table ready for us to enjoy.

We sat with mum and aunt Margaret and drank many more cups of tea and ate many more scones with Devon double cream and jam. Although still early in the day it was dark. In winter in England it starts to get dark early in the afternoon. It was now time to sit down for dinner. The meal in the middle of the day that everyone calls lunch is, for the English, dinner. You see, one more example that the English do everything the opposite way from the rest of the world.

A short time after that Janet's father and brother came in from work. This was followed by tea being served at the usual time of between five and six in the afternoon. By the time supper was served, just before going to bed at about ten thirty, I was very tired. I was also drunk with happiness and the not inconsiderable amount of sherry that had freely flown in the house since the arrival of brother Bill and dad William, for short also called Bill. I was given Janet's old room and Janet was set up in her older sister Marion's room. Marion is ten years older than Janet and by that time she was married. Marion, her husband David and their three boys lived in a low rent council house which is municipality subsidised housing awarded to families unable to afford a decent place otherwise. I crashed in a very comfortable and high metal bed like the one I had in my own home while growing up.

I slept like a log all night long only to be woken up the next morning by mother Jane with a piping hot cup of tea. I guess that the tea was the excuse to come into my room to find out if her daughter had, in the middle of the night, suffered a sleepwalking attack and wandered into my room to be with me. After she was reassured that I was alone she gently deposited the cup on the bedside table and left the room. I felt I had to get up and, since there was no shower in the house, I did what everyone else did, I took a bath. Back in 1971 in Europe, people did not take showers or baths every day. The norm was one bath on Saturday evening after finishing work for the week. Janet's family were more fortunate and had a bathroom with a bathtub and running hot water.

Breakfast was waiting for me in the dining room downstairs. Fried eggs, bacon, sausages, grilled tomatoes and mushrooms were all steaming on my plate accompanied with three slices of toast, butter, jam and marmalade. It is important to know that in England, only jam made with Seville oranges is called marmalade, all the rest are jams. What a feast. It was just Jane, aunt Margaret, Janet and I as the guys were already off to work. By the time we finished eating it was almost ten o'clock. Guess what? when eleven o'clock came around more food appeared on the table.

This is the second meal of the day. It is called 'elevenses' and is normally just the proverbial tea with cold milk and a couple of dry biscuits. Shortly after that, Janet, aunt Margaret and myself set out in Janet's rented car to go to visit Marion and her three boys at their council house. We reached the house at about twelve-thirty in the afternoon. Following the formal introductions being made and pleasantries exchanged you will surely guess what happened next? Yes, we sat down for lunch.

Cabbage soup, roast beef, brussel sprouts, roast potatoes and Yorkshire pudding all covered by a generous amount of brown gravy was the fare presented to me by Marion and with all the proper pomp and circumstance. Bread and butter pudding and apple pie with custard was the dessert. Then following, in the English style, a wheel of Stilton cheese which had been marinated in Port wine for the last two weeks was served with Carr's water crackers. What a delicious treat. A glass of Port wine was a must. The conversation was very fluid and friendly. I was embraced by the family as a gift from our Lord and yet I was only the boyfriend and nothing else at that point.

After such a meal I would have liked to sleep but this was out of question as the three little brothers were ready to play. Even with the snow, ice and sub-zero temperature they dragged me outside not understanding that I had been living in the bliss of Bermuda's weather for the last year. I just wanted to escape them and run into the house to stand in front of the fire. That, of course, was out of the question. For the love of Janet I endured the cruel frost and biting wind for about an hour or so. It was a long, tormenting afternoon after such a royal meal.

Eventually Marion's husband David came home from work; of course it was tea time and we had to eat again. Slices of gammon, cheese, cucumbers, watercress, bread, butter, jam, scones and copious amounts of tea were put on the table with everyone devouring everything as if we had not seen food for days. Yet only about one and a half hour earlier we had, quite literally, stuffed our faces in a shameless manner.

This tea operation took about two hours and David was pleasant enough. He seemed to have taken a liking to me or, at least, that was the impression I got. Now I had met all of the family members who could be influential in Janet's decision regarding what I had in store for her some days later. I had yet to meet brother Bill's fiancée Ronnie who was a registered nurse and loved horses. I learned that, as a child, Ronnie had spent many years living in hotels as her father had been a hotel general manager but was now retired. This meant that she understood better than anyone else in the family what having a husband in the hotel restaurant business would mean to Janet's life if we decided to spend our lives together. There was no resistance on her part to our relationship and when I got to meet her it was a cordial and pleasant encounter.

Now, with all the formality of meeting the family completed, Janet decided that it was time to go around and visit the many friends she had left behind when she left England to move to the US. It felt to me that this list of friends was longer than the number of cardinals in the Vatican and that list is long, as of today there being two hundred and sixteen. In the rented car we drove for miles all over Kent and London for Janet to say, "Hi," and for me to be introduced and meet all the people close to Janet's heart. A few of these people have since passed away but, even after forty-five years, every time we go to England we visit the ones still alive. Friendship and devotion have always been strong in Janet's life.

Finally, after about five days of this running around, we had two days to ourselves and this meant playing the tourist. London had to be visited with the Tower of London, Tower Bridge, Buckingham Palace with the changing of the guard ceremony, the British Museum and, at the top of the list, Soho. I knew Soho a little as I had worked in an Italian restaurant there for one week a few years previously. These visits took up one of our precious days. A second day was spent visiting Greenwich, where Janet was born. We saw the Cutty Sark tea clipper (one of the last to be built), the Royal Observatory and the National Maritime Museum. It is remarkable how well all these beautiful places and pieces of art are maintained.

Two days before I was due to leave England for Italy, Janet and I went to the Crook Log Pub and sat cosily next to the fire place. We enjoyed the soft and romantic music while sipping our gin and tonics. I had put on my woollen double breasted blue suit and was looking pretty good, or so I thought.

After my second gin and tonic, I mustered the courage and asked Janet if she would marry me. Janet was not surprised as I had written a letter to her every day since we had met that Friday evening at the London Town discotheque. She accepted to become my wife without hesitation.

MEETING CENTONARA

Very happily we returned to the house for supper but decided we would not share the news with her parents or brother just yet. For the next two days I was in heaven and found it very difficult to keep all that joy inside me. Alas, as everything has a beginning and an end, this moment too ended the morning Janet drove me to the station for my train to Heathrow and from there a flight to Milan and home to my mother. Janet and I had agreed that I would spend three weeks at home with my mother and she would join us the third week before we would fly to spend two days together in New York. My mother was bursting with joy to see me. I had kept my promise to return home and see her at least once per year. She was even more delighted when I told her that we would have a young English lady visit for the third week of my stay.

Following my father's death my mother had moved out of the master bedroom and into the room my sister and I had slept in. This room was in the inside of the house with only one wall exposed to the front. It was small, sat right above the kitchen and had two single high iron beds. Its location meant that in winter it was slightly warmer than the master bedroom which was over the dining room and with two walls exposed to the outside weather. By that time my sister was married and had moved to her house which was attached to our one but totally separate. My sister's former bed in the room now occupied by my mother was empty and mother made it clear to me that I was to sleep in that bed in the same room as her. Janet would sleep in the big bed in the master bedroom. This arrangement would ensure that no secret encounters between Janet and I would take place under her roof and her watchful eye.

I knew the score long before of course and played by the rules. She was a wonderful mother and even now that she could have taken it easy in her almost total blindness she kept helping my sister and her husband in their household. We enjoyed a great time recounting the times of my childhood, the good and naughty things I had done. And now I was bringing a young lady home to introduce to her. She was interested in my future but never for a moment did she become nosey and inquisitive as to what our intentions were. Never once did she ask me if this girl was the one I intended to marry and to be the mother of my children but my mother had a natural soft spot for the English and was secretly hoping that Janet would be 'the one'.

Soon the time for Janet's arrival was upon us. Armed with a bouquet of red roses, which were hard to find at that time of the year, my brother-in-law drove me in his small car to the airport to meet her. She wore a black overcoat and she was just the most beautiful thing I had seen. She stepped out of the custom area and fell into my arms, kissing for as long as our breath would allow. My brother-in-law, half shocked at our public display of affection, waited discretely a few feet away. Following the introductions first priority was to treat Janet to her first taste of a real Italian cappuccino. With that accomplished, we settled in the car for the 30 mile (48 km) drive to Centonara and to my excitedly awaiting mother.

Almost needless to say that my mother and Janet had an immediate and genuine affinity for each other. The first hurdle was over. My sister too took a liking for Janet and graciously tried to make herself understood by whichever means she could. She turned out to be quite funny as she invented words in English hoping to hit the right one along the line. When all these attempts failed she would use her hands and even make drawings on a sheet of paper. At the end, exhausted, she would call for me to translate their conversation. In due course this became the preferred method of communication between my family and Janet.

My mother was by now almost totally blind but that did not stop her from producing a most fantastic dinner. She pulled out of her magic hat the same menu she had traditionally produced once a year in former times when we were all alive and at home as one big happy family. Her starter was veal in tuna fish sauce followed by hand made ravioli in broth. The main course was ossobuco with saffron risotto and a gigantic salad. For dessert she produced her favourite angel bread sponge delicacy topped with a masterfully made chocolate sauce. I was given the honour of buying the wine to wash all this down.

By the time evening came I was so worn out that all I wanted to do was to go to bed and sleep soundly until breakfast time next morning. Janet got the hot water bottle that I had enjoyed for the two weeks I spent alone with my mother. Now I was going back to the same thing as when I was growing up, having mother's hot water bottle put in my bed first just to take the chill off the sheets and then the bottle was put in her bed for the night. I sure was not about to complain as I was not feeling the cold. Knowing that Janet was sleeping on the other side of the wall kept me warm enough - even on a cold winter night in a room without heating. So sleep soundly I did.

Janet was shocked when she got up next morning to find that there was no shower and that nobody in the family bathed. The breakfast my mother put on the table was typical of our home. It consisted of coffee, a stale roll from the day before, fresh butter made by our distant cousin, Maria, and home-made jam. This was a far cry from what Janet was used to in England. But she was a good sport and did not complain about the lack of bacon, eggs, sausages, grilled tomatoes and mushrooms. See what love can do?

Next it was time to take Janet around the village and introduce her to everybody, friends and foes alike, as all had to be made part of this event. After all a local boy was bringing home an English girl. Naturally gossip started immediately and went around the village like wild fire, the old ladies had a field day. Some said Janet was not pretty enough for a boy like me, some said she was too skinny to be able to bear children and some said she was outright ugly. Fortunately Janet did not understand a word so I translated all those negative comments into the most flattering compliments a person could wish to hear.

It was good to know that the village had not changed much from the times of my childhood when gossip was the norm and that it still continued to these days. After we had made all the most important introductions including the mayor, the priest and the mother superior we returned home for another magnificent lunch. Later that day we walked the 2 miles (3.2 km) down to the village where my aunts, uncles and cousins lived. There it was a repeat of the introductions in the village except that Janet was welcomed with open arms from the rest of the family, not with the mean gossip as ignited by village dinosaurs. This was a relief as I had feared that Janet might catch on to what they were saying from their facial expressions.

With all the formalities behind us we could now walk around and see the sites I was eager to show this wonderful woman who had agreed to become my wife. No one knew of our marriage plans. Had people known it would just have generated another round of gossip which could have turned malicious had some of the old village ladies really disapproved of my choice. The next day, again without a shower and following the same skimpy breakfast, we borrowed my brother-in-law's car and travelled to town for market day. In those days the market occupied almost every street in the centre of town. Everything and anything could be found there from shoes to cheese to salami to clothing and local handcraft leather goods. Janet had a great time rummaging through the stalls and she naturally wanted to take something back with her to remember those happy days.

Even if it was winter a visit to Lake Maggiore was a must. My brother-in-law was kind enough to lend me his car and that made it easy for us to visit Stresa, a real pretty town on the shores of the lake. From there we took a ferry to the three Borromeo Islands in the middle of the lake. It is a must for all visitors to go to Isola Madre, to Isola Bella and to visit the Borromeo Castle with its magnificent afreschi and impeccably manicured gardens. Large numbers of peacocks roam free there, fanning their tail feathers in a multi-colour display comparable to the prettiest rainbow in the sky. Lunch had to be eaten on Isola Pescatori where fresh pesce persico (perch) is the king of fishes.

Keeping in the good Italian tradition the meal started with a

Campari and soda to prepare the stomach to take in and digest the amount of food we would be eating. A generous antipasto was the starter, fettuccine puttanesca followed and then the grilled perch with roasted potatoes and green string beans. We could not miss out on a freshly home-made tiramisu dessert - so we didn't. We drank a Soave Bolla white wine with the meal and finished off with an espresso correto (coffee with brandy). After taking a leisurely three hours to enjoy the meal, the view of the lake and the surrounding mountains we took the ferry back to Stresa where I had left the car. In this day and age we could not have a Campari, a bottle of wine and coffee with a generous dash of brandy and drive the car but back then it was not a problem. By the time we arrived home at around six, because we had stopped to enjoy a Cappuccino and a home-made gelato, it was about time to have dinner.

Mother, with her usual concern that we would be hungry, had prepared the same delicious, potato and leek, French style parmantier soup which she had regularly made every Sunday night for dinner while I was growing up. Because she herself grew potatoes and leeks in the field she worked it was cheap and yet one of the best soups you can eat. The main course was roast rabbit with rosemary and a leaf of salvia. The dessert was a mouth-watering apple tart and Bialetti coffee was the norm. All of it, it goes almost without saying, was washed down with three bottles of Barolo which comes from the same Piedmont region in which our village is situated and is classified as the best Italian wine.

With our day of departure fast approaching I entertained Janet by taking her to as many of the local sites as I could. That included a trip to the foot of Monte Rosa, the second highest mountain in the Alps and just a few kilometres from our home. The last evening at home turned out to be a very interesting one. My sister and her husband invited us to have dinner at their house as they had a formal dining room. They also invited Chiaro, a boy with whom I grew up and with whom I am still in touch. He was at that time a heavy drinker but the good thing about him was that the more he drank the funnier he became. I really do not remember what my sister Anna, also an outstanding cook, had made for dinner but, as the evening progressed, it become clear that Janet and Chiaro were hitting the bottle pretty hard. I was not drinking that night as I figured that one of us had to be sober next day to tackle the flight from Milan to New York.

By the time I went to bed I couldn't tell how many bottles of Barolo had been drunk in addition to Chiaro's favourite after-dinner drinks which were limoncello and, being a northern Italian, grappa. By midnight I helped Janet into her bed. This incidentally was the only time I had been to Janet's room in the week she had been with us under penalty of certain death from my own mother. At 5.00 am I had to return to her room to wake her up. The poor thing couldn't open her eyes and had a splitting headache. I helped her to get dressed and gave her some of the hot coffee mamma had prepared but she could not swallow the standard stale roll with butter and jam.

In the shortest time possible my brother-in-law, Janet and myself were on our way to the airport. By the time we got there Janet was feeling better and after the departure formalities were completed enjoyed her last real cappuccino as we waited for our flight to be called. The flight was very smooth and we could see the snow-capped Alps below us. Heading towards Paris the view turned to the vineyards of Burgundy and soon to the blue water of the Atlantic all the way to St John's island in Canada. This is one of the few places in the globe where standard time is on the half hour rather than the full hour. After a stop long enough to refuel we took off again and the next stop at JFK and a taxi ride into Manhattan. Back then the airlines were competing for business and even in economy class the wine and alcoholic beverages were free. Janet was still feeling really bad and would not even take a glass of red wine to wash down the food. I, on the other hand, drank two glasses of wine and landed at JFK happy and relaxed.

In the city we met up with Virgilio and his Italian girlfriend who were also on their way back to Bermuda after visiting their respective families in Italy, his in Tuscany, her's in Naples. The next two days were great fun. We went for huge steaks with baked potatoes and sour cream with chives and a huge salad at Tod's for just 1.59 dollars each. We also went to see the Rockets at Radio City and all the usual sight-seeing tours that people do in New York. Time flew by. Soon it was time for Virgilio, Lisa and myself to go back to Bermuda and Janet back to the YWCA at White Plains and to her job as a bank teller.

MARRIAGE PLANS

Back in Bermuda the routine started again. Only this time I had other plans to consider as Janet and I were deciding when we were going to get married. This event, like many others in our lives, was shaping up in strange way. Because our plan was that we would be in Bermuda for a while after getting married, I was preparing the cottage to make it presentable and up to par to receive my new bride. I was out shopping for bed linen, new dishes, decent cutlery and all the other stuff I thought was important to Janet. Finally we settled on June the 12th of that year as our big day, no messing about for us!

There was one small detail still pending, I had not asked Janet's father and mother for her hand. This had to be done. I penned a nice letter to her parents and asked for the honour of becoming part of their family as their son-in-law. Both mother and father gave their consent and expressed just how happy they were to have me in such a position of responsibility within the family.

With that formality out of the way it was time for me to buy Janet's wedding ring and for Janet to buy my wedding ring. We decided to get married in White Plains, then board the Amerikanis ship and cruise back to Bermuda. We would honeymoon there for a month before getting a Green Card and moving to the US. Janet, being also a trained cake decorator, was very firm about making our wedding cake herself. Sandy and Millie were also let in on the special news and were very happy for us. The photographer and the church had also to be found.

We were going to get married at a Methodist church in White

Plains. Because I was raised a Catholic the minister told Janet that she had to see a priest as well. The priest was okay with that but Janet had to attend several classes at the Catholic church and learn about catechism and what it meant to be Catholic. Eventually the rings were chosen and a photographer booked. Janet baked the heavy English fruit cake which was left to soak in rum for the five months we had left before the wedding. Sandy had agreed to be my best man. I ordered a made-to-measure Hong Kong suit as it was normal in those days that tailors from Hong Kong would come to Bermuda to sell their suits. They would take your measurements and, after you picked the material and paid in advance, your suit was made in Hong Kong and shipped to you.

Everything was advancing as planned. I was only concerned that, once we got married at noon and got to the ship for the cocktail reception, we would run into the Greek boy from whom I had stolen Janet that night at the Forty Thieves night club. I must say that, to my relief, that never happened.

During these months I continued writing every day to Janet a love letter, romantic as I could be. It was then decided that three days before the wedding I would fly to New York, get a blood test done, get the marriage license issued and be ready to get married. I did indeed fly to New York and Janet picked me up at JFK and took me to the hotel in White Plains where I was booked into until the 12th. First thing the next morning we went to the license office for the blood test and to get the license. Here we had a challenge.

We had not known that it would take a week for the results of the blood test to come back before the license could be issued. That was a shock. After explaining to the clerk that we did not have that time she said that she could arrange for us to meet with a judge. He would decide if he could waive the need for a blood test based on his interviewing us both. We must have impressed him as he said, "You have an honest face and I believe you. I will give you the permission to get married this Saturday." Wow that was a relief! With all that behind us we were ready.

The day before the wedding we went back to visit with the

minister who was to marry us at the Methodist church. Here there was one more surprise. He informed us that he had forgotten to tell us that the church had a bazaar the next day and he had made arrangements for us to get married at a Presbyterian church at the other end of town. All the invitations to the fifty or so invitees had gone out with the address of the church on them and now, with less than twenty-four hours to go, the minister had pulled the rug from under our feet. We did not know what to do. The minister realised what he had done and offered a solution. He put up a notice outside the door of the church letting everyone know of the change of venue and we hoped that we would not lose anyone in the shuffle.

Karl, a friend and an admirer of Janet, was working as a chauffeur for some big shot business man and his boss had agreed that he could use his Cadillac to be our wedding carriage. Janet chose to wear her friend's wedding dress but purchased a beautiful outfit she would wear for the cruise to Bermuda. This was all a bit stressful as so many things seemed to have gone out of our control.

THE WEDDING

That night, in my hotel room, I prayed to God to be with me and Janet in the step we were taking. Being brought up in Italy and by a devout Catholic mother there was no room in our household for talk about divorce. At that time in Italy the only way out of your marriage was as in the movie 'Divorce Italian Style' which showed you how to shoot your wife! ... not a pleasant alternative to a marriage gone sour. As Janet also recorded the marriage in England so did I in Italy. Now I was going into it for life. I was so happy to do that. Never for one minute would I have thought of a divorce let alone shooting Janet. Nevertheless I could not sleep that night.

Because of money and the incapacity to undertake a trip like that none of our families were present. My mother and sister would not dare to travel to New York. Janet's parents, older sister Marion and her husband David, her younger brother Bill and his then fiancée Ronnie, did not have the money to do so. This meant that Sandy and Millie were the closest people we had. Until they eventually died many years later we were always grateful for all they did for us.

Saturday morning came and I was getting very nervous. After a light breakfast I got dressed with Millie's help. My new Hong Kong blue suit had a badly cut collar - too late to do anything about that. While Millie was with me at the hotel ready to walk me to the altar, Sandy went to the YWCA to be ready to play the part of Janet's father and give her away. For him it was a dual role as he was also my best man. What a task he had undertaken. As the time approached Millie and I had a car, paid for by Millie, take us to the church. The wedding was scheduled for 12.00 noon.

I was standing at the altar looking impatiently back down the isle. At the stroke of twelve Janet, looking like an apparition, walked into the church holding on to Sandy's arm. She smiled at me and I could not believe that such happiness as I experienced at that moment could be felt by any human being. I was so full of joy I felt like screaming to the entire world that I was the luckiest man on earth. But I kept quiet and the ceremony proceeded beautifully with hymns sung by another of Janet's friends. Passages from the Bible were read and the minister spoke about us as if he had known us all his life rather than the few months he had known Janet and the two days he had known me.

I was very stiff. When I look at the photos now I can remember that, by the time the ceremony was over, my back hurt and all the muscles down my legs felt as if I had run a long way up a very steep hill. The ceremony finally ended and, after the formalities of signing the wedding certificate, we were ready to leave. Karl was waiting outside with his employer's Cadillac to take us, first back to the YWCA for Janet to get out of the borrowed wedding dress and into the beautiful blue and white dress she had bought for the cruise and second, to New York harbour to board the Amerikanis. We reached the ship at about 3.30 pm. A corner of the lounge bar was reserved for our party. There were other wedding parties occupying other corners of the lounge and that really made for a nice atmosphere with lots of music, chatting, a lot of canapés and even more champagne on offer. There were lots of hugs and some tears too but above all much happiness and barrel loads of good wishes. Everyone was happy. One of the best things about having the wedding reception on the ship was that at 4.45 pm the sirens were sounded to signal all invitees to leave the Amerikanis for the ship to be able to set sail at five o'clock. Slowly our friends left and the last ones to say goodbye were Sandy and Millie. Finally alone!

There was lots of hand waving and throwing kisses from the deck to our friends who were now standing on the quay with smiles on their faces, lots of them brought on by the amount of champagne consumed and more of them just by the sheer joy of sharing the most beautiful day of our lives. Exactly at five o'clock the ship gave a long siren blast and was pulled back by powerful tugs. We were on our way to a new life, the two happiest young people on earth.

As it was too early for dinner we went downstairs into the cabin to unpack our luggage and settle in for the three days sailing to one of the most beautiful places in the world - the island of Bermuda. It was bit disappointing to find that the cabin had two single beds. I thought, "What the heck, in the worst scenario we would have to sleep frog style," - not at all an unpleasant way to spend three nights with my beautiful bride. After unpacking we changed into more casual clothing and went to explore the ship. We checked out the restaurant and asked the maître d'hotel which table was assigned to us. We were delighted to find that we had been given a nice corner table. This meant looking out at the other voyagers rather than being in the middle and feeling like a gold fish in a bowl.

Our familiarisation tour continued by visiting the spa, the gym and the sun deck pool. We stopped again at the bar and, as if we had not already had enough, we had one more glass of champagne. Now dinner time was approaching. We wanted to be among the first people to be in the dining room as I found that walking down the main staircase my legs were turning to jelly. This was mainly due to the champagne but also because I had started feeling nervous about my new life and about now being a husband.

I had purchased a beautiful white tuxedo, black trousers, dinner shirt, Bordeaux bow tie and a matching cummerbund. Janet was radiant in her new two piece blue and white suit. At the appointed time for our seating we were all ready, dressed to kill - and famished. We walked to the dining-room to have our first dinner as Mr. and Mrs.Peter Giacomini. Myself and the maître d'hotel who received us at the door were the only two men in the dining-room to wear a tuxedo. Fortunately his was black; had mine been black too then most likely the other passengers would have taken me to be a maître d'hotel working in the dining-room. As we sat at our corner table looking at the other passengers getting seated I felt that, without any doubt, we were the most handsome, the best dressed, the most sophisticated and certainly the happiest couple of them all. It also occurred to me that we were one of the youngest couples and one of the few without walking sticks or wheel chairs. I counted my blessings.

The menus were placed in front of us by an olive skinned, black haired, good looking and most courteous Greek waiter who, without much ado produced another couple of glasses of champagne. The a la carte menu was long and very impressive. After much consideration we decided on a fish dinner. We chose smoked salmon with capers as our appetizer. Our main course was north Atlantic sole belle meunière with rissole potatoes, French string beans and, to add some colour to the plate, the chef masterly prepared carrots Vichy. The white wine to accompany our main course was a bottle of perfectly chilled Mosel.

While slowly eating our dinner I took the opportunity to call Janet 'Mrs.Giacomini', partly for the novelty of it and partly to get her used to other people addressing her by that name. Then, with the bottle of wine empty, it was time to order dessert. This was a particularly difficult choice as the dessert menu was about a yard long and the offerings so sinful that we had to take a break to think about it. The band was playing some beautiful music and the moon was shyly glancing into the dining-room reflecting on the dance floor, so I invited my new bride to dance with me. Janet willingly agreed and up we were in each others arms dancing cheek-to-cheek to the sound of 'She Is A Lady', 'Help Me Make It Through The Night', 'I Love You For All Seasons' and 'Where Do I Begin?' We could have danced all night but we had one more important mission to accomplish. Our dessert had to be ordered and eaten before we could dance some more.

Deciding on the dessert was even harder than choosing the main course. After much indecision, we settled on crepes suzette flambé at the table. As the crepes were being prepared by an expert pair of hands, the sommelier brought to the table a bottle of 1962 Château d'Yquem, Sauternes, one of the best vintage in its history. He poured two generous glasses for us to accompany the now ready and steaming crepes suzettes. If Janet was impressed with the dinner up to that point the dessert was the crown that topped everything we had relished before. They just melted in our mouths. The taste of the Grand Marnier and fresh orange juice were so well balanced that we will never forget the sensation on our tongues. That dish was not made by human hands but created in paradise by some kind of master angel. The Château d'Yquem was no less perfect. Our first dinner together as Mr. and Mrs.Peter Giacomini was not just a culinary perfection, it was an experience of a lifetime. I thought to myself, "If getting married is like this then I want to get married every day!"

The night was progressing magnificently. With the dining experience perfectly concluded, the music soft and romantic brought us back to the dance floor for more cheek-to-cheeking. Then we took a long walk on the top deck under a starry sky and a full moon which, by that time, had turned the ocean into a fairy tale scene like a shining mirror. It was now well past midnight. It had been a long day for Janet and I and time to retire to our cabin ... the one with the two single beds! Holding Janet in my arms as Mrs.Giacomini was the most wonderful and happiest sensation I had ever experienced. Sleeping frog style, which I thought would be a major problem, turned out to be sensational. (Try it yourself some time, just make sure it is with the right person)!

Sleep was bliss but waking up was another story. As I tried to get out of bed my legs were telling me that something was not right as they were refusing to hold me up. The steward brought a breakfast of fresh orange juice, a selection of rolls, Danish pastries, a variety of toasts, two humungous omelettes, crispy bacon, sausages, hash browns, sliced pineapple, sliced bananas, kiwi and a steaming pot of coffee with a choice of cream or milk, to our cabin. A breakfast fit for a king - and queen. But I was feeling sicker by the minute and looking at all that food made me feel even worse. As I wanted to be a macho husband I was trying to dismiss the seasickness that was building up inside my stomach. I thought, "If I just can eat this glorious omelette, a few rolls and drink some hot coffee I will be fine." What an illusion that was.

I did eat the food and drank the coffee but I had to run to the upper deck, lean over the rail and give all that 'fit for a king' breakfast to the scavengers of the sea. So much for my ego as the newly macho husband. Janet meanwhile continued to eat her breakfast in the cabin, not letting this minor detail distract her from the experience she was enjoying. I returned green-faced to the cabin, lay down on my little bed, rolled over and wanted to die. As the day passed, I felt worse. The vomiting continued even if there was nothing else to throw up. Janet spent the afternoon feeling sorry for me and trying to alleviate my discomfort and also my shame. Soon it was time to get dressed for the Captain's dinner.

Janet got made up and into her best clothes. I tried to get up to make myself ready for the most important event of the cruise but no way could I stand, let alone get dressed. I fell back on the bed again and urged Janet to go to dinner and not to miss it because I was such a wimp. She took a bit of convincing but eventually she agreed to go to the dinner while I was rotting away in the cabin feeling like an idiot and certainly not like the exotic Italian lover which we Italians were always told we were.

While Janet was in the dining room having dinner at the

Captain's table, eating lobster bisque and all the other delicacies, I was getting worse by the minute. I became convinced that I would die before she returned. In due course Janet did come back in the wee hours of the morning. After the glorious dinner she had stopped in at the bar and had another glass of champagne. For me the night was nothing more than an excruciatingly painful experience alone in my single bad. There was no frog sleeping that night. When breakfast was served to our cabin next morning the tray was just as beautifully loaded as the day before. This time I tried to eat a little. It did stay in my stomach, no feeding of the scavengers was to follow.

Janet, being a 'water person', had absolutely no problem with the sea, the waves and the rocking of the ship. We walked to the deck and I lay down on a chaise longue by the small swimming pool. It really was nice. I kept looking at the horizon and felt like Columbus on his voyage when he could not see land for what seemed an eternity. Like him I was praying to see land in order to save my life. Like him I could not see it. I knew we were still a long two days from seeing the shores of one the most beautiful places on earth. I had never to that point longed for Bermuda as much as I did then. I knew that if I made it there alive I would survive whatever came after.

Eventually the sea calmed down and the ride became smoother. Not so smooth as to improve my disposition. Not only was I feeling poorly physically, the worse part was the emotional distress of having failed my new and most loved bride on her honeymoon cruise. The next two days were eventless and certainly not very exciting to say the least. Early morning of the fourth day, looking out of the porthole I could see land. It was small at first but gradually getting bigger. This was such a relief. I knew that the moment I set foot on terra firma I would feel great; no more stomach aches, no more dizziness, no more of any bad feelings.

ON DRY LAND

Our trusted friends, Virgilio and Rodolfo, were waiting for us at the dock. Virgilio could not transport us on his Lambretta but

Rodolfo could in his VW beetle. The ride to the cottage was short. I was looking forward to getting there and settling in with my new bride. It promised to be a month of blessed hours and days.

Shortly after arriving Janet figured out that the first thing she needed to do was to go to do some food shopping. Off we went on our moped to Hamilton, the capital, where there were food stores and restaurants. By then the seasickness was all gone and I was a happy bridegroom again. After the shopping was carried home in the basket on the moped and properly stored, a little lunch was skillfully prepared by Janet. She was eager to show me how well she could cook. I felt obliged to wash the dishes, the least I could do after she had slaved to make me such a wonderful first lunch. I too was eager to impress on her what a good choice she had made in marrying a man who would have no problem washing dishes - even after being married for just four days.

The month in Bermuda was flying by with so much to do. Spending hours on the beach had become a daily routine and eating in good restaurants had become the norm. Our favourite pastime though was just to stroll hand-in-hand on balmy nights under star spangled skies. One evening I decided to really splash out and took Janet to the night club at the Hamilton Princess to see the Three Degrees performing live. This was a singing group made up of three African-American ladies who sang, as told in Greek mythology, like the sirens on the islands to lure the sea farers to shore. Still today, although they do not exist as a group, their songs are sung all over the world; one of their famous ones was 'I left the cake out in the rain'.

My next priority was to get my 'green card' work permit from the US embassy. This proved no problem. I also took three days off to get a nasal polypus operation taken care of since I still had a health insurance I could use on the island. Janet was so sweet and caring that I was convinced that I would almost like to get ill just to have her fretting about and taking care of me.

Now was time to start thinking about our return to the States. San Francisco was our destination. For me California was the ultimate paradise on earth; where I always wanted to go to live and maybe even in due course die. An old trunk was found and most of our belongings, mainly my clothing, was diligently packed and shipped. Some farewell parties took place and, just as had happened at New York harbour, some tears were shed.

The day of departure finally arrived and I was just as happy as a pig in mud. I was going to California and I had a new bride whom I loved to boot. Nothing else could have been added to my life at that time. After a few more parties, more eating, more drinking, more walking at night bare foot and under the stars on the still hot sand of the Pink Beach, the time came to leave behind this terrestrial paradise to go to the next one.

The day came to say bye-bye Bermuda, San Francisco here we come!

Chapter 10

THE STREETS OF SAN FRANCISCO

And so we arrived in California on a warm and clear July day in 1971 to be greeted by my good friend Renato from my time in Rome in the early 60s, and his wife Branka. They had been living in San Francisco for some time, Renato working as a chef in a restaurant at Fishermen's Wharf and Branka working in a hospital. I had attended their wedding in London in the mid 60's but Janet didn't know either of them. I was hoping that they would get along well. Fortunately that happened from the moment they picked us up at the airport.

They lived in a modern building at 1250 Leavenworth Street and we had rented a very nice, fully furnished, one bedroom apartment in the same building. The trunk we had sent ahead in which we had packed bed linen, kitchen utensils, dishes, cutlery and glasses, had been safely delivered. We were all set to look for work and did not waste any time. The very next morning Janet started scouting bank and savings institutions while I started on top of Nob Hill at the Fairmont, then down to the Tenderloin at the Notlih and every hotel in between.

For Janet it was a reasonably short task as, by the third day, she had landed a job with the Crocker National bank on Fourth and Market and the very next day she was working. It was a different story for me. In spite of my experience and knowledge of foreign languages I could not locate work as a waiter anywhere. My ego was bruised. I couldn't believe that my new wife would get a job before me; me the macho man, macho husband and Latin lover. So I made the decision to change tack and not look at hotels but to take the restaurant route. The next day bright and early down I marched to the Fisherman's Wharf and started knocking at the door of any restaurant that looked semi respectable. In no time at all I had a job. I was to be a host at Pier 39 Restaurant which was at that time one of the most popular restaurants in San Francisco. My job was to stand at the door, receive the guests, lead them to a table and go back to the door. The waiters made all the money and I had absolutely no chance to earn any. It seemed kind of strange to me that the position of host was the entry position to working in the restaurant and, if you were lucky, you would eventually be promoted to waiter. Such a chance was slim however, as the waiters would rather die than quit; there was just too much money to be made in tips which, in those days, were not taxed. All the old waiters owned apartment buildings, shops and restaurants of their own.

I quickly decided that I wanted to be back working as a waiter in a five star hotel and quit Pier 39 after just two days. I started again canvassing the hotels, from Nob Hill all the way down to the Tenderloin and every five star hotel in between. Then, on the third day of my quest, the Fairmont offered me a position as a banquet waiter. At the time I did not know that banquet waiters in the US made lots of money as the fifteen per cent service charge was distributed directly among the team working on that particular banquet. As the saying goes, 'when it rains it pours'. The very next day I got an offer from the Notlih to be a waiter in their elegant gourmet restaurant, the Gourmet's Table. This posed a difficult choice.

The Fairmont was known to be the best hotel in San Francisco. It was family owned but that meant that possibilities for promotion were few and far between. The Notlih, on the other hand, was a major hotel chain in the United States and the sister company, Notlih International, already operated hotels all over the world. Also I had worked at the Berlin Notlih as a waiter several years previously and enjoyed a good experience. After some soul searching and talking it over with Janet, the decision was made to work at the Notlih. The following day I went to meet with Mr.Jacobi, the maître d'hotel of the Gourmet's Table restaurant.

Mr.Jacobi was a kind, older gentleman who had survived a Japanese concentration camp. He wanted his team to be happy at work and treated everyone with respect. He reminded me of the benevolent grandfather I had never had. The team was a mixture of European waiters, Chinese and some American. It was easy to assimilate as everyone was nice and eager to help the newcomers. My work schedule was from 4.00 pm to midnight five nights per week. Janet soon had her first taste of what it meant to be married to a waiter.

In spite of my work schedule we still found time to enjoy each other's company. We spent every spare minute exploring together our new city. To my surprise I discovered that San Francisco was similar to Rome. Like Rome, the original city is built on seven hills. Of course the modern, expanded city can claim to be sitting on as many as seventy-one hills but the jury is still out on this one. We walked everywhere. Ghirardelli square was one of our favourite spots, the Ghirardelli Chocolate Factory our favourite sweet spot! We rode up and down Nob Hill on the famous cable cars and discovered Lombard Street, known as the most crooked street in the world, with its trees and beautiful flower beds. We also discovered that the light in the city was the same brilliant light as that of Bermuda, free of pollution and smog. What a beautiful city we had made our own.

By now two months had gone by and we had realised that we could not afford to pay our 250 dollars per month rent, so we started to look for a cheaper place. A few days into our search we came across an apartment of which the building's management was looking for a young couple to act as guardians of the building. This was a common practice; the guardians getting free accommodation in return for keeping an eye on the whole property, helping other tenants and generally assisting and liaising with the owner of the building. I was concerned that, with Janet and I both working, this arrangement would not work but Janet convinced me that we could do it.

With the help of a Columbian friend, we moved our belongings in his car to our guardian's apartment. It seemed nice enough until we went to bed on the first night. The previous tenants had been a gay couple with a large number of cats which had been kept inside twenty-four/seven and allowed to use the carpet as their sand box. The harsh smell of cats' urine was so incredibly pungent that there was no way to breath without passing out. Needless to say we moved out next morning.

This time Renato came with his car. While Janet was at work he helped me move our things into a studio just a few hundred yard away and back on Leavenworth Street. This place was very small with just one bed-sitting room where the couch converted into the bed at night. This operation involved the morning and night moving of the coffee table that Karl, Janet's German friend who had driven us around on our wedding day, had given us as a wedding present. The kitchen was so small that only one of us could be in it at a time. There was no worktop space and the refrigerator was just a tiny, under counter ice box which constantly leaked on to the floor. We cooked on a two flame gas burner. But we were happy, in love and paying only half the rent we had paid previously in the nice apartment ... and it didn't stink of cat pee. It was also ideal because, with Janet working banker's hours and I working waiter's hours, we were rarely there at the same time.

Soon I discovered that there was a general manager in the hotel called Klaus Loewe. He was the younger of two brothers working there. His older brother, Godhardt, was the vice-president of Notlih's western US region which included their emerging Las Vegas operations. While Klaus was supposed to manage the hotel, it was in fact Godhardt who did it. He was one of the biggest egomaniacs that I have ever met.

Each morning, as early as five o'clock, he would come to the office and telephone at their homes the thirteen general managers of the hotels under his control, demanding to know why they were still in bed and not at work like he was. His office was at the end of the corridor where the sales, catering, food and beverage and convention service offices were located. The walls of his office were covered with photos of himself in the company of some personality or another or of him receiving some kind of award. On the outside of his door hung a big plaque which read - 'Before entering kneel and worship'. Now if that is not ego please tell me.

While in his office he shouted at everyone working there, either in person or on the phone. He was ruthless in business, a diabolic person who used and abused everyone who allowed him to and he knew nothing of moral principles; cheat and lie was his standard of business. He was also heavily involved with the gaming operations Notlih had in Las Vegas and with characters there of little integrity. Godhardt was married and had three sons who also followed him into the hotel business.

There was another part of Godhardt's life that was most intriguing to me and which I found difficult to understand. He had a German girlfriend working as a cocktail waitress in one of the hotel's bars and he made no secret of the affair. He was quite brazen about it. Almost as if to defy anyone to challenge him, he would disappear to his room with her every afternoon at about five o'clock for two hours after which she would return to serve cocktails at happy hour to Godhardt's powerful friends.

Why would a prestigious entity such as Notlih Corporation tolerate a person like Godhardt Loewe within their ranks? Probably a case of 'money covers a multitude of sins'. For sure there were a multitude of sins out there but the amount of money he earned for the corporation was so huge that Bart Notlih, also a very arrogant man, would look the other way and let him do his thing.

As for me I had no problem with Godhardt. From the day I started to work as a waiter at the Gourmet's Table, where he would entertain his side kick waitress at least three times a week when he was in town, he took a liking to me. At the time the six hundred room tower addition to the already twelve hundred room hotel was being built. This tower was forty-six storeys high and a restaurant called Klause's Cellar was created in the basement and another called Godhardt's Room was built on the top floor. Naturally Godhardt put his brother in the basement and himself at the top. Nothing to do with ego of course.

INTO MANAGEMENT

After only three months of working as a waiter I was promoted to assistant restaurant manager for the opening of Godhardt's Room on the forty-sixth floor. The restaurant served a buffet lunch and a buffet dinner with dancing every night to a live band. The band played from a hanging cage above the dance floor - very much a novelty in 1971. I worked lunch from 11.00 am to 3.00 pm and returned at 6.00 pm until 1.00 am, six days per week. My only day off was Tuesday. Janet of course had to work all day but in the evening we would have dinner together, mostly at home, and then go dancing at the Tonga room in the Fairmont Hotel. There we would drink a cocktail called Scorpio which was made with fruit juices and rum and served for two people in the same huge, coconut terracotta shell.

The Tonga Room still exist today and, judging by the description on Trip Advisor, nothing has changed. It still has tiki torches everywhere, a lagoon in the middle with a live band floating around on it and, every fifteen minutes or so, a tropical shower which falls from the sky just long enough to make you feel like you are in the South Pacific. It was a wonderful experience for me as I did not have to get up early the next morning but for Janet, to get ready for work at 9.00 am, it was much harder. Nonetheless she was a willing companion and we thoroughly enjoyed our Tuesday evenings there.

My salary was 750 US dollars per month and I was no longer in the union as I was now in management. Even if Godhardt had the union leaders in his pocket, I was now the 'enemy' of the workers so to speak. Not that I cared about not being in the union as I had long since concluded that it was just another mafia run racket. The restaurant team now comprised of myself, Angelo, the restaurant manager and the other assistant restaurant manager, Werner from Germany. Then there were twenty-five waitresses, each one more gorgeous than the next. All were personally interviewed and selected by Godhardt himself. These interviews consisted of the girls dressing in the blue and white extra short hot pants and tight fitting tops waitress outfits and parading before him like prize poodles at a fair. No words were spoken, no questions asked. The selection criteria was simple. If they looked good in hot pants they would sell a lot of booze.

Angelo was an older Greek-American guy who had worked with Godhardt at the Fairmont and paid no attention to his screaming fits. He constantly smoked while receiving the guests at the restaurant entrance, was very handsome with silver white hair, wore an elegant white tuxedo and had a kind word for everyone. Werner was a bit of a wimp and would shake in his boots whenever Godhardt arrived. Godhardt loved it and used poor Werner as a door mat. He sadistically enjoyed screaming at him at the entrance of the restaurant and seeing him shrivel up, turn red and purple and blabber meaningless apologies. Immediately following such a session Werner would run upstairs to the toilet to take a pee. I was surprised that he could make it to the toilet and that he didn't just urinate right there at the door like some poor kicked dog would do. Strange the effect some people can have on others.

Then there was me. I had learned, by observing other managers when I was a waiter, that for Godhardt to respect you, you had to stand up to him. When he screamed you had to scream back at him. In other words you just had to be as nasty as he was. He did not understand anything else.

So far so good. About three months had gone by and Godhardt was leaving me in peace to perform to the best of my ability. By now it was New Year's Eve. Naturally I was at work and it was Janet and I's first New Year together. There was no way that I could leave her in the small studio by herself at such a time so we decided that Janet and our Columbian friends would come to Godhardt's Room and spend the evening there. I chose a nice table for them in a corner overlooking the harbour side of the city. They ordered a bottle of Californian champagne and had dinner at their leisure. I could join them for dinner and even for a glass or two of champagne as, back in the seventies, it was very acceptable for a manager to drink while at work. At the stroke of midnight I was with Janet at the table enjoying hugs and kisses and more champagne. As the evening progressed, the atmosphere just got better and better. The wine, cocktails and champagne were flowing, the guests were dancing and having a real ball – and then it happened!

An elderly gentleman dancing with a much younger lady got too close to the edge of the dance floor and, in the euphoria of a cha-cha-cha, stepped backwards and tumbled over. He hit his head on the glass window and split his forehead badly, blood gushed from the wound. The dancing stopped and Godhardt was there in a flash. Because he was very quick thinking he immediately asserted that the accident could not have been the fault of the hotel but was due to the man's carelessness while gazing down the deeply cut front of his dance partner's dress. So the old man was taken by ambulance to the hospital. He got stitched up, an X-ray of his head and of his ribs taken and he was kept there overnight. By now the party was dead with no dancers on the dance floor, no more drinking and people leaving. By one o'clock the room had emptied.

Following our usual routine, Janet, myself and our friends walked to our studio a half mile or so from the hotel, had one more drink and called it a night. The next morning was not a working day for Janet but it was for me. At 11.00 am I was back at work for the lunch service. Not five minutes had passed than in rushed Godhardt, finger pointing at me and yelling something about the champagne served to my wife and my friends the night before. After a few moments of surprise and astonishment I deduced that he was accusing me of having had two bottles of champagne and dinner for my wife and two friends and not paying for it.

Fortunately I had kept the bill which clearly showed that everything was accounted for and that I had paid in cash. I was so livid and upset that, full of rage I took the bill from my pocket and threw it in his face. I shouted that I was not a thief, nor a crook like he was. I told him not to judge me by his own standards and, just for good measure, threw in that he was an egotistic, womanising, idiot unfit for the position he held in an organisation like Notlih

Hotels. I had heard some other senior managers shout back at him before but never had an assistant manager of a restaurant dared to berate him as I had done. No one had ever thrown anything at his face, nor called him the names I had and in front of Angelo, Werner (who was shaking just as I was but from fear not rage), the waitresses and the entire restaurant crew. Then the most amazing thing happened. Without a word Godhardt turned on his heels and left.

Angelo, Werner and the twenty-five waitresses who had by that time gathered around to witness my hanging by my testicles from the band cage suspended over the dance floor were open-mouthed and speechless. The scene they had witnessed was like a bad Hollywood movie. Or like David beating Goliath. I myself fully expected Angelo to tell me that Godhardt had called him with the instructions to get me out of the building immediately. That did not happen and I worked the rest of the day as normal. I went home that afternoon and Janet, it being Saturday, was waiting for me to go sight-seeing with her and enjoy a cappuccino together before I went back to work at six o'clock.

When I told her what had transpired she was certain that I would be fired on Monday, if not before. But we put that out of our minds and took the cable car to Ghirardelli Square where the sun was shining, the breeze pleasant, the light bright, the cappuccino superb and the chocolate at the factory even better. How much better could it have been? A beautiful young wife who loved me, the love I had for her and the fact that, daring the consequences, I had stood up to Godhardt, the most powerful person in the Notlih organization.

I must admit that returning to work at six was a bit scary. By that time all of the one thousand five hundred employees at the hotel had heard about what had transpired between Godhardt and myself. Some of them were silently cheering for me, some were totally surprised to see me still there but most were wondering what kind of punishment was Godhardt planning to dish out to me. I was actually quite relaxed about it all as I was sure my fate was sealed. I expected that I would, on Monday morning at eleven o'clock as I walked through the employees' entrance, be stopped by security and taken to human resources to receive my last pay cheque and the proverbial pink slip. That night I slept better and started making plans as to where I would start looking for my next job. Would I go back to the Fairmont? That would have possibly been a bad choice because the Fairmont hated the Loewe brothers and I had turned down their offer in favour of the Notlih. I had gone to bed with the enemy. By that time I was tired, stressed out and didn't need to create a problem that did not exist and possibly never would. So I went to sleep.

The next morning, Monday the 3rd of January 1972, Janet got up, quietly made her breakfast, showered and left for work. At about ten I got up, showered, shaved, dressed in my tuxedo, ate some cereal and went to my work. As I walked through the employees' entrance I was not stopped by security and to my surprise not called in by the human resources manager either. I went straight to the service elevator and rode to the forty-sixth floor. Angelo and Werner were already there and somewhat surprised to see me. By 11.30 I was getting nervous as nothing had happened and by 12.00 o'clock I really was falling apart.

Then the phone rang. It was Godhardt and in his usual thick German accent he said, "Peter, I vant you to come to my office now." I had resolved to be strong in front of him, no matter what he was going to dish out. As I approached his office door and read 'that' plaque, I had to smile thinking that this was going to be my day of judgement and whatever came down was final. Heaven or hell, which will it be Lord?

I entered through that door and I am sure that I have never stood more straight and defiant. Godhardt Loewe, the most mighty, the most powerful of all people was about to hand down his sentence to me for standing up to him and giving him a dose of the same medicine he so freely dished out. He did not look up at me when I entered but motioned for me to sit on the lower-than-his chair positioned opposite him at his desk. He finished shouting at some poor soul on the phone, slammed down the receiver, stared hard at me for a few seconds and then … burst out laughing! I did not know what to make of it. He did not say a word for what seemed like an eternity but when he finally spoke said, "Peter you have more guts than brains. In all my years of screaming and abusing people only a few have stood up to me. No one ever called me the names you have done and no one ever threw anything at me. Honestly I like that and admire you. Because of your courage, I am going to promote you to assistant catering manager starting tomorrow. Now you can go."

Had I not been sitting down then I am sure I would have fallen down. What a shock! When I went home that evening Janet was asleep and I did not have the courage to wake her up to tell her the news. You can imagine her surprise when we got up the next morning and I told her what had happened. I had not slept a wink that night. I was too excited and scared and so many thoughts were going through my head. Will I be able to make it as an assistant catering manager? What would I have to learn to do? Is this a step that would advance my career? What will I do next? The proverbial 'promote people above their capacity and see them sink or swim' came to mind. But I was able to tell Janet that in this position I would be home more often and be able to enjoy more dinners with her.

ONWARDS AND UPWARDS

Next morning at nine o'clock I was in the catering office reporting to Joseph Karl, the director of food and beverage and Gaas, the catering manager. Karl had been in a Shanghai prison camp with the Loewe brothers and Mr.Jacobi; Gaas was a fine Dutch guy with enormous global experience. My office had a common door with Gaas's office and after the introduction to the rest of the team he asked me to sit in my office and just listen to his conversations with the customers. I did that for three days and was soon anxious to get going. Like a sponge takes in water so I was trying to learn all there was to learn in the same way. I only needed to be a bit more patient. The next step was to sit in with my first customer and have Gaas coach me along. He was the most organised person I had seen. His desk was always spotless with no piles of paper or files lying around and his files were immaculate. Just a few days after that I took off like a rocket. Now I was receiving customers who wanted to book social events like weddings, bar mitzvahs, dances, school graduations and not least, the annual San Francisco gay pride parade ball.

For this event the big ballroom was extraordinarily decorated for the two thousand attendees who wore the most spectacular costumes imaginable. A big band provided the main entertainment and during their break a smaller rock 'n roll band took to the stage. Whisky, champagne and wine flowed non-stop all night and everyone was on the dance floor. I had never experienced anything like that in my entire life.

Growing up in a small village in a family whose mother was very Catholic, gays were looked upon as abnormal and nasty terms were used to describe them. While it was acceptable for two girls to dance together during the village patron saint celebration, had two men done that in public a scandal would have erupted. Short of stoning them right there and then, anything could have happened. Now I was confused and could not distinguish between who was a male, who was a female and who was in-between. Then again I was in San Francisco, a city known for its liberal approach to life. Nevertheless, to me it was very much like Sodom and Gomorrah all over again and I thought that maybe I should not have booked that business. Gaas very quickly put my doubts to rest.

He reminded me that it was an annual event at the hotel, had the support of top management and as long as I could charge them plenty it was fine to have it. At that point I learned two new things. The first one was that one of Godhardt's favourite phrases was 'charge them plenty', the second was that Gaas, in all his elegance, was also gay. This came to me as a shock. He was the most handsome man working at the hotel. He was tall and slim with a full head of black hair and stood as upright as a bean stalk. He wore the most fashionable, made-to-measure suits with matching shirts and always shiny shoes. My discovery of him as being gay did not change one iota my opinion of him as a professional and as a gentleman. He continued to be my biggest supporter and mentor.

My initial thought that becoming an assistant catering manager would give me more time with Janet turned out to be untrue. Now my working day started at the latest at 8.00 am and it was expected that the catering manager who had booked an event be present when it took place. This meant that if Gaas and I had contracted an event in the same evening we both had to be present until at least the dessert had been served. I clearly remember one evening at around midnight when I was leaving the hotel to go home that Godhardt saw me and asked if I was only going to work half a day that day. In addition to that my office was now just 20 feet (7 m) away from Godhardt and Klaus's offices and the shouting that went on all day was tiring and stressful.

Sundays were more relaxing as Janet and I normally had the day off together and had found a Methodist church where we attended the morning service before going home for lunch. The afternoon was normally spent strolling the streets of San Francisco (no relation to the TV series). One of our favourite walks was in Polk Street which, at that time, had many little family owned shops, cute cafés and no Starbuck's. Renato and Branka were also outdoor people and loved to go to a lake not too far from the city in his big, blue Buick which he would often drive us around in too.

Janet was doing well at the bank and had become popular there. Particularly so with the manager Mr.Oppenheimer who treated her like an adopted daughter. He liked the fact that we were both young, with the desire to succeed and that we were working hard and saving our pennies in order to eventually buy our own house.

The studio apartment was getting smaller and smaller by the day so soon it was time to move, on this occasion into a larger apartment just a few block away from the Notlih and from Market and Fourth where Janet worked. It was perfect for the two of us. Not too big a place and at an affordable rent and not so small that that we couldn't both be in the kitchen at the same time.

Back then I liked to cook dinner when at home in the evening. My specialties were river trout and roast rabbit and, on special occasions, I'd make a crepes suzettes dessert with Grand Marnier and brandy. But our earnings were still not in line with buying such extravagant delicacies on a regular basis. One evening I came home from work early and, as I opened the door, I saw Janet running from the bedroom to the door and standing there in the middle of it. I laughed as I did not know why she would be doing such a thing until she told me that she had learned an earth tremor drill at the bank whereby the staff were instructed to go quickly to the nearest doorway and stand under it. Apparently, it was considered the safest place to be. Many years later, when we lived through an 8.8 magnitude earth quake we learned that this was pure nonsense.

While one would think that the contrary would be the case at the Notlih, only one famous visitor came to dinner during the time I was working there. He was Sir David Frost the English journalist, satirist and television presenter. In 1977 he famously interviewed President Richard Nixon for the revelationary documentary 'The Original Watergate Interviews'. He conducted interviews with many other personalities. People such as Mohamad Ali and Henry Kissinger. He also got into the movie business, setting up his own company in 1960 which he called David Paradine Ltd.

One could talk about David Frost and his achievements for a long time but for me the thing that stands out in my mind is the photo of me taken with him. It was my first photo with a famous person. I was very tense. He noticed this and put his arm around my shoulders and started to laugh like a madman. In no time at all everyone else, myself included, was laughing hysterically too and it was at just that moment that the professional photographer, who accompanied Frost everywhere, clicked the shutter. I still have that photograph today and it brings back fond memories of my days rubbing shoulders with the rich and the famous.

By now a few months had gone by. I felt more secure about my job and Mr.Oppenheimer, Janet's boss, encouraged her to buy a house. I was scared to death by such a prospect, I just couldn't get my head around the idea. While I had grown up in a house, it was one which was already there, built by my grandfather. But after years of travelling and working in different countries my attitude was that to live in a house was not necessary, renting an apartment was just fine. Being encumbered by a mortgage was distinctly undesirable. In addition to that we believed that to find a house we first had to have a car to get around in and look for open houses and areas where we could afford a house.

I continued scared at the prospect. To make matters worse, Mr.Oppenheimer told Janet that she could have a special interest rate of only six percent. While this might sound good to informed ears, to me it was like hearing a death sentence being handed down. I made the calculation that, with my 750 US dollars monthly salary and the 450 US dollars Janet was earning we could make it ... just. I had, however, to eat twice a day at the hotel six days per week in order to make that happen.

We also had to buy a car and, coming from the old countries, buying something on credit and having to pay interest was not a thing either Janet or myself had grown up with. With the help of the husband of one of Janet's friends from work, we bought a brand new, white, 1973 VW bug at a cost of 2,000 dollars and paid in cash.

Janet had a New York state driving license and I had a German license. Neither of these licenses would allow us to drive the car legally in California. We got hold of a driving school and started taking lessons on the California highway code, how to drive on the hills of San Francisco and how to park at the side of the road whether driving up hill or down.

The instructor suggested that we take our tests in Daly City as it was less hilly there and, he reckoned, easier to pass. We took his advice and one morning, very eager to get our California licenses, off we went. We were fortunate as we both passed the test the first time. Now we were licensed drivers and we owned a car, albeit a German made one.

A MAN OF PROPERTY

Now it was time to get into real debt. We were looking to buy into the American dream to own our own house. We were advised that looking for a property within the city limit would only be a waste of time as we couldn't afford to pay the prices and that Daly City (once again) was the best option for us.

For the next few Sundays we drove around every afternoon to look for 'Open House' posters placed at the roadsides by real estate agents keen to make a sale. Finally, after a few Sundays of searching, we found our first dream house. It was a typically Californian one, built on a cement slab and with wooden support posts. It had a garage at street level and the main entrance off to the right side up a set of wooden stairs. The garage was big enough for two cars with a place for a work bench and makeshift sleeping accommodation where the drug-addicted son of the previous owners had slept. The main accommodation had real oakwood floors, the living room had a fireplace and from the living room and the dining room there was the most magnificent view of the Pacific Ocean ... but, being in Daly City, only after mid-day when the fog had lifted! There was a decent size kitchen, three bedrooms and two bathrooms.

The asking price was, to me, a fortune, 28,000 dollars. On top of that we would be required to pay the utility bills, the real estate tax and the insurance. Also there was no furniture, so hunting down garage sales became our new specialty. Every Saturday Janet would scour the city for them. The first thing we needed was a bed but, with not one to be got, we had to incur the additional expense of buying a complete bedroom set from a wholesale store.

We also acquired three orange crates and for several months these became our two chairs and table. They were set up in front of the fire place as it was winter. It turned out to be quite romantic to eat our meals together on weekends in front of the blazing fire while listening to music from a small portable radio I still had from my days in Germany. The mortgage payments, my main reason for many sleepless nights, turned out to be easier than I thought. We had jobs. We had a car. We had a house - even if a scantily furnished one - and we had each other. There was nothing else we wanted nor needed at that time.

While I would have liked to have babies around, Janet smartly wouldn't hear about that subject. She knew that it was too early in our married life to load ourselves with the responsibility of raising children. Besides which, my Italian upbringing would have had a terrible conflict with the need for Janet to go to work and have some stranger looking after 'my baby'. We were now accustomed to the American life style even if our table and chairs were still three orange crates. Many material things had to be given up in order to maintain what had become a luxurious life style for us. One thing though which we never gave up was our one evening out in town each week, to either a movie or to our favourite night spot at the Fairmont, yes the Tonga Room.

Time was flying by and eventually we purchased a cheap dining table and some mismatched chairs. A few months later a small sofa and two armchairs to set in front of the fireplace were added. Everything was moving fast and we had just started to get used to being a home owner and to living in San Francisco and Daly City when I was offered a job as catering manager at the Eastgate Plaza Hotel in San Diego. My salary would go from 750 dollars per month to 1,200 which made me think that it was a move well worth making. The chances for promotions to catering manager at the Notlih were non existent as Gaas was not about to leave. There was even less chance of Joseph Karl moving as he was stuck to Godhardt Loewe's shirt tail and couldn't or wouldn't let go if his life depended on it. It seemed just too good an opportunity so, after some hesitation, Janet and I decided to take the chance and move.

By June of 1973 I was in San Diego while Janet stayed behind to sell the house. I was staying in a room in this magnificent new hotel with all the charm of an old European classic hotel. I had known these hotels because I had worked at the Grand Hotel in Rome, the Grand Hotel in Paris, the Beau-Rivage in Lausanne, Switzerland and even the Castle Harbour Hotel in Bermuda was an

211

old one. This hotel, however, had things that the others did not have. The water taps were gold plated and the bathtubs were square and large enough for three or four people to take a bath all together - if they were at least good friends.

The gourmet dining-room was named after the Fontainebleau Castle in France and it did measure up to it. The décor was very much like the château and the food creatively and masterly prepared by a toque noir chef from Montreal called Joel. It was hard to believe that in his free time he smoked pot and wore ear rings. The small ballroom was the replica of the dining room at the château of Versailles with even the fireplace an exact replica of the one in the château in France. The crystal chandeliers also were Baccarat, masterfully made in France. The bar was no less impressive with its mahogany counter and enormous oversize chandelier hanging from the ceiling in the centre of the room.

The team of managers was, however, weird to say the least. As the saying goes 'the fish starts stinking from the head'. The hotel was owned by J.C.Pierce, a financier, owner of the San Diego Hijos baseball team. He was also a major investor in the tuna industry, owned a bank and Air Blue Sky. He was eventually convicted of grand theft and tax evasion in connection with the collapse of his bank and of the airline. At the time I was working at the hotel he was married to Concepcion Sanchez, who, back in the '40s, was working for a radio station in Dallas as secretary and goffer. She was definitely a smart woman.

She knew which buttons to push in order to get to where she wanted to in life and she wanted more than to be just the co-owner of the TV station which she eventually had become. So marrying J.C.Pierce was the greatest move she could have made. She had free rein to do what she wanted with the hotel as, for him, it was just a game. She went to France, visited all the châteaux and purchased all the antiques pieces she could get her hands on. When the time came to transport all that she had bought in France to furnish the hotel she had to rent a cargo ship to get everything to San Diego.

The general manager was a banker who was a trusted friend of

Mr.Pierce but his knowledge of the hotel business was non-existent. Worse still, he was running the hotel like a bank in which the customer has no rights and the rules of the bank prevail at all times. One of his most idiotic decisions was that the bar would not serve coffee. He felt that everyone crossing the threshold had to consume strong drinks. The San Diego newspaper quickly got wind of this and a full page was written up the next day with the headline, "Bartender, give me an Irish coffee but hold the whisky!" The rest of the story was a denunciation of all the stupid things which the most expensive and most beautiful hotel in San Diego was doing.

The executive chef (Joel from Montreal) was married to a much younger wife and had five children from a previous marriage. The oldest of his sons had moved to London where he lived as a hippie and a drug addict. Years later I was told that his wife had had enough of the 'tribe' as she used to call the family and left him.

As I was on my own from June to August, after work I had dinner almost every night in the Fontaineblue restaurant where an old gentleman was the maître d'hotel and the most gracious of hosts. I loved to watch a soap opera on Mexican television called Muñeca (doll) which was full of mischief and intrigues. Every two weeks I flew home to see Janet for the weekend or Janet would fly down to San Diego to see me. Fortunately these two months went by rather quickly and the house was sold for 32,000 dollars.

I intended to fly up to San Francisco and drive Janet down to San Diego in our VW Beetle but just prior to that Janet took the car to the VW dealer for a service. On her way home with the car it broke down on the freeway. There were no cell phones then and Janet had to wait until someone stopped and helped her. It turned out that the garage had emptied the oil from the engine but had forgotten to replace it and the engine had blown. A new engine was required so the garage loaned us another car and we drove south first thing the next morning. A week later the young mechanic who had forgotten to replace the oil was made to drive our car to San Diego and return to San Francisco with their car.

Now Janet was finally in San Diego with me so the search for an apartment was the next thing to do. After just a few days we found a one bedroom, fully furnished apartment (we had sold the little furniture we had with the house). The location was great as it was a short walking distance from the hotel and from the bank where Janet had found employment very soon after arriving. It was on the ground floor of a tall and modern building with two tennis courts and a sun terrace with a large pool on the roof. We settled in quickly and started the mission of finding out all about San Diego, its surroundings and Tijuana, just 15 miles (24 km) distant across the border.

At that time Janet and I played tennis so we made good use of the tennis courts. It was during one of these game that I shot a high ball to Janet who stretched to get to it and landed badly on her left leg. She couldn't get up and I had to lift her up and put her in the car and on to the hospital emergency room. The X-ray results revealed a torn left knee cartilage with which to this day, at age seventy and a few operations later, she still has problems.

San Diego was on the missionaries route from Mexico to California and this activity produced many interesting sites with churches and monasteries peppered all over the region. Then there is the San Diego zoo which ranks among the most famous zoos in the world. I do not believe that animals should be kept in cages, but nonetheless it was a good place to spend a Sunday afternoon with an ice cream and feel like a child again.

Tijuana was something else. The first time we went there was on a Saturday evening. Because we had heard all the horror stories about taking the car into Mexico where, for sure, it would be stolen or the wheels would be taken and the car left standing on bricks, we drove to the border, left the car on the American side and walked over to Mexico. What a totally different world. I had some idea of the music, the colours, the food and the abundant tequila from watching the TV soaps I mentioned, but those proved to be a pale shadow of the reality. The people were a happy bunch with Mariachi music pouring out on to the dirt roads from every possible hole in the wall which the locals called homes.

Every corner had a mini market selling everything from papier-maché flowers, ponchos, tequila and guitars to riding boots, whips, spurs, leathers bags and music cassettes. The pick of all these exotic items were the enormous sombreros, black full Mexican cowboy suits with silver embroidery and white ladies' campesinas dresses (cowgirl dresses) with enormous colourful flowers either printed or sewed on the cloth. It was just incredible and almost out of this world. After walking street after street and exploring market after market we were ready for dinner.

We found the Centro Comercial Plaza Madero (it still exists to this day). Among its maze of narrow walkways there was available everything you might ever want made from cast and wrought iron. We were so mesmerised by all that we saw that, for a while, we even forgot that we were hungry. I bought a wine bottle rack which became part of our furniture for many years to come. Then eventually we chose a rustic restaurant called La Placita from the plethora of eateries catering for every taste from tacos and tamales to burritos, quesadillas and chili con carne. You name it and they had it.

We plopped ourselves down on a wooden bench with a wooden table made out of a tree trunk and chose huevos con chorizo (fried eggs with a spicy hot sausage) and a cerveza Carta Blanca (a local beer). Our amazement continued as groups of strolling musicians paraded by every few minutes with their happy sounds of guitar, trumpet and singers. All too soon we had to make our way back across the border.

On our way we stopped at a shop and bought ourselves a good bottle of tequila. The salesman assured us that we were allowed to return to the US with it but he lied. When we arrived at the border, a border policeman took it away from us and then, in front of our unbelieving eyes, opened the bottle and poured it down the drain. I felt so angry I could have strangled that guy. By now it was late at night and we walked over the border into the US of A.

Tijuana became one of my favourite places as it is so Latin that I could relate to it well. I did not speak Spanish like the Mexicans do but after having worked in San Francisco I was understanding what they were saying most of the time. I spoke Spanish with a Spanish accent as my Spanish speaking friends in Europe, with one exception, were from Spain. Mexicans laughed at my accent but they did understand everything I said and that was great.

Tijuana now became part of our regular agenda with our visits there becoming more pleasant with every crossing. One of the highlights was to walk across the borders and climb aboard a local bus known as blanco y azul (white and blue) to go downtown. These buses were an absolute riot, shaking and rattling their way along pothole filled roads with drivers who must have bought their drivers' licenses at the local print shop. It was a miracle that we never rolled over. The passengers were generally a mix of Americans courageous enough to get on one of these buses and visitors from all over the world out to experience the real Mexico. There were also some gypsies and some 'wet backs' who had just been deported from the US and were accompanied to the border by bulky immigration officers.

The greatest thing on the bus was the music. There was inevitably a group of at least four or five mariachi musicians with their guitars, trumpets and singers. The music was lively, the songs delightful and they created a real sound of Mexico ambience. Even the most stuffed-shirt travellers had to relax in such an atmosphere. Before getting to our destination shots of tequila were passed around followed by a large black sombrero in which you were expected to drop at least a dollar for the entertainers. These guys went back and forth all day and sometimes all night, singing and playing to entertain everyone and earn enough money to support their usually large families. I loved it. By the time we got downtown we were in the mood and ready for the street vendors, the ever present beggars, the noise, the fumes of old cars and buses and the food and Carta Blanca. What a country - Viva Mexico!

As time went by we became more courageous and soon we were

ready to drive our VW Beetle across the border. This was a less rewarding experience than crossing on foot and taking the bus downtown. The positive side of driving was that now we could venture outside of Tijuana and to the seaside which was only a few miles out of town. Tijuana junta al mar (Tijuana by the sea) was a new development with new houses and apartments and a totally different world from the main town. We were fascinated by the contrast and I really fell in love with the rolling Pacific Ocean and seriously considered buying a property there. Today I wish we had done that. Who knows we most likely would have retired there.

SICK OF THE SEA

The desire to get to know this part of the world kept growing in me. Before winter came I wanted to go further south. Encenada was the next choice. While only 84 miles (135 km) from San Diego by car I did not want to drive. I decided to take the ferry down from San Diego in the morning, allowing us all day to explore before returning at night. What a great way to spend a Sunday.

This was all well and good and the first hour on the water felt just fine. However, soon the ocean got rough with waves as high as 5 feet (1.5 m) and I quickly turned green and started to re-enact my honeymoon by vomiting my breakfast to the eagerly awaiting shrimps. It was horrible as I thought that by now I had passed that stage of feeling seasick, especially on just a short trip along the coast ... but wrong I was. Sometime after we arrived and set foot on land, my stomach settled. By now I was ready to explore the town. It was almost a carbon copy of Tijuana. The same street vendors, the same beggars, the same gypsies, the same colourful shops, the same tequila and the same lively mariachis everywhere. Gosh, I loved Mexico.

We walked and walked around for hours until finally it was time to eat. We found a hole in the wall eatery with dirt floor, wooden tables and chairs and which served the most delicious enchiladas prepared with love by a big mama who clearly devoured her fair share of corn tortillas every day of her life. My favourite Carta Blanca beer washed it all down and we partied on until it was time to catch the ferry for our return journey. I was, not surprisingly, dreading the moment. When we got on board I went below deck and found a seat about midway in the ferry. It is common knowledge that if you place yourself in the middle of a ship the rocking is diminished and therefore, normally, you don't get sick. Well, it was all fine for about half-an-hour. Then my stomach started to churn again and my face turned green. Faster than lightning, I was running up the stairs to the side of the ferry, grabbing the rail and delivering my delicious enchiladas lunch to the shrimps for their second free meal of the day. I am certain that on that day there were no happier shrimps in the whole world than the ones swimming off the coast of Baja California. For the rest of the trip I hung to the rail and puked until nothing was left in me. Then I started puking bile. It was actually scary to see a part of my inside which I had never seen before being fed to the fishes of the ocean. Once in San Diego I fell on my knees and thanked our Lord I was still alive.

Now we wanted to pursue the American dream of home ownership once more and started looking for a house to buy. After seeing about a million of them we finally settled for one in the town of Mira Mesa. It was a lower middle class area 17 miles (27.5 km) and a twenty minute drive north of San Diego. There was also a good bus service, handy for Janet on those occasions when I had to stay for dinner service at the hotel and couldn't drive home 'til late.

The house had three bedrooms, an open plan living and dining room, a small kitchen, two bathrooms and a two car garage. It didn't have the view that our Daly City house had enjoyed but it did suit us well at that point in our lives. In the month of November we moved into our new home.

A few months before that we had met two English girls, Pat and Helen, who were taking some time travelling around the US on the back of odd jobs here and there. They were nice kids, a little younger than ourselves but no less adventurous and were living in a studio apartment in the building. We soon became good friends and did a lot of things together. Naturally my friend, Richard, was brought into the fold of our friendship. They helped us to move our few belongings from our apartment to the new house. With Christmas Eve approaching, the five of us decided to have dinner together in our house that night, go to midnight Mass and then return home for more champagne and panettone (traditional Italian Christmas cake).

Following a scrumptious steak dinner and lots of wine we headed out for church. Nobody seemed to be too worried about DUI in those days. I am not sure that I can remember now where the church was. As a matter of fact, I don't think I remembered even then where it was because the wine had already taken over my brain. Remembering anything about the Mass or why we were there seems even less likely. The hour spent in church helped to clear our heads a little and the drive back home was a straighter and less curvy one than on the way to the church. We made it home and the party quickly recommenced with the champagne corks popping and panettone being devoured. Before we knew it was five in the morning.

Richard was in no condition to drive Pat and Helen back to their apartment in San Diego or to get himself home to La Jolla where he lived. So he took the second bedroom and Pat and Helen took the third and we all crashed out. By nine o'clock on Christmas morning we were all up and about, even if we could not walk a straight line nor talk any sense. We cooked a breakfast of bacon, eggs, sausages, pancakes with maple syrup and strong black coffee. By eleven o'clock we were on our way to walk the beach in La Jolla, one of the most beautiful spots on earth to be on a sunny Christmas day in California. By 2.00 pm we were ready for lunch. What better than a BBQ on the beach? Richard was a master at the grill. In no time he presented us with the most delicious meal which we devoured with great gusto while sitting on the warm sandy beach. The beer and wine were flowing again as if there was no tomorrow.

Work was becoming more stressful as J.C.Pierce was arrested, jailed and then let out on bail many times. Janet was a pretty heavy smoker at the time but one evening she announced that she intended to stop smoking as she wanted to have a child and had been told that as long as she smoked she would not get pregnant. I thought that that was a bit of an old wife's tale but who was I to dispute it? She told me that she would attend the Schick Institute in San Diego where they would teach her how to stop smoking for 350 dollars. I was smoking too at the time, albeit much less than Janet. When I heard how much we would have to pay to stop smoking, I stubbed the Malboro which was in my lips at that moment, flung it and the half full pack of cigarettes which I had in my pocket into the garbage bin and stopped smoking right there and then. I figured that to pay 350 dollars to stop Janet from smoking was bad enough but to pay 700 for the two of us amounted to total madness!

Sure enough Janet went to the first session at Schick and all was fine. Then, at about the eighth or ninth session I got a call at work to please go to the institute to pick up my wife and take her home. I was told that she was not in any condition to take the bus, let alone drive the car. Worrying myself half sick I rushed to the place to find Janet slouched on an armchair, her face as white as a bleached sheet, her arms as limp as the arms of a puppet and her legs turned to jelly. With the help of an attendant we sat her in the car and I drove her home. Once there I put her to bed and she fell asleep, totally oblivious of where she was and what had happened to her. The next morning, after drinking a strong black coffee she regained enough strength to tell me what had happened.

This is what she said. "When I entered the small room where the sessions were taking place I was told to sit down on a chair at a table on which stood a mountain of cigarette butts. The stench was awful. Imagine an ashtray left overnight with just two cigarette butts. Now multiply that by the contents of two thousand ashtrays, sit in front of them in a space no bigger than 5 feet by 5 feet (1.5 m square) and take a deep breath. After about five minutes of trying to breathe in that stench came the pièce de résistance of the treatment. I was given a lit cigarette and told to follow the instructions sounding from a tape recorder.

The instructions were very clear. About every five seconds a voice would shout out, 'Inhale', so I inhaled. For the first few minutes I was able to blow out the smoke I had inhaled before the five seconds were up. But by the tenth inhalation my lungs were full of smoke yet this terrible voice kept telling me to inhale. Eventually there was no more room in my lungs for oxygen, they were full of nicotine and I couldn't breathe any longer. I puked all over the giant mountain of cigarette butts and kept on puking until I had nothing left in me to puke. Then I passed out and collapsed. I knew nothing else until I woke up in my bed this morning."

This is how my beloved wife stopped smoking, at least for the time being. With that out of the way now was time to get serious about having a baby. That was a task in which I had a part to play too!

WHEN ONE DOOR CLOSES .....

At work things were getting worse as Mr.Pierce had finally lost the bank and the airline and was now spending more and more time in jail and less time out on bail. News often arrives in strange ways and this time was no different. One afternoon we were told that the hotel had declared bankruptcy and that we would have a court appointed receiver to manage the hotel until such time as a buyer was found. Not good news. Then the self same evening I arrived home to find Janet very happy indeed. She rushed to me, wrapped her arms around me and beamed, "Congratulation daddy, we are pregnant!" Janet has always said, and would still say today, "We are pregnant," rather than "I", but either way what joy I felt at that moment. I knew immediately that our lives would change and become fuller and richer than they already were. We opened a bottle of champagne to celebrate and that was the last drop of alcohol Janet would drink until after our beautiful daughter Emily was born.

Now I had a dilemma. Do I stick around at work and hope things get better or look for a job with what would hopefully be a stable company? I was genuinely concerned as I had a new responsibility looming, one bigger than just me. After some serious praying and discussion with Janet we decided that it was better that I look for new employment. In the event, this proved easy.

On the recommendation of my old friend Renato I applied to both the Marriott and the Jerik in Los Angeles. Within a few days I was called to go to the Jerik in downtown Los Angeles for an interview. Full of enthusiasm, I journeyed to L.A. for my meeting with the general manager of the hotel. The interview was the most uncomfortable one I have ever had to endure. When I arrived I informed the front desk that I had an appointment with the general manager. His secretary came out and escorted me to the executive offices where I was kept waiting for more than half an hour without even an offer of a coffee. Eventually I was ushered into the general manager's office where two smartly dressed executives sat but I was directed to a chair in the corner with no introductions being made.

Eventually though one of them introduced himself as the general manager and introduced the other as the regional vice president. They pulled up their chairs in front of me and the inquisition commenced. The questions came thick and fast but none of them had any bearing on me, my feelings or my family. It was all about how would I make money for Jerik hotels. Soon I was sweating then, after about an hour of the torment, they revealed that they were looking for a food and beverage director and would let me know within two days if I had passed the interview. I left with a totally negative view of the company and felt less than enthusiastic about the prospect of joining such an impersonal organization.

I was pretty sad by the time I arrived home in Mira Mesa that evening. My mood changed quickly when Janet greeted me at the door with a huge smile on her face. She asked me how the interview had gone. While I described my miserable encounter she, strangely, kept smiling. When I had finished my tale she pointed me to the answering machine and pressed the button. I heard the voice of Paul Turano, director of catering at the Los Angeles Airport Marriott asking me to call him ASAP.

Within minutes I had called him back and arranged to drive to the L.A.Marriott to arrive at 6.00 pm the following day, stop overnight and have a look around the hotel. I drove there next day, arrived smack on six and checked in. On going up to my room I was surprised to see that a huge basket of fruit, a plate of cheese and a bottle of wine were waiting for me alongside a welcome card, hand-written and signed by the general manager himself. What a difference in approach to that of the Jerik people the day before. After I got over the shock I went to Paul's office accompanied by a charming and smiling receptionist. Immediately he received me and, after inquiring about my trip up the freeway, took me to the Hangar bar on the eighteenth floor which had magnificent views of all the planes landing and taking off at the airport.

We had a couple of glasses of wine and the conversation revolved entirely around our personal lives, our families and all those things dear to our hearts. Not once was business mentioned. About an hour later Paul invited me to have dinner in the Capriccio Italian restaurant. First he proudly showed me the banquet areas, meeting rooms and the two large ballrooms. I was impressed because this looked more like the San Francisco Notlih, except the ambience was more refined. I had not heard anyone screaming, calling names or belittling anyone! The décor was very different. I found out that that was down to Mrs.Marriott being in charge of the decoration of the hotels. It was clear that her favourite colour was red. Everything was red. At dinner a few glasses of wine (red of course) were put away and the conversation remained on life in general, sport, travelling, politics and religion. Once again the subject of work was never touched upon. As the evening came to a close Paul asked me to report to his office at 9.00 am the following morning.

That night I did not sleep for one minute. I was excited about the prospect of working in this hotel and with a company that had, after all, a heart. All kind of thoughts came to me, most of them positive. I could picture myself working with the people I had seen in passing so far, all good looking and professional in their demeanour, courteous and respectful but having fun too. Next morning I reported to Paul in his office at 9.00 am and we went straight from there to the Capriccio restaurant and a scrumptious breakfast of bacon, eggs, sausages and hash brown potatoes all washed down with a pot of coffee.

Now Paul informed me that they were looking for a catering manager and the next step, if I was agreeable, was for me to meet the general manager. The position of catering manager was, of course, a step back for me as I was already a director of catering at the Eastgate Plaza and was looking at a promotion to director of food and beverage with the Jerik. Paul was not really interested in finding out what I knew about the business, he trusted me.

I found out later that there was a saying within Marriott at the time - 'There are three ways of doing things; the wrong way, the right way and the Marriott way'! Paul took me to meet the general manager, Mr.Jerry Best, a chubby jovial Chicagoan with a firm handshake and a wonderful smile. He was completely different from any general manager I had met before. He transmitted warmth, made you feel good and possessed not an ounce of misplaced ego. What a great man.

The conversation with him lasted only ten minutes. I was then asked to wait in Paul's office while the two of them had a pow-wow. The three minutes this conversation took seemed to me to last an eternity as I really hoped that they'd make me an offer. I was fairly shaking in my boots by the time that Paul returned. He was smiling and said, "Jerry and I like you very much and we would like to make you an offer to join our team. The only position we have now is the catering manager one but our company is growing fast and you will have every opportunity to develop yourself into a future director of catering. The Oldport Beach Marriott and the Lincolnshire Marriott in Illinois are currently under construction. We will pay you 350 dollars per week, we pay weekly and not monthly like everyone else does." I accepted the offer without hesitation. Even if it meant a demotion I knew that with this kind of company I could go far. For me it was a marriage made in heaven. We agreed on a starting date and I drove back home singing at the top of my voice all the way to Mira Mesa.

Janet was at work and I couldn't give her the great news. On the answering machine there was a message from the general manager at the Jerik. I called him and he offered me the position of food and beverage director of the L.A. Jerik Downtown at a salary of 2,200 dollars per month. This was forty-five percent more than Marriott was paying me and I would have been an executive. My reply of, "Thank you for you generous offer but I just accepted a much lower offer from Marriott!" fairly knocked him back. I was after all declining a substantial offer from the great Jerik Corporation in favour of a demotion with an unknown company, as Marriott was at the time.

This done I had to resign from the Eastgate Plaza. I went to the hotel and asked my secretary to type a letter of resignation which I presented to the court appointed receiver. Returning home that evening I was just too eager to tell Janet that we were going to move to Los Angeles and that I would be joining Marriott. By that time a purchaser had been found for the Eastgate Plaza. My last day there coincided with the first day the new company took over.

The new owner was not at all happy with me stopping work that very day. He offered me the position of director of food and beverage had I wanted to stay. But nothing on earth would stop me from joining Marriott at that point.

Chapter 11

A MARRIAGE MADE IN HEAVEN

Now 'we were about two months pregnant' as Janet would put it. As part of my welcome package Marriott moved our cheap furniture and few belongings to an apartment which was so close to the hotel that, when I sat up in bed, I could see the hotel's red neon Marriott sign reflected in the dresser mirror. We rented our Mira Mesa house to a German couple. The Marriott had been open just one year when I started work there on July the 14th of 1974. The hotel had a solid team of people and immediately I felt at home.

I had purchased a new brown suit in order to look good for my first day at work. When I arrived, with the expectation of meeting the team and starting in the office, I got a surprise - the first of many. After meeting all of the team in the catering department I was taken to the banquet office and introduced to Hunter Hansen, the catering service manager, a fancy title for what the Notlih Hotel would have called head houseman. He was the person in charge of setting up the rooms for the various events, be they a meeting, a dinner or some other function. I was told that I would be working under Hunter's direction for a week, carrying tables and chairs, like every member of the set-up team.

At the time I thought that that was ridiculous as, with my experience, surely I would be more useful given a desk and a telephone from where I could be making and answering calls and booking business. I did not want to upset the apple cart although I was a bit put out to be carting around tables and chairs like all the housemen – and in my new suit. They had the physical strength and experience of heavy lifting while I was totally wasted after just the third table. Then, half a day into my labour, I tore a large gash in the leg of my trousers. I carried on nevertheless. I thought, "Well I wanted to join Marriott and here I am, not only with a demotion but working as a houseman in a new and ruined suit."

After a few days I was transfered to work under the Dutch maître d'hotel serving the meals. He was a nasty sod and took an immediate dislike to me which he made no attempt to hide. Even later on when I was selling the most expensive dinners which earned him substantial money through the service charge, he would do everything possible to undermine my work. But this was better than carrying tables and chairs and I enjoyed re-enacting the service of meals which I had done for so many years before. The kitchen was next and the executive chef with whom I got along famously was a very nice, young Dane named Reinhard and who I knew from my time at the San Francisco Notlih Hotel. This too proved to be a totally new experience. The famous saying about the three ways of doing things - the right way, the wrong way and the Marriott way - was so prevailing here. I was shocked for example to find that in the pastry kitchen the black forest cake wasn't a chocolate and cherry one but an almond tart. There were many such anomalies so I decided to write them down in order that I could, once I started selling, properly inform clients and thus avoid problems further down the line.

Finally my week of hands-on training was over and I moved to the office. The welcome I received was beyond any expectation and imagination. A welcome party had been organized and all the managers were there. I had never seen a spread of food and booze anything like that. I soon learned that all managers could drink for free at the bar and have their drinks charged to the hotel. At the Notlih only the Loewe brothers were doing that and at the Eastgate nobody was doing it. I thought this is not real, all the managers drinking free in the bar every evening before going home. I soon got into the same swing of things and I still can't say if it was a good or bad thing. In retrospect I'd have to say it was a bad thing because some managers abused the system, getting drunk every evening.

My team was made up of the director of catering, Paul, with whom I had spent time at the interview, and Peter Dannemann and

I were the two catering managers. Then there were the assistant catering managers Jerry Pitelli, John Drahos and Rick Strycker plus four secretaries. I quickly got to like all of these people. They soon became super friends rather than just workmates.

Janet found a bank job very soon after our arrival in L.A. Every morning we would leave the apartment together, with me walking to work and she driving the car downtown. It was a joy to see her so happy. Every evening I laid my head on her tummy to try to hear our baby's heart beat. When Emily started kicking it was just the greatest sensation in the world.

I was doing well and I was liked. Karl Kilburg was the director of food and beverage at the hotel and was just being promoted to corporate director of the same at the Marriott HQ in Bethesda, MD. Karl was German and had joined Marriott as a pastry chef in the first Marriott hotel. He ended his career many years later as the vice president in charge of all the Marriott properties in Europe. I only worked with him for a day or two before his move but he took an immediate liking to me and, as of today, forty-two years later, we still call each other and stay in touch. He was quite an athlete and ran 10 miles (16 km) every day of the year. He regularly ran marathons, cycled throughout Europe each year and had a standing desk in his office. He was a firm believer in thinking that it's better to be standing rather than sitting, so he never sat down in his office.

At work it was just great, the phone never stopped ringing and we were all going full steam from dawn 'til dusk or whatever hour we left at night. So too were our colleagues in the sales department led by Jon Loeb, director of sales and marketing, and one of the most obnoxious men I had ever met up to that point. Either he liked you or he hated you. If he liked you he would immediately find a nickname for you and if he hated you he would just ignore you. Fortunately for me he liked me and proceeded to call me 'pizza face'. I didn't mind as long as it helped to create a good working relationship between me and the sales guys and girls. For me it just continued to be such a treat to be part of this team of professional people and, more importantly, super human beings; so the days and months just flew by. Thanksgiving came and went uneventfully and then Christmas too. When New Year's Eve came around, that was another story altogether.

The two ballrooms were completely sold out for the celebration with more than a thousand guests scheduled to attend the New Year's Ball. A band played in each of the banquet rooms which were decorated in the latest 60's style with the finest crystal, china and silver candelabra laid out on the freshly starched table cloths. Balloons, hats, confetti and feathers had been placed on each chair by the most attentive waiters in all of Los Angeles. As the guests arrived, both bands struck up Kool and the Gang's big hit of the year, 'Jungle Boogie'. The atmosphere ignited like wild fire. Before you knew it all thousand guests (whose names had not been checked off at the door on entry) were on the dance floor dancing even before they'd gone to their table places. Getting them seated at their places for dinner became a nightmare. Somehow it all worked out and people just sat wherever they wanted to and the party continued. A five course dinner with non-stop champagne and wine flowing was served until midnight came. I was, once again, surprised to see that all the waiters, cooks and other staff were given a glass of champagne served by the managers. All of our spouses were also there and we all joined them for a toast, a hug and a kiss.

Janet was holding up well although by now her tummy had become so big that she had to walk sideways through the doors in our apartment. Shortly after midnight she was tired and decided to drive back to the apartment with my promise that I would follow her shortly. This was one of the promises I broke. The party was winding down in the ballroom by that time but Paul, our director, had other plans for his team. He suggested that we should go to the Capriccio Restaurant and help the waiters there to pour coffee as the evening was still going strong and it appeared that the end of the celebration was still a long way off. So we did that, even if by that time the glass of champagne we were supposed to have had at midnight had turned into at least a bottle each. We were all tipsy at best if not all out drunk. Never before had I experienced anything like that in all the fifteen years I had been in hotels. The directors, the managers, the waiters were all drunk and smelled of alcohol a mile away.

Arriving at the Capriccio we all got hold of a coffee pot and went around to every table pouring coffee. The guests were surprised and surely confused by the sudden appearance of a bunch of tuxedo clad drunkards serving them coffee whether they wanted it or not. This circus went on for an hour or more by which time we were all worn out and thirsty. Paul fixed up a table and we sat down to even more champagne. This was actually a bit scandalous because by that time, not only were we all drunk out of our minds, but also our tongues were loose and the most colourful vocabulary was flowing. We could have been a crew of truck drivers or construction worker. These were the managers of a five star Marriott Hotel on New Year's day morning of 1975!

I was as drunk as everyone else and had completely forgotten my promise to Janet that I'd be home shortly after her. By now it was eight o'clock on January the first and we were all still drinking. I left the hotel and walked the few hundred yards to the apartment. As I gingerly staggered up the stairs to the door it opened. There stood poor Janet in her night gown, tears rolling down her face and so pale that I thought she would pass out. I wasn't feeling too good myself of course. My head was spinning, my stomach churning, my heart aching and shame took over my inner-most feelings. How could I have done this to her? I really must be a monster. However the colour returned to her face as her worry eased and she realised that nothing drastic had happened to me. I was just drunk and tomorrow I would be sober again. Going to sleep was the only thing either of us could do at that time and so we did. Janet was getting bigger by the day and eventually gained 44 pounds (20 kg) before the end of the pregnancy.

Time was certainly flying. Peter Dannemann was transferred to Lincolnshire, Illinois, to open the first Marriott hotel with a theatre in it. Then, just five months after joining Marriott, I was offered my first promotion. Chet Baket, the resident manager at the hotel was being promoted to his first general manager role opening the Oldport Beach Marriott Resort and Tennis Club just 43 miles (70 km) south of L.A. and he wanted me with him. This move, if I accepted it, would take place in the second week of January. Emily was due to arrive in the first week of February and it would mean moving away from the doctor and the clinic where she was going to be born. Marriott convinced me that all would be fine. They would pay not only for the moving to the new area but also for totally packing and unpacking our belongings; it was all sealed and delivered, so to speak. Yet I was still worried.

OLDPORT BEACH

Not only would we be moving away from the doctor and the Daniel Freeman hospital near the apartment we lived in but the work situation concerned me. Chet Baket was very appropriately known as 'the Bear'. He was not the most polished nor diplomatic man I had ever met up to that time. A Chicagoan, like Jerry Best, his background was in sales. He had joined Marriott as a bartender at age twenty six at the Marriott O'Hare airport in Chicago and made his career brought along by Jerry. While Jerry was a refined man and a real gentleman Chet was really what his nickname said. I was scared to work with him as he could at any time cut me loose and then what? I had a very pregnant young wife, in just about a month I would have a new baby and we were going to move. To any normal person it did not make sense to accept this job. Then again, we were not normal people. I accepted the move before even talking it over with Janet.

That very Saturday, the 4th of January, Janet and I drove to Oldport Beach to take a look at the construction of the hotel. The location was great, built on top of Fashion Island, the newest and most fashionable part of town. All the luxury shops were there along with the Rolls Royce dealership. While there we also looked around for an apartment to rent. It soon became apparent that, even with my increase in salary, Oldport Beach was out of the question. Janet had stopped working on December 31st so I was now the only bread winner. We did find a two bedroom apartment with car port a bit more inland in Costa Mesa, a more working class area and within two weeks we were on our way to Oldport Beach and our new life. The move itself proved stressful, particularly to Janet, as the removal men were clumsy to say the least. They finally tipped her over the edge when one of them opened a box of kitchen utensils and literally poured them into an open drawer. That was the end of their help. Janet sent them on their way and completed the unpacking herself.

I was by then getting to know the hotel and was putting together my team. The best source for that was the Los Angeles Marriott from which one of the two assistant banquet maître d'hotel had been promoted to the actual maître d'hotel in Oldport Beach. I needed a catering manager to be my second in command and I only wanted one guy to fill that position. Rick Strycker one of the assistants from Los Angeles was a jolly fellow, always laughing and telling jokes. He was also a hard worker and a good professional. With Jerry Best and Chet Baket's agreement I called him and asked him to come to the pre-opening office in Oldport Beach for an official interview. Rick came on a Thursday and before the day was over we had made him an offer which he accepted. He arranged to start with me the following Monday.

He was doubly pleased because his very pregnant wife, Diane, was from Costa Mesa where her parents and siblings also lived. A win-win situation for all. The next Saturday evening the hotel gave him the traditional going away party given to all managers who were being promoted to another hotel. Following the party, Rick and Diane decided to take a Porsche, which Rick was considering buying from a friend, for a trial drive come joy ride to Malibu. Going round a bend Rick hit sand on the road, lost control of the speeding car and crashed. Fortunately for Diane she was not wearing the seat belt because of her already large tummy. She was thrown out of the car on to the sidewalk. Rick was less fortunate. He was crushed against the steering wheel. They were taken by ambulance to the nearest hospital and laid on two stretchers side by side in the emergency room. Diane was actually uninjured and conscious. Much to her dismay, she overheard the medical staff say that Rick, although alive, had no chance of survival. Sure enough two days later Rick stopped breathing and was pronounced dead. That was devastating for Diane of course, she was several months pregnant with their first child (whose well-being was still uncertain) and now a widow to boot. Why do things like these happen? A beautiful young family in the making, two wonderful young people in love and with an unborn baby all destroyed by some sand blown in the wind on a road in Malibu.

The shock was almost impossible for many of us to bear. My daughter Emily was due to be born in a few days. I felt that, by hiring Rick to work with me, I had taken his life and the joy of fatherhood away from him while leaving a new baby to be born who would never know her father nor how great a guy he was. Diane moved back to Costa Mesa and resettled in her family home where Regina was born. Janet and I were given the honour of being her godparents. We always kept close ties with Diane and Regina. Some years later, Diane married a nice young man named Kimmer who took Regina as his own daughter. They had twin girls together.

Regina in due time followed in her father's footsteps. She attended a hospitality college and became general manager of Marriott and Hyatt hotels. Regina still has Rick's briefcase and his name tag from the hotel. Rick would have been so proud to see her progress with such success into a world that he loved so much. Regina met Cregg, also a hotel manager, and they were married in November of 2009 in a wonderful traditional ceremony on the island of Kauai, to which Janet and I were invited.

With Rick's demise I was now faced with a dilemma. Who could I find to take his place, help me shine and keep 'the Bear' happy? Once again I got lucky. I hired Ginny who had never worked for Marriott but she was a quick learner and a very capable young woman. Plus Bruce, who also had never worked for Marriott but was also a brilliant find. They both learned very quickly how to do things 'the Marriott way'. I hired two secretaries and now we were all ready to go. The first week of February was approaching and I knew Emily would be on time. It has turned out that she actually is in life always early, and she started that trait at the very moment she was born.

I was working on my first opening and my first as the department head. While I felt pretty sure I could do it well there were times when I was wondering if I could please 'the Bear' and not get fired. My direct superior, the director of food and beverage, to whom I technically reported was a gentleman who really had no knowledge. He was a procrastinator and had the habit of hitting the booze which made him less than reliable. This in turn meant that 'the Bear' was very much involved in the planning of the opening and he was also nervous as it was his first one too.

We also had a weak executive chef brought in from the company's largest hotel, the one thousand three hundred room New Orleans Marriott, where he'd been a bit of a failure. This was his last chance. If he didn't work out in Oldport Beach he would be dismissed (in the event that did happen about a year later). I was working six days a week as hard as I could to make sure I stayed ahead of the game and shone.

HOW TO HAVE A BABY

On Saturday February the 8th of 1975 I went to work after agreeing with Janet to pick her up at the supermarket at 1.00 pm where she would be waiting with her groceries. I arrived to find her slumped over her shopping trolley. She told me that she had been experiencing fits of pain all morning. I took that to be contractions so took her straight home and called the doctor in Los Angeles. He asked me how far apart the contractions were, told me to stay calm and to take Janet to the hospital only if the waters broke or if the contractions were five minutes or less apart. We started counting and by 6.00 pm we were there, five minutes apart. The waters had not broken but I called him and he told me to go immediately to Daniel Freeman hospital.

There is a song that says, "It never rains in Southern California .... ", well it sure picked the most inappropriate time to prove those words wrong. It was chucking it down cats and dogs as we set off on the drive to hospital with Janet doing her best to deal with the increasing pain and the more frequent contractions. The rain was not easing up. I was praying and making every effort to stay calm and drive, but there arose another unforeseen obstacle. To get to the hospital we had to drive by the Forum where, unbeknowns to us, a football game was to be played later that evening. The traffic heading there was already heavy and building. That and the rain were becoming a serious challenge for me. As one known to be capable of 'getting lost in a tea cup', this was not the time for me to take a wrong turn or wander from the route we had practiced driving many times before. Nonetheless I got us to the hospital by 8.00 pm by which time Janet was in tears, in constant pain and with the contractions so close to each other that she had no time to breathe in between.

A nurse received us and escorted Janet to a toilet, sat her on the bowl and went to call the doctor. The nurse must have forgotten Janet was there because for almost an hour she was left there alone and in pain. Eventually the nurse must have remembered, as she returned and took Janet to a bed and told me that the doctor would arrive shortly. After what seemed an eternity the doctor came and examined Janet. Back in those days Daniel Freeman hospital did not permit husbands in the delivery room so I had to wait outside.

By now it was almost 11.00 pm and I was pacing the little waiting room in such a state of anxiety that I'm surprised I didn't faint. When the doctor finally came out he put his arm around my shoulder and told me, "The baby is too big for Janet to be able to deliver it, she could die in the process and the baby too." I was naturally shocked and panic overtook me. He continued, "The best solution is to give your wife a spinal injection and for me to get the baby out using forceps."

I had no idea what he was really saying but the fear was so great that Janet and the baby would die that I would agree to anything he said. He then returned to the delivery room and, without saying anything to Janet, turned her upside down and injected a long needle in her back. Janet screamed in pain and then she didn't feel anything anymore. In just a matter of minutes Emily was pulled out of the comfortable heat of her mother's womb by a pair of gigantic pliers into this cold and strange world. The forceps bruised our poor Emily's right eye but she looked so beautiful to me even with her little eye black and half closed. Janet was just happy to have this little creature, who was already loved from the moment of conception, now laying over her breast and looking so peaceful after the exhausting work of her birth.

It had been a long day and a stressful one for both mother and child. Now Emily was hungry. After being bathed she attached herself to Janet's breast and sucked out the last drop of life poor Janet still had in her. Both of them fell asleep so peacefully that they were quite a sight to behold. I was told that Janet would sleep all night under the effect of the spinal injection and the exertions of the birth. I wanted these moments of watching them sleep never to end but I was ordered home under protest. I was told to return the next morning at anytime I liked as visiting hours were waived for new fathers. I drove all the way back to Costa Mesa as happy as any new father could be. No sooner did my head hit the bed than I too passed out.

By seven on Sunday morning I was awake again and ready to drive back to the hospital to be with my two women. A coffee and a stale roll were my breakfast and off I went sure that all would be well and Janet happy to see me - wrong! The effect of the spinal injection had worn off and Janet was in more severe pain than during the contractions. I felt so sick to see my beautiful wife, now a mother of my child, suffer so much. All I could do was to sit by the bed and hold her hand while Emily was brought back to her for yet another feeding. She was oblivious to her mother's pain and, almost like a milking machine, sucked and devoured all the milk on offer. Her black eye and the rough pulling of her head during birth was forgotten, all she needed now was to eat and to be held.

As time went by Janet's pains seemed to ease a bit. She was forced to eat some hospital food, not quite gourmet, but good enough for someone who had not seen food for more than twenty-four hours. All day I stayed there trying to be of comfort, admiring my beautiful wife and my most beautiful baby. What a joy it was to be a father. Every man should experience it, no words can describe the feeling. Before I realised it was time to leave and go home. I must have been a bit of a pain in the neck to the nurses as they almost had to call security to get me out.

The next day, being Monday, I had to go back to work. On my way to work I stopped to buy cigars for the men at work and chocolates for the women, a must in those days. These gifts, given to friends and colleagues, would be an omen of good fortune and luck for the baby. As I entered the hotel everyone knew that my baby was born because of the big smile I had on my face. I quickly gave away the chocolates and cigars and asked 'the Bear' for a day off. He readily agreed. I returned to L.A. and spent all day in the hospital practicing holding Emily, changing her diapers and even bathing her. She felt so small or my hands felt like the paws of a giant around her little and seemingly fragile body. What a delight to do all those things. Because Emily was breast feeding the only things I could not do was to give her food.

By then Janet felt better. As I presume all new parents do, we counted all Emily's fingers and toes just to make sure she had everything a little person ought to have. Yes, she had five fingers on each hand and five toes on each foot. While driving home that evening I planned the welcome home dinner for Janet and decided on the menu and wine I would treat her to. By the time I reached the apartment I too was exhausted. Next day I did not dare ask 'the Bear' for another full day off but did ask if I could leave around three in the afternoon to drive back to the hospital and see the now two loves of my life.

I repeated the routine of the previous day, driving there, cuddling my two women and driving back to Costa Mesa at eleven at night. The next day I was supposed to drive them both back home in the morning. 'The Bear' was once again generous and told me I certainly could go. Janet had given me clear instructions as to which dress to bring for her to wear going home. Early that morning I took the dress as instructed and returned to the hospital, happy at the prospect of finally having my girls home.

The obstetrician gave Janet a final once over and declared her fit to leave. We had to wait a further three hours before the pediatrician could check Emily and give her a clean bill of health. Then, when Janet got around to putting on the dress I had brought for her, she realised that she couldn't fit into it. With tears of disappointment flowing down her cheeks she had to leave wearing the same maternity dress she wore when she arrived even though she now weighed 40 pounds (18 kg) less. Janet was wheeled out to the car in a wheelchair with Emily on her lap and me carrying her suitcase just a few steps ahead.

I had bought a baby car seat but quickly realised that Emily was too small to be strapped into it. After some debate we decided that Janet would hold Emily in her arms in the back seat except that the car did not have safety belts in the rear seats. So we settled for Janet in the front seat with my promise not to drive faster than 50 mph (80 kph).

Driving at that snail pace it took us about two hours to make it back to the apartment in Costa Mesa. The nursery had been ready for the last month since we arrived at the apartment and Emily was placed in her comfortable bassinette, a kind of giant crib made out of twisted bamboo. As we had not known if the baby was going to be a boy or a girl all of the sheets and bed linen were neutral to yellow and white in colour and our baby loved it immediately. Janet took a rest. By seven she was awake and Emily was being fed once again.

Now it was my turn to set to preparing the welcome home dinner. The table was laid out with a white table cloth, cutlery, glasses and a white candle on a crystal candle stick. Smoked salmon with finely chopped onions, capers, a drop of olive oil and a dash of black pepper was the starter. Chilled Frascati white wine from the hills of Rome washed it all down admirably. Filet Rossini with turned carrots, French green beans and rissole potatoes was the main course. To help us enjoy it to the highest level a bottle of Moulin-a-Vent from Burgundy was savoured. The conversation was flowing, Emily was peacefully asleep and the love we shared was heart-warming.

After all that was eaten it was time to get back to the kitchen and prepare the dessert. One of the desserts I had learned to do well over the years of working in fine restaurants of luxurious hotels was the famous crepes suzettes. With all my ingredients ready I proceeded to caramelise the sugar, adding a teaspoon of unsalted butter and OJ, Grand Marnier orange liqueur. Slowly, and with well mastered precision, I added the crepes turning them over and folding them in an almost perfect triangle. It was now time to set them on fire. With the best cognac I could afford I lit them to the delight of my beautiful wife who had endless love for me and for what I was trying to do to impress her. The crepes were brought to the table with a bottle of well chilled Moet et Chandon French champagne. It was like living in a dream, such perfect joy.

Eventually the evening came to an end and by then Emily was ready for another feed but Janet's eyes were slowly closing. I am sure that we men do not understand or appreciate what a traumatic experience it is to carry a child for nine months, go through the painful event of giving birth and through all of that to stay serene and smiling. I do admire women for what they must go through to keep this world turning. So, while Janet changed into her night gown I did the last change of diapers before going to bed. I laid Emily down and in the bedroom found Janet already sound asleep in Morpheus' arms. She was a beauty to behold!

It was around three in the morning that Emily woke us up crying. I thought that she either needed a diaper change or she was hungry again. After checking that her diaper was not the guilty party I carried her over to Janet being certain that a feeding was required. I was wrong, Emily would not eat. She continued crying. We could not fathom the cause nor get her to stop 'til about six when she seemed to fall asleep exhausted. The sleep though was short lived as, just a little while later, she started screaming again but even louder.

As we were living in an apartment building we were afraid that, apart from the disruption to our sleep, the neighbours might call the police but fortunately that did not happen. What did happen, however, was that we took her to the doctor the first moment we could and the diagnosis turned out to be not good, severe colitis and allergy to the breast milk. What a nightmare this eventually became as day and night Emily cried and cried. We took turns at carrying her around and trying our best to calm and reassure her but the results never changed. Plus, as the problem persisted, both myself and Janet were becoming more tired and irritable. It took months before Emily got over her problems, stopped crying and started to eat baby food. Then, with the crying stopped, the colitis gone and her growing fast, she was a bundle of sheer joy.

MORE AMERICAN DREAM

Now it was time to think about buying a house. Our house in Mira Mesa had been rented to a German couple on a one year lease which was now up and they had moved on. We put the house on the market and soon after that it sold and we started looking for our dream home.

Mission Viejo was a vibrant community not too far from work with mostly young families living there. Because my dream was to never move from the Oldport Beach Marriott I wanted to buy a house in which to live out the rest of our lives and add another child to our family. We found a beautiful ranch house with two bedrooms, a nice living room, a den and a small front and back yard. We still had only one car but Janet was able to get to the shops by walking and proudly pushing the pram with our little Emily in it. We soon made friends at the church we started to attend. Life was good and we were happy.

My work was going well, I was really appreciated. Soon the company asked me to move to a bigger hotel in Philadelphia. I pleaded that the weather there was colder than California and not to my liking. I turned the job down as I was happy in Oldport Beach. The job had become an easy routine and I had spare time on my hands.

As I was so determined to spend my life in California I decided to take a real estate course, get myself a real estate license and possibly leave the hotel business to make it big in real estate. After enrolling in a class at the community college I realised that it was not as easy to do as I had thought. It meant getting up at 4.00 am to study, being at work by 7.30 am and doing classes again in the evening 'til ten. Also I decided to take the class twice before taking the state exams as I didn't want to fail it or be told that I had to take the class and the exam again. After completing the course for the second time I felt ready to drive to San Diego to take the exam.

One afternoon Janet, Emily and I drove down and checked into the Eastgate Plaza for two nights. As I left to go to the exam centre I told Janet to chill the bottle of champagne we had brought with us to celebrate my passing the exam and becoming a licensed California real estate agent. Luckily I whizzed through the exam without any hitch. That evening we even splurged out on a dinner at the Fontainebleau restaurant in the hotel, very expensive but extremely good. My friend the chef, Joel, was still working at the hotel and he prepared one of the fanciest dinners Janet and I had ever experienced up to then. After a great dinner, a bottle of champagne and a night of rest we were ready to drive back to Mission Viejo the following morning.

Now what can I do with the real estate license? At the church we had met a couple and he was a broker. When he found out that I had passed the state exams he offered to hang my license with him, this was a way that I could start selling houses. Within a short time I was keeping open houses on Saturdays and Sundays and soon found out that I was now away from Janet and Emily seven days a week. Finally, after spending several weekends showing houses, I sold one. And that was my real estate career over, short lived but a lot of fun. It was really a big ado about nothing as I never made any money as an agent.

Life was moving on and I was feeling really settled. It was time to have a second child. Janet had a specific idea about children, either there had to be two or four. As she was a middle child she did not want to have three. They also had to come very close to each other so that all the diaper changing would be over in one concentrated period and then never start again. Fortunately from that perspective, Paul was conceived just nine months after Emily's birth. As we were now living in Mission Viejo, an obstetrician was visited in nearby South Laguna. Janet liked him immediately. That was a great start as that had not been the case with the one she had with Emily. She had felt a lack of trust with that first obstetrician and it had indeed turned out that her mother's instinct was right; although unfortunately not until delivery did it become apparent with the spinal injection and Emily's rough forceps delivery.

This time the doctor was gentle, had patience and took all the time in the world to coach Janet and myself through each step of the pregnancy. We also went back to the La Leche classes. By the time of delivery came around we were real experts at the process. It was agreed with our friends Ann and Larry, who lived in Garden Grove, that we would call them at any time of day or night when the time to leave for the clinic came.

It was not a surprise to them that on Tuesday August 17th of 1976 at five o'clock in the morning we called them to come and fetch Emily as we were leaving for the clinic. By that time the contractions were just minutes apart and we knew the baby was going to rush into this world very quickly. I was allowed to be in the delivery room this time and my job was to wipe Janet's forehead with a clean cloth. This act of kindness was repaid with a punch in the stomach by a screaming Janet as the delivery was in progress.

Paul was soon born and this time we had the name all set. For a girl it would have been Charlotte or Elizabeth but for a boy there was no doubt it would be Paul, no hesitation. The delivery was much simpler this time and Janet, coached by this good doctor, delivered Paul without any medication by eight o'clock. We were now the proud parents of two beautiful and healthy little babies. After stopping at the cigar shop and at the candy store I drove to work to announce to everyone the news of the new arrival and to distribute to all my co-workers and friends their cigars and candies. I didn't stay long at work and went back to the clinic to be with Janet and Paul while Emily was taken care of by Ann and Larry. Just two days later I picked Janet and Paul up from the clinic, drove them home, settled Paul in the bassinette in the room with Emily and prepared the welcome home dinner for Janet.

Paul was fine for the first week. He was breast feeding and slept well all night and day. But soon we started smelling something rotten in the room where he and Emily were sleeping. We could not figure out what it was. It was not dirty diapers from either one of them but Paul was now constantly crying. Finally we unwrapped his circumcised penis to find out that it was infected, red and purple beyond recognition. We immediately rushed him back to the hospital. After a period of medication, the infection went away and Paul stopped crying. We took him back home to where he returned to his happy self, eating, sleeping and filling diapers all day and night long.

On the work front things continued really well. Business was prospering and the department I headed was the most successful one in the hotel. Only one thing started to worry me a bit. The social life and the parties at work as well as those outside of the working circle were increasing and so was my drinking. Many a night, after work, I would stay behind at the hotel and drink at the bar.

One evening, quite late and quite drunk, I was driving home to Mission Viejo. At the entrance to the community some sprinklers were on and splashing water on to the road. The tyres of the Beetle were slightly worn. At the speed I was driving plus the impediment of my reflexes due to the overdose of cabernet sauvignon, the car span around twice and hit the kerb. One wheel promptly fell off the axle. The rear of the car sat on the side walk and the front was half way into the road. What was I to do? There were no mobile phones in those years.

Once again divine providence came to my rescue. A California Highway Patrol car came along and pulled up. I was a bit scared as I knew I was drunk. Fortunately the two police officers must have taken pity on me. Instead of doing any breath test or asking me to walk a straight line like you see in a movie, they just asked if I had been drinking. I thought to tell them the truth rather than lie and try to fool them so I said, "Yes." I was surprised when they offered to call the pick-up truck to take the car to a repair shop and to drive me home. Not even a ticket. Wow, how did I get away with it? This should have served as a lesson to me and a warning to stop drinking and driving but no it didn't. I continued to do just that for many more years to come.

Arriving home in a police car and telling a very worried Janet what had happened was also a task and a half. She was sympathetic and did not make any fuss. Next day I had to sober up, rent a car and go to the repair shop. Back at work, I found a lot of people sincerely concerned about my accident. This included some of my colleagues who had been drinking with me the night before but knew better than to drink and drive.

A few months later 'the Bear' invited me for a corridor walk for one of his friendly chats. He started off by saying that I had done a great job for almost three years and that the company now needed my expertise at their big hotel with the second largest catering department in the company at Atlanta. While I could not claim the foul weather as an excuse this time around as I had with the Philadelphia job proposal, I did simply say that I really loved the Oldport Beach Marriott and loved working with him. While he was not a man who cared much for compliments he must have liked that one and he fended off the company's overtures once more on my behalf.

In the meantime in the food and beverage department a Latino mafia had formed. The godfather was the Argentinian director of food and beverage, Pedro Almovar, who had all his 'pawns' in place around him. He had a Cuban restaurant manager in one restaurant and a Costa Rican named Pablo Contrera in the other restaurant. He had a Nicaraguan executive chef, Octavio Adidas, and all of the kitchen and waiting staff were either from Mexico or Cuba.

After a short while he was promoted to be the director of food and beverage in Los Angeles. The position he vacated gave me hope that I would get that job and secure a long tenure at the hotel. I was wrong as I was not even considered. Instead the Costa Rican restaurant manager was promoted into the job. As expected he failed and 'the Bear' regretted that he had been railroaded by Pedro.

It was not long after the disappointment of not having been promoted that he yet again invited me for one of his corridor walks. This time I was really worried as to what he might offer me as I was running out of refusal options. Sure enough the company now wanted me to move to Chicago to open the Chicago Marriott Downtown. This was at the time the second largest hotel the company had. It boasted one thousand two hundred and fourteen rooms, a ballroom with the capacity to seat two thousand people, another one with a one thousand five hundred person capacity plus many smaller meeting and conference rooms. He saw me hesitate and read my mind about the weather in Chicago and my desire to remain in California forever.

He cut it short and to the point by saying, "Listen to me, this is the third time the company offers you a promotion. This is the largest catering operation the company has and it will be a long time before a larger one will be opened. If you turn the company down your wish to remain here forever will become reality. You will be forgotten and never be considered again for any promotion." I asked him to let me think about it and discuss it with Janet.

I was really concerned about what he had to say. The idea of a move to 'the windy city' was becoming less and less attractive. When I got home and, with a long face void of enthusiasm, passed the news on to Janet her face lit up. I told her that I really did not want to move anywhere and especially Chicago. She quickly took steps to change my mind. She organised a party to which she invited all the Chicagoans who had run away from that city to move to California and who now were out there bragging about how great Chicago was!

Chapter 12

NANOOK OF THE NORTH

And so it was that Janet and I went to Chicago for a formal interview with Bud Davis, the general manager of the hotel. He would have the final word on my promotion. It was also an opportunity to house hunt for a suitable property should my interview with Bud prove successful. Sure enough Bud and I got off on the right foot and before the lunch was over I was hired. Then Janet and I set off house hunting with an agent whose services had already been arranged by the hotel.

As most people in the US in those days wanted to live in the suburbs of big cities and commute we started looking in Wilmette, Winnetka, Skokie, Glencoe and Evanston. The most important consideration for me was the proximity to a train station so that I could take the train into town to work when the temperature fell below zero, the snow was 6 feet (1.8 m) high and the wind was blowing at 50 mph (80 kph). The very next day we found a lovely house in Wilmette. It had three bedrooms and just one bathroom but, because the children were still babies, that did not matter. It had a nice living room with a wood burning fire, a large bay window and a formal dining room. Beneath all this was a great basement also with a wood burner and a work shop. This last room became the family room and we spent all of our time in winter watching TV and playing games together there.

With the house purchased and ready, we settled on the date of November the 5th for our arrival. We moved into the Marriott O'Hare hotel while our household belongings were delivered to the house. But there was a tragedy in the offing.

In October my sixty-eight year old mother passed away in Centonara. To add to the problem my sister, Anna, was very sick and fighting breast cancer. Her husband, Tullio, was not of great help as he was really screwed up in his head with religious fanaticism and spiritualistic beliefs. What a mess.

The moment I received the news I immediately left home to go to Italy for the funeral and to sort out what needed to be done after the last parent dies. The house and the meagre inheritance my parents had worked hard all of their lives to leave to my sister and I was what needed to be dealt with properly. I knew that my crooked, miserly and egotistical brother-in-law would take more than what mother had stipulated in her hand written will. After a few failed attempts to take more than he was supposed to have he gave up. My sister was, on this occasion, able to resist him and insisted on doing strictly what our mother had wanted us to do.

So the house, the few little pieces of land and the bank account were divided. My sister and I became the proud owners of a roof over our heads and half a million liras each – about 500 dollars at the time. The amount was immaterial. What mattered was the sacrifices that our parents had made to save that money. In their hearts they always wanted us to have a better life than they had and to them that meant financial betterment.

One of the most appreciated gestures was that 'the Bear' sent, via Interflora, a beautiful flower arrangement which arrived at the house just as the funeral procession was leaving for the church service and burial. It brought additional tears to my eyes knowing that back in California people cared about me and the pain I was suffering at that time.

With all that done it was time to go back home and make the final arrangements for yet another family move. This time it was a bit harder as we had never before moved with two very young babies. This meant prams, diapers, feeding formulas, toys and a ton of baby clothes had to be packed and transferred. We were also going from sunny southern California to the windy city. For those of you who know what Chicago is like in November you sure can appreciate what a shock this was to our systems. The removal men had come to our little house that we had come to love in Mission Viejo and packed everything up. The VW Beetle was given to one of the driving services and we were now ready to take a flight from Los Angeles to Chicago.

As was common practice at Marriott in those days a lavish going away party was given on the last working day. This was a great excuse to eat, drink and be merry for all the managers and the employees working directly under the manager being promoted. This meant that I received lots of presents and therefore additional stuff to carry on the plane. This included the traditional photo of the hotel signed by everyone with best wishes and sometimes not so nice comments about your tenure at the hotel. It was all in good spirit however and consistant with the great camaraderie which existed in those days within the Marriott family. And so we were off.

Arriving in Chicago was a different story altogether. The wind was howling, the snow was falling, the frost was biting and reality settled in ... what on earth had I let myself be talked into? How could any sane person trade southern California for Chicago, Oldport Beach for Michigan Avenue, Mission Viejo for Wilmette? I must have been mad. But the damage was done and I could not undo it. The moment I landed at O'Hare that evening I made myself a secret promise to take my family back to California within the next two years.

At the Marriott O'Hare we were treated like royalty as we were coming to open the largest and the most luxurious Marriott in the city. On top of that we had a Michigan Avenue address, very prestigious as everyone knows.

On the 7th of November at nine o'clock I went to the pre-opening office to meet Bud Davies, the general manager. He introduced me to the rest of the team. Some of them I already knew. Jon Loeb, the director of sales and marketing and I had worked together at the Los Angeles Marriott. He was a genius at his work in spite of being the craziest person I ever met. He could not do a knot on his shoes nor tie his tie. He came to work with both of these items undone and his secretary would do them up for him. Every night he would go to the bars on Rush Street and would not go home until he was absolutely plastered.

As the hotel was to open non-union and was in the heart of teamster union territory there was a picket line outside the hotel with union pickets parading, carrying huge placards condemning the hotel for unfair labour practices and all other kinds of nonsense. They set up a kind of mini office complete with desk, telephone and even their own Christmas tree on the sidewalk at the employee entrance so they could canvass support from and/or harrass hotel staff as they entered and left work. One night Jon exited blind drunk from the hotel as was his custom and decided to 'teach them bastards a lesson' by running off with their Christmas tree and chucking it into the Chicago River. What Jon had not taken into consideration was that 'them bastards' (as he called them) would chase and catch him. They gave him such a kicking that the next day he could hardly walk and his eyes were black and blue. Fortunately for him he did not come out of his beating with any broken teeth, ribs or, worse still, the broken legs which some who crossed the union had been known to receive.

This event though in no way deterred Jon from carrying on in his inimitable drunken and couldn't care less way. One day he turned in an expenses claim for approval to Bud Davis, the general manager. The expenditure of 80 dollars was identified only by the letters 'MHS'. Bud called him into the office and asked him what these three letters meant. His explanation went something like, "You see Bud before going out to Rush Street last night I put a 100 dollar bill in my pocket but when I woke up this morning and counted the money there were only 20 dollars. 100 minus 20 means that I Must Have Spent .. MHS .. 80 dollars in the bars!" Bud could not believe what he was hearing, found Jon's explanation not funny at all and promptly punched him in the face. Thus finishing off the job the union tearaways didn't by sending him to hospital with a broken nose. Today, after many more adventures and misadventures, Jon is driving a taxi in Las Vegas, riddled with debt and poor health due to his excessive drinking.

The executive chef was Reinhard Danger, the tall, skinny Danish fellow I knew from the San Francisco Notlih and the Los Angeles Marriott. He was a good guy and very caring. While at the hotel he met a girl who was a restaurant manager and they got married and lived happily ever after. This young lady was the daughter of a Sicilian immigrant family who were in the cross state trucking business and, not un-naturally, financially well off.

Lee Cockerell was the director of food and beverage operations. I did not know him but his reputation was one of a hard task master. He was a great manager but at that stage still had a lot to learn about being a good leader. He was extremely demanding and the management team in general were quite afraid of him. I fared better as he took a liking to me and never mistreated me in any way. I have however seen him, at the hotel and in following years, totally intimidate people. One of his redeeming graces was that he hired an outside, armed security company. He himself rode shotgun in the company truck as it made the early morning rounds of garbage disposal and supply collections which the unionised garbage collectors and suppliers, dissuaded by the pickets at the hotel entrance, would not do. Lee grew up in Oklahoma so he knew well how to use a shotgun. With Lee and the armed guards in the trucks all of our supplies got delivered and our garbage got taken away.

As the hotel swung into action it was evident that the going was going to be tough. However, we had a great leader in Bud with his background in the Notlihs. He really was a father figure. He had worked many years in this market and he knew the clientele well. He knew that we had to have a kosher kitchen and a kosher catering manager if we wanted to attract the lucrative Jewish wedding, bar mitzvah and bat mitzvah business to Marriott. After interviewing every kosher catering manager in the city we settled for the lady who had a good reputation within the community and was at the time working at the Beech Tree Hotel. Man that was a mistake. She was pure trouble. Jon immediately christened her as 'the Jewish princess'. Fortunately for all of us she herself soon realised that the Marriott ways of doing business clashed with hers. She quit and returned to the Beech Tree Hotel.

In the meantime I had learned enough about Jewish habits and requirements that I had become the specialist in that area. I knew that I had to deal with the rabbi who would come to prepare the kitchen before every function. We had a dedicated kosher kitchen as all the cutlery and china had to be prepared for the kosher functions and could not be used for anything else. The rabbi was a nice old gentleman who, I discovered, enjoyed a good shot of French cognac. In order to make life easier for everyone, especially him, when he came to do the routine kitchen preparation I made sure I gave him a comfortable room on an upper floor and a nice bottle of Remy Martin VSOP. It was easier to 'kosherize' the kitchen ourselves and by the time he came back down we were well into the food preparation and all was kosher!

The banquet maître d' was Eddie Towfighnia, as smart and hard working a guy as I have ever met. He came to the US from Iran as a student, met Joyce at the University, married and never went back to Iran. We took him from the Hyatt Hotel in New Orleans. His organisational skills were incredible as he could manage a banquet for two thousand people in one banquet room, another for fifteen hundred in the other and any number of small events all at the same time and never miss a beat. He was eventually promoted and enjoyed a good career until Franco Habana, regional vice president at the time, pushed him out of his post of general manager at the San Juan Marriott. Eddie retired in Colorado after his two daughters married and moved out of the house.

The banquet chef was Thomas Buehner. He was as cool as a cucumber. I've never seen him lose his temper. No matter how busy he was he always looked as if he had just came out of the shower. He too made a career with the company. After many international assignments, he eventually retired when he was the general manager at the JW Marriott and Courtyard in Kuwait. He divorced his first wife and, a few years later married Jina, a Korean model. He lives in Italy near Milan as his wife is still very much involved with the fashion world. He is one of the five retired

Marriott friends with whom I have dinner once a year somewhere in the world.

A LOVE HATE RELATIONSHIP

Janet loved Chicago and the house in Wilmette. I hated the city and the weather. One reason I felt that way was that our time there coincided with two of the worst winters Chicago has ever experienced. The winter of '77 to '78 had the lowest temperature ever recorded in the city and the winter of '78 to '79 recorded the heaviest ever snow fall. As a result of this freezing weather I gained the nick-name 'Nanook of the North'. I would show up to work wearing a face mask, a heavy woollen hat, thick hand-knitted gloves, long johns under my suit, the heaviest overcoat I could find and heavy snow boots with galoshes on top to protect them from the snow. Today, with all the fear of terrorists about, I would probably be arrested as only my eyes were visible and nobody could recognize me.

We also bought a new car as Janet needed it to take the children to Montessori, go shopping and generally move around. And I needed a car so that, when the weather was not so harsh, I could drive to work rather than take the train which was a twice daily stressful event. To start off I had to shovel the snow off the VW which was always parked in the driveway as we only had a one car garage. This meant a five o'clock rise to shovel the 6 foot (1.8 m) of snow off the car and clear the driveway to the road. Usually by the time I had done that the snow plough had come by and rebuilt a snow wall between my driveway and the road. Finally I would be off to either the drive to the city or to the rail road station to catch the train. Arriving at the train station had its own complications.

To find parking was a task and a half, spaces were all metered and the meters were totally covered with snow. The first thing to do was to dig out the meter, guesstimate the time to pick up the car in the evening and then fumble, with gloved hands, to pull out coins sufficient to cover the expense. This last operation inevitably resulted in coins dropped deep into the snow and buried, to lie there hidden until they bloomed into money trees when springtime eventually arrived. With the meter feeding eventually accomplished I could proceed to the train station and to my usual purchase of a large hot coffee with two creamers. This was not so much because I was crazy about the coffee but more because it was warm and comforting to hold in my half frozen hands.

I also carried the traditional briefcase of every real, or pretend business person. I had never really understood why everyone carried a case ... but I was about to find out! On the dot the seven-twenty train pulled into the station and that's when the briefcase became a means of survival. By the time the train arrived in Wilmette it had stopped in at least seven or eight stations and all the seats were taken. The corridors were transformed into commuter packed sardine cans. There was no civility in the process of boarding the train, briefcases were used to push people out of the way, hit them, push them aside and clear a passage to the carriage door without, hopefully, leaving any casualties behind. Once on board, the train would resume its run to the next station and the next rugby scrum and then to the next and so on until it arrived downtown about half an hour later. Getting off the train wasn't too bad as all the people walked in one direction ... but now everyone was headed for the buses.

The bus stops were not organised with one bus to one stop. No, all the buses going in their various directions stopped at whatever stop was available. If your bus stopped 100 feet (30 m) away from where you were standing it meant that you had to frantically rush through the mass of people whose bus had stopped just where you were standing to get to your bus. Here my briefcase came into full play. The mass of people directly confronting you made it resemble more a game of American football with heads butting and ribs cracking as briefcases swung and struck. Sweating and swearing, I would normally finally make it to the door of the bus. Here stood the bus conductor, an African-American guy, 6 foot 5 inches (1.9 m) tall with shoulders the size of Mohammad Ali's. He sold the bus tickets and, once again, I had to fetch coins from my pocket.

My choice was to either take my mittens off and have my hands freeze or attempt, once again, to take the coins out of my pocket with them on and for sure drop some in the snow again. This last was a very dangerous thing to do because the conductor had no sense of humour. If you didn't have the right coins for the ride to hand, he would select the most foul words from his personal collection and use them on you. The nicest of them always was 'white trash man' but, as we had to board the bus to go to work every day, we all had become immune to these insults. We just wanted to get on with the day and our lives. Eventually, after two hours of freeze, sweat, stress and pure hell I arrived at work. Most of the time I felt like turning around and going straight back home to go to sleep again.

The mitigating factor was that the work was pleasant. I truly enjoyed working with the real team which we were. Bud had the ability to make you feel good and showed his appreciation for a job well done at every opportunity. Also, soon after I started at the hotel, more people from the L.A. Marriott joined me. One of them was my secretary Linda Norton (we are still today LinkedIn friends). Her Jon Loeb assigned nickname was Linda Boomer. I'm sure you can imagine how she earned that title. Linda was a Southern Bell and loved to speak with an almost impossible to understand southern drawl. She was witty, a lot of fun and never turned down a good party and a glass or two of Southern Comfort. Also there were the Kings, a couple of young and very dynamic people. They worked in sales and were great fun too. I was disappointed to learn that some years later they divorced.

On my team I had Dick Texas, recruited from the Sheraton in Washington DC, as the catering manager. He was married to an English girl, Gil, who had come to the US as an au pair a few years earlier. They had three boys of different ages. Dick was a friend of Mike Napolitano who at that time was the corporate director of catering. More interestingly, Dick's mother was the last of the Gunner family who had made their fortune by killing people. Not literally of course but they were one of the largest and most successful gun manufacturers in the world. She had married six times and all of her husbands had either left her or they had died.

With such a dysfunctional family background it came as no surprise that Dick's life turned out to be equally chaotic. He loved to entertain in his house. His favourite gig after lots of liquor had been consumed and a lot of food ingested was to go to the top of the stairs in the house and ask one of his children to introduce him as the President of the United States of America. He got a kick out of it. The first time he did it we all had a good laugh. By the third time it was no longer funny and the guests were hoping that this time it would not happen. But it happened every time.

One day he told Gil that he was gay and was leaving her to go to live with his boyfriend. This came as a shock to everyone, no one ever suspected him of being homosexual. Gil, broken hearted and financially broke took the three boys, moved back to England and started a new life. She got a job, rented an apartment, put the boys into schools and was slowly pulling her life together. Then, two years later out of the blue, Dick showed up at the house. He was crying tears of repentance and asked her to come back with him to the US as he was a changed man and no longer gay. He told her he missed her and the boys and Gil believed him. She turned her back on her new life and relationships, moved back with him, put the children back into school and got a job. The 'new' life was short lived. Six months later he told her that he was gay again and he went back to live with his toy boy gay friend. Sad but not surprising.

The other catering manager was Linda. She was a white South African married to an African-American policemen. Their life was made hell every time they went to visit the family. He was a pleasant chap but the marriage did not last very long. She was however a proud mother - to Pixie a cute little Yorkshire terrier.

With a team of three people and the kosher manager doing the Jewish business, in our first year of operation we turned in sales of 4 million dollars. By today's standards that is really not a great deal of money but in those days it was. Our most expensive dinner menu at the time sold for 18 dollars. The hotel had in a very short time become the place to see and be seen in for Chicagoan society and the well to do.

One of the first society events to be booked was a dinner for the Society for the Prevention of Child Abuse, a huge fund raising event with over a thousand guests. The ballroom was set up magnificently and the stage was enormous as the star turn was to be Bob Hope. The menu was a gourmet delight and the wines were so good that Bacchus himself would have had a feast. What the organisers had failed to tell Bob Hope was that the hotel was surrounded by a union picket. The evening was going great and the time for Bob Hope to perform was approaching but, when he arrived at the hotel entrance and saw the union picket, he made a u-turn and left. He would not cross the picket line to perform even if those thousand plus people had paid a fortune to buy a ticket and donate for a good cause. There were lots of disappointed people that night at the Marriott. Fortunately for us the dinner itself was a success and we did not get a bad rap.

By now December of '78 had come around and without any doubt the most prestigious of all Chicago balls was to take place at the hotel. This is known as the Crystal Ball, also an evening with more than a thousand people in attendance. All the ladies were wearing the most beautiful evening gowns and jewelry to blend with such splendour and the men had their name branded tuxedos and gold bracelets as thick and heavy as handcuffs; what a display of wealth and elegance. The room was decorated with huge, real crystal balls hung from the ceiling and palm trees made out of Baccarat crystal. Naturally the menu and the wines were up to par. The two bands were set on a revolving stage. As one band disappeared for a break, the other would strike up the same tune as it revolved into view. I had never seen anything like that. The dinner went off without a hitch. Eddie and myself were mastering the service while Lee and Thomas were overseeing the kitchen part of the job.

At about one in the morning it was all over. Lee and I decided that we had earned a drink. We did not have to go home that night as we had both decided to stay in the hotel. We crossed the street to our watering hole on Rush Street where there were other people from the hotel drinking the night away as usual. Jennifer, a stunning blonde who was the reservation manager, was among them. One glass of wine took us to the next and by three in the morning Lee, Jennifer and I had drunk our fill of cabernet.

By five in the morning the bar finally closed and we were put out in the street. I only had two hours to sober up before work. Back in my room I decided that going to sleep would give me real difficulty getting up on time and that taking a warm bath was the thing to do. So I ran the water as hot as I could stand it and went into the bath hoping it would ease my drunken stupor and the headache I felt coming on. I was in the hot water less than three minutes, I believe, when I was fast asleep. The alarm went off at ten to seven and, jumping out of the tub, I was dressed and at work in five minutes flat. I don't remember what I looked or felt like but, in the circumstance, it's probably better that I don't!

A MAN FOR ALL SEASONS

Chicago was nice in spring and in autumn. In spring the snow had melted away, the roads were cleaned up, the flowers were rising and the birds, happy to be alive, were singing beautiful melodies. The people seemed reborn again after a long and dark winter. Bright clothing came out of their closets and laughter filled the air. I liked spring there. The children were now a bit bigger and Janet and I had two bikes with child seats on the back. On Sunday afternoons we would go to the woods or parks and pedal away happily with Paul on Janet's bike and Emily on mine. We had a good life after all and had also made some good friends through the Montessori.

Autumn was also nice. One of our favourite things to do as a young family was to go to the woods and walk in the leaves that had fallen by the millions to the ground. The sound of dry leaves while walking in them, the brisk air and the still blue sky were things I came to treasure. We had to make the most of it as winter was coming again. The snow, the sub-zero temperature and the wind were to be with us again soon. The train routine would restart too and with it the dislike I had for the city and its weather. My heavy jacket, my facemask, my heavy hand-knitted mittens, the woollen hat and the scarf long enough to wrap around my neck at least twice would come out of storage and be used again for many months to come. The one good thing about winter was that it was dark early making the nights longer to be spent, first with the children until their eight o'clock bed time, and then with Janet, cuddled on the couch watching a TV movie in front of the wood burning fire place. That was the good life of winter.

Then in January of '79 while I was at a citywide catering conference, Janet received a call from her sister Marion, in England. Janet's mother had passed away. She had been a heavy smoker and sick with cancer for some time. She gave up the battle one afternoon while having her last fag and her last cup of tea. She was courageous and strong and had fought a long battle before giving in. After the meeting was over I arrived home to find Janet in a state of shock and desperate to get to England. First thing next day we booked her the next flight out while I arranged time off to look after Emily and Paul. This was a sad time as, when one parent dies, it affects everyone who loves them. My mother-in-law had always been nice and kind to me, from the moment she opened the door of the house that cold morning in January of 1971 with flour all over her apron, to the last day of her life.

The occasion did cause me to have mixed feelings as it afforded me a rare opportunity to be at home all day and night for a week with my two babies. One of the most exciting things to do with them was watch Sesame Street every day at five o'clock in the basement with the wood fire lit, lying on the floor drinking hot chocolate. This was very helpful in taking the children's minds off the loss of grandma. Soon Janet returned home and we were all just so happy to see her. Summer came. The bicycle rides in the woods started again and so did the mosquito bites, especially to Janet. She always was and still is the prime target for all biting insects. Be it mosquitos, spiders, ants or just anything that bites, they always go for her first. Only then would they go after me, Emily and Paul - and in that order.

Slowly Autumn came around. The walks in the woods and stepping on dead leaves became the routine again. It was really a beautiful time of the year, not yet too cold but fresh and pleasant enough to stretch out for long walks on Sunday afternoons. After Autumn came winter. This reminded me of the promise I had made to myself to take everyone back to California before the winter of '79/ '80 blew in freezing and furious.

CALIFORNIA RECALL

In those days, contrary to how it is done now, manpower planning was done in Maryland at Marriott headquarters. The four regional directors and the disciplines directors would meet to decide which personnel had demonstrated the most suitability in aptitude and attitude to be considered for upcoming job vacancies. John Donald had been discipline director in the west coast for several years and I had known him and Karl Kilburg, the company director of food and beverage, since I joined Marriott in 1974. Both gentlemen liked me and felt that I was ready for promotion again - my lucky day.

The day following the meeting I received a call from John, "Hello Peter, this is the man who made you a star!" I knew he had some good news as the tone of his voice was excited and anyone who knew John knew that he rarely got excited. He was a good guy but with absolutely no sense of humor nor any display of emotion. This made it very difficult to know what he was thinking or to predict his next move. After a few more pleasantries he asked me if I would be interested in a move back to California, and specifically to the Marriott's Santa Barbara Biltmore. I immediately replied, "Yes. When do I leave Chicago?!" He calmly ignored the fact that he hadn't yet specified to me the position in question nor any other detail but went on to tell me that the job on offer was as director of food and beverage.

This hotel only had one hundred and seventy five rooms, all of which could fit into just two floors of the one thousand two hundred and fourteen room Chicago Marriott. That mattered not a jot to me. The promise I had made to myself was going to become reality - and to top that I was being promoted.

The trip to Santa Barbara was arranged and off Janet and I went to interview with the general manager, Jeff. It was a mere formality as he didn't have anything to say about the decision the 'wise guys' (as he called the regional directors) had taken. I was to be the man and that was the end of the story. Our short time there was mostly spent looking at houses. We found a lovely California ranch house at the end of a cul-de-sac, ideal for us as there was no through traffic to endanger our children riding their tricycle on the sidewalk.

Returning to Chicago after a few days in southern California was like dying all over again but the holiday season soon came and I was counting the days before the move. Our house sold quickly. On New Year's Eve Janet, the children and myself moved into the hotel as all of our belonging were packed and gone. By that day I was no longer working. Dick Texas had been promoted to my position of director of catering and it was time to celebrate New Year's Eve, my promotion and our return to life in California. In the ballroom we had arranged a huge celebration with a four course meal and wine and champagne enough to float a battleship. The bands were delivering a magnificent atmosphere for dancing and simply being happy.

Janet and I were sitting at a table for ten. One of the other guests there was Samir El Fayumi, an Egyptian who had just been hired as the director of human resources at the Sakkara Marriott. He was a fervent Muslim and under no circumstances would he touch a drop of alcohol. This was the wrong place for him to be that night. As the night progressed the eating and dancing continued at pace and the drinking was getting out of hand. By the time one o'clock came around the huge ballroom crowd had turned into a noisy, loud and unruly bunch of drunks. I was no exception. We had a baby sitter to stay in the room with Emily and Paul and this gave me the liberty and the license to drink myself silly. So I did. The only sober individual at the table, probably in the room, was Samir. He was gobsmacked, staring open-jawed at how a bunch of Christians would behave in what they considered having a celebration and a good time.

By the time three o'clock came around I could barely stand. Most likely crawling on all fours, I found the elevator and somehow reached our room. The baby sitter was paid and left. I still had to face the not inconsiderable challenge of getting undressed and into bed. That's when I fell over and cut my head open on the corner of a bedside table. Blood was gushing from my wound and on to the carpet. As I was totally gone, I could do little about it other than to press a towel to my head and fall asleep.

I had no idea what had happened to Janet until the next morning when I woke up with a double headache, one from the cut and one from the hangover, to find her asleep on the bed. She was totally unaware that I had fallen over and cut my head. If this were to happen today I would be so ashamed of my behaviour that I could not show my face in public but, because everyone except Samir was also drunk, it made no difference. Anyway we skipped breakfast that morning and went down to the restaurant at noon for New Year's Day brunch. Even after that my hangover persisted so I spent the rest of the day asleep in our room. A somehow appropriate finale to my time spent in Chicago.

Chapter 13

TEAM GIACOMINI

On the 4th of January we flew to Santa Barbara. We were chauffeur driven to the hotel and our second floor suite with a beautiful view of the garden facing east and the majestic Pacific Ocean to the west. We quickly settled in and set off for our first dinner without having to wear heavy coats, gloves and all the paraphernalia that we had become accustomed to during our time in Chicago - what a relief.

Next morning I reported to Jeff at the hotel at nine o'clock and was introduced to the team. That was quickly done as I didn't know any of them. Settling into my office was a bit harder as my new secretary insisted on telling me how great the former director had been. This despite the fact that he had been fired for poor performance. In her eyes he was the greatest and Marriott were wrong to have fired such a wonderful guy. This went on for a week at the end of which I told her that if she missed him so much she should quit and rejoin him at the hotel in Los Angeles where he was now working. Sure enough that worked. The following Monday she came to work with a nicely written resignation letter. My first challenge was overcome with little difficulty.

Having moved from Chicago to California, and especially to Santa Barbara, made it easy to recruit people who, like me, had got sick of the weather in the mid-west. It took just one phone call to get my former Chicago secretary Anne to pack her suitcases and fly out with her husband to join me in sunny southern California. With that part taken care of I settled into the job with all my body and soul. The first thing I had to do was to clean up the kitchen and the pastry kitchen. It proved harder than expected. The previous year the health inspector of the city of Santa Barbara had closed down the pastry kitchen and had fined the hotel 12,000 dollars because of poor sanitary conditions. The inspector was now a regular visitor to the hotel in order to ensure that everything was up to scratch and that we were now complying with the city code. Here I had to overcome another obstacle - the executive chef.

He was a tall, slim, handsome, French-Canadian who wore black trousers, a starched white jacket and a 'toque' about a foot and a half (45 cm) high on top of his head. This made him look as if he were wearing a crown and he sure believed himself to be a king. With such an imposing appearance and the personality to go with it my first impression was that he would have everything under control – wrong! A community of plump cockroaches were unwelcome inhabitants of the Santa Barbara Biltmore kitchen. As I listened to the chef explain how great he was, how many medals he had won and how clean and efficient was his kitchen, I was watching a giant cockroach climb up his trouser leg. That did it. I made him an offer he could not refuse. Either he resigned and worked out his resignation period or be terminated on the spot. He chose the first option and gave me one month notice.

The hotel world is indeed a small one and I found that the maître d'hotel was a French fellow who had been my boss's boss at the San Francisco Notlih. Now I was his boss and this hurt his French pride. I also discovered that he was very fond of good French wine to accompany his dinner. With no intention to offend him I explained that, due to the miserable financial position of the hotel, he would have to forego the pleasure of his nightly bottle of top end plonk. He did agree to desist the practice but I wasn't convinced of his good intention. I felt that he would most likely continue with his bottle of expensive wine regardless. I gave him a few days to relax over the issue. About a week later I said goodnight to everyone at six in the evening and left the hotel only to return at ten when I knew that the maître d'hotel would be eating his dinner. Sure enough, as I walked into the restaurant, I found him at his usual table with a filet mignon dinner and a full bottle of one of the best wines we had in the cellar. Needless to say that was the last bottle of expensive French wine he ever drank at Marriott expense. I fired him the next day.

I had seen off two of the most important managers in the food and beverage department and a secretary in my first month on the job. I was a bit scared to say the least. I had to find an executive chef and a maître d'hotel and, while at it, add a pastry chef too. This last was the easiest to find as I quickly established with a dinner there with my wife that the Montecito Inn had the best dessert in town. I invited their pastry chef, a very talented young woman, to come in for an interview and before noon on the same day she was hired. Then I located a German executive chef working in another mid-west Marriott who, like me, was only too keen to escape the cold and snow. So within a month the executive chef position was covered too.

The maître d'hotel position was more complex though. In the US nobody knows what a maître d'hotel is, never mind what he is supposed to do. First I changed the title and the position on offer to director of restaurant. At the next manpower planning meeting in Washington DC, John Donald the regional director, came up with just the right person for the job. He was Frank Garahan, a single New Yorker working in Connecticut with a real passion for the business and whose good looks and constant smile guaranteed his success with the girls on any California beach. Now the three key positions were filled. Boy was I relieved.

The hotel laid on a Sunday champagne brunch which served one thousand two hundred people each week at the ridiculous price of just 12.50 dollars. People would stand in line for hours to get in. The queue could be a mile (1.6 km) long. Fights often broke out as people got tired of waiting. This was not good for the hotel which, at the end of the afternoon, grossed a mere 15,000 dollars. This paltry sum was not worth the damage to the reputation of the hotel so I took the decision to change the programme.

I increased the price to 17.50 dollars with the aim of reducing the number of diners to a more manageable six hundred in number. I replaced the stainless steel cutlery with silver plated sets, the plastic salad bowls with crystal ones and the paper napkins with good Egyptian cotton ones. Slowly the hotel's reputation improved. The quality of food served was much superior and the pastry chef had become what would now be known as a 'celebrity chef'.

With the reputation on the up and up it was now time to bring in a real maître d'hotel to ensure that the service in the restaurant, bar and room service would keep pace with the rest of the hotel. As no one in the company was really trained for the job I had to look outside. I was seeking someone who would concentrate solely in the area of service in the food and beverage areas and not drink a bottle of wine every night with their dinner. The name of Virgilio, now a partner in an Italian restaurant in Atlanta, Georgia and who had in the past worked as my assistant when I was a waiter at the Delta Hotel in Ascona, Switzerland, came to my mind. In Georgia he met Anastasia, the wife of his partner in the restaurant. He fell in love with her and, since he was no longer married to the Neapolitan girl, they got married - all in the space of six months. Not unsurprisingly given the circumstance, the partnership in the restaurant did not work out so when I called him he was more than ready to come to Marriott with me.

Now, with all this great help, I could become more creative - my best part. I decided with Jeff to start a cocktail hour and call it 'Fiesta Brava'. We were at the time sitting at our usual table in the bar and there were no guests there at all. Our plan was to go to Tijuana, south of the borders in Mexico and have a typical carreta Mexican food street cart made. We would also buy real sombreros for the waiters and the bartenders and colourful campesinas dresses for the waitresses plus a full display of paper flowers, pinatas. That's just what we did.

Life was going well. Emily and Paul were getting big and Janet had settled in and had even had her knee operation done. We were all thriving but there was a problem. Jeff, the general manager, was an alcoholic and soon found out that I too liked a drink. He had started the routine of picking me up from my office at five each evening to go to the bar and drink far too much before going home. He drank whisky, I drank wine. Nibbling at the spicey Mexican food being served from our (now very popular) carreta made it easy for me to down glass after glass of wine until I had reached my quota of five glasses and at the stage of making a monkey of myself. Meanwhile Jeff would still be sober enough to enjoy the show I was putting on. It was a dangerous road we were walking – or rather driving.

After drinking myself to the limit I would get into my VW bug and drive home. I was not in a condition to drive most of the nights but I drove anyway. It was only a miracle that I never killed anyone or caused an accident. Jeff too was totally wasted by the time we left each evening. Janet was putting up with my errant behaviour and Jeff's second wife, his secretary, kind of tolerated his drinking but was trying to get him off the booze.

The turning point for Jeff came on the evening of his birthday. His wife had prepared a candlelight dinner with all the trimmings and had planned a romantic evening on their terrace overlooking the sun setting on the Pacific Ocean with a violinist and singer to serenade them. All Jeff had to do was be home by seven; but gone nine and he and I, both drunk beyond recognition, were still at the bar. By ten we made it home. I remember going straight to bed without even giving Emily and Paul a good night kiss, never mind greeting Janet who was in no mood to kiss some foul smelling drunkard.

Jeff experienced an altogether more sobering welcome home. His wife was waiting with three suitcases ready packed and a rolling pin in her right hand. I don't believe she hit him over the head with it but the message was clear and harder than any blow - "Either you start rehab tomorrow morning or I will pick up those three cases and you will never, ever see me again!" Jeff loved his wife and the very next morning first thing he was at AA. I lost track of him for a few years but I heard that he had sobered up, never touched a drop of whisky again and lived happily ever after.

I loved California and was dreaming of buying a house in Ojay, working at the Biltmore until retirement and just being very happy. The house we had purchased had a small back yard. The children could spend a lot of the time outdoors just like all the healthy, sun-bleached-blonde, tanned and athletic Californian kids. Montessori was their school and church activities also featured heavily. Janet felt settled to the point that she got herself a job serving meals to the children in a public school. We were all so happy there, all in all a real Santa Barbara life style. But, if I hadn't realised it before, I soon came to understand that when working for a large corporation you have very little control over your life.

A MAN IN DEMAND

The Biltmore was a great little hotel, Santa Barbara one of the most beautiful spots in the world and the California life style suited me to a 'T'. A home in Ojay would have been the cream on the cake. But no, it was not meant to be. Just eight months into my dream job the call came once more from John Donald, regional director of food and beverage. He told me that Chet Baket, my former boss in Oldport Beach, had moved to manage the opening of the seven hundred and fifty room convention Anaheim Marriott next to the original Disneyland Park there. Chet needed a director of food and beverage with convention experience as the main business would be in catering for enormous groups.

The hotel had two restaurants, a bar, a big swim-up bar and an extensive room service. While I was a director already, the size of the Santa Barbara Biltmore was so small that it could fit into the smallest banquet room at the Anaheim hotel. On top of that Chet was desperate, his opening date was approaching and he needed me. He asked me to drive down from Santa Barbara to Anaheim to meet with him. I'm pretty sure that he was still hoping for an older and more qualified candidate to show up but no such person materialised and I was offered the job.

I really didn't want to go but, just as happened before in Oldport Beach when it was recommended that I go to Chicago, I was again subtly informed that by stepping up to the plate and helping the company out I would be rewarded in the future. Janet too, was less than happy at the prospect of quitting her home in Santa Barbara, her friends at the church, the parents and children at Montessori,

Virgilio and his wife, Anastasia and her personally rewarding work at the school feeding the children. Needless to say, we moved again.

The routine of looking for a house restarted and we found one rather quickly in a lovely community called Turtle Rock in the town of Irvine. Janet loved it. The Montessori was not far and my work was less than thirty minutes away. Everything was just perfect. Quickly I dived into my work to get ready for the opening. I was lucky that Annie, my secretary from Chicago and now in Santa Barbara, wanted to come with me to Anaheim. There was therfore no interviewing or settling in to be organised in that department. A big plus.

The executive team now consisted of Chet Baket (aka the Bear) as general manager, Paul Avena as resident manager, myself as director of food and beverage, Debbie Smith as human resource director, Rick Shrecht as director of engineer and Horst Rotterdam as director of sales and marketing. With the exception of Paul Avena I had worked with all these people in Oldport Beach. They were all nice human beings and believed in the Marriott philosophy of helping people to work as a real team for the benefit of all. I felt immediately at home. The hotel was coming along well and the opening was only ninety days off so I had to get my team together.

I recruited Bill Countryman as executive chef, another snow refugee from the east coast, and Ken Fullmore came to be my director of restaurants from the Los Angeles Marriott. The banquet maître d'hotel was easy to find as he came from the Oldport Beach Marriott which I had taken him to from the Los Angeles Marriott when we opened Oldport. Sharon Sola, also from the Los Angeles Marriott joined me as the restaurant manager for the Italian restaurant and I found an outstanding chef called Salvatore Troia to be my restaurant chef at the JW Restaurant. Unfortunately, I found out later that he had an alcohol problem and would come to work inebriated several days in a row. The restaurant manager was a German fellow whose problem was pride rather than alcohol. I had my hands full with two primadonnas in the one show.

The restaurant turned out to be immediately successful as those days were at the advent of nouvelle cuisine and chef Troia was a master at that. The restaurant manager was soon replaced by a very nice single Austrian guy called Joseph Wiener. In his mid forties, he immediately fell head over heels for my married secretary Annie who, even if she didn't care much for her husband, cared neither for Joseph as a lover. So fortunately for me, as there was no romance between them, I could keep them both on the team.

In those days we still had the freedom to drink in the bars after five in the afternoon on a daily basis. One of my first moves was to introduce 'my' cocktail hour and the carreta was ordered from Mexico. The routine started all over again. This gave me the excuse to go to the bar every evening and drink two Dos Equis beers and eat some Mexican food before going home. My new drinking buddy was Paul Avena, the guy on the team I did not know. At first he seemed to be a good fellow but after just a short time of working and drinking with him the true Paul came out. He was an arrogant and mean individual who would not hesitate to stab anyone in the back if that served his purpose.

Life continued to be good. Janet, Emily, Paul and I enjoyed the walks and the bike rides in the park near our house and our Tijuana trips became more frequent as we were closer to the border. My days off were Sundays and Mondays which were really good because one day was totally dedicated to church and family and on the other I could catch up with chores and work in my garage and in the house. We were near Ann and Larry, our friends with whom we are still close to this day, and it was one of the very best times in our lives. It really flew by, we were only there nine months when the call came.

AN OFFER I COULDN'T REFUSE

This time it was Karl Kilburg who called Chet Baket to tell him that he would like me to go to Sakkara to open the Sakkara

Marriott as the director of food and beverage. "Not again!", were Janet's first words when I told her that I had been offered a posting to Egypt. The Bear was a bit concerned about losing me so quickly. On the other hand he had told me that the company would reward me if I stepped up to the plate and helped him open Anaheim. I am not sure that he didn't have something to do with that move. He was a hard boss to please but he was one of the fairest people I ever met.

On October the 6th of 1981, President Sadat of Egypt was killed by an agent of the Muslim brotherhood fanatical group which would come to rule Egypt for a short time and I was asked to fly to Sakkara with Janet to be interviewed by Juergen Schlank, the general manager there. Janet and I were kind of excited to board a plane and have business class seats as we had never flown in business class before. We found it really cool to enjoy champagne upon arrival on the plane, have huge seats and the best wines and food all the way to Sakkara. I thought, "If this is the way expats live, then count me in." After a long but very comfortable flight we finally arrived in Sakkara and were welcomed at the airport with a chauffeur driven Cadillac to whisk us to the Sakkara Sheraton Hotel. This was a very nice hotel at the time, albeit that it was something of a brothel for Arabs guests visiting Sakkara in the summer months.

The next morning it was arranged for me to have breakfast with Juergen while Janet was to have the same chauffeur driven Cadillac and the guide/interpreter take her to Maadi where the Sakkara-American college was located to inquire about the schooling for Emily and Paul. The conversation with Juergen went reasonably well despite the fact that he had little respect for anyone coming from the US to a place like Sakkara in the early '80s. He believed, not unreasonably, that unless you already had Middle East experience you were set up to fail. After breakfast he took me to visit the building works. The hotel had been under construction for almost seven years. That was no surprise after I saw the way the poor Egyptian labourers had to toil. Everything was done by hand with a long line of barefoot men carrying bricks and cement in a container up twenty floors to the top of the tower they were completing. Their supervisor carried a long stick and quickly beat any worker who was not moving fast enough. I was shocked.

The hotel consisted of the old Sakkara Palace, two twenty storey towers connected by a horse shoe shaped building. It housed three hundred and fifty rooms, a beautiful health club with an indoor/outdoor pool, magnificent gardens, three restaurants and a traditional style lounge bar. I was so impressed with the hotel that for a moment I forgot what I had seen happening to the poor building workers who, it turned out, did not have the use of any toilets on the site. They used any available corner not in open view for the purpose, creating a horrendous stench and swarms of flies in the process.

One redeeming feature in the midst of so much poverty and inequality was Juergen's secretary, Nagla. She was a French educated Egyptian woman who spoke fluent Arabic, English and French. The classes of society in Egypt are well defined by the level of formal education you receive as a child. The aristocracy were French educated in the best French schools; the middle class did not speak French but were educated at English speaking schools; the lower class only spoke Arabic and had very little formal education.

Time for dinner came around and it was arranged that Juergen and his wife Michelle would dine with Janet and I at the Sheraton. When the time came to ask for the bill, Juergen told me to charge it to my room. Although the hotel was paying for the meal, we were the guests. It showed me very little respect on the part of Juergen to ask me to do that.

That night neither myself nor Janet slept. We had to make a decision the next morning whether to take the job or not. At breakfast we decided that we could not live and work with Juergen. I informed him of our decision. He was astounded to hear that I would turn down the opportunity to work with him and in the biggest Marriott hotel outside of the USA. I told him frankly that the hotel was not the problem but rather his personality and that I didn't appreciate the fact that he put the dinner bill on my, his guest's, account. For good measure I threw in that I didn't like the way his building workers were treated. (On this last point I did not understand at the time that this was a cultural issue over which he had no control).

Juergen's response was to call his boss in London, Marshal Dunant, the regional vice president. When Marshal heard that I was not going to take the job he apparently went berserk. He told Juergen to have us change our tickets and fly to London to see him rather than go directly home. Nagla swung into action and in no time we were booked on a flight to London and left immediately. As Marriott had no hotels in London at the time, a reservation for us had been made in a very old and traditional English hotel not far from the regional office.

The morning after our arrival, Janet and I enjoyed a leisurely English breakfast then caught a London cab to meet Marshal and the regional team at his office. Marshal quickly revealed himself to be a really nice bloke. A gem to deal with. His team were great too. Renato Sandmeier was the regional director of food and beverage. Although his name is Swiss-German, he grew up in Lugano, the Italian speaking part of Switzerland. We straight off discovered that we could talk together in our own dialect.

That evening Marshal and his wife, since divorced, took us to dinner at the Carlton Tower Hotel's finest restaurant called Prime Rib. The meal was superb, the company charming and reassuring. I candidly informed Marshal of the reason I had turned down the move. He confided that he himself had communication difficulties with Juergen. He told me that he would have a heart to heart conversation with him and I could be assured that Juergen would change his style. With that commitment, Janet and I decided to give Sakkara a go.

Back in California we were questioned about our sanity ("Are you crazy?") about leaving Turtle Rock, California, the Anaheim Marriott and the USA to move to an uncivilized, backward and so religiously different country. Ann and Larry were so much against the move that it was hard for me to prevent them from influencing Janet to stick to our decision as a family. My colleagues and friends at the hotel were not so much against the move, some could see the advantages and some were even a bit jealous that I had been presented with such an opportunity. By now Christmas and New Year had come around. The parties and celebrations were more emotive than ever now that we knew it would be a long time, if ever, before we would be back celebrating with our friends again.

With the preparations for the move going ahead full steam the excitement was mounting every day - and along with it the anxiety. I was questioning the wisdom of the move. Did I really want to leave my friends and lifestyle behind to go to live in the dusty streets of Sakkara? Did I really want to leave the most comfortable home I ever lived in to find who-knows-what kind of apartment in a city which, at the time, already had fifteen million inhabitants? I couldn't share my fears with anyone, especially Janet. After all I had accepted the job and now I was committed. I had to go.

By the 8th of February the removal men had been around and everything that was not going to Sakkara had been put in storage. The 11th was the date set for our departure so on the 10th we were given our going away party. In those days Marriott had just opened their one hundredth hotel in Maui but was still small enough to be a family oriented company. Family and spouses were always invited to these fantastic, elaborate and full of fun celebrations to toast the person promoted to leave. That was the best bit of the party as the rest of the team would normally prepare little sketches about the successes (but mostly about the failures) during the individual's time with the team. It was all done with humour and in the best of spirits.

At the height of the festivity three guys dressed in full mariachi garb and accompanied by three real mariachi musicians blasting their trumpets entered the room pulling the Fiesta Brava cart I had had made in Tijuana. It was loaded with goodies and presents.

These created a new challenge as the shipment of what we were taking by air had already gone to Sakkara. We had to figure out how to carry this unforeseen load with us on the flight. One of the most challenging gifts was the traditional framed photo of the hotel and the staff with their comments written around it. It was so big and bulky that I didn't know how we could carry it to Sakkara. Rick, director of engineering, came to the rescue. A perfect wooden box complete with locks was built overnight and the framed picture went into it – problem solved.

GOODBYE AMERICA

The next morning, with heavy hearts and even heavier heads due to the amount of cabernet sauvignon and Dos Equis beer consumed, we were driven to the L.A. airport and boarded the flight to Milan. It had become a kind of family tradition that every time we moved we would all four wear a red golf shirt emblazoned with the name 'Team Giacomini'. Emily and Paul really enjoyed that little game and, to tell the truth, Janet and I enjoyed it too. Naturally, expecting to land in cold Milan in February, we had to still wear heavy coats on top of our short sleeved tee-shirts.

As the company was very generous in those days and was run by directors who came from the food and beverage discipline, we were all able to travel in business class. What a treat. Champagne flowed all the way to Milan. Back then the drink and drive rules were not enforced anywhere in the world and renting a car half inebriated at the airport upon arrival was not a problem. A bit more of a problem was how to drive out of Linate airport which is on the other side of Milan to where we needed to go without crossing the city centre. Janet is usually the designated driver. I am the navigator but trying to read maps (GPS didn't exist then) was a challenge for me as I also had to read road signs. Fortunately, all the signs were in Italian but, given the speed Janet drives at, it still presented me with a real test in speed reading and patience. Soon however we made it to the circular road around the city and were able to head for Centonara with no major complication.

There we were treated to a joyous welcome by my sister Anna.

We stayed in the old house. Janet and I slept in my parents' bedroom with Emily and Paul in the other room. It was February, cold and with snow on the ground. The house didn't have heating of any kind. As we were eating with Anna, Tullio and Maria Ester, not even the stove in the kitchen of the old house was lit. There was no hot water in the house nor in Anna's house and no way to shower or take a hot bath. For one week we had to revert to the old fashioned way of washing by taking hot water in a pail from Anna's wood burning stove and then washing ourselves down with a cloth.

This was a very primitive experience for two American children used to having a bath every day since the day they were born. It was not only a new experience for them but they could see, for the first time, how I grew up. The winters were especially hard for us growing up. We didn't know any better than that bathing or showering was something reserved for rich people and to be practiced only in the cities.

That week was so busy going around to visit with the relatives, aunties, uncles and cousins still living at that time. My favourite visit was with my cousin, Iuci. She was a heavy set lady of about fifty years of age, always jolly and loved to both cook and eat. Additionally she always had a good bottle of wine and a good glass of Marsala sweet wine at the end of the meal. Not surprising that she weighed a ton. She had a daughter of about thirty, Dolly. She was the exact opposite of her mum and a picky eater. Maybe she didn't want to have all those extra pounds to carry around like her mother had.

My favourite aunt, Zia Pina, was also always generous with her meals. She too always had a good bottle of wine and a glass of sweet Marsala wine at the end of the meal. In that one week I must have put on ten pounds in weight. All the meals were home cooked with lots of risottos, ossobuco and my favourite, polenta. Plus we were fed every kind of dessert and accompaniments imaginable.

Soon the week passed and it was time for goodbye. The plane was waiting and the excitement rose. Tullio took us to the airport in his flashy, red car. Once again we were off and on the last leg of our journey. The very beginning of a brand new adventure for Team Giacomini.

Chapter 14

A SAND DANCE TO TREASURE

The Alitalia Milan to Sakkara business class flight afforded us stunning views from the east to the west of Italy with the Apennines and their snow-capped peaks straddling it majestically. A delicious Italian lunch with lots of champagne accompanied our crossing of the Mediterranean to Cyprus before Alexandria with its port and gardens came into view beneath us. As the plane approached Sakkara airport we flew over the pyramids of Giza with the last rays of the sun casting an enormous shadow of the pyramid of Keops on the ground which made it appear even bigger than it is. What a phenomenal first impression of our host country. Splendid was the word that came to mind and landing at Sakkara airport really was like entering another world.

Waiting for us inside the airport was Mr.Sope, general factotum at the Sakkara Marriott. There was none of the present day terrorist inspired security so, in no time at all, he had retrieved our large amount of luggage from the conveyor, had our passports stamped with the required visas and we were on our way to the Sakkara Sheraton Hotel where we were to stay until we found suitable living accommodation. We were picked up by the hotel driver in the Cadillac normally assigned to Juergen Schlank. The ride from the airport in Heliopolis to the Giza area of Sakkara took almost as long as our Milan to Sakkara flight such was the traffic and chaos of the city.

There were cars everywhere incessantly blasting their horns, donkey drawn carts, horses with huge loads and garbage collection carts with barefoot children in grimy galabiahs on top sorting the filthy loads. It was one of the most shocking scenes I had ever experienced up to that point in my life. Emily and Paul's eyes were wide in disbelief. I think that then and there they realised how fortunate they were to have been born where they were born. The camels seemed to have priority, wandering around the road with impunity. The already snail pace traffic had to stop whenever a group of them decided to park themselves in the middle of the road. Wow, what a scene, but we were in it and had already decided that the best way to face it was to embrace it.

Arriving at the hotel our next surprise was to see how many Russian built Ladas were parked there; the cars' presence a remnant of Russia's years of alliance with the former left wing president Abdel Nasser. On entering the hotel we received another, quite different surprise. Our nostrils were immediately assailed by the delicious aromas of spices and of roasted lamb, the smell that would follow us everywhere we went for the next three years. It took a while to get used to but it was lovely. It was a particular blessing in that location as it somewhat camouflaged the altogether less pleasant odour wafting from the Nile just 10 yards (9 m) away.

Two connecting rooms were provided, one for Janet and me and one for Emily and Paul. This was a good arrangement as we would not have been very comfortable had our rooms not been accessible from the inside. Then, not having bathed for over a week, we all luxuriated in long, hot showers before collapsing into our beds and instant sleep. The windows of the hotel were not sound proofed from the noise in the street below but, exhausted with the excitement of our day, that didn't stop us from enjoying a wonderful night's rest.

Arising next morning in this new world was another experience for all of us. The shower and the bathtubs in the two rooms were dandy. We enjoyed the first morning bathing and getting Emily and Paul ready for their first day of school at the American International School of Sakkara. It was located in the town of Maadi about 8 miles (13 km) from the hotel. We went down to the restaurant for breakfast and found a buffet table which was a display of abundance as I had hardly seen before. From the typical local food like tamya, casserole of whole baked beans, lamb kebabs and huge platters of roasted fowl in heavy spices to the western dishes such as scrambled eggs, smoked salmon, French cheeses and baguettes, German pumpernickels, American donuts and Danish pastries, there was every kind of dish imaginable. Considering that we were in a poor country that was a shock in itself. It was just such a contradiction to what we had seen the night before on our drive from the airport.

At the table next to ours there sat two men and one elderly lady. I heard them talking about the Marriott and laughing loudly at the mention of Juergen Schlank. It took a while for what I was hearing to sink in. I was really tempted to approach their table and talk with them. With a real effort, I managed to stay put and eat my breakfast. As the three got up to leave and passed by my table, they threw a suspicious glance my way which I only came to realise the meaning of when I got to my work at nine that morning. With Emily and Paul, their backpacks loaded and accompanied by Janet, off on the school bus to start their first day at the Sakkara American College, I took a taxi to the hotel's pre-opening office located in a residential villa about a mile and a half (2.5 km) away.

Upon arrival there I found Juergen enthroned pharaoh-like in his office with Nagla seated outside. Without much ado he informed me that my office would be in another building just two blocks away. As I was leaving the villa I heard two of the voices which I had heard earlier laughing over breakfast at the Sheraton come from behind a door I was passing. I could not resist the temptation to look inside. There, sitting opposite each other at a small table serving as a desk, were the man and the elderly lady who had breakfasted at the next table to me in the restaurant just a short time before. Now they were working quietly, none of those jokes about the Marriott and certainly none about Juergen.

They invited me in, got up and introduced themselves. The man was Marc Elchupe, an Egyptian married to a Swedish lady and the resident manager who was also number two in the hierarchy of the hotel. The lady was Constanza Kurtz, German in every way, and director of service or housekeeping manager. Each had very interesting pasts.

Marc had returned to his post from a Marriott in the US as he spoke Arabic and knew the culture and the people. Constanza had worked with Juergen in Saudi Arabia. What made her interesting was the fact that for a woman to work in Saudi Arabia she had to have special permission to do so granted only by the king himself. She turned out to be Juergen's eyes and ears in the hotel, reporting to him all that she heard or saw, a regular snitch in fact. In the next office sat the third man from breakfast. He turned out to be Ed English, the director of sales and marketing. Ed had joined from a Marriott in his native UK. He was married to Brigit and they had a small girl called Charlene. He was pleasant enough on introduction but for now working quietly and a far cry from the boisterous guy at the breakfast table.

I left them for my office which was, like most of Sakkara in those days, in an old building. It was a fairly large apartment, skimpily furnished and with ancient plumbing which made use of the toilet embarrassing as the racket of the flush informed the entire building of your visit. There were a few old tables, a few chairs and two old, black dialing phones which normally didn't work. I was there alone for about one week. The first thing I had to do was to find a good secretary who could speak and write Arabic and English as all correspondence to the outside world was conducted in English but within Egypt was conducted in Arabic. Also the bureaucracy was quite concerning and you could easily get in trouble through pure ignorance.

During that week two more members of the food and beverage team arrived. The director of restaurants was Nagui Salamat, a Coptic Egyptian from the Marriott in Los Angeles. He was married to an Egyptian lady and they had a boy and a girl, both a little older than Emily and Paul. They also went to the Sakkara American college at the hotel's expense. The executive chef was Robert Dalruff, a German from the Marco Island Resort in Marco Island Florida. He was married to a Swiss lady and they had a baby daughter. As we settled into the office I soon detected that Nagui was weak and devious and, because he spoke Arabic, no one ever knew what he was up to. Robert was a gentleman.

The search for the secretary continued. Nagla's husband Nimani (front office manager at the Holiday Inn Pyramids) came up with one candidate. Her name was Jasmine Butassy, a twenty-four year old devout Muslim. Another candidate, a Copt, was introduced by Nagui ... Muslims helped Muslims, Copts helped Copts. Following an intensive interview from the three of us, the two candidates were sent to Nagla and Juergen for the final interview. Nagla was so taken with Jasmine, especially when she found out that she too was a Muslim and prayed five time a day, that she convinced Juergen to employ her. With that decision made one big obstacle was overcome. This was mid-March and on April the 4th Jasmine started work.

The chef and I busied ourselves in finding what ingredients were available to create menus that would appeal to the local customers as well as to the international clientele we expected to be our main stream of business. Moustafa Khorany was the purchasing manager and a decent fellow. We involved him from the beginning of this process and as a result he took a liking to both of us. We collected some information from other hotels such as the Nile Notlih (open since 1955), the Sakkara Sheraton where we were staying, the Mena House Oberoi and the Sheraton Heliopolis.

We also believed that it was imperative to bring in food from the US in order to perform the grand opening in suitable style. After determining our requirements Jasmine translated and wrote out the purchase order. The cost of this container load of goods came to over 70,000 US dollars. An enormous amount in those days.

Nagui was busying himself with the recruiting and selection of the front of house management staff while Robert was looking for kitchen managers. It was commonly held that Egyptian chefs were not up to par (a theory that was proved totally wrong in years to come) so a French sous-chef was recruited from Canada. He was married to a lady from India. The restaurant chef was also French, his name was Pascal. He now works in Florida in a retirement home and still writes to me via LinkedIn. The butcher was Mark, a Swiss guy married to a Chilean lady and they had a little daughter. The pastry chef was German. He was a great guy who years later was transfered to the JW Marriott in DC. After a while there he went to the San Diego Marriott, a large hotel with over a thousand rooms where Chet Baket was general manager.

This pastry chef was a real genius and possessed the stamina and work ethic of a typical German. He was also very kind and giving, a great teacher adored by his team, one hundred percent efficient and one of the best people I worked with in over fifty-five years in the hotel trade. A lone Egyptian sous-chef was hired who had worked in Italy and who turned out to be the best of the bunch. Years later, under the food and beverage leadership of Thomas Buehner, he was promoted to executive chef.

THE FAMILY TAKES TO SAKKARA

On the family front things were also going well. The idea accommodation-wise was that Janet, who has a much better sense of orientation than I have, would walk around Sakkara looking at buildings from the outside. If they appeared newish and clean she would make a note of the location. After six that same evening, we would all go together to ask if there was an apartment with three rooms available to rent in the building. This was hard as our Arabic was non-existent and the first person to deal with was the bouhab, the doorman hired by the owner of the building. This poor sod at best lived in the garage of the building with a wife and many children. He was considered one of the lowest class of people, rated only marginally above garbage collectors. They had absolutely no education and could not read nor write Arabic - let alone English.

After a few days of such searching Janet found a building that looked new and which was only two storeys high. The height of the building was critical. We had learned that, when an owner of a two storey building wanted to increase his rental revenue, he simply added two or three more storeys on top without any planning permission or proper building practices. More times than not the whole building would subsequently collapse. As we approached the gate a loyal bauhab wearing a decently clean galabiah sat there cross-legged, smoking and with his ever trusted glass of tea to hand. In our very rudimental Arabic we tried to tell him that we were looking for a three bedroom apartment to rent. He gestured for us to wait, mentioned the word 'doctor' and disappeared up a stairway; only to reappear a few minutes later accompanied by the 'doctor'.

This turned out to be an extremely well dressed young man of about thirty who was indeed the owner of the building and a real medical doctor. His English was perfect, accent and all, as he had studied medicine in England. He was a single man living with his parents and younger brother on the first floor. He had one brand new and very nice apartment available on the second floor which, by Sakkara standards of the time, was a real plush place. It had three bedrooms and three bathrooms, an enormous living-room and a kitchen. It had no furniture but he said that Janet could go with him to the furniture shop to choose furnishings and that he would buy them. We asked him to hold on to it and that we would come back the next evening with Ismail Ramadan, our Egyptian director of finance, who would negotiate the rent and the terms. Dr.Mohammad, as was his name, agreed to that and we parted.

The apartment address was on 7, Sharia Moussaddak, 100 yards (90 m) from the main road called Gamet-el-duwal-el-Arabia or the Road of the Arab Universities. Also at the corner of the first crossroads there was a mosque with a gigantic minaret. We were happy with our find and went back to the Sheraton to have dinner with the children who were there doing their home-work.

The following day after six, Janet, Ismail, Emily, Paul and myself went back to meet Dr.Mohammad. He was waiting for us with the customary hospitable glass of steaming tea ready. There followed some animated bargaining as is expected in that part of the world before Ismail and Dr.Mohammad shook hands. This signified to us that the deal was completed and all parties were happy, not least us. We had found a new building two storeys high, Janet would pick the furniture, Emily and Paul had their own room and bathroom, we had a medical doctor as the owner and living on the floor below. To top it all it was only 2.5 miles (4 km) from work and 100 yards (90 m) from the main road where getting a cheap taxi ride would never be a problem.

The next day, after Emily and Paul went off to school and I to work, Janet was picked up by Dr.Mohammad at the hotel and went to search for furniture. It turned out that he had very much set a budget for the purchases and he wasn't too flexible in going with what Janet really liked. As he was paying for it, and because he was a man and she a woman, she ended with good furniture but far from what she really wanted. Janet wasn't too thrilled as she likes to manage her own life and be surrounded by things of her own taste and choosing. However, the little setback on the furniture selection was a minor issue and not one to deter us from enjoying the apartment. In the next few days we were ready to move in. The only delay was that our belonging had not arrived from California. Although we didn't take a lot of things, there were some basics that were absolutely necessary.

The next step was to look for a car. On Gamet-el-duwal-el-Arabia there was a Volvo dealer. We had decided that for us to drive in Sakkara with Emily and Paul in the car we needed to have a very well built and secure car. The Volvo seemed to be the perfect sedan for our family. We bought a four door, white 244 at the unbelievable price of only 11,000 dollars.

Inside the city you couldn't have a serious accident. The traffic is too heavy to go fast with five rows of cars normally crammed together on a three lane road. Janet quickly pointed out that you could put out your cigarette in the next car's ashtray as you were travelling so close together with the next vehicle. The standard joke in Egypt was that a car only needed a horn. We also learned that Egyptian drivers did not turn on their lights at night because it would use the battery power. We got Mr.Sope to get us two driver's licenses and we were ready to become Egyptian drivers.

Shortly after that we moved into the apartment and we were all set. Janet had found a church right behind the hotel where she met many other expat wives with whom she could participate in various social activities and the children were enjoying the new school.

Work was moving along well too. During the pre-opening we all took Friday off, as that is the day of rest in the Islamic world. One sad factor for me was that Sunday, being a normal work day, I could not go to church. For all of the time we spent in that country I only went to church during Christmas and special holidays. Now with the school for the children going well, the apartment set, the car purchased and drivers' licenses in our possession all the foundations for a trouble-free life were in place.

The next big challenge was the food shopping; food was available but supermarkets were non-existent. This created a daily task for Janet of going from little shop to little shop for this, that and the other. Certain things such as rice, flour and sugar were only sold at governmental stores called gameah.

The first time that Janet went to the gameah to buy sugar, rice and flour, she got the shock of her life. When she entered she saw two lines, one very long, one very short. Not un-naturally she joined the shorter one. As she stood in line there a woman in the longer line looked at her sternly and beckoned her to move to the longer line. Janet paid no heed but the woman kept waving to her and soon more women joined in, waving their arms and getting distinctly heated about it. Janet kept ignoring them. Eventually two huge women in their black overall dress came one on each side of Janet and, without further ado, physically lifted her up and carried her over to the other line. Only then did Janet understand that she had been standing in the men's line.

The rule was that at the counter three men were served to one woman. Three men, one woman, three men, one woman ... and so on. What a cultural shock that was for an English woman who had lived most of her adult life up 'til then in the US. There, before the womens' lib fad, it was always the women who would be served first, who would have the doors opened for them and who would have the chairs pulled up for them in a restaurant. Now she had to adapt to a new reality, at least outside of the home, this was a *real* man's world. She broke down in tears to the scorn and laughter of all the women in the line who believed that Janet was being disrespectful to the superior gender by standing in their line.

Janet was and still is the best driver in the family. Driving the new Volvo through the streets of Sakkara for her had become second nature. Soon she ventured into the inner parts of the city looking for little hidden away shops where to buy the most interesting items. She found an old master making mashrabella, the finely carved furniture typical of the Islamic world and ordered a living room hexagonal coffee table and two side tables. She also became an expert at navigating the Khan-el-Kalili market where she found all the spices and the best jewelers still making all their pieces by hand.

In one real gem of a shop, the original founder and two elder brothers had gone to Florence at an early age and learned their craft from a master goldsmith there before returning to Sakkara to open their business in the market. They crafted amazingly delicate work with twenty-four karat gold. Janet couldn't resist and bought me the most beautiful pair of cufflinks I have ever owned. One day Paul will be the proud owner of them. She also had her eye on a magnificent bracelet so, on her next birthday, I bought it for her. It was so cheap compared to the prices in the west and of far superior workmanship.

Summer was now approaching and the children were on their summer holiday. I couldn't take leave for vacation as we were now advancing towards the opening. Janet, Emily and Paul however left for Centonara to spend some times away from the tremendous desert heat to which we were not accustomed. At the beginning of July the entire management team moved into the hotel as the first section that became ready were the offices. It was towards the end of Ramadan. By that time devout Muslims are tired of the so-called fast which actually does allow eating and drinking but not during the day. So they stay up late for the suhur (dinner before sunrise) and getting up for prayers at sunrise. Tempers tended to run short at this time. People were very quarrelsome and would burst into heated arguments and fights for no reason other than that they were worn out. As we packed up our office furniture and equipment for the donkey cart to come and move them, Jasmine fainted. This was a problem because she was the only woman in our office and Muslims considered it improper for men to touch her, even with the good intention of helping her. She herself would also not want to accept even a drink of water as that was considered a sin.

As an aside, menstruating women are permitted to eat and drink in daylight hours during Ramadan but must then make up for the days missed by fasting at a later date before the next Ramadan. However, most women will not take advantage of this because they feel embarrassed. It is very harsh on them but so is Islam in general. The brutal practice of female circumcision of young girls, while outlawed, is still common today throughout the Islamic world. Old women perform the mutilation using just an old razor blade.

Finally the move was completed and we were settling into our new offices albeit with the smell of recently laid moquette and the fumes emanating from the glue. Now was the time for the major task of taking in the equipment that had arrived for the opening of the hotel and which was stored all over the city. Because the ballroom was the largest open space in the hotel it was separated by areas and all the containers and packing items were brought there. The ballroom had been one of the first places to be completed specifically to accommodate this function.

So, after the carpet was laid, it was completely covered by sheets of plywood professionally installed. A team of people was assembled and a captain was appointed to take responsibility for the proper reception and invoicing of all the materials to their proper area. This proved to be a difficult mission in Sakkara as the hotel had been under construction for seven years and the hotel's needs had been determined by people back in Washington DC who had never even been to Sakkara. In the event Yako El Mattum, assistant director of finance, and I, were appointed joint captains.

As we started our task, it soon became apparent that the ballroom was too small to accomodate all the goods arriving.

As a consequence, as the donkey carts arrived, we received boxes that had been stored for seven years under the most primitive of conditions. Most of them had been torn open and there was no way of knowing what contents had disappeared. Even so, there still wasn't sufficient room for everything to be housed in the ballroom so we improvised places all over the hotel. We specifically commandeered the staff canteen to store this huge quantity of 'stuff'. One result of the shambles was that I became the proud owner of thirty six thousand unwanted and surplus to requirement water glasses.

When all was done and every area had received what we believed belonged to them we were opening the hotel. This was October the 16th of 1982. Emily and Paul had returned to school. I was busy with the hotel opening. Janet had made friends with Juergen's wife Michelle who, as a good Dutch woman, was making pearl jewelry in their nineteenth floor apartment to sell at ladies' luncheons.

EQUESTRIAN GAMES

By that time we also had started horse-back riding at the Giza pyramids every Saturday morning. I had switched my day off to Saturday so my Muslim department heads could be off on Fridays to go to the mosque. I preferred that too as the children were off from school Friday and Saturday and we had a day to spend with family and friends. The group spending Saturday together was usually us four, Nagla and Nimani, Jasmine, Ismail and Jacqueline and anyone else who would join in. Janet had been riding before but the children and I had never done it. Now at age forty it was my turn to learn.

Nagla owned a beautiful horse which was housed in a stable and well looked after by an old and very kind groom. This old gentleman had never been outside of the pyramids area in his life. Yet he spoke perfect Queen's English which he had learned during the British colonial days when teaching English children how to ride. We were now advancing from the tourist pastime of riding camels to being real riders of magnificent pure blood Arabian horses.

Janet knew how to ride and Emily and Paul learned quickly under the tutelage of patient Said. I struggled along and eventually got the hang of it. Whereas Janet and the kids could ride and control strong horses, I was always asking for a meek and mild tempered one. Usually I got to ride a very nice mare who treated me well and seemed to know I wasn't an expert rider. She would take over and get me around in the desert for about an hour and finally bring me back to the stable were I could dismount without being thrown from the saddle.

One Saturday I got courageous and asked for a more powerful horse and disregarded Said's advice not to do that. So he gave me a stallion. Man oh man! That was an adventure that could have ended much worse than it did. As we were all in line crossing a dune, my stallion decided that he had had enough of this amateur on his back. He broke line and galloped off at full speed across the desert. I was petrified. Then after what felt like an eternity of blind terror, the stallion decided it was time for him to be rid of me and proceeded to catapult me off his back right on to a big heap of fresh horse manure. That however proved to be a good lesson in horsemanship for me. Just as a child who falls off their bike should do, I got straight back in the saddle and rode off again at full speed as if nothing had happened. Now I was a qualified jockey.

After the ride it was a choice just which hotel pool to go to – the Hotel Meridien, the Mena House Oberoi, the Club Med or the Sheraton Heliopolis. We would have lunch consisting of mezzah (a selection of Egyptian food), drinks and tea. Swimming, or at least being in the water, lying in the sun, laughing and pushing each other into the pool was common practice. This, without any doubt, was the best group of people ever put together.

Janet, Emily and Paul's horsemanship was so good that it was time to make our rides more challenging. One of the longest rides, which made it more rewarding, was to ride from the Giza pyramids to the Sakkara pyramid at least once per month. This meant getting up at 4.00 am and getting everyone ready and to the stable by 5.00 am when we left Giza for the three hour ride.

We arrived at our destination at 8.00 am. We all sat on the still cool sand and had our picnic breakfast which I had carried in a backpack. This took an hour also with the intention to rest our legs and more so our bottoms. By 9.00 am we were ready to remount for our ride to Giza before noon. One of the rules there was that only 'mad dogs and Englishmen go out in the mid-day sun'. That was the real truth as to be out in the sun at mid-day in the Sahara is probably one of the things that only the two above mentioned subjects would be daft enough to undertake.

Now, after a six hour horseback ride, the lower spine, the buttocks and the legs had become numb and walking painful to impossible. I, more than all the other more experienced rider, felt like one of those heroes in old cowboy movies who had become bow legged from spending so much time on the horse. But what an experience this was ... enjoying breakfast with the people I cared the most for in the world in the shade of the King Djoser step pyramid built between 2,667 and 2648 BC was one of the greatest experiences one could ever enjoy in life.

My first year in Egypt was coming to an end and the Zamalek Tower which would house all the expat executives was nearing completion. Juergen, Michelle, son Bram and daughter Aya were in a gigantic apartment on top of the tower which had a beautiful view of the Nile and the city. Because they were so high up they had less dust coming in and day long sunshine. We were allocated an apartment on the nineteenth floor which had a small kitchen with a small refrigerator, a two-burner electric stove, dish washer and small counter top. There was a living-room and three bedrooms and it was located in the inside of the hotel overlooking the gardens and pool. We also had a nice view of the Sakkara tower from our balcony but this was short lived. On his next visit, Marshal Dunant, the regional vice president told Juergen to keep the top apartments for paying customers. As a result we were moved down to the fifteenth floor. The apartment and everything was identical to as before except the view of the Sakkara tower had gone.

Moving into the hotel meant that we could now get all our basic food from the hotel kitchen. This ended the need for Janet to have to stand in line at the gameah to buy sugar, flour and rice or to have to trek from little store to little store for the other supplies. Now she only had to fill out an order and have me pass it to the chef for delivery to our door by room service two hours later. Payment was deducted from my salary each month. This afforded Janet more time to socialize, explore the surroundings and especially old Sakkara. She was so 'local' by now that she would stop in the streets to buy a 5 piastras (3 cents) tamiya sandwich for lunch from a local vendor. No foreigner would do that and get away without what was known as the Pharoah's revenge, meaning a nasty dose of diarrhea. Janet never got it once in all the years we spent there. As she ventured more into the little streets with the car, the more adventures she encountered.

One that she will never forget was the time that she parked the car in the street and went to explore by foot around the area and the little shops. Arriving back at the car she discovered that she couldn't move it. The army had dug a deep trench behind it as there was (yet again) a burst water pipe. She was desperate to get home as the children were due back from school. Then, as she was wondering what to do next, the officer in charge yelled some orders to the soldiers. A bunch of them lifted the heavy Volvo over the trench by hand and deposited it on the other side!

A HOTEL AWAKENS

At work I had accumulated some skills which were to prove invaluable to me when I became a general manager later in my career. Juergen did not like to meet VIPs coming to the hotel. While he was very handsome, tall and well groomed, he considered famous people to be a nuisance and did not care for them. To him they were just a burden. When Prince Charles of the United

Kingdom came he asked Nimani and I to be the welcoming party. Later, when the then famous singer Dalida came he asked me to receive her too. I welcomed the latter with an enormous bunch of red roses. I still have a photo of me giving her the flowers and receiving two kisses on my cheeks from her as reward. Sadly, and not as far as I know as any consequence of that meeting, she committed suicide years later.

As part of my work I was also involved in organising a monthly get-together with the other five star directors of food and beverage. This was an informal meeting over a beer to share experiences and learn of what new rules the bureaucratic Egyptian government had come up with. One day the food and beverage director of the Nile Notlih told us that all of the knobs on their kitchen stoves were always broken but they couldn't figure out why. He decided to hide in the kitchen early in the morning when the stoves had to be turned on. What he saw was the cook arrive, take a wrench from his pocket and, instead of simply pushing in the knobs and turning them to light the stoves, forced each knob around until it broke.

At my hotel we also had some funny things happening. A lot of our stoves were electric and the cooking plates were always cracked. We couldn't find out the cause of that problem. Following my colleague's advice, I too went to the kitchen early in the morning but I found nothing untoward until I made another visit at midnight. Then I discovered that the cleaning crew had figured out an easier way to clean the cooking plates than the usual scraping of them with steel wool. They had worked out that by turning the plates on to full blast until they were red hot and tossing a bucket of cold water over them, all the dirt would loosen up and all they needed to do was to was to pick it up. That sure was easier. Who says that people who can hardly read or write are not clever? But we were lucky that no one ever got electrocuted. Not in that way at least .....

One of the most dramatic experiences at the hotel was the death of a twenty-five year old houseman. While all the maids were women, the housemen were the ones who carried out the heavy physical work. Constanza Kurtz, the much loathed German director of services, forgot one morning to turn off the water tap in her bathtub in her apartment in the hotel tower. A few hours later water was seen pouring out of the apartment's door into the corridor. From the balcony facing the garden it was running like a Nile water fall and was filtering down into the floors below. The alarm was activated and the housekeeping team swung into action.

The young houseman took a wet vac and ran to the apartment where by now the water was quite deep. He set it down in the water and, metal extractor hose in hand, plugged it into an electricity socket. The shock catapulted him across the room and turned him to charcoal in a fraction of a second. The incident created great distress throughout the hotel. Following the local culture, wailing by the staff started immediately. They considered the already disliked Constanza to be a murderer for forgetting to turn off the water in the bathtub. This was the worst accident I witnessed during my time at the hotel. There were others, such as knife cuts in the kitchen, but no one else ever got killed. Thank you Lord.

ALEXANDRIA

During our time in Sakkara we enjoyed some fantastic excursions. The resort city of Alexandria by the Mediterranean Sea became a regular day outing, sometimes two days. Usually the same group went and, if staying over, we would all stay at the Sheraton Montazah which at the time was the best hotel in the city. It was just one minute from the beach and just a short walk from the Montazah gardens and Palace which was the summer residence of the former King Farouk. Trips to lake El-Fayoum, an oasis in the middle of the Sahara desert just 43 miles (70 km) from Sakkara, were also frequent.

When Janet's father came to visit we had lunch in a restaurant on its shores. I ate so-called Saint Peter's fish. I didn't realize that it was not cleaned out and that it was grilled with all the intestines still inside. Before I realised, I had eaten a whole mouthful of fish intestines and excrement - not an experience I wish on anyone. The rowing boats were great fun. Janet's father had had one when she was a child and this meant that he and Janet were two excellent boat people and skilled at navigating. The five of us would rent one and go around the lake enjoying the scenery and each other's company.

THE HOLY LAND

One of the nicest trips was to the Holy Land. As Egypt and Israel had signed a peace treaty there were direct flights between Sakkara and Tel Aviv. It was really easy to reach, only 251 miles (402 km), less than an hour by plane. We took a seven day vacation during the week of Passover, stopping first in Tel Aviv. There we rented a car and drove to Nazareth and the Sea of Galilee, Haifa and Caesarea.

At Netanya we visited a diamonds factory where Janet designed two rings, one each for me and for her. We had to trust the owners that the finished articles would look like the drawing Janet had made, paid for them and left. The next day we were leaving for Jerusalem and the rings were to be delivered in three days to the Ramada Hotel where we would be staying. The hotel was large and below expectations but was nevertheless comfortable.

Here we joined guided tours to visit all the sites where Jesus had supposedly been. I say 'supposedly' because there is no certainty that the places referred to in the Holy Bible are the same places but that point is not really relevant. What is relevant is the feeling that more than 2,000 years ago Jesus stepped on those same stones of the Via Crucis on His way to Calvary; that somewhere in that town Jesus had shared with His disciples his last supper; that somewhere in that town Jesus had been crucified and died and that somewhere in that town He was buried and came back from death. I found all of this mystery was just overwhelming. I could feel His presence.

To start from the beginning we went first to the Church of the Nativity in Bethlehem. Also this is 'supposedly' the right place but it really didn't matter. From the humble stable in which Jesus was born to the cathedral now sitting on top of it there really is no comparison, nevertheless I could feel His presence. There were what felt like millions of people from all around the world there. People of all faiths, races and backgrounds, Jews, Muslims and Christians. All seemed to get along and behave with respect to each other and their beliefs. There were no fights and no discourteous behaviour between them and back in Jerusalem it was the same among the visitors.

What was scary and horrifying was to witness the continuous pelting with stones by Palestinian youths of any Israeli military or police vehicle going by. The Israelis did not take it lightly and shot back with rubber bullets. It was the anniversary of the attempted terrorist attack on the Dome of the Rock, the holiest Muslim site in all of the Holy Land. This action by a Jewish extremist group had already escalated the tension between the two factions. Every Israeli, male or female of military age, even if not serving in the army, was carrying a gun while walking in the streets. For us it was unusual and rather unnerving to see.

We discovered a small Palestinian run restaurant called the White Horse and serving excellent Middle East food just inside the city walls. The clientele was mostly Christian monks who came from all over the world and had one thing in common, a love of good food. As we continued our touring we wanted to walk up to the Golgotha by way of the Via Dolorosa but, as we went up, an enormous crowd started to press towards us. It became seriously frightening as panic set in and the start of a stampede seemed imminent. I found myself fighting to get to the side of the narrow street but was making no progress ... one step forward, two steps back ... until finally, gathering all my strength, I made it to the side and into a doorway. I pulled Janet and the kids in behind me. There we were safe and out of the way of the crowd. By now the descending mass had gained so much impetus that people were falling over and being trampled. After a while, the danger subsided and we continued the ascent to the top of Gethsemani.

This was the place where Jesus and the two thieves were

crucified. The tour guide explained that, under Roman law, crucifixion was the way by which criminals were dealt with. In order to ensure that the condemned individual did not die too quickly by bleeding to death from the wounds inflicted when being nailed to the stake, the nails were heated until red hot before being hammered into their wrists. Also, contrary to all the images we see of Jesus on a cross, victims were crucified totally naked. This meant that, as the body lost the strength to retain urine and excrements, these were let go to the delight of the spectators.

The old temple wall also provided the dramatic scene, and sound, of hundreds of Orthodox Jews (all male) with their braided hair and string belts, bowing and praying before it. The cracks in the millennial wall were filled with little pieces of paper with prayer requests. It was a very emotional moment to see so much faith - or is it fanaticism?

Not far from there, at Muslim prayer time, there were in every corner men prostrated on their knees and pushing their foreheads into the dirt in order to secure a black mark on it. This was to show that they were devout Muslims who prayed the regulation five times a day. Once in a while they would lift their heads up to make sure that, just as the Jews were doing, people were looking at them and witnessing their devotions. All this while the mohazzin were reciting prayers from hundreds of minarets.

This brought back to me childhood memories of home and of mamma. She was the leader in the house in almost everything, especially religion. My dad would go to Mass on Sunday only when this did not interfere with his fishing for trout in the rivers or with his picking of mushrooms in the wood. Mamma on the other hand would never miss Sunday Mass, attending devoutly with my sister and I, both dressed in our Sunday best.

As distances from one place to another in Israel are very short, we took a trip on public transportation to Hebron. This is in the middle of the occupied territory of what would be Palestine should the 'two state solution' ever become reality. This small town is known for its beautiful blown glass work. As we walked the narrow street taking in the music, the smell of the food and shopping for a glass of mint tea we admired the fine glass objects on display on the tables at the side of the road. Janet fell in love with a cute flower vase and bought it. We also visited Beersheba with its well of the oath or well of seven, reputedly dug by Abraham. This is the fourth largest town in Israel with about 200,000 inhabitants and known as the capital of the Negev desert.

Retuning to Jerusalem and the Ramada Hotel, we found our rings delivered as had been promised by the diamond factory. They were exactly as Janet had designed them and they looked very beautiful. We wore them for many years until, with our advancing age, they became too small to wear. We were now coming to the end of our vacation in the Holy Land but there was one thing left for us to do.

Ever since I had started working in hotels at the age of fifteen I had been fascinated by hotel brochures. In Rome I would make a point of going into the lobbies of all the good hotels to find brochures of hotels from all over the world and collect them. I would spend hours looking at them and dream about visiting them and maybe working in them one day. One of these brochures which I'd collected was from the King David Hotel, in Jerusalem. Now, all these years later, we were actually in Jerusalem and presented with what might well be my only opportunity to see it and even have lunch there. On our last day in Jerusalem, we did just that.

I had told Janet, Emily and Paul all about this great hotel, its history and about all the famous celebrities and statesmen who stayed there. I built the expectation so high that I was fervently hoping it would live up to my hype. As we arrived there, my hopes sagged. I detected a distinct lack of kerb appeal. It was actually quite a run-down building from the outside and my expectations sunk even lower when we entered the lobby and saw that it was very old and badly maintained. The curtains were hanging loose, the marble floor was dull and the windows dirty. In the dining-room we were received by a surly young Palestinian. An equally sour-faced young Israeli waiter took our order. The white table cloth and napkins were stained and more yellow than white and the glamourous silver cutlery settings I had expected were but ordinary stainless steel. But we were there and I kept trying to build it up.

We ordered the meal. When the meal came I asked the waiter for a glass of milk for Emily and Paul. He refused to serve it because it was Passover. I explained that the children were Christians and not Orthodox Jews. That didn't work. I begged, I cajoled, but no joy. By that time I was at the end of my tether. I had a really tough time remaining calm, civilized and not doing or saying anything in front of my children which I would regret later. This was the last straw. All my great expectations were gone. I was really feeling bad but the children and Janet didn't seem to be overly concerned with the experience. The next day we were taken the 37 miles (60 km) to Tel Aviv Airport and flew back to Sakkara.

THE ISLAND OF APHRODITE

Things quickly returned to normal. Work for me, school for Emily and Paul, lots of exploring and socialising for Janet, our Saturday horseback outings and luxurious swim pool lunches and parties. Our next trip, this time to Cyprus, soon came around. The short flight to Larnaka took us there in no time. My first impression was of a rather desolate landscape and rough people but I soon started to see the beauty of the place. The sea was a magnificent, clear turquoise colour and, contrary to the polluted air of Sakkara which turned the sunsets greyish, the sky was truly blue.

The ride from the airport to Limassol took fifty minutes along the sea front. Here is where I started to see why people who had been there before had so many nice things to say about the place. From thereon the holiday became a continuous adventure absorbing the beauty, history and legend of the island. Archaeological evidence has demonstrated that Cyprus has been inhabited since prehistory. The Neolithic (8200-3800 BC) and Chalcolithic people (3800-2400 BC) left behind remnants of their everyday lives which includes simple single-room huts, stone tools and pottery. Cyprus is a real treat for lovers of archaeology.

Our hotel wasn't anything too glamorous but comfortable. Anyway we didn't plan to spend a great deal of time in it. Having settled into our rooms, off we went to explore the town. Limassol is pretty, set on the sea-shore and is the business capital of Cyprus. The many international companies doing business there enjoyed big tax breaks which brought people from all over the world into this city and its mild Mediterranean climate.

The modern sea front areas had wide, clean avenues in contrast to the old, back alleys of the inner town. These fairly bustled with the noise, shouting and frantic activity of street vendors selling anything and everything under the sun. I loved the smell of the fresh gyros roasting and of the tea brewing every few yards on the sidewalks. Old men sat in cafés on the squares playing cards or dominos. They were drinking wine or the Greek liquor ouzo which is like French Pernod in taste and character. It is made from aniseed and changes colour from clear to cloudy when water is added. I felt very much alive there.

The next morning we took off on the forty minute drive to Paphos. This is, according to mythology, the home of Aphrodite, the Greek goddess of love, beauty, pleasures and a few other things besides. Homer, in his book Odyssey, mentions Aphrodite's secret precinct in Paphos with an altar fragrant with incense, where she went to be bathed, anointed with immortal oil and clothed in lovely garments by graces. There are many legends around this mystic figure and the Romans adopted her too. They changed her name to Venus. Our next visit entailed making the two hour drive to Nicosia, the capital city of Cyprus. We took the slower and more scenic route through the middle of the country where the vista was very different from the seaside areas we had visited thus far. The terrain was rough with peaks and valleys and cattle, goats and sheep grazing everywhere. We stopped at a small café full of locals and enjoyed the wonderful experience of a rustic breakfast of goat and sheep cheese, olives and local bread washed down by strong Turkish coffee.

On July the 20th, 1974, the Turkish army invaded Cyprus helped by the US in the background. This followed the coup d'etat which had taken place on July the 15th. As a consequence of that act of aggression the island is still divided into two countries today with the northern part of the country under Turkish control. In this part of the island the majority of the population is made up of Turkish Cypriots and Turkish is the official language.

The southern part of the island is an independent country, part of the fragile European Union. Here the population is made up of Greek Cypriots and Greek is the official language. The dividing line cuts through the centre of the city of Nicosia and this point is a UN controlled demilitarized zone. Janet, Emily, Paul and myself wanted to live the experience of walking through the 'green line', the buffer zone patrolled by the UN forces. This was hairy to say the least. It is a narrow street where pedestrians can walk. On the north side the Turkish military point their guns over your head at the Greek army who, likewise, point their guns over your head at the Turkish army. All this happens while jeeps, loaded with yawning UN soldiers, drive up and down the alley totally indifferent as to what their mission is.

One must remember that as of today Nicosia is the only world's capital still divided. There have been attempts at reconciliation with elections held on both sides of the island in 2004. The results were not promising. Sixty-five percent of the voters in the Turkish controlled area voted against a united Cyprus and seventy-five percent of the Republic of Cyprus voters voted against a one country solution. This clearly means that we will not see a united Cyprus any time soon. Even back then the Greek part of Nicosia was very westernised with foreign investment, malls and hotels everywhere; the city was alive and busy. It reminded me so much of my times in Berlin, almost twenty years earlier. There one could see the squalor of East Berlin and witness the true face of communism from the high viewing points erected on the west side of the wall. It was our last day in Cyprus and we wanted Nicosia to be our lasting memory of the place, especially for Emily and Paul, so as to see and realise the evil that man is capable of. The next day we flew back to Sakkara. That city, even with all the noise and pollution, seemed like a veritable heaven after having seen what real depression is like for some.

Our routine activities resumed as before but at work it was time for me to come up with a new concept for the food and beverage area. From the balcony of the apartment I could see that the number of people, hotel guests and Egyptians, walking in the garden was really huge. The idea came to me in a flash ... Why not build a café on this very wide sidewalk? After brainstorming with the team, the idea became concrete. The Promenade Café was born! Getting down to the planning was a lot of fun. Engineering helped to design the bar and the necessary outdoors tables and chairs were purchased. The required staff were hired and trained. In no time at all, we had the largest outdoor café in the Marriott system. It was real fun to see how successful it quickly became.

Arabs in their garb, scratching their toes, would lounge contentedly drinking for hours on end; while western business people would sit there doing business with their Egyptian and Arab counterparts. And tourists of all nationalities would stop for a cool Stella beer following a long, hot day in the sun taking in the beauty and the exhilarating sites Sakkara and its surrounds had to offer (this last included a good deal of Sahara sand which our cleaners cleared by the bucket load each day). My whole team, cleaners and all, were mighty proud of our achievement. Even Juergen, normally very short on praises, was delighted with the results and said so in public many times.

ATHENS

Our last trip outside of Egypt to Athens and to Jordan came a short time afterwards at New Year. On Hogmanay the hotel was a seething hive of activity with the restaurants full, the night club packed, the ballroom heaving with more than eight hundred guests and music, dancing, eating and drinking in full swing everywhere. We were also in the ballroom celebrating with other members of the executive committee. All worked out well and it was 5.00 am on the 1st when I finally went up to the apartment. Janet and the children were already prepared to go off on our trip. After a quick shower and change of clothes I was ready too. Off we went to the airport for the short flight from Sakkara to Athens and to the Ledra Marriott Hotel. We found Athens to be an attractive city with all white buildings, mostly excellently kept. Even then the city was very polluted although, coming from Sakkara, that was no big deal.

As countless others had found before, and no doubt have since, there are so many historical sites of antiquity and places of interest to be seen in Athens and its surrounds that it's impossible to see and do everything in the allotted time ... so we started with a visit to a pizza restaurant just behind the hotel. Next up was the Acropolis and the Parthenon. The Acropolis is an ancient citadel located on an extremely rocky outcrop above the city of Athens. It contains the remains of several ancient buildings of great architectural and historical significance, the most famous being the Parthenon.

Construction of the Parthenon, a temple dedicated to the goddess Athena, began in 447 BC. There is much controversy about the original site and what came after this original one was supposedly burned down by the Persians during their occupation. But what is left of it, is sure worth a visit. Its foundations are carved out of lime stone and its columns are marble. The primary reason for the building of this temple was to house the monumental gold and ivory statue of Athena. The temple and the chryselephantine statue were dedicated in 438 BC and work on the sculpture continued until completion in 432 BC.

To have a good grasp of what Athens has to offer to historians would take months, if not years, to explore and study. The Greeks were just such an advanced civilisation those thousands of years ago. It is shocking to compare those glory days with what is happening now, not only in Greece but with other bygone civilizations such as those of Rome and Egypt. All of these are now practically bankrupt, poor economically and socially struggling to survive. More recently we have seen the same occurring with the

British Empire which begs the question as to what will happen when the power houses of the USA, Russia and China go the same way?

With the time we had available to see and to explore we had to make some serious decision on what not to miss. We decided that Delphi, a three hour drive north-west of Athens, was a must see. It houses the temple of Apollo, the ancient theatre, the stadium and the sanctuary of Athena Pronaia with Tholos, the Kastalia spring and the treasures that adorn the sacred way. The archaeological museum on the site contains many important ancient Greek artifacts from the excavations at Delphi. One of the most interesting historical facts is that it is here that the Olympic games were born. At the origin of the games only men participated with the athletes performing naked. All and any wars being fought at the time of the games were suspended during competition and only resumed once the games were over. Not a bad idea. We returned to our hotel late that evening, exhausted but happy to have been able to take in so much history and culture in a day.

The next day was Sunday and we wanted to go to church to attend a service. This naturally had to be a Greek Orthodox church of which there was one at walking distance from the hotel. The Greek churches are extravagantly adorned. Unlike their Russian counterparts, they have pews. We sat on a pew near the aisle. Janet on the outside, then Emily, then Paul and with me in the inside. The aroma of incense washed over us. As the service started we were sitting down, following what the other people were doing as we couldn't understand what the priest was saying up in front.

At one point during the service Janet crossed her legs. One elderly lady from across the aisle, dressed in the traditional all black of latin European countries, became rather agitated and motioned to Janet. Just as the time in Egypt at the gameah, Janet didn't pay any attention to her. A few minutes passed and the woman kept making signs but Janet continued to ignore her.

Eventually the woman couldn't contain herself. She jumped off her seat, bolted across the aisle, grabbed Janet's leg that was crossed over the other, pulled it forcibly to the floor and scolded Janet in such a loud voice that all the people in the church turned around to see what was happening. Janet's face went red with embarrassment. She indignantly jumped to her feet and strode out of the church. Naturally, I and the children followed. This was our adventure in trying to attend a Greek Orthodox church service.

JORDAN

Shortly afterwards it was time to leave Athens to fly to Amman in Jordan. When we arrived at the airport in Amman we proceeded to the passport control before picking up our luggage. The first officer to look at our passports returned them to us and waved us through. As we arrived at the next group of officers we had to show our passports again. Here the officers looked at them and passed them from one to another in a very agitated way. After what seemed like an eternity one of them motioned to me to follow him. I was puzzled but certainly was not going to argue. We went through a labyrinth of corridors packed with officers smoking cigarettes, people shouting and children crying. It was depressing to say the least.

Finally we reached an office and there, sitting at an enormous desk full to capacity with files, was the moudir kibir (the big boss). He must have been important given the large number of officers running around him, bowing and scraping, bringing him Turkish coffee and lighting his never ending chain of cigarettes. His head was down looking at some papers and he never lifted it as he spoke through an interpreter. Now I was told that the problem with our passports was that we had been to Israel the previous year and that any person who had an Israelis stamp on their passport could not visit an Arab country.

This was a complicated matter as we travelled with passports from different countries. Janet's was British, Emily's and Paul's were American and mine Italian. The moudir kibir informed me that under no circumstances were we going to be allowed to enter Jordan. After very patiently explaining to him that we lived in Egypt, a friendly Arab country, and were learning more about

Islam and visited Jerusalem to see the Dome of the Rock he seemed to relax and made me an offer I could not refuse.

He gave me the choice between being put on to the next flight and leaving the country or keeping my passport and returning the other three to me. The action I needed to take was the following : That very day we would have to go to the American Embassy in Amman and get new passports for Emily and Paul and also go to the British Embassy and get Janet's passport exchanged. I was then required to return to the airport with the three new passports at which point he would return mine to me to do the same at the Italian Embassy the next day.

In the meantime Janet, Emily and Paul were worried sick that I had been taken prisoner or worse. Haile Aguilar, the general manager of the Marriott, where we were going to stay, had come to pick us up but had left the airport thinking that we had missed our flight. So I accepted the offer and left the airport without my passport but with the intention of making all this happen in the shortest possible time. Finally we reached the hotel and, after explaining to Haile what had happed, we set off on our tour of the embassies. At both embassies we found out that ours was a routine situation and immediately the passports were replaced.

Returning to the airport I was again escorted to the moudir kibir who returned my passport, stamped the other three and kept them until I would return with my new passport the next day. At last we returned to the hotel after a completely wasted first day in Jordan. Haile and his wife Teresita were brilliant hosts and made us feel very welcome. We enjoyed a relaxing swim in the hotel pool, then a lavish dinner with Haile and Teresita before we crashed totally exhausted into our good Marriott beds.

The next morning, armed with my passport, I set off for the Italian embassy to complete the same task for me as for the others. Only to find upon arrival that the embassy was closed for some kind of Italian holiday. This was particularly annoying as we were scheduled to travel to Petra that day where we had a reservation at the Forum Hotel. Needless to say how disappointed everyone was when I returned to the hotel and told them of the forced change of plans. Haile was very sympathetic and understanding as he had experienced the same situation previously with other friends visiting the city.

In Amman, like so many places in the Middle East, there are a host of beautiful sites to be explored. There is the citadel where the remains of the Roman temple of Hercules are to be found and the eighth century Umayyad Palace complex, known for its grand dome. Then there's the six thousand seat Roman theatre built in the second century and still the site of present day musical shows and plays.

That same afternoon Haile drove us in his Mercedes to Jerash, the Roman city built in 2000 BC and beautifully maintained so that you can fully appreciate the magnitude of the task undertaken in its construction. The main colonnade avenue, the Oval Forum, the Jerash Nymphaeum, the south theatre and Hadrians Arch at the entrance of Jerash, just to name a few, are the most impressive Roman ruins I have ever seen. It's always hard to believe that anything like these could be built by human hands so many thousands of years ago. What a marvel. With Haile there were always two priorities. One was great automobiles and the other was great food and excellent wines. Today was no exception. After a nice glass of tea we returned to the hotel for a short break and clean up before getting ready for dinner in his and Teresita's apartment. As usual the menu was well planned from beginning to end and the wine flowed very nicely but without excess.

The next morning at 5.00 am we drove to Petra in Haile's Mercedes which he had kindly lent us. We were now one day behind on our schedule but decided that that unforeseen delay was not going to spoil our visit. The trip to Petra turned out to be quite an adventure. The drive took us through mostly desert, harsh terrain, hills of reddish stones and scorching heat but we were well equipped with plenty of water and food. Janet loves to drive whenever possible so she drove and I planned the route, read the maps and played the navigator. We had decided to take the shorter route on the way there so as to take the longer one on the way back via the Dead Sea to stop for a swim. We didn't get lost on the way there and after three hours arrived at the Forum Hotel, checked in and enjoyed a delightful breakfast as it was only gone 8.00 am.

Now it was time to explore Petra, originally known to the Nabataeans as Raqmu and also known as Rose City due to the colour of the stone out of which it is carved The city is famous for its rock-cut architecture and water conduit system. It was established possibly as early as 312 BC as the capital of the Arab Nabataens. It is a symbol of Jordan and is its most visited tourist attraction.

A short ride from the hotel took us to the parking lot where we left the car. From there we rode on horseback through the narrow Al Siq canyon cut out in the rocks to reach the splendour of the pièce-de-résistance of Petra, the Monastery. It is a site not to be missed in a lifetime. Carved into the sandstone hill by the Nabataeans in the second century AD, this towering structure, called Al Khazneh, with its ornate Greek-style façade, may have been used as a church or monastery by later societies, but likely began life as a temple. This is just one of the marvelous carved constructions there. Living quarters and tombs are all carved into the rose colour rocks high up on steep, almost vertical rock faces. From there the day continued with a barrage of non-stop revelations of more and more archaeological treasures, each more amazing than the last. By four in the afternoon, we were completely 'wonders of the world bedazzled' – and exhausted. We remounted our waiting horses and hacked back through the canyon to our car.

Back at the hotel we made a point of meeting the general manager, always a good professional courtesy. He was a very congenial, young Englishman who told us with some excitement about a trip to the top of the mountain the next day. We booked the mule and donkey ride up the twisting paths with the climax of a champagne lunch in the 'Cave in the Sky' as the fitting finale. We asked him how on earth he could get the chilled champagne up there, to which he ecstatically replied, "Where a donkey can go so too can champagne!"

Quite early next morning and after a robust breakfast we set off with Janet and I on mules and Emily and Paul on donkeys. The general manager accompanied us and the many other guests, guides and servants. After about three hours of climbing through rough terrain and several rock falls we reached the Cave in the Sky. While we were outside taking photos and just admiring the beauty of it all, the guides and the cooks set out rugs on the floor for us to sit on and prepared the lunch. There were probably about a dozen of us there and we were about to experience the eating adventure of a lifetime.

An array of delicacies, seemingly impossible to have been produced on little camping stoves, was served Bedouin style. This involved sitting cross-legged on the plush goat skin and lambs' wool rugs to tuck in to huge platters of lamb stew with rice, salads, vegetables, mezzahs and karkade. While cutlery was provided, the more adventurous in the group attempted to eat in the Arab way of scooping the food up in their fingers. This worked for some but others soon reverted to using spoons, knives and forks. The chilled magnums of champagne kept flowing like rivers as if there would be no more champagne tomorrow. Turkish coffee followed and then we were given a water pipe to smoke whilst leaning back to rest our overloaded stomachs.

After an hour or so of pleasant relaxation, and almost slumber, the staff produced from nowhere the dessert. Platter after platter of Lebanese, Egyptian and Moroccan pastries overflowing with honey were served. This orgy of food lasted all afternoon, it felt almost like a Roman bacchanal. Eventually, as the sun started to set over the distant tips, the mules and donkeys were resaddled to carry their now considerably heavier passengers back to the hotel again. That night the four of us took a shower and opted to skip dinner. Just the thought of more food made us feel quite ill.

The next day was time to say goodbye to Petra and head back to

Amman taking the Jordan valley highway north. After about two hours we spotted the southern tip of the Dead Sea which, bordering Israel, the West Bank and Jordan is the lowest place on earth at 1,410 feet (430 m) below sea level. We had come prepared, with our swimming gear already on, to have a dip in the world's most salty sea. The water was very warm and so dense with minerals and mud that it was impossible, even for a poor swimmer such as I, to sink. Janet, Emily and Paul, who are great swimmers, had a real fun time trying to dive underwater but always being pushed back to the top. It truly was a once in a lifetime experience to bathe in those waters.

A little further up is the Mujib nature reserve which is the lowest nature reserve on earth at 1,344 feet (410 m) below sea level. When we were there this reserve as such did not exist as it received that designation only in 2008. The magnitude of nature, the rocks and waterfalls and the generally breathtaking scenery which makes the reserve one of Jordan's most popular natural attractions was on full view.

Mujib's complex river system and all-year water flow enable it to support a rich biodiversity with over three hundred species of plants, ten species of carnivores and numerous species of resident and migratory birds already identified and recorded. Some mountain and valley areas are difficult to reach, so offer safe havens for rare species of cats, mountain goats and other mountain animals. The wadi Mujib trail which allows trekkers to take in all of these areas has been created since we were there. It's a pity it didn't exist then. By now sunset was approaching. We resumed our journey back to Amman, arriving there tired but overflowing with emotions about what we had lived in the last three days. It was time to pack our cases and head back to Sakkara.

UPPER EGYPT AND ASWAN

Now we were approaching the summer of 1984 and, in spite of the heat we were sure to encounter, we were determined to take a Nile Cruise from Luxor to Aswan before leaving Egypt. The first week in June we flew to Luxor and boarded the Nile Maxim, the

The Cardboard Suitcase

boat which would be our home for the next week. Before sailing to the south, known as Upper Egypt, we visited the Valley of the Kings one day and the valley of the Queens on the next. In the scorching sun the temperature was well over 120°F (45°C) and Paul and I had to wear long sleeves and long trousers. Janet and Emily wore skirts floppy enough to serve as fans.

The Valley of the Kings is the place where for five hundred years, from the 16th to the 11th century BC, tombs were constructed for the Pharaohs and powerful nobles of the 'new kingdom', the eighteenth to the twentieth dynasties of ancient Egypt. The most famous site there is the tomb of Tutankhamun, the child king, but the most impressive to me was the Hatshepsut Temple. This is the tomb of Pharaoh Hatshepsut and considered to be one of the incomparable monuments of ancient Egypt. Even today there is speculation that Hatshepsut was actually a woman.

The following day it was the turn of the Valley of the Queens. This is the place where the wives of the Pharaohs were buried. It is also known as Ta-Set-Neferu meaning the place of beauty. The tomb of Nefertari is one of the most beautifully maintained and nothing short of spectacular. An unforgettable site and sight.

Upon returning to the boat Janet, Emily and Paul made the not uncommon mistake of taking cold drinks to assuage their thirsts (I chose a cup of hot tea). Within half an hour all three of them had to rush to the toilet suffering from severe Pharaoh's revenge, meaning diarrhea. The fact that the three of them had the same problem was made even worse by the fact the occasion required three full time toilets and we only had one in each cabin. This meant that Janet had to stay close to the public one on deck while I stayed with the children in the cabin for a whole night and part of the next day. Fortunately this situation didn't persist and soon everyone was running on full power again.

It was time to sail south towards Aswan. The first stop was Esna but we didn't disembark there to see any of the antiquities. Soon the boat moved on to Edfu and the Ptolemaic Temple of Horus (built between 237 and 57 BC) and the settlement of Tell Edfu.

Although unassuming and unglamorous to the tourists, this settlement is a monument that contains evidence of more Egyptian history and is of more archaeological interest than the Ptolemaic temple.

From there the boat proceeded, against the strong currents of the Nile, to the agricultural town of Kum Umbo famous for its unusual double temple. The southern half of the temple was dedicated to the crocodile god Sobek, god of fertility and creator of the world as well as Hathor and Khonsu. The northern part of the temple was dedicated to the falcon god Haroeris, also known as Horus. It was originally an Egyptian city called Nubt, meaning the city of gold, but became a Greek settlement during the Greco-Roman period. It also boasted a crocodile museum where three hundred mummified crocodiles were on display.

From there we headed to Aswan with no more stops en route and that was just fine with us. By that time we were 'antiquified out'. Much as we enjoyed history we had taken in so much in such a short time that it was hard to absorb never mind remember.

Aswan is one of the most picturesque places I have visited, a place where time stands still. The view from on top of the hill to the blue and white waters and scattered islands of the Nile, with faluccas gliding by and the jasmine and honey scented breeze, combine to create a veritable heaven on earth. Aswan has been southern Egypt's strategic and commercial capital since antiquity. Apart from its natural beauty, it is home to significant archaeological sites such as the Philae temple complex on Agilkia Island.

The Aga Khan spent his winters in the mild climate of Aswan because he suffered from severe arthritis. His mausoleum is set on the bank of the Nile and is built in pink limestone and Carrara marble in the style of the Fatimids tombs. He lived in Aswan with his fourth wife, Begum Om Habibeh Aga Khan, who he married just thirteen months after divorcing his third wife. Begum was born in Sete, France, on February 15th, 1906 and became Miss France in 1930. She died in Le Cannet, France, on July the 1st of 2000 at age ninety-four and is buried in the mausoleum in Aswan with her beloved husband.

As we were so close we couldn't miss a visit to Abu Simbel. We were quite tired at that point as the dry air and the heat had drained our energy so the decision to take a forty-five minute flight there in a light aircraft, rather than an eight hour round trip by bus, was an easy one to make. There are two principal treasures of antiquity in Abu Simbel that every person in the world should see. They are the Big Temple dedicated to Ramses II and the Small Temple which is dedicated to his wife, Nefertari. Both temples were completed in approximately 1264 BC, after taking twenty years to build.

Ramses II dedicated the Big temple to the sun god, Ra, and to himself. Gigantic statues of Ramses II guard the entrance. The Small temple is no less impressive and the dedication text on one of the buttresses reads, "A temple of great and mighty monuments for the great royal wife Nefertari Meryetmut for whose sake the very sun shines giving life and love." The two colossal standing statues of Nefertari in front of the small temple are equal in size to those of Ramses II. She is shown holding a sistrum, she wears a long sheet dress and is depicted with a long wig, Hathoric cow horns, the solar disk and a toll feather mounted on a modius.

Besides being really colossal it is extraordinary that the statues of Ramses and Nefertari, and indeed both the entire temples were, stone by stone, removed from their original location to where they stand proud today. This was because of the construction of the Aswan Dam. Among many challenges faced by the team of engineers working on the dam project was the one to find the right spot to set the temples and their guardian statues as the sun had to shine through the entrance to illuminate the gods at sunrise. But between 1964 and 1968 this monumental work was accomplished (and twenty months ahead of schedule) to the universal acclaim of all the world who wanted to save these temples and not have them disappear under the waters of the dam.

For us it was a very exciting day to behold this extraordinary three thousand plus years of history and try to understand how life was for people living then. What conclusions could we draw? Were they very different from us today? Were they better or worse people? What motivated them to excel in what they were doing? It seemed to me that they had the same passions, the same desires and ambitions as we have today - the need for recognition, the need for admiration and, most of all, the need for love. And so this most memorable of trips drew to an end and on the following day we flew back to Sakkara and to our familiar routine.

FINAL DRAMA

Janet and I were in the final stage of planning Emily and Paul's summer camp in northern Italy. We settled for a children's colony in Valle d'Aosta, Gressoney, because the camps there had a reputation for being well organized, clean and with a Christian approach. Also the distance from Centonara, where my sister Anna lived, was relatively short.

I was also informed at this time that, before the year end, I would be transferred back to the US for four months of training to become a resident manager, my next logical career progression. This kind of retreat for Emily and Paul should have lasted about two months. Janet and I would in the meantime have enjoyed each other's company back in Sakkara while preparing once more for the unknown.

The first week in July the four of us took a flight to Milan, rented a car and drove to Centonara. The usual welcome was afforded us by my sister and we settled into the old house. Maria Ester, our niece, was now a snotty teen and quite jealous of the attention that her mother gave Emily and Paul.

Two days later we set out to leave for Gressoney. As the crow flies the distance between Centonara and Gressoney is no more than about 40 miles (65 km) across the Alps but to get there on the freeways took about two hours. However we were not in a hurry and chose a more picturesque and naturally slower route. It was an opportunity for us to see new places and for the children and Janet to absorb some mountain culture while taking in fresh air. We eventually arrived at the camp, liked what we saw and were comfortable to leave the children there.

The first night, after settling Emily and Paul into their accommodation at the colony, Janet and I booked in to a chalet style small hotel. It was an absolutely charming and romantic place, all wood and with flowers running down from the balconies. Janet and I relived enchanting honeymoon moments then next morning, after visiting Emily and Paul to have breakfast with them, we departed for the airport on our way back to Sakkara.

Lo and behold - the minute we arrived in Sakkara the phone rang. It was my sister Anna calling to tell us that overnight Emily had been taken to the hospital emergency room in Ivrea suffering from suspected appendicitis! Janet grabbed her unpacked suitcase and we headed for the airport to find her the first flight to either Milan or to Turin. When Janet arrived at the hospital in Ivrea Emily was in a miserable state. She had been operated on but her condition was worsening and she was in real danger of dying.

As she was not getting any better a German lady specialist was called in and she had the foresight to ask Janet where had Emily been living up until now. When Janet told her that we lived in Sakkara this confirmed to the doctor her suspicion that Emily had contracted typhoid fever. The Italian doctors were not experts and, because she had horrible tummy aches, they had believed it was a simple case of appendicitis.

Emily was immediately moved to the quarantined infectious diseases department where, for the first two days, not even Janet could be with her. After that Janet had to wear hospital gowns and masks in order to spend a few minutes a day with our daughter. Poor Janet spent long nights trying, and failing, to sleep on chairs in the hospital corridor until the German lady doctor took pity on her and arranged for a bed on which she could lay down at night. Emily's quarantine lasted for forty days.

In later analysing what might have happened, Janet determined that Emily had been invited by another school friend in Sakkara to sleep over and had eaten dinner there. The vegetables were, most likely, not properly washed with disinfectant as Janet did at home and this was the source of the typhus infection. Paul was not allowed to visit with Emily. He was left all by himself at the colony but Janet went to visit him on a few occasions during this time. Janet and I could only communicate by land line phone (mobiles didn't yet exist) and this was tricky as the telephone system in Egypt was still somewhat antiquated.

Back in Sakkara I was given dates on which to return to California for the training. This wouldn't be until the end of October. By mid September, when Emily had finally recovered and was able to fly, she plus Janet and Paul left directly for California. There they were temporarily put up in the Anaheim Marriott until I arrived. Then we would move into a condominium we owned at Laguna Niguel. Denny Pit, the new Sakkara director of food and beverage had already arrived from his former position at the Athens Marriott. He came with his wife Angie who then became the director of restaurants. October the 25th arrived and it was my day to leave Egypt - supposedly for good.

Because the Volvo was going with me to America I had to do some interesting work. The rule was that if you took a car out of Egypt you had to return the license plates to the department of motor vehicles and leave without plates on the car. That created quite a problem for me. My plan was to pick up the car in Venice, drive to Centonara and then, a few days later, to Frankfurt where the car would be taken by the shipping company and delivered to me in California. But, because of 'kullo momquin fee el Saqqara' (a widely used expression meaning everything is possible in Sakkara), I got new license plates made in a sweat shop in the centre of the city, got a crooked company to prepare the export documentation and have the car taken to Alexandria to be on the same boat as me heading for Europe.

Now came the time for the traditional going away party which was scheduled to be held in the hotel night club. In the lead up to that I could not understand how Denny Pit would not spend proper time with me for the hand over of the department. Instead he was always gone and I noticed that Jasmine and the department heads were missing at the same time. I couldn't however figure out if there was a connection there until I walked into the night club for what was supposed to be a very low key goodbye party and was amazed to see that the club had been transformed into the temple of Karnak complete with its avenue of the Sphinx and the complex labyrinth of columns.

The show began and a man-made circus camel appeared on to which I was promptly hoisted and paraded around the club to the sound of old Pharaonic music. All of the managers were dressed up in traditional old Egyptian costumes and my fortune was read out. I was pleased to hear my destiny proclaimed as very positive and the stars predicted that I was bound to accomplish great things in life. The food, Egyptian wine and Stella beer were plentiful and everybody enjoyed a great time.

I received an enormous number of gifts, lots of silver and ivory gadgets like letter openers, miniature fallukahs (the typical one sail Nile river boat), silver trays and so much more. Plus there was, naturally, the traditional framed photo of the hotel with all of the signatures and best wishes from the team. The gifts were so many that a suitcase was also provided for me to put them in.

Juergen and Michelle invited Nimani, Nagla, Denny and Angie, Jasmine and I to dinner at the Sonesta that evening where Alfredo of Rome was presenting a food festival with his famous fettuccine. Alfredo was a very fat and famous chef who had become renowned for his golden spoon and fork with which he would toss his pasta dishes at diners' tables. Actually it was quite disgusting as he would sweat profoundly while he was working and drops of sweat would fall into the pasta, fresh cream and parmesan cheese mix you were about to eat.

Also I was told that night that he drank a bottle of Fernet Branca Italian liquor each day. This liquor is made from herbs and, if a person has bad digestion and drinks a shot of it, his stomach is immediately cleared, either up the way or down! In the event neither such catastrophe occurred and the show marked an impressive conclusion to a day when I had received so much appreciation and care from all the people who had become my friends ... and who still are today.

Sadly the next morning Nimani, Nagla and Jasmine took me to Alexandria and dropped me off at the harbour from where I would sail to Venice via Piraeus accompanied by my illegally registered car. After a tearful goodbye they departed and I was left to the tender mercies of the same crooks who were supposed to have all the paperwork ready for me to take my car out of the country. They had figured out that they could milk some more money out of me. They explained that there were problems in taking the car out of the country and that more paperwork had to be completed. I knew it was all a show but decided to play along. After two hours of pretending that they were resolving the 'new problems', the car was finally loaded on to the ferry. They asked me for 400 dollars for their efforts. I indulged in the traditional haggling and agreed eventually on a reduced fee on which we shook hands and hugged in the traditional manner.

Now I was on my own, sitting with Stella beer in hand on the ferry's deck as the sun was setting. I contemplated what a beautiful experience my stay in Sakkara had been. Although professionally very trying and hard I also felt that life there had taught me patience, tolerance and a passion for life and to do things which I wouldn't have considered doing before. Things like daring to ride a horse and crawling inside the Great Pyramid had become a normal part of life to me and only at that moment did I realise how much I was going to miss that country.

I had stumbled in full of misgivings and doubt but had been drawn trance-like into a sand dance to treasure, a paradoxical rythm of chaos and enchantment. It is so true that Egypt is a magic place. One either loves it or hates it. I loved it.

Soon it was dark. The lights of Alexandria were switched on. The ferry left the shore behind and I cried. I sat there weeping and motionless, just staring at the dark sky, the dark water and Egypt slipping away from me. I wanted to hold on to it. I wanted to lean over the rail, stretch out my arms and firmly anchor my hands on to that land and never let go.

But life moves on and so did I.

Chapter 15

BREAKING INTO DESPAIR

When the last twinkle of Alexandria's lights had faded from view I went down to the dining room for a good Italian dinner; I was after all, on an Italian ferry. Before going to bed I went to the bowels of the ship where the cars were stored to put my home made license plates on my car. Now I was legal and could safely drive off the ferry when I arrived in Venice. Returning to the bar I knocked back two more Stella beers before wobbling weak-kneed to my cabin and crawling into bed to wake the next morning with a mild hangover. The rest of the trip was unremarkable; eating, drinking, socialising and sundeck bathing.

It took thirty-six hours to reach bustling Piraeus, the main port in Greece. It is just 7.5 miles (12 km) from Athens and one of the busiest ports in Europe. We had a twelve hour stopover there. I spent the day taking in the commotion of passengers and cars landing and embarking from the vantage point of an upper deck. As darkness fell, I took the opportunity of turning in early. Next morning I was awake and up at the crack of dawn as I wanted to take in the sights and sounds of the port as the ferry left and to view Athens from the water. I also wanted to experience the navigation of the Corinth Canal, that incredibly narrow strait which cuts through the Isthmus of Corinth to join the Saronic Gulf to the Gulf of Corinth. It saves a long trip around the Peloponnesus Peninsula and it really is an astonishing piece of engineering.

As the ferry glided over the still waters, the distance between the side of the ship and the walls of the canal were so minute that you could almost reach out and touch the rocks. The 26 feet (8 m) deep and just short of 4 miles (6.6 km) long canal is only 81 feet (24.5 m) in width at the Saronic end and a mere 70 feet (21.3 m) wide at the Gulf of Corinth. It is a short ride but a heart-stopping one. I breathed a huge sigh of relief when we made it through out of the the squeeze.

The first short stop thereafter was a three hour one in Bari, a town in the Puglie region in the south of Italy. Although the port here is of less magnitude than Piraeus it is still among the largest ports in the Aegean Sea. Here again the hustle and bustle of people and cars coming and going was repeated. Then the ship made the short hop to, and a brief stop at, the port of Ancona in the Marche region of Italy before carrying on to its final destination of Venice. Venice was, and remains, the most important port in the Aegean. It is modern and equipped to serve the largest cargo vessels as well as the very biggest cruise liners of all the major passenger cruise ship lines. All the ferry boats to the Balkans, the Middle East and Africa leave from here.

The ferry arrived in Venice at mid-day and the customs' formalities were mercifully brief; unlike the shenanigans in Alexandria. All I had to do was buy temporary motor insurance to cover me during the days I was driving in Italy and to Frankfurt where I would give the car to a shipping company to be taken to California. With that done, I downed one more cappuccino and was soon out of Venice and en route on the four hour drive to Centonara. I passed through the hilly region of the Valpolicella where the popular Soave white wine is produced along with the famous Ripasso and Amarone wines. When I was a wine drinker Amarone was one of my favourites and I over-indulged on it on more than one occasion. I didn't stop to enjoy some this time as my goal was to get to my sister Anna before dinner.

Once in Centonara, my Volvo with the Egyptian number plate quickly became the centre of attention. Such a vehicle had never been seen in the village before and the fact that it was owned and driven by Pierino the 'wonder kid' who had left the village many years previously with just a cardboard suitcase rendered it all the more spectacular. In all honesty I had to try hard to stay humble with all the attention I received. Older folks had seen people who had been abroad return to the village before but never with a foreign car and exotic license plates. When I took my car to the

Volvo dealer in town for a service, he was amazed to find the carburettor full of fine Sahara sand. He had serviced many cars but never seen anything like that.

The usual treats were put in place and I enjoyed my time with Anna. But Tullio and Maria Ester were not nice. Maria Ester was now a teenager with all the moods of that age and this obviously stressed her mother out. One afternoon Anna and I took a trip to Switzerland to enjoy some precious sibling time together. She was then forty-six and had been sick for five years. She had endured several operations culminating in the removal of both her breasts, as a result of which she now felt only half a woman. Tullio had openly kept lovers – Divina, Algibra and Valenska were well known ones. Anna knew but pretended not to. Maria Ester had met Batman Bin in Sakkara and continued to stay in contact with him unbeknowns to her mother. I am still convinced that her father knew but he had other dark reasons to be part of the cover up. The week I spent there was a week of discoveries I would have rather not made. The worst of these was that a conspiracy between Tullio and Maria Ester to destroy Anna was brewing ... and they were slowly succeeding.

BACK TO BADEN-BADEN

Early one morning I left Centonara. My first stop was Baden-Baden, the spa town in Germany where I had worked for one year earlier in life. That previous connection apart, there were two other reasons for my visit. One was that I wanted to stay one night at the best hotel in the city, the Brenner's Park Hotel. The other reason was that the maître d' hotel there was Castelletta, the fellow I had taken with me to Rome to the Grand Hotel as an assistant waiter in 1961 and not seen since. As he always did, the maître d'hotel at the Grand Hotel had sent Castelletta to Baden-Baden to the Bellevue Hotel for the summer season. When this closed for the winter Castelletta chose not to return to Rome and moved instead to the Brenner's Park Hotel where he eventually became the maître d'hotel. He married a German girl and there he spent his life. It had been twenty-two years since we had seen each other and I was curious if he would recognise me. To complicate things I had grown a beard for the trip.

As the drive from Centonara took less than six hours I arrived at the Brenner's Park shortly after mid-day. After checking in I decided on a walk around the town to see what was what. My first stop at what had been the Bellevue Hotel yielded a huge disappointment. It had been transformed into a Kurhaus, a luxury spa centre where mostly elderly and rich people go to treat ailments real or imaginary. Then I walked to the town centre and visited the casino. This brought back memories of Cristina my German-Jewish-Argentinian girlfriend from my time in Baden-Baden twenty years earlier.

By this time the sun was setting and I returned to my room for a luxurious long bath after which I donned a good suit and walked to the Europaeischer Hof. There I parked myself at the bar and ordered a Campari and soda. As I was still smoking at the time I purchased a pack of Ernte 23, the brand of cigarettes which I had always smoked while living in Baden-Baden. After a leisurely drink and a couple of cigarettes I slowly walked back to the Brenner's Park, pausing here and there to admire the expensive items displayed in the shop windows.

When I arrived at the hotel I first established that Castelletta was indeed working there then asked for a table. I was told that there was a wait of about thirty minutes (the usual trick to get you to the bar to have a drink before dinner). I knew the game but played along as it served my purpose. I sat there and had one more Campari and soda. Presently Castelletta, properly dressed in his black long tail outfit, came to get me. He recognised me not.

During our days at the Grand Hotel in Rome, the maître d'hotel would not call us assistant waiters by our names as he never made a point to learn who we were as people. His way of getting our attention was either to kick us in the shins or call us all 'Nino'. So, as Castelletta led me to the dining room door, I softly called out 'Nino'. He paused and half turned but, sure that he had misheard, carried on. A few steps later I called again – 'Nino' - but a bit louder. This time he stopped and turned abruptly with a surprised look on his face and his mouth open. He still did not recognise me. Hesitatingly he sat me at a table near the wall. As he handed me the menu he took the opportunity to study my face, desperately trying to make a connection between this bearded mystery man and 'Nino'; for all his mental efforts he could not connect the two. As he was speaking German to me I replied in German as he took my dinner order.

This was becoming a game that I enjoyed. Then, quite suddenly, I remembered my father telling me that a good game ceases to be fun if it lasts too long. So I called Castelletta over speaking in the broad Italian village dialect we both knew so well.

At first I thought that he was going to faint. He must have thought that he was seeing a phantom. Finally he put two and two together and recognised me. We had a lovely long chat about our lives, our careers and our families. We exchanged tales of what we had each been up to in the intervening years and reminisced over the escapades and madcap revelry of our younger days. I ate too much, drank too much, smoked too much and talked a lifetime. As I had to get up early the next morning, we eventually had to bid each other farewell and, with big Italian hugs, call it a night. But what a night!

The next morning I had to make the two hour drive to Frankfurt to deliver the car to the shipper for transfer to California and I had to catch my flight to Los Angeles. Such was my hangover from the night before that I sure didn't feel like driving. Yet drive I did. I had put the pack of cigarettes I had bought the night before on the front seat of the car beside me with the intention of smoking some as I was driving north. My head was pounding and seriously hurting and I made a decision – a big decision. I opened the car window and flung out the half empty pack of cigarettes never to smoke again. It is now thirty-three years since that day and, boy, am I glad.

When I arrived in Frankfurt I took the car to the shippers. With the usual German efficiency all the paper work was processed in a matter of minutes. Then I was on my way in a Mercedes taxi to the airport. The flight was very comfortable as business class paid by the hotel was still the norm for all employees on international assignments. Janet had rented a car and came to pick me up at the airport. As I emerged from arrivals, she turned pale and I thought she would drop dead. I knew there and then that my idea of growing a beard was not my brightest move ever. In spite of the fact that we had not seen each other since July and had had Emily's illness to contend with, the conversation from the airport to Laguna Niguel, where we had moved into our condo, was not very fluid. Hardly anything was said and I felt really bad. The reaction from Emily and Paul however, when Janet and I went to collect them from school, was totally different. They were really happy to see me and thought my beard was great - children's love is unconditional.

This was almost the middle of November. We had never lived in that condominium and we found life there very different as we had always lived in our own home. Here it was community living. The garage was separate from the house in what was like a garage row and every time you went there you had to walk by other people's doors. There was very little privacy. Everyone knew what the neighbour did all the time and it felt as if everyone knew your business.

As our Volvo had not arrived yet we rented a large station wagon to get the essentials into the place and set up the house. Also we had a visit from Janet's brother, Bill, his wife Ronny, son Will and daughter Rebecca on their way to emigrate to New Zealand. It was a nice time. Emily and Paul spent a few days playing with their English cousins and we were playing hosts. My training started too. I was assigned to train as a resident manager which meant that I was learning the room managment part of the hotel operation. I was very fortunate in that there were three hotels all within easy driving distance in which my training could take place. They were the Oldport Beach, the Los Angeles Airport and the new Irvine Marriott hotels. The four months of intensive education covered learning how to take a reservation for a hotel room, checking in and checking out guests, familiarisation with the functioning of the laundry and knowledge of the workings of the security department.

MUSTASHAT ISLAND BECKONS

But on February 11th of 1985 I got a call from Everhart Proud, the New York regional vice president. Without ceremony he informed me that I was promoted to the position of general manager of Sir George's Castle Resort on the island of Mustashat. I couldn't believe what I was hearing. I was skipping the position of resident manager altogether. The location sounded exotic too. It was agreed that I would go to New York the following week to meet him and then fly on to Mustashat to see the hotel and meet Adolph Adler, the incumbent general manager. Adolph was being moved to Washington as the hotel manager for the opening of the Marriott Washington Marquis on Freedom Plaza which, with one thousand nine hundred and seventeen rooms, was the biggest hotel Marriott had at the time.

When I got home that evening and told Janet the news, she was delighted. I had kind of expected that she would not be too thrilled with the idea of repacking everything, storing it again and moving on but she had heard that in Mustashat the schools were very good and the children were educated according to the old English school curriculum. The following week, full of enthusiasm, I flew to New York to meet with Everhart Proud and his wife. They didn't have children and lived in a nice apartment at the Sussex House Hotel, a very nice but old hotel on Central Park. I expected that we would have dinner in the apartment and get to know each other. I bought a nice potted plant for his wife and took a taxi to the hotel.

When I rang the bell of his apartment Everhart opened the door with a great show of impatience, grabbed the plant from me and called to his wife. She already had her coat on and they hurried me out of the door. I was completely taken aback with the curt 'un'welcome and the evening progressed no better. We rushed to a restaurant, sped through dinner and his message was simple. "Go down there and let me know if you want the job or not!" It wasn't an inspiring start to our relationship and it was to end no better three years later.

In Mustashat I was picked up by Adolph and taken to the resort which was impressive at first sight. He gave me a tour of the property from the one mile (1.6 km) long beach and the three swimming pools to the various restaurants and bars scattered around the site. We ate lunch in the main restaurant and he invited me to the cottage for the evening meal. There I met his Spanish wife Jimena and their little daughter, Cosita. Next day I checked out the schools and took a look around the island.

One of the most distressing things which I noticed straight off was that everyone, from beach vendors with enormous suitcases on their heads to rastafarians smoking weed and just about any other beach bum, took a short cut to and from the beach over the front lawn of the hotel. Also disturbing was the fact that I returned to the hotel to find Adolph involved in a shouting match with a mob of men in his office. As I was about to enter, the door burst open. Adolph rushed out and immediately asked his secretary Jane for a cigarette. Jane later explained that she kept Adolph's cigarettes for him as he was trying to cut down. The row I'd chanced upon was due to the fact that a scam had been discovered involving pilfering from the hotel bars at night. This last fact didn't surprise me as I had seen all that in Bermuda when I worked there as a waiter.

While I was less than impressed with Adolph's management style I was quite taken by Mike Riby, the director of engineering. He was a naturalised Canadian with a Canadian wife Rosie and a son, Eddie. Andrija Pieroff the food and beverage director and Antun Mignon the resident manager were less impressive and both were married to nasty women; between them they would make life harder for all of us. The management occupied separate cottages. All were next to each other and a rife environment for gossip among the team. None of this deterred me from wanting the job and accepting the challenge. Even before leaving the next day, I had called Everhart Proud and accepted the position. We agreed on the 17th of March as the date for my move.

I returned to California. In order to make the prospect of yet another move more appealing to the children, I took them to the local sports shop and bought them fishing rods. The idea was to get them looking forward to the move, the new schools, new friends, a new environment and (another) new house. Once more the removal company came, took all our belonging to storage and off we went to the rhythm of the calypso and 'beautiful Mustashat the gem of the Caribbean Sea'! This turned out to be the only time I was happy that our luggage got held up in transit (at New York) and did not make it with us. This because Adolph and his family were still occupying what would be our villa for the next week of turn-over and so had rented another villa for us in the same complex.

After he picked us up at the airport (minus luggage), it was dinner time. We walked the short distance to the hotel to eat. There we were introduced to the staff as the 'new manager' and all seemed very friendly. On our return to the villa however we were shocked to find that someone had broken in. The intruder(s) had smoked cigarettes, broken open the pantry door, made tea and had helped themselves to the pineapple and the rest of the fruit that was in the 'pirate chest' welcome gift the hotel gave to its guests. They had pretty well trashed the joint. Now you understand why it was a blessing that our luggage didn't make it. It would all have gone too. That was our 'welcome to Mustashat'. Not exactly a steel band sound and the melody of calypso!

Turn-over week went smoothly. It included a visit to the Prime Minister's office and one to our lawyer, the former prime minister, Henry Ford. In a way this was my first mistake. The Adlers moved on to Washington and we took possession of our villa. We soon realised that, while the house was quite adequate for the Adlers, it was small for us. We had two children and the house only had two bedrooms. However Everhart Proud gave us approval to add an additional bedroom and the construction started. By now it was

July and the children were on summer vacation. I had to go to New York for my first quarterly reporting to Everhart. Janet, Emily and Paul came with me to meet Sandy and Millie, our friends. While we were there the building of the additional room had created an opening between the part of the house we lived in and the new room. We got a call from Mike Riby, the engineer, that someone had broken into the villa again. Two hits in less than four months was getting to be more of a routine than a problem. At least we were not there and it was not such a shock.

THE UGLY FACE OF POLITICS

Meeting Sandy and Millie proved to be a wonderful experience for Emily and Paul. They felt as if they had found new grand-parents; they were showered with gifts and treats. It sure was a lovely time had by all. On our return to Mustashat I paid a visit to Henry Ford to share my concern regarding the issue of the beach vendors trotting through the resort's beautiful gardens. I explained to him how their boom box radios and enormous suitcases were not conducive to the 'idyllic island' and 'deserted beaches' expectations of our guests who had come to Mustashat for a well-earned vacation of peace and tranquility. Henry Ford's suggestion was to close the current gate of the hotel and re-route the public entrance to the beach by building a wooden stair off to the side. Then he said to open a more majestic main entrance to the resort and man it with our security. This was done. It was my second big mistake.

While the measure stopped the vendors from traipsing through our property, it upset them no end. It also upset the opposition Labour Party. We were able to control that for a while until our security guards, sympathetic to their countrymen's plight (and bribed too no doubt) allowed the vendors access through our majestic new main entrance. Now they had even more ground to destroy as the walk to the beach was longer. I discovered that there was on the island an ex-Amsterdam police officer who owned a security company. He had fled Amsterdam because he had crossed the mafia and they were after him. Here I made my third mistake.

I hired him and his guards and moved them in one Monday morning and put them at the gate. When the hotel security came to work they were denied entrance and fired on the spot. This led to the rest of the staff coming out on strike. I called Everhart to inform him of this only to be told that I had made the wrong decision. He said that I should have left things as they were as the resort was considered nothing but a tennis escape for him and the regional team. In trying to put things right I had stepped on his toes and made him an enemy. The only good thing turned out to be that the strike was illegal. The union president came and told the staff to go back to work or we could and would fire the entire team. The strike did however, last for four hours and that was enough to eventually seal my fate.

Now life returned to what one could consider normal in the Caribbean. To entertain the guests we had a band playing in the bar every night until midnight, except Sundays. Although we could hear the music from our villas it was no real problem for us. However it was a considerable nuisance for the older English folks who lived there most of the year. We received an enormous amount of complaints, especially from one particular elderly lady who wanted us to stop all kind of noise in order to get her beauty sleep from nine o'clock onward. The thing is we were on the wrong side of the island from where the action was and our guests had nowhere to go to have fun and dance. We had little option but to ignore the complaints and carry on business as usual.

One evening the children were in their rooms asleep while Janet and I were watching TV in the living room. Janet said, "I hear a noise in the bedroom." I laughed, thinking it would be impossible for a noise to happen there. There were three windows all with metal bars, therefore impossible for anyone to get in. Or so I thought. When Janet repeated the same concern, to make her feel better, I went to the bedroom. There I saw a long arm reaching through the bars of one window. The hand at the end of it held a stick with which the thief was trying to hook up Janet's handbag which was resting on a chest of drawers. The thief hadn't seen me so I moved the bag back a little and tip-toed to the kitchen. There I got hold of a hammer, returned to the room and smashed his outstretched arm as hard as I could. The recipient of the blow let out a loud screech of pain. He (or she) dropped the stick and ran off, jumping the high fence to the next property. Another attempted robbery foiled.

Another evening while out for dinner with Janet at a friend's house, I received a call to say that a bomb had been planted somewhere in the hotel; apparently because the New York chapter of Haddassah was in the hotel having a conference. I dropped everything, took the car and rushed back to the hotel. There I mobilised a group of people and we, as discretely as possible, scattered in all directions to search for anything that looked suspicious. After about an hour of searching without success I thought that, if there had been a bomb hidden somewhere, it would have exploded by now so I called off the search and went home.

AN ILL WIND

I was there only five minutes when Janet arrived in the car of our friends with whom we had been dining. She was not alone. An enormous dog jumped out of the car in front of her. Janet told me that after I had left, the conversation turned to our friends' many dogs. They had a large estate which was a former sugar plantation with lots of space for ferocious dogs to roam around. They had adopted a street dog who was anything but ferocious and this poor fellow was constantly attacked by those other aggressive animals. With chunks of his fur bitten off his neck and legs he was a rather pitiful sight. Faced thus with a fait accompli I had little choice but to take him in.

The children were delighted to have him and soon named him Sandy due to his rather weird colour. His wounds eventually healed and, well fed and cared for, he became a happy dog with a safe home and a large garden to run around in.

The villa had all tile floors and rattan furniture which made it possible for Sandy to roam around inside the house too and sleep in the living room. He was a real sweetheart of a dog. With him inside the house when we were going out at night we felt secure that at last we would not be robbed again. What were we thinking?

One evening Janet and I went to a cocktail party on the other side of the island. The children had a sleep-over night at the house of little friends and Sandy was in his corner in the living room asleep. Upon returning home that night we were terrified at the scene we found. Someone had come into the house, beaten Sandy (who had urinated all over the floor) and taken a gold chain and cross which Janet had left hanging on the handle of the bedroom closet. We had a safe in our house but, in the rush to leave for the party, the chain had not been locked away.

We called the police who by now were habitual visitors to the villa but nothing was ever found. The jewelry I had given Janet when Paul was born was now gone. We were later told by our babysitter that Sandy had previously belonged to a black man who regularly beat him. We concluded that it was someone who knew the dog's history who had broken in that night. This revelation also explained why, if a white person went by in the street, Sandy did not react but when a black person, male especially, passed by then he went totally berserk.

Janet and the children had taken up dinghy sailing lessons. The children had become strong swimmers and routinely participated in competitions. Going to the beach had become our regular Sunday pastime. We would take a baloney sandwich and a bottle of wine and spend the afternoon playing frisbee or trying to build sand castles. Driving home from one such day out we encountered a turtle slowly crossing the road. Emily and Paul had the terrific idea to take it home with us. Janet was driving, so I stepped out of the car and picked up the turtle. Emily moved to the front seat while Paul and I, with turtle on my lap, occupied the back seat. What a disaster. The turtle, probably terrified and in distress, let out a flow of stinking diarrhea all over me and Paul. It was hilarious for Janet and Emily of course, they were laughing their little heads off. It was less fun for Paul and I who were covered in slimy, green turtle poo. Despite that we got the turtle safely home. She stayed in our garden for a few days and got on fine with Sandy who took a liking to her. One morning we found that the turtle had gone out through the fence never to be seen again.

Antun Mignon, resident manager at the resort, was eventually transferred to New Jersey. He was replaced by an Egyptian fellow I knew as he had been part of the training team during the pre-opening of the Sakkara Marriott. He was not a well man. At times he was hospitalised with breathing difficulties and confined to an oxygen tent. Also, he believed that he could treat the Mustashat staff in the same way as he was used to treating Egyptians. He shouted and bullied whenever he wanted something done. The Mustashat staff of course just looked at him, laughed and quickly nicknamed him 'the crazy pharaoh'. It took little time for him to realise that he was out of his depth. He returned to the US with his tail between his legs.

He, in turn, was replaced by Steve Solberg, a very smart guy who had already been director of sales and marketing at Clair Point Marriott in Alabama. He quickly fitted in. He was a divorced father who had his five year old daughter with him. This never become a problem as he hired a local lady to be at home with her all day while he was at work. Thanks to LinkedIn we are still in touch today. The executive chef position was one of the hardest to fill. We brought in a young Belgian guy with whom I had worked in Egypt. What a mistake that turned out to be. He was drinking heavily and, like the Egyptian resident manager before, he couldn't lead people. Even though he came from the London Marriott he still had the idea that people only responded to bullying. He too failed and had to be relieved of his post after only six months.

Next up as executive chef was Carlyle, a tall, dark and gleaming-smiled Mustashat divorcee returning to his native island home from a posting in the US. In no time he had a queue of the most gorgeous American Airline stewardesses waiting in line, almost taking a ticket for their turn, to be entertained by him. Frank

Basmati, originally from Niger, was also transferred to Mustashat as director of engineering. The combination of Carlyle and Frank soon proved to be catastrophic. Both were serial womanisers and serious drinkers. There was also a third character on the scene, a local supplier named Ed.

Soon after that we started the renovation of the restaurants and the building of a smart entertainment centre. We also had a change in the director of finance. Scott Glasgow was now our man. Scott was a very extravagant individual who had married a Brazilian prostitute he had met when he was driving trucks in Brazil. They had three boys, one still a baby. His wife unfortunately was always smoking marijuana and stoned out of her head most of the time. It had come to the point that Scott would bring the baby in the crib to the office in order to feed and change him.

Notwithstanding that, one day Scott showed me an invoice for fifty cases of demi-glace, a concoction seldom used in our kitchen. This got my attention. The invoice was from a company called FREDCAR, a new supplier to the hotel. We were intrigued by this name and the low sequencial number on the invoice. It had to be a new company that Frank and Carlyle were purchasing from, but who was it?

In reviewing the invoices for the renovation I spotted an item which I did not recognise, which Frank had bought one thousand units of at an astronomical price. I sought the help of the regional director of engineering in identifying this item. It turned out to be simple light bulbs but listed as something else. This switched on a light in my head. I sat in my office studying the invoice when, all at once, the name of the company fell into place ... FREDCAR equalled FR= Frank, ED= Ed, CAR= Carlyle!

The three of them had formed a company with the sole purpose of ripping off the hotel. The fifty cases of demi-glace purchased by Carlyle and the one thousand light bulbs purchased by Frank now made sense. Frank was called to New York to the regional office and fired. It was harder to fire Carlyle, he being a Mustashat. Of course we stopped buying from Ed and their company quickly died.

NEVER A DULL MOMENT

There was never a dull moment, day or night in Mustashat. One night I got a call from the night manager at 2.00 am to say that there was a dead body floating in one of the swimming pools. I dressed and rushed to pick up the resident manager. We arrived at the pool just a few minutes after the phone call to find that there was indeed a body in the water. I asked the night porter to walk into the pool and push the body to the side. He refused as his superstitious belief was that touching a dead body would bring bad luck. I took my trousers off and went to retrieve the body myself. As I put my hand on the shoulder of the 'corpse' the man suddenly moved, let out a scream and jumped about a foot out of the water. I almost died from fright myself. He was alive.

After assisting him from the pool and reviving him further with hot black coffee, he told us that he was a flight attendant with American Airlines. He and a stewardess had been drinking champagne all evening in the pool. He got drunk. The girl left him there and he fell asleep. He had a lucky escape. We helped him to bed and that was the end of that story.

On another occasion I was called out during the night to attend to a young drunkard smashing up the furniture, antique desks and chairs in the reception area inside the castle. The night manager and the security supervisor were already there when I arrived but were afraid to get too near to the vandal because of his extreme aggressiveness. Fortunately I was able to calm him down and coax him outside to sit on the steps overlooking the garden. The sound of the waves lapping on to the beach relaxed him somewhat and he opened up about what had happened.

It transpired that he had hired a taxi from outside the hotel to take him downtown to a night club. As he wanted to ensure a return ride later on from the same driver, he had ripped a one hundred dollar bill in half and given one half to the taxi driver with the promise of him receiving the other half when he picked him up and took him back to the hotel. The young guy then got totally drunk at the club and then either missed or, for whatever reason, was not picked up by 'his' driver. Having to take another taxi back to the hotel upset him so much that, in his drunken state, he decided to get even with the taxi driver by smashing up the hotel.

It was now 5.00 am. I took his passport off him and got him to bed with the instruction to see me in my office at 10.00 am to settle the issue. By that time I had assessed the damage at 2,000 dollars and informed him that he'd have to pay up before he would have his passport returned. The young guy was genuinely sorry for the havoc he had caused. He had to call his mother to get the necessary cash and have it wired to the hotel's bank account. His mother immediately wired the money and next morning I gave him his passport back. Off he went on his merry way happy that I didn't get him arrested.

One day a guest rushed back to the castle from the beach to see me. He had a black eye. He told me that he had been beaten up by a beach vendor high on marijuana. This guest was divorced and had come on vacation with his daughter. While the two were enjoying the sun on the beach this vendor had approached them to offer his rasta bracelets and other trinkets for sale. The man and his daughter had told him that they were not interested. At this point the vendor had turned aggressive and had laid hands on the teenage girl. Not surprisingly, her father had jumped up to push the vendor away. That's when the vendor punched him in the face and ran off.

I called the police who told me that they knew the vendor in question and that he had history of violent behaviour. As for the guest, he was from New Orleans and threatened the hotel with a law suit. Although the assault was not our responsibility he was afforded a complimentary week at the hotel on a future date for his pains. A small price to pay for keeping a satisfied client.

Mustashat had by now become a fashionable holiday destination for Europeans. Apart from the Brits who still believed the island to be part of the empire, Germans and Italians had started to come and I received a group of my countrymen at the castle. Italian tourists are a special kind, their routine is always the same. The morning after they arrive at their destination an Italian's first priority is to buy postcards to send to family and friends to show off the beautiful place they have discovered. It's an all morning operation as, with Italians, there's always a heck of a lot of people who need to be informed. Only after this essential task is concluded do they set off for the beach and their real holiday activities. Knowing this, I had informed the hotel gift shop to be well stocked up on postcards.

While in most of Europe topless, and even naked, sun bathing had become common practice it was still prohibited in Mustashat. Among our guests we had a famous Italian TV star. One afternoon, while taking my usual walk on the beach, I was surprised to find her lying stark naked at the far end of the one mile (1.6 km) long beach with her knees bent and legs spread wide. A young local guy was sitting on the sand looking directly at her most private parts. I deduced that he was aroused as he was salivating out of both sides of his mouth.

For her own well-being, I suggested to her that she should put her bikini bottom back on. My goodness, what a reaction. The celebrity made it clear to me in no uncertain terms that she had not travelled all those miles to return to Italy with her body showing the difference in her tan between a total body tan and a bikini clad one. I concluded that she either did not understand the danger to which she was exposing herself or that she actually wanted to have rough sex on the beach in full daylight with any stranger willing to oblige. So I left her to it.

On another occasion a guest came to my office to inform me that he'd been awakened in the middle of the night by a strong body odour. As he woke up he saw a rasta by the chest of drawers at the bottom of the bed holding his wallet in his hands. He shouted out. The rasta took flight and jumped from the room's balcony to the ground one floor below. Fortunately, by being awakened by the body odour, he had avoided being robbed of the cash in his wallet.

Andrija Pieroff, the food and beverage director, was transfered to Syracuse in up-state New York and replaced by a Pakistani fellow from the Marquis Hotel in New York called Nussrat. With both the 'troublesome wives' now gone, it was like a breath of fresh air. Nussrat was polite and good with people and soon won the respect of the staff. But a tragedy was in the offing.

Nussrat had been with us only two weeks when he took the director of catering with him in his car (which he had bought on his arrival) to visit other hotels on the west coast of the island. On the way back Nussrat lost control of the vehicle, drove off the road and crashed down an embankment. The director of catering had both his knees broken. Nussrat's injuries were much worse. He was in a coma, totally immobilised and in danger of dying or of being paralyzed for life. I received a call about midnight from the hospital in Watertown. I immediately drove there with Steve Solberg the resident manager to find that we really had a problem much more serious than anything we had so far encountered.

The director of catering, after many operations, was eventually sent home to his family to be cared for while his knees were healing. For Nussrat it was a totally different story. He hung in there between life and death for about a month. He could not be flown back to the States and he could not go back to Pakistan where he did have a caring family to look after him but no adequate medical facilities to cater for his condition. Once the doctors determined that he could be moved, we contacted Mary, a friend he had back in New York. She and her parents agreed to take him in and look after him. He was flown there by ambulance plane and, after a full year of careful nursing from Mary and family, made a full recovery.

I met Nussrat many years later at one of the general managers' conferences. He had become general manager of a Renaissance Hotel in California. He was so grateful for what we did for him that he kept telling everyone that I had saved his life. A bit of an exaggeration but I was mighty happy that he had made it through. He was married, not to Mary, had children and life was good for him. The young director of catering also recovered and opted to sue the hotel, claiming that the accident was caused by an officer of the hotel in the line of duty. He never came back to work.

During the next six months our house was broken into four more times. By then we were so used to having that happen that we kind of missed it when two or three months went by without an unexpected guest trying to relieve us of our goods and chattels. We had become used to living with break-ins.

Uninvited guests apart, home life was good. Janet was kept busy with Emily and Paul, driving them the 14 miles (22.5 km) to school in the morning and taking dinghy sailing lessons during the day. Then, in the afternoon, she would pick up the children from their two different schools and take them to either swimming, piano, ballet lessons or cricket practice. Paul had his all white cricket outfit and was looking rather handsome in it. Both kids did twenty minutes piano practice each evening before they sat down to their home-work. It was a good life for everyone.

KICKED INTO TOUCH

The election to select the new Prime Minister came and the opposition Labour party won. This was a government likely to support the beach vendors and the unions. They'd also be anti-business for no reason other than that entrepreneurship and business was seen as exploitation of the poor locals. This especially applied to foreign owned businesses. This is when it hit home to me the mistakes I had made in trying to clean up the hotel and have separate access to the beach for the vendors and the local people. I had made political enemies.

The new government quickly introduced hotel inspections to check the operation for all kind of issues. If it was not the labour inspector checking that all the employees were scheduled correctly at all times then it was the health inspector who would always find that something was not done in strict accordance with the local regulations. It soon became evident that a conspiracy was afoot to have me removed from my position. Everhart Proud, in his wisdom, sent a former general manager of the hotel (who knew all the Labour party politicians) to stay for a week. This visit was ostensibly to celebrate his wedding anniversary but the real purpose was to find out what was going on within the government about me. Shortly after this guy's departure Everhart informed me that he would be coming for a regional visit. I had the feeling that this was going to be a very uncomfortable visit.

After the usual meetings and wining and dining the regional team convened a separate session behind closed doors. The next morning Everhart came to my office to tell me that I had until July to find a job. His reason for my dismissal was that I had caused too much trouble with the government by wanting to make the hotel an efficient and well functioning operation. In other words, because I had accomplished what had not been accomplished in the previous eighteen years of Marriott ownership of the property, I was fired for it.

I was destroyed. I walked over to the cliffs and slumped there head in hands thinking that this was not real. My first position as general manager and I had failed. I felt that I had let everyone down. I had shuffled my family from place to place, had Emily and Paul moved from school to school and all to give them a better life than the one I had had. Yet here I was jobless on an island in the Caribbean. I wanted to roll down that cliff and drown. After composing myself I returned to the hotel. The regional team had departed. I gathered my hotel team around me and made the announcement that I had been fired. They could not believe what they were hearing. Scott Glasgow, the director of finance and Steve Solberg, the resident manager, were particularly flabbergasted.

Janet had told me many times that I should have learned to be more of a politician and less of an hotel operator. She had long held that such an approach would have given me less troubles and more success. Now I knew that she was right and I had to go home and tell her of my dismissal. This was not an easy task. It is never easy to tell your wife you have been fired. Your self-esteem is gone, your courage is shattered. I understood that there is no such thing as 'fair' in life ... only reality. I was done!

As the news spread around the company I had sympathy calls from several people who, like me, had received unjust treatment from Everhart Proud. I learned that he was lazy and arrogant. I could now see how he had promoted Adolph to the Washington position. They were both of the same style. They were not leaders, just unscrupulous individuals.

I tried my best to resume an attitude of business as usual - hard as that was - but even the children could feel my tension. In the evening I would become more argumentative with Janet and finish a bottle of Soave Bolla wine with dinner. This was in early January. In February, Karl Kilburg rode to the rescue once again. With customary frankness he told me that there was no way that I would be reassigned as general manager to another hotel. Everhart Proud had smeared my name very badly and no other regional vice president would support me.

He came up with the solution that I could stay in the company in the position of food and beverage director at the eleven hundred room Boston Ulysses Grant Marriott. While this was effectively a demotion I chose to accept it. Among other reasons, I had less than two years to complete in order to become fully vested in the Marriott's profit sharing plan. This was the plan that allows Janet and I to live the life which we do now that we are retired in the Algarve. I was not about to give that up.

Chapter 16

NOT QUITE A TEA PARTY

By now it was March. Janet tried her best to keep everyone in positive spirits but I was beyond consoling. We made the move to Boston and found a forty year old house in the quiet suburban area of Sudbury, an easy 23 mile (37 km) drive from the city. It didn't have all the modern comforts but it was alright. I thought it a good idea to buy it as I was sure that my career was over and that I'd probably die there. It was right across from a high school. That suited Emily fine as she was starting high school a year early as her years in Mustashat had put her one year ahead of the American kids. She was a brilliant student.

Life returned somewhat to normal at home with school, ballet, American football, swimming and skiing in winter, occupying my own and my family's time. I tried to settle in to my new position with my chin up but found the general manager to be a real big head. A Frenchman, Jules Paillard spoke English with an almost incomprehensible French accent. He directed all his conversation to 'his greatness' (the general manager). Jules thought I needed to be retrained into the American ways and to achieve that he paid for a Dale Carnegie course for me on how to make friends and influence people. Ironically, if anyone needed that course it was himself. Michele Jacobini, the resident manager, was an okay guy and an Italian-American whose family name had been phonetically changed at Ellis Island.

I dived into the job, leaving home early in the morning to see the breakfast operation and working hard all day to show my metal. I also stayed late at night to see the dinner operation. We had an Italian Restaurant called Bello Mondo. From its misspelled name to the food that was served the restaurant was a total disaster. The only thing Italian in the restaurant was the family name of the Italian-American chef. He was a willing young man but without experience in Italian food to the point that he had his grandmother write the recipes for the restaurant. Something had to be done quickly about that. I arranged for him to go to Milan for two weeks training at the Savini Restaurant. This is to Milan what Maxim's is to Paris, the cradle of traditional cuisine. He came back full of enthusiasm and the restaurant made a phenomenal change.

I was also lucky to find a couple of Italians from Naples who produced fresh pasta at home and sold it to the hotels and restaurants. To have them added to the Marriott list of approved suppliers, both their premises and their work practices had to change. They were very eager to become our pasta supplier and easily agreed to all the required alterations. Soon we were in business serving the best ravioli in Boston.

I myself had developed a taste for real Parmesan cheese and Barolo wine. As this was the time that managers and directors could still eat and drink at work, I had taken up the habit of staying for dinner in the restaurant almost every evening. I'd dine on nice veal dishes, the best pasta in Boston, Parmesan cheese and never less than three large glasses of Barolo. Drink driving was still condoned in those days and drinking three glasses of heavy wine with dinner was normal. I knew my limit to be totally drunk was five glasses, so I thought with just three glasses that I could drive the 23 miles (37 km) home in reasonable safety. This drinking was of course not conducive to my health nor to my family life but I was still a confused and angry guy.

To make me even more angry, my cash and credit cards were stolen in the gym one evening where I sometimes worked out before going to dinner. I had locked up my clothes and my wallet in my locker but I foolishly left the key underneath my towel on the bench while I went into the sauna. On my exit from there my clothes and the contents of my wallet were gone. There had been two other guys, strangers to me, in the changing room. Clearly they had seen me leave my key on the bench and availed themselves of the 'free' opportunity to clean me out.

Six months into the stay in Boston we took a family vacation to

Niagara Falls and Toronto. The plan was to see the falls then drive to Toronto to visit with Mike Riby, Rose and Ed and another couple of friends from Mustashat. The return trip was planned to be via Montreal. When we arrived in Toronto our car broke down. The local Volvo garage loaned us a car to drive to Ottawa to see the changing of the guard at Government House while they made the necessary repairs. This we did and 1,000 dollars later and one day delayed we were on our way back home. We had to skip Montreal because of the lost day. This however was not nearly the worst thing that happened on that trip. While we were visiting with Mike and Rosie we were informed that Jules was moving to Los Angeles to open the Marriott at Forum Centre and his replacement was to be ... Adolph Adler!

I knew this to be bad news for me. Adolph was not only a pupil of Everhart Proud but, when I replaced him in Mustashat, the changes and improvements to the hotel I made had made him look bad and inefficient. Now he was going to be my superior. When I returned to work my fears were quickly confirmed. Adolph was an even more self-centred individual than Jules. He came in like a whirlwind of shouting and bullying which brought back memories of the Loewe brothers at the San Francisco Notlih. I could hardly believe that this was happening in a Marriott. He shattered all the principles I had come to believe in during the fourteen plus years I had been with the company. The 'take care of your employees and they will take care of your guests' principle of the founder was gone out the window. Under Adolph's regime of terror everyone worked in fear of being stepped upon.

Adolph was also a heavy smoker with a cigarette permanently fixed in his lips all day but he did make some 'friends'. These were mostly people who had figured out how to take his shouting and abuse as a positive rather than a negative. That wasn't me of course and I could see my day of judgement coming. This feeling was confirmed when, sitting directly opposite me at a celebratory dinner, I overheard him say to Michele Jacobini, the resident manager, that, "Peter has fallen asleep at the controls." These words acted like a light switched on in my brain. I knew I had to quickly find another job and move on. I contacted two headhunter agencies and put myself on the market. Failing that I would be fired and I would have no chance to ever work for Marriott again. One of the head hunters came up with a couple of places who wanted to interview me. I went to those interviews but nothing came of them.

Then one day I got a call to go to interview in Pittsburgh for the job as general manager at the Horse Shoe Bay Marriott in Florida. This hotel was a Marriott franchise, the franchise company being Cross States Hotels, the largest franchisee Marriott had at the time. When I arrived at the HQ of Cross States I met George Fatherson, the regional vice president with whom I had become good friends at general managers' meeting. Like me he understood island life having worked on Key West at the tip of Florida. (Key West of course, is not really an island but anyone living there thinks of it as such). Things went well with George but less so with one particular regional director. I returned home that night convinced that I wouldn't get the job. In fact I got a call from the headhunter next day telling me just that. A short while later though I got a call from George asking me to go back to Pittsburgh to interview again. He had convinced this other guy to reconsider. Sure enough, after a second interview, I was hired.

Upon returning home I had to tell Janet and the children that we were moving again. Janet had studied hard to become a dental assistant and had been only two days in her first job. Not unsurprisingly her reaction was less than positive. She exclaimed without hesitation, "I will never work one more day in my life!" She didn't keep her word though. We agreed that I would go to Florida alone and that Janet and the children would remain in the house until the end of the school year and then join me in the summer. My contract included a paid trip home to my family every two weeks or alternatively the family could come to Florida and visit me. I was also given accommodation in the hotel during the time until my family joined me. And so, in March of 1989, I drove to

Florida in our Toyota Camry and I was gone.

THE KEYS TO FLORIDA

In Florida I found a whole new world. The resident manager had worked for Cross States for many years. He disliked Marriott with a passion. He was a big talker and sported a beard, something Marriott Corp. did not allow at the time. The food and beverage director was ex-Marriott and one of the laziest people I have ever encountered. Needless to say he didn't last long with me. The director of marketing, Jim Bode, was a nice guy – and huge. He perpetually had in hand one of those enormous McDonalds 'big gulp' supersize drinks guaranteed to make you fat and give you diabetes overnight.

The director of human resources was a nice lady who also had worked for Cross States many years. She was George's favourite member of the team and she didn't hate Marriott, so that was nice too. The engineer was a likeable fellow, also with a beard, and skinny as they come. He and his wife lived on a boat in the marina in Fort Lauderdale and we got along well. My routine visits back home to the family were just that, a routine and becoming tiring. During these months the family visited me only once. As they arrived at the airport in Fort Lauderdale and Emily stepped out of the plane her first words were, "Dad really likes to live in a sauna!"

That weekend I drove them around to look for a house. We decided that we would not buy as the house in Sudbury had not sold. Until that happened we wouldn't have the money for a down payment. We did find a house for rent in Boca Green, an area which we liked. It had a golf course and was a typical Florida community with lots of waterways where alligators lurked. Soon after that school was over and the family moved. I flew back home to pack and drove the Volvo down with Janet and the children. The house goods arrived and we moved into the house. Life was quite good at first. I was fine at work in spite of not really liking the Cross States way of doing things. Paul adjusted fairly quickly to the new climate and environment but Emily found the heat tough. Janet? … Janet resented having studied hard to become a dental assistant only to be brought to Florida by my work and was not adjusting easily. All this weighed heavily on the family. I was caught between a rock and a hard place. I knew that I would have been fired had I stayed on in Boston. Drinking was also becoming a problem for me.

I was home every night for dinner which should have helped but it didn't. In fact it made matters considerably worse as arguments were escalating. After a heated exchange one evening, Janet packed a suitcase and walked out leaving the children and I alone. By that time Janet was working for a Jewish funeral home selling plots and funeral services. The next day, after dropping the children at their schools, I set off to her work to find her. Before Paul went into his school he gave me a small package he had wrapped and said, "Dad if you see mom today give it to her please, this is her Christmas present." That did it, I broke down in tears. When I found Janet she agreed, after much tearful persuasion, to come to the house the next day at 2.00 pm for a chat. Later, when I picked up the children from school to take them to their activities, I realised just how hard being a mum is. Emily and Paul didn't talk, their eyes were red and the mood sombre. My heart was broken. I wanted Janet back.

At home that night there was hope among the children that mum would come back but, knowing Janet, I was more cautious. This was in case Janet had decided that life was better for her out there in the world on her own without us three to be concerned with. The children were more upbeat. When I dropped them off they told me to make sure to get mum back and have her pick them up from school at 4.00 pm that afternoon. At 2.00 pm I was home and waiting for Janet. When Janet arrived we sat together on the couch. It was a tearful conversation as we both realised what we had missed and messed up on. Janet told me that she had stayed in a motel just like one sees in the movies. I explained to her that I now realised that there was a significant outside factor which had contributed to the situation and it was called – wine! From that moment I decided not to drink any more.

Life resumed much as before but minus wine and beer for me. It wasn't that hard to be without drinking and soon it became the norm. Paul joined the Boy Scouts, Emily did her ballet. Both of them continued with their music lessons and chose an instrument. Emily opted for a clarinet, Paul for a saxophone. We bought them their new instruments. Paul's saxophone has followed us around the world to this day where it sits on the top shelf of Janet's closet. We had found a nice church called Spanish River to attend as a family. Reverend David was an excellent pastor and an eloquent preacher. He led a Bible study class for men one evening per week in his house. I had become more religious and found it a better way to live. Both the children were doing well at St.Andrew College, a top private school in Horse Shoe Bay. Paul made it to Eagle Scout and was the youngest in the troop to make it to the top.

His final test was to pilot a monoplane. I was invited to fly with him. Although I was a bit scared I could no way show it and climbed into the aircraft with Paul and the pilot. The pilot took us up and then handed over the controls to Paul saying, "Okay Paul, take us for a ride." I could see that Paul was nervous as he was biting his lips. I, sitting in the back, was even more nervous. All went well (I am here to write this book today) and Paul of course, passed with flying colours.

At this time we sold, at a loss of 50,000 dollars, the house in Sudbury and bought a smaller one in Deerfield. This is a blue collar community south of Horse Shoe with none of its frills and sophistication but the neighbours were nice, friendly and down to earth working people.

At work things were going alright. IBM was our prime customer, Siemens was also a big account and Toyota too. The manager of Toyota was a nice guy and one weekend he loaned us a test Lexus car to drive to Key West. We spent a nice weekend in the Keys and drove back. Approaching our house, we smelled smoke and started to wonder whose house was on fire. The smell became stronger as we got nearer to the house. As we drove up to it, we had the fearful sensation that it was our house burning. Paul and I got out of the car, went to the front door of the house and cautiously touched it.

It was red hot! Paul ran to the electrical box at the side of the house and turned off the power. Our next door neighbour called the fire department. In no time fire trucks, ambulances and all arrived with sirens screaming. The firemen got their hoses ready, smashed a panel in a window, inserted the nozzle into the living room and turned on the water. Half an hour after that we were able to enter the house. What we saw was the most horrifying thing we had ever seen up to that point in our lives.

Everything was smoke damaged. The smell was obnoxiously pungent. It was impossible to breathe without a wet cloth over our mouths. The heat was almost unbearable and the plastic cabinets had melted. The carpets were burned to a cinder. The Fire Chief soon deduced what had happened. In my wisdom I had left a small lamp switched on at the end table at the side of the couch in the living room. The lamp was connected to the wall outlet with a long extension cord with multiple points and which ran under the couch.

A tropical storm had hit the town on the Friday night and lightening had hit the roof causing sparks to come out of the multiple outlet at the end of the extension cord. These sparks set fire to the carpet but, because the house was closed, the lack of oxygen prevented the carpet from bursting into flames. Instead the carpet had slowly smouldered, melting the cabinets and burning the couch and all the furniture around it. He also told us that at one point the temperature inside the house could have reached 1000°F (538°C), the same temperature which a self-cleaning oven reaches during the cleaning operation. Now I understood why nothing had survived.

There we were, in the street with nothing but shorts, t-shirts and the sandals we had on. We were lucky that our two cars were in the garage and nothing had happened to them. The first thing we had to do was all get new clothes. As for those in the house, we tried to have them dry cleaned but the smell of the smoke never came out. Everything had to be dumped in the garbage.

As regards accommodation, we were lucky to be friendly with

the manager of the top resort in the city. I went to see him the morning after the fire. He took pity on us and gave us one of his luxury apartments for considerably less than the cost at a Residence Inn. This also meant that we had free access to the resort pool, gym and other facilities. It was three months before the mess was all sorted and we were able to move back into the house.

What an experience that was. Losing your home with everything in it is definitely one of the most traumatic things that can happen to a family. It feels like all your life has gone. The damage to and loss of treasured photographs and mementos seemed to particularly affect us but the whole disaster certainly changed our outlook on life and our sense of priorities. The event demonstrated to us that mere material possessions are nothing, they can disappear in a puff of smoke. Family, love and life itself ... these are the real treasures.

MY CAREER IMPLODES

By now summer was approaching and business was not good. IBM, our biggest account, decided to limit how much they would pay for their employees' hotel stays while travelling on business and informed us of the amount. Jim, the director of sales and marketing and I, turned down their offer. As a result we lost all their business, half of our turnover, overnight! What a shock. A new CEO was appointed at Cross States. He was Rupert Kicks who had been fired from Notlih and many other companies and always under suspicious circumstances. He came to visit us with George on the 2nd of August 1990 (the same day that the first Gulf war started). The moment he walked into the meeting room and looked at me, his eyes told me that I would be dismissed from my post. He didn't remember me, of course, but I had met him once before. When Janet and I were recently married and I was working at the San Francisco Notlih we had taken a vacation in Hawaii. We stayed at the Notlih Hawaiian Sandy Beach Resort. It was one of the largest hotels in Waikiki and Rupert was then the general manager. Before leaving the hotel that evening George informed me that

Rupert wanted me out and they would let me know when that was to happen. From my hotel they went to Fort Lauderdale South Marriott and fired the general manager there. I was later told that he fired four general managers in total on that day.

I was now working every day under tremendous stress. When would the axe fall? Every morning I was going to work wondering if this was it, was this my last day at work? Well the day came soon enough. On the 17th of August I received a visit from George to officially terminate me that day, Paul's fourteenth birthday. But Rupert was generous and kept me on the payroll for four months.

I had met a man who was a retired hotel general manager from the Princess group and a 'pieds noir' of Moroccan origins. He was a smart guy and running a meeting planning agency. When I told him I was looking for a job he made me the offer of a desk in his office, free of charge, for me to set up a place from where I could call, look for and eventually find a job. All I had to pay was the cost of the telephone. What he never told me was that he really wanted me to pass on all the information I knew about companies holding meetings and conferences. Now my job was to spend ten hours a day in the office making calls, making contacts and sending my resumé out to try to get someone to interview me. I called Bud Davies, my former Chicago general manager who still had many contacts with Notlih. He put me in contact with Peter Kleiser who was now the vice president of food and beverage for the entire Notlih chain and who I knew from my Notlih days.

I flew to Los Angeles for an interview and before lunch was over I was offered the job of regional director of food and beverage for their western region operation. It consisted of thirteen hotels spanning from New Orleans to Alaska. This was only two weeks after I had been fired but I returned to Florida actually sad that I had been offered a job at a corporate office. The reason? - I didn't want a travelling job. I was gone from home working in the hotel enough as it was but at least had dinner at home most nights and slept in my own bed. I could spend quality time with Janet, Emily and Paul. Maybe misplaced pride came into play too. After all, if I was offered such a big job with a major corporation just two weeks after being fired, then I thought what else would come along if I held out? I turned the job down and went back to my makeshift office and endless phone calls.

The months passed and nothing was materialising. A few interviews came and went but I was getting desperate and started to panic. The money from Cross States had stopped coming after four months and I was receiving unemployment cheques. My self-confidence was at zero. How could I be standing in line at the welfare office, me, the guy who had come from a small village and was blessed to make it big in the American corporate world? How can I tell my wife and children that they are the only people who would talk to me while the rest of the world had shut me out? I considered changing profession, perhaps to a painter, as I had repainted every house we had ever owned. I thought to attend classes in the trade at the local community college.

Then I seriously thought about suicide! I had been thinking of which would be the way to die easily with not too much pain. I wanted to die but I was still afraid of pain and did not want to suffer. I had heard that you could kill yourself by connecting a hose to the exhaust pipe of your car, bringing it into the car through one of the windows, closing all the other windows, starting the car, inhaling and falling painlessly to sleep never to wake up again. With this plan in mind, I started to construct the system. The problem was how to ensure the hose stayed attached to the exhaust pipe? I had got as far as figuring out that if I wrapped a towel around a water hose and secured it with steel wires it would work. It was now six months into my unemployment.

It was a headhunter who distracted me from my dastardly suicide plan. He came up with the suggestion that, as the Berlin wall had fallen, the cold war was supposedly over, President Reagan and President Gorbachov of the Soviet Union were talking to each other in a more or less civilized manner and the Soviet Union was still alive but not well, I should consider opportunities in that part of the world. I said, "Yes." In no time I got a call to go to Vienna for an interview regarding the position of general manager opening a hotel for an Austrian company in Novoburg in the USSR. I went to Vienna. After an interview with the executive team of the Polarc company I was offered the job. The executive team of this company did look decidedly dodgy, a real band of crooks in fact. But did I have a choice? After all this time unemployed I needed to work to put bread on the table. Our resources were getting low and my self-esteem was pretty well non-existent. I accepted the job.

Returning home I explained my decision and my motives to Janet, Emily and Paul. I tried to paint a really positive picture of the scenario. The plan was more elaborate and complicated than with previous moves. This was to be a total disruption, different from anything we knew or had done in the past. We realised that we couldn't go as a family as Emily was in her last year of high school and would go to college the year after. And there were no schools for Paul in Novoburg, the nearest school was in Germany. The house and everything else had to be sold. What could not be sold had to be stored. I was to leave in two week for Vienna.

The house, furniture and the Toyota Camry were quickly sold to the new director of sales and marketing at the Marriott. The Volvo was sold, as his first car, to the son of a friend of mine. It was organised that Emily would become a boarder at St.Andrew for her last year there. Janet would stay in Florida to clear things up and organise everything prior to our next new life behind, what had been until then, the iron curtain.

Chapter 17

THE TORN CURTAIN

Now I was in Novoburg trying to get the town's first international hotel up and running. Novoburg was called the Soviet Silicon Valley but the reality was that there were a handful of factories making some extremely poor quality TVs and not much else.

On August 19th myself and the team were out for dinner at a typical Russian restaurant called Detiniez. The restaurant was located inside the first Kremlin walls (Novoburg was the first Russian capital and therefore had the first Kremlin) and it was packed with so many Soviet soldiers that it was really kind of frightening. We were able to communicate with a few of them and asked why they were there. We learned that they had been told that they were on their way to Moscow for a parade the next day.

After dinner we went back to our hotel and didn't give this matter further thought. Getting up the next morning to go to work, we noticed that the receptionist, a pleasant elderly lady who spoke good English, wore a very worried expression. I asked what was bothering her but she was hesitant to reply until she was sure nobody was listening. Eventually she pointed to the radio from which some sombre classical music was playing and whispered in my ear, "Something is happening. When there is only such music on the radio and nothing is spoken it is because something is changing at government level."

I didn't entirely understand the significance of what she was telling me but we soon learned that a military coup had taken place and tanks were rolling down the streets in Moscow. All telephone communications were cut and I couldn't make my usual calls home. In the US the news was of course on television so my family knew of the situation and were worried sick.

To complicate matters further, Janet and I had an appointment to get our US citizenship in September of that year; and in the same month Janet took Paul to Germany and settled him in to the Black Forest Academy, a school mainly intended for the children of Christian missionaries. Paul was the only non-missionary child there but he was a strong Christian and that helped him to settle in well. We returned to the US for the citizenship ceremony on the 18th of September and we left for Russia immediately afterwards. It was an unhappy trip with tempers running high. We had travelled a lot as a family but this time we were leaving our children behind in the care of strangers.

The opening of the hotel was a bizarre experience. Galina, our human resource director to be, was still working in a factory so we hired two hundred employees to staff the hotel for business that never came. Winter was approaching and there was no reason for anyone in their right mind to come to Russia. Soon after the opening we had the first snow fall and in no time at all we had about 10 feet (3 m) of snow on the ground. We were almost reduced to recluses behind the hotel walls.

Poor Janet tried hard to get into the swing of things but felt that she had abandoned Emily and Paul. She found it difficult to get over the fact that she had left them behind. The empty shelves in the shops were another reality we had to live with. We had come from the US where abundance was the norm to a country where you had to wait in line for possibly two or three hours just to buy a pound of dry biscuits.

ENTER THE MAFIA

Everyone in Russia at the time wanted to be a friend with a foreigner. The simple reason being that the dream of every Russian was to be able to get a passport to get out of there. The general belief was that if you were friendly with a foreigner you could get a passport. Young Russian women sought to get married to men from anywhere else in the world. We had a restaurant manager from Vienna who made the big mistake of getting involved, and secretly planned to elope, with a girl that belonged to the mafia.

They had arranged to catch the same night train to Moscow and from there to Vienna ... but the mafia boss knew of the plan. When our restaurant manager got to the station he was met by four thugs who gave him a severe beating and threw him on to the train. They took the girl away and she was never seen again. I never asked what had happened to her. It was pretty obvious that the answer would have been found at the bottom of a lake.

My assistant at the hotel was not chosen by me. The Russian owners had put him in. Rumour had it that he was ex-KGB. He spoke perfect English, naturally with a very strong English accent, and he was the only hotelier on the team. He was exactly the type of guy I didn't want but I soon realised that I needed him. It was all new to me how business was done in Russia so, if I wanted to get the hotel open and functioning, he was the guy to make things happen.

The company decided to buy only equipment that was produced and available in Russia to stock the hotel. Under my assistant's guidance, we visited the china factory. There was only one type of white, poor quality and visibly porous china available. Even so, we bought it. Then we went to the only existing glassware factory and met the manager. His only glasses produced were of a straight line, almost triangular design engraved with fancy patterns.

We requested to have them plain without the design. The manager wouldn't hear about that. He insisted that he had produced the same line of glasses all his life and it was prohibited by the regime to do anything different. After some straight talking and a hefty bribe changing hands, my man persuaded him to produce the glasses to our specification. Getting linen was not difficult as there was no choice at all. There was only one colour, white, and one size table cloth. As our banquet tables were round and large we had to have the hotel seamstress sew two table cloths together to cover one table. We had to import cutlery (from Italy) and we bought all of the furnishings from different sources throughout Europe.

The hotel had a good restaurant and it became popular with the local community. I organised a businessmen's club which soon, not unexpectedly, became mafia dominated. I quickly learned that the mafia controlled everything else, inside and outside of the hotel too. They set up a prostitution ring. I was told how many girls I was going to have working the lobby. Whenever a single male guest checked in, a girl would ask at reception which room he was in, call him on the house phone and offer 'Russian hospitality'. We also opened a disco which hosted a get together of about thirty mafia guys every night. The boss would come in surrounded by his boys. They'd stand at one end of the bar, drink all night, get drunk and leave without paying the bill. There was absolutely nothing I could do to make them pay.

One night one of the boys approached me with the intention to intimidate me. He held his clenched fist right under my nose and looked me straight in the eyes with the most menacing stare I had ever seen. I was petrified but couldn't run away as that would have meant turning the hotel completely over to them. I stood and prayed hard that he wouldn't hit me. After what felt like an eternity he lowered his fist, slowly smiled, took my hand and shook it firmly. From that day on he was respectful of me.

The team had agreed that one of us would stay on duty in the disco every night until closing time. One night while I was on watch I went to the toilets but found the door locked from the inside. Yet I could hear people inside crying and shouting. Eventually the noise stopped, the door opened and 'my friend' mentioned above emerged. He brushed past me and left. Behind him he had left a man lying on the floor in a lake of blood and urine with his head kicked in and six or eight teeth scattered around him. I couldn't call the police as they were themselves mafia. I just called an ambulance to come and take him away. Then I woke Frau Feuerbrandt, the housekeeping manager, who came down and helped me clean up the mess as best as we could.

One of the most serious beatings happened one night outside the main door of the hotel. The young Finnish manager of a Finnish company dealing with the export of timber from Russia to lanlandни

Finland made the mistake of flirting in the disco with the girl who 'belonged' to the mafia boss. On his way out of the hotel he was attacked by four mafia thugs. He was thrown to the ground, kicked senseless and left for dead. I was awakened by the commotion and immediately rushed out. There to find the bloody sight of a body with an eye ball popped out and hanging from the head.

While there was a beating inflicted by the mafia every night this was by far the worst. I had the front desk call for an ambulance. After it arrived and the medics got the lad inside, I followed it back to the local hospital in my car. However, there was nothing that could be done for him there as his situation was so bad. I had the phone number of his boss in Finland so I called him and an air ambulance was dispatched from Finland immediately. By that same evening this young man was back in Finland being cared for in a hospital. I hope he recovered.

Our family life was totally disrupted with the children all over the world, Janet and I miserable, work in a shambles and no business in the hotel. I also found out that the secretary I had been given by the owner was actually put there to keep an eye on me. Fortunately for me she was a decent young woman who decided to quit rather than play that game. The director of food and beverage and I decided to share his secretary. After all, other than translation, there was really very little for her to do. It was now October and the place became even more miserable. The trees were bare and the Siberian wind was blowing all day and night. The queues at shops to buy the bare minimum of groceries and supplies were longer, cold and tiring to stand in. Janet was patient and coped admirably. Contrary to Egypt, here Janet could at least stand in line with both men and women.

One day a lorry load of bed linen and towels arrived. The entire shipment was offloaded and locked in a fourth floor storage room by the director of security. The room had one window to the outside. I had learned that anything that was not nailed down would be stolen because the Russians believed that everything belonged to the people and, as they were the people, they could take it. The next morning I asked the director of security to open the door of the storage so I could check out the goods. At that his face turned bright red then ashen. I immediately guessed that all was not well.

Sure enough on entering the storage room I found that a pile of the linen near to the window was missing. I looked out of the window and saw a large dent in the snow about the size of a bulk of linen. There were foot prints leading to and from it. It was obvious to me that the director of security, probably under instruction from the Russian owner, was the guilty party. For a moment I wanted to hit him but I thought better of it. I had no intention of facing up to the mafia. It was widely known that a couple of German hotel general managers who had resisted the mafia in St.Petersburg were fished out from the bottom of the Neva river.

Christmas came ... and with it Emily and Paul. Their holiday visit was the highlight of our entire time in Russia. We skied cross country and went ice fishing on the lake. We visited St.Petersburg, all the interesting places around Novoburg and generally jammed all the activities we possibly could into the little precious time we had. Emily and Paul also received a short, sharp lesson on what communism was all about. The vacation was all too brief. Soon they left to return to Florida and to Germany. Janet's life and mine returned to its same sad routine.

During the hiring process for the hotel I had found that Russian men are, in general, unemployable. The main problem is their drinking habits. Women were the driving force in the economy. Women worked at jobs, laboured in fields, raised children, stood in line for hours to get the basic food needed and then went home to find a drunk husband who would beat them every night. We had, however, one driver out of two hundred employees who was more reliable than most. Or so it seemed. He was dispatched with the mini-van one morning to the table linen factory some distance away to pick up an order of linen. By evening he had not returned. We were worried about him. My ex-KGB Russian assistant put out some feelers and by 4.00 am next morning he found out that the driver was in a hospital two hundred kilometres from Novoburg.

Now the roads in Russia were just horrible, full of holes and covered with ice. Nonetheless we jumped into my car and eventually got to the hospital. We found him with his left arm broken in six places and stretched out on a mattress in a corridor. There was no medical attention as we were told there was no doctor available. His arm was also stripped of all skin and by now, a full twenty-four hours after the event which had caused the damage, infection was setting in. We decided to get him back to Novoburg for treatment. We carried him out to my car and got him on to the back seat and covered by a makeshift blanket. After another exhausting four hour drive we deposited him in the hospital in Novoburg. This hospital was horrible too but it was like a Mayo clinic compared to where we had found him.

The story of his accident was simple enough. On his return drive with the load of linen he had been smoking, drinking brandy and driving with his arm hanging out of the open window. He had drunkenly lost control of the mini-van and flipped it into a field with his arm trapped under the vehicle. Fortunately it was his left arm but it took three months to get better. When he returned to work I had to fire him.

By that time I was contacting every headhunter I could in the hope of finding a job somewhere else in the world - anywhere else! It was now February and each year in that month there is an international tourism fair in Milan. There, hoteliers and tourism operators from all over the world meet to present their products to travel agencies, tour operators and the like. Polarc had decided to participate. Janet and I saw this as a wonderful opportunity to get out of Novoburg and fly to Milan. We took the night train to Moscow. The trip was so cheap that we bought a whole cabin with four couchettes for the two of us so as to avoid having strangers in the cabin with us. We slept little as the train rattled about a lot but eventually we arrived in Moscow with time to kill before our evening flight to Milan. We decided to visit the Kremlin, Red Square, Saint Basil's Cathedral (where we witnessed a wedding ceremony), Lenin's Mausoleum and the State Historical Museum. Driving by the Bolshoi Theatre we thought how nice it would be to come one evening to see the Nutcracker performed - but that was never to happen. By that time we were pretty tired. Nonetheless, it had been a very pleasant day and one never to be forgotten.

A FRENCH RESURRECTION

Soon we stepped on to our Alitalia flight to Milan ... and into another world. During the three hour flight we were served real Italian ravioli and Janet had a nice glass of Chianti. It was like being born again after the dark months in Russia with the lack of every basic comfort, including toilet paper.

In Milan Mike Hill, the company director of sales and marketing and also ex-Marriott, was waiting for us. The hotel chosen for our stay by the company was a good distance from the fair ground and from the city centre with its fashionable shops, fancy restaurants, museums and the Duomo. Janet still made the most of seeing all of these, and everything else she could of the city, while I attended the fair. It was quite sad to see the pathetic box in a corner of the exhibition hall which was our Polarc stand compared to the well decorated and professionally manned booths of all the major operators ... but Polarc wouldn't pay for anything better. However, we met up every evening at the hotel to go out with colleagues and friends, many Marriott people. That was just so enjoyable. The highlight of the trip though, was a visit to Centonara to see my sister Anna. Then, sadly, we had to return to Russia. The flight on Alitalia was our last connection with the world we knew.

In Moscow we shared a quick meal with Adalhard Adalbreach, the vice president of operations, and with the general manager of Polarc's hotel in Baku. This is when I definitely made up my mind to leave the company as soon as possible. It was so obvious that I didn't belong in that group. Their interests were totally different from mine and consisted of drinking, chasing women and stealing from the company. Returning to Novoburg was painful. Now I was contacting the headhunters every day. Eventually, in June, one of them arranged an interview for me with the Grand Hotel de l'Arc in Paris. The job on offer was for the position of director of food and beverage. I didn't mind stepping back in position one more time as I just had to get out of Russia. I had met Pierre Ferchaud, the general manager of the hotel, when he was general manager at the Marriott Prince de Galles in Paris. Pierre was and is a real gentleman. We are still in communication to this day.

A few days before leaving for the interview I had a phone call from Fritz Fikle, the man in charge of the hotel part of Polarc. As I picked up the phone, instead of hearing a polite, "Good morning," from the other end, I got a crude, "You fucking idiot!" shouted at me. I hung up the phone. A few minutes later I called him back but he continued to insult me, albeit in a lesser way, about something I was doing and with which he didn't agree. So, at the end of the one way conversation, I gave him my resignation.

Now that was a bold move. I had not yet gone to Paris for the interview with the Grand Hotel de l'Arc and could still end off out of work as I had been a year previously. There is a limit however to the abuse anyone should have to endure regardless of their situation. I had reached that limit. I knew that I couldn't and wouldn't accept such behaviour. I went home and told Janet that I had resigned and we were going to Paris for an interview the following week.

God smiled on me once more. We went to Paris, the interview went well and I was hired. I was also promoted to vice-president of food and beverage for the Grand Hotel de l'Arc and Paris Convention Centre. This was at the time the largest convention centre in Europe. We returned to Russia and proceeded to arrange our departure. Janet went to Germany, collected Paul and moved into a hotel in Paris where they met up with Emily. She had by now finished her last year at St.Andrew in Horse Shoe Bay. I continued to wrap up my work to pass on to the new general manager. He turned out to be the general manager of the Baku hotel I had dined with in Moscow. Adalhard flew in from Vienna to give me a small farewell party. It was a real cheap affair typical of the entire company way of doing things. The event embarrassed both me and my team. All the staff had come to say goodbye to me but they were treated miserably with only small canapés, soft drinks and water. All the while Adalhard and the new general manager treated themselves (not me) to a bottle of Russian champanski. I was glad to get out of there.

The next day was the 14th of July. I arrived in Paris in the midst of a spectacular parade on the Champs-Elysses with tanks rolling down the avenue and aircraft zooming overhead leaving behind vapour tails of red, white and blue. This was not a military coup as had greeted my arrival in Russia the year before but the Bastille Day celebration, France's most revered public holiday. It could have been specially arranged to celebrate the arrival of me and my family. We were overjoyed to be there.

It was terrific for Janet, Emily, Paul and myself to be together again, even if Emily was leaving shortly for Davidson College in North Carolina. Paul was accepted at the International School and also signed up at the Alliance Française where, in just one year, he completed his French language class achieving a grade four pass. That was one higher than I had achieved when I was in Paris as a young man.

We also started to look for an apartment. Pierre was very generous in giving me time off to visit ones which Janet had preselected with an agent beforehand. We chose one with two small bedrooms, one small bathroom, one small kitchen and one small living room. Soon after moving in, a leak appeared in the ceiling. I contacted the agent, who contacted the owner, who refused to do anything about it. Two weeks later, we found another apartment on the first floor at 7, Rue de l'Etoile in the 17th arrondissement.

This one was just a five minute walk from the hotel and a short metro ride from Paul's school. It was a small apartment too but it had a huge terrace, as big again as the whole rest of the place. Our room was pretty tight for space. Paul's was so small that he could only have one of those pullout bed/desks where, when you want to study at the desk, you have to close the bed and, when you want to sleep in the bed, you have to close the desk. Our kitchen was a one person one, long and narrow.

But the location was to die for, just the best you could wish for in Paris. We didn't have a car, didn't really need one. The apartment was just 150 yards (137 m) from the Arc de Triomphe and all the glamour of the Champs-Elysees was but a stone's throw away.

Janet was near everything she wanted, particularly the Louvre. Going there was like being in heaven for her. She's an extremely artistic person and joined the club Les Amis du Louvre which meant she could come and go there as she pleased. Even by going to the Louvre several times each week, Janet was never able to see all of the treasures on display there nor the many special exhibitions which came from all over the world. She thoroughly enjoyed her walks there, often stopping on wet winter days to enjoy a warming mug of hot chocolate in a café on the Champs-Elysees.

Galleries La Fayettes was another of her favourite 'homes from home' as she could spend hours there just wandering around, window shopping and admiring the elegant displays. There was also a delightful café inside with the best coffee and pastries to die for.

Paul adapted quickly to his new school. At last he had the chance to complete high school in the same school without being constantly moved about as had happened in the past. Beside his normal high school work and the Alliance Française he took up acting in the school drama society. They performed a play in which Paul had the leading role. The school headmaster's daughter was the principal actress and the play ended with Paul having to kiss her. I am sure that that was one of the most embarrassing moments in his life.

My work was hard but extremely interesting. This was because of the complexity of the hotel, it being home to Europe's largest convention centre and the fact that it was fifty years out of date in the way it was run. This latter, not because of Pierre, but because of the hotel's proprietors who were the Perigeaux family of champagne fame. They had owned the business for many years. The president and supreme leader of the family was Monsieur Gerard Perigeaux.

At hotel level, the purchasing manager had more power than the general manager. Nothing happened in the hotel without the approval of Monsieur Musico, the purchasing manager. He was from Naples, had worked many years for the family and, crucially, belonged to the same masonic lodge as Gerard Perigeaux where he outranked his boss. This meant that Monsieur Perigeaux would not dare to contradict or over-rule him at work. Musico operated a totally corrupt alliance with the executive chef whereby they creamed a tremendous amount of money from all the hotel purchases which were made only from members of the lodge.

The uniforms in the hotel were so old and outdated that they reminded me of the early '60s. From the top down, everything was managed in an arrogant manner devoid of any consensual lower management participation. The hotel had fallen into decay and a state of disrepair. The linoleum tiles on the floor of the main restaurant were so worn that guests were actually walking on the bare cement. The bar on the thirty-eighth floor, with a magnificent view of the city, had couches and tables which were falling apart. I concentrated first on the kitchen which had old wooden cabinets and stinking open drains. My priority was to seal the drains and replace everything with stainless steel.

The standard of service was also deplorable and antiquated. We were not doing plate service but employing the outmoded French service system. This meant that, by the time the meal was served, the food would be cold and almost inedible. I proceeded to purchase the hot boxes to start doing plate service and portable bars so as to stop using tables as bars at cocktails. I selected the vendors, mainly from the USA. This didn't sit well with Monsieur Musico as it curtailed his ability to earn a hefty commission. I also went to Balenciaga, a top designer in Paris, to get new staff uniforms.

One day I walked into the cellar and was shocked to find thousands and thousands of francs worth of wine and liquor that had been taken off the beverage list more than ten years earlier. It was still sitting there instead of having been rotated out and sold. I made a promotion to sell them off at special prices, by the bottle and by the glass. I was grateful to Pierre for being with me on all of this.

The resident manager, a half Swiss half Chinese international hotelier called John, was experiencing the same difficulties as me in trying to modernise the rooms department. He possessed all the expertise needed to make things right but he too faced opposition to his initiatives. Just to do some promotion, either in the rooms area or in the food and beverage area, met with constant resistance from the top of the executive chain to the bottom; with the exception of Pierre who was doing his best to help John and I achieve what we had been hired to do.

One good thing was that my days off were Saturday and Sunday. This meant that Janet, Paul and I could go to the American church in the morning and after that, either take a train ride out of the city or simply walk for hours enjoying the sights. Janet loved the many water fountains and architecture around the city and kept a note of them all in a special album. I believe she was able to locate and log the majority of them.

At work I had found that two assistants managers in the food and beverage department and the director of catering responsible for the banquet department were working without any clear job descriptions. As a result, their jobs were overlapping and nobody could be held accountable for anything. I wrote a clear job description for each of them and put one of them in charge of the restaurants and the other in charge of the bars.

There was also a nice young secretary called Corinne in the department. She tended to be a bit depressive at times but we got along well. She was willing to learn to do things in a more modern way. I found that, while I had more free time than I had ever had in previous jobs, the complete inefficiency of the operation and the old ways of doing things were very tiring. The politics played, the power games and the back stabbing were slowly getting to me.

My sister Anna, niece Maria Ester and her then boyfriend, Alfredo, came to visit us in Paris. As our apartment was so small we could not accommodate them. Pierre was again generous and came up with two rooms for them. Anna told us during the course of the visit that it had turned out that Maria Ester had kept up a secret relationship with Batman Bin, the young man she had met in Sakkara when she was fifteen. Once before she had run away from home to go to Paris with him.

Soon after Anna and the others had returned to Centonara I received a desperate call to say that Maria Ester had run away from home again. She had come to Paris to be with Batman Bin. Anna gave me the address of the apartment where he lived. It was in an area of Paris where white faces were not welcome and where even les flicques wouldn't venture alone. Along with the hotel's chief of security, I went to visit them.

When we got there Batman Bin was home but Maria Ester was at the Alliance Française. He told me that they were going to get married and regardless of what anyone said or felt that is what was going to happen. He said that they were both adults and could marry without consent from the parents.

I called Anna back and told her all this. Maria Ester later called home too and it was agreed that the two love birds would return to Centonara where Batman Bin would sleep in a room in the old house and Maria Ester would go back to her own room. The arrangement would be for one year and they would marry the following year. This is exactly what they did and they have been happily married since July of '93 and have two daughters, Emma and Greta.

OPPORTUNITY KNOCKS

Paris Fun & Family Resort had opened its doors in May of '92. I had tried, unsuccessfully, to join them from Russia. Now two former colleagues from Marriott had acquired leadership positions with the company. Lee Cockerell, previously general manager at Marriott, was the vice president of food and beverage for all hotels and for Restaurant Row. Sanjay Varma, also a former general manager at Marriott, was the vice president in charge of all hotels and Restaurant Row. This was the same Lee who had been my boss at the opening of the Chicago Marriott Downtown many years before. Ever since my arrival in Paris, we had been in touch. My hope was that one day I'd leave the horrible French company I was working with and rejoin an international organization. Paris Fun & Family Resort, I thought, would be perfect.

In March of '93 I got a call from Lee asking me to come over to Val de Marne for an interview with him and Sanjay. Full of enthusiasm I took the train and arrived forty minutes later at the Fun & Family Resort station. It took me a few minutes to walk to the meeting place where they were both waiting for me. The interview was more of a 'hello how are you' than anything else as we had known each other for years. The offer came soon enough. The position was to be the director of operations for the one thousand room Oldport Bay Club Hotel within the Fun & Family Resort complex. Jan, a Dutch guy, was the general manager there. I was thrilled to accept the offer and rejoin a large international company.

My contract with the Grand Hotel de l'Arc called for a three month notice period. I turned in my resignation to the new general manager, Jean-Paul Claude, on the 1st of April – April fool's day! (Pierre Ferchaud had been dismissed as it was the company policy to only keep the general manager for a period of two years and then fire him). Jean-Paul couldn't believe that I would leave the hotel. He was really concerned to have to find someone else who could put up with all the stupidity of that job.

Easter was on 11th of April and Jean-Paul invited me to take Janet and Paul to Biarritz for the Easter weekend and stay at the Grand Hotel du Palais. This is an old and traditional hotel dating back a very long time. His intentions were honourable. He wanted to give me time to reconsider the Paris Fun & Family Resort offer and hopefully decide to stay at the Grand and help him out. The three of us enjoyed a memorable weekend of gourmet dining, spa treatments and spectacular views of the Atlantic ocean; all in all a perfect getaway from the hustle and bustle of Paris. Returning to Paris after four days of luxury hospitality and living in paradise might well have changed my mind ... but it didn't. I was more determined than ever to make the jump to the Fun & Family Resort. I worked my three month notice as diligently as I had always worked before with no slacking off.

Then, on my last week at work, something unprecedented in the history of that company occurred. Monsieur le President, Gerard Perigeaux himself, summoned me to his office. I was so shocked that I almost dropped dead with surprise when Jean-Paul told me to report to Perigeaux's office at three o'clock that very day. In the typical French manner I had never even been greeted by him before; whenever he had passed me he would go straight by as if I were invisible. Now I was received by him in the most cordial way. He asked me to sit down and even offered me coffee. I thought he would ask me to stay and make me some kind of offer I would find hard to refuse. To my surprise, he instead asked me what was going on in the hotel.

Although somewhat taken aback by his request I let rip with my views regarding the malaise pervading the hotel and the rotten people who worked for him. I told him of all the stealing, the bribes, the corruption and that the two people he valued most highly were the ones who were robbing him blind.

These two were of course Monsieur Musico, the purchasing manager and the executive chef. I also revealed to him that the executive chef was coming to work at 10.00 am and, by 11.30 am, he would sit in his private dining room with his entourage and consume a tremendous lunch with the most expensive bottle of chateaux wine possible. By 1.00 pm he would leave with his secretary for some hotel room in the city and, returning at 6.00 pm without his secretary, would indulge in a repeat of the lunch feast before going home to his wife. I told him that the only honest person in the hotel, meaning Pierre, had been fired.

He congratulated me on my move to Paris Fun & Family Resort. He revealed that he was on their board of directors and knew the financial condition of the company. He asked me to try to help them out. He absorbed all I said to him about the hotel but didn't give the impression that he wanted to, or cared to, do anything about it. I was wrong to think that.

A few months later the executive chef was fired. However he couldn't fire Mr.Musico as he was his superior in the masonic lodge. What could he do to take him out of that role in which he was causing so much damage? He promoted him to the head office as the special assistant to the President. This is how bad people achieve high positions. Definitely a case of keep your friends close and your enemies closer!

Chapter 18

A FRENCH FARCE

My employment with Paris Fun & Family Resort started on the 1st of July with a one week introductory course at the resort's 'university'. There I was taught all about the company policies and values. I also had to learn the names of all the resort's characters and their popular ballads and songs. My measurements were taken and I was assigned a dog character costume which I was required to wear at parades and on other occasions while cavorting in the resort to entertain the visitors.

While I was taking the university course for executive recruits in one room, our daughter Emily, who was staying in Paris with us for the summer, was in a room next door learning the same stuff. She had also been hired by the Fun & Family Resort as a sales person in the pirate shop. This meant that we could meet for a snack lunch and have a good laugh together at what we were learning. Then, with my induction training completed, I started work at the Oldport Bay Club Hotel.

On my very first day I discovered that the company had considerably more problems than might be apparent to a casual observer. The European executives had fallen into the arrogant French way of doing business rather than follow the established international practices. The general manager, Jan, was one of the worst. He put me on a daily alternating rota. One day start early and finish at 6.00 pm and the next day start at 1.00 pm and finish at 11.00 pm and so on. The first day it worked but by only my second day he instructed me to come in at 7.00 am and then made me stay at work until 11.00 pm that night. He was just an arrogant sod.

I left for Maria Ester and Batman Bin's wedding as planned and, on my birthday, the 30th of July we all came back to Paris. When I returned to work that Monday I was summoned by Sanjay and Lee to be told that I was being moved over to be director of convention service operations. In over a year since the opening of the banquet/convention department, it hadn't been able to serve even a simple coffee break on time. I was just glad to leave the Oldport Bay and Jan.

I met with Bruce, the director of convention services, and found him to be a real nice guy and very intelligent. His only problem was that he had never worked in a hotel nor in any convention department anywhere in the world. Bruce had an administrative management staff of American, Dutch, German and French women who reported to him. This team had little interest in working with the service staff who reported to the director of convention service operations – now me! The disconnect between administration and operations had been catastrophic and was now patently obvious to me. Bruce did not really understand the problem but was, nonetheless, delighted to learn that there was a solution. It was that only one person should be in charge of both areas of the convention department - and that person had to be me! I was not going to make a big noise about it, just take over the day to day operation. He would still be the director representing the department. He readily agreed.

I set up a meeting for all my service managers and the administrative staff to attend. I first informed the dysfunctional team that the next person to send a CYA (cover your arse) inter-departmental mail would be fired on the spot (there had been an epidemic of these). I added that, when there was an issue of any kind, the manager in question had to get off their fanny and go to the other person and resolve the issue face to face.

One American female manager retorted that I was not her boss and that she didn't have to listen to me. I had to make it crystal clear to her that I was now in charge of both the office and the service departments and that I would run the operation in the most efficient way I saw fit. I gave her, naturally, the choice to stay or to go as from now on the rules of the game were changing. She decided to stay.

Another major difficulty was that the entertainment section and the hotels were fighting each other rather than working together. Management of entertainments felt that the hotels were there to serve them but, as the office of convention services would book functions in all of the restaurants in Restaurant Row, total co-operation was essential. I established a 3.00 pm daily meeting with all the personnel in charge of servicing the events in each venue of the Fun & Family Resort, to which they had to bring their banquet event orders. I also requested that the kitchen chefs be present.

In typical French chef attitude they were not initially agreeable nor happy with this. Nor with the way I conducted the meetings. After arguments and protests a compromise was reached and they agreed to attend the first part of the meeting. By then they had figured out that it was much easier to work this way than the way they had been working previously. The entertainment section also started to follow suit. We were now able to organise events there in the many different venues and be sure that they would happen.

The next task was to train the banquet staff to give service. The way it had been done was incredibly disorganised with a last minute arrival of personnel coming from various hotels to the Convention Centre to serve a banquet. All of the most modern equipment was available and yet staff had never been trained on how to use it. The first time I witnessed a banquet there, five hundred guests were in attendance, ten to a table. The waiters took five plates at a time on a large tray and served half of the table, then returned to the kitchen and stood in line behind the other waiters to get the next five plates. The result of course was cold food for everyone. The very next day I trained the managers in the service department of every hotel how to carry ten plates on a tray in one go so that each table could be served in one trip and thus provide hot food for all. I was making progress.

For me this was the easiest year of my life. I was getting up at 5.00 am every morning and walking to the boulangerie for the day's fresh baguette. Then Janet prepared Paul's snack lunch to take to school with him while I got ready to catch the 7.00 am train at the station just 200 yards (180 m) along the road from the apartment. I always picked up the newspaper at the kiosk there and arrived at the Fun & Family Resort train station at 7.40 am. From there I walked to my office and was ready to start work for the day at 7.50 am. Then, except if there was a major function taking place, I left the office at 6.00 pm to be home to have dinner with Janet and Paul by 7.00 pm. What a life.

Yako el Mattum, the general manager of the Marriott's Prince de Galles Hotel with whom I had worked in Sakkara many years before, wanted me to give a young colleague some career advice. I met this lad in a café on the Champs-Elysses one Sunday morning in September. As we sat there sipping hot chocolate I had the urge to go to the toilet. Once there a tremendous pain siezed my tummy and looking down I saw a bulge in my lower belly/groin area the size of two tennis balls. I barely dragged myself up the stairs and got the café owner to call an ambulance. The young man I had been talking with ran over to our apartment to tell Janet but, by the time Janet arrived at the café, I was already on my way to hospital. The young guy drove Janet to the hospital where doctors at the emergency department had already diagnosed me as suffering from a hernia. Janet contacted the American Hospital in Paris and I was operated on the next day and invalided off work for two weeks.

By that time Emily had returned to the USA to start university in North Carolina. Because she was ahead a year when we had come to Boston from Mustashat, she started at seventeen years old instead of the normal age of eighteen. Janet kept busy with her various activities such as bible studies at a centre just outside of Paris. There she made friends with Beryl who, years later, would end up living nearby us in Portugal. Janet and her get together quite often for coffee and meals. One of the highlights of Janet's Parisian life was to visit the fresh produce markets and to wander around smelling the cheeses, picking up fresh vegetables and flowers and bartering with the old market traders. Janet got a real kick from that.

Back at Paris Fun & Family Resort the team had finally come to terms with being organised and following the rules I had dictated. Now I could revert to my style of management and lead from the front as I always preferred doing rather than pushing from the back. With Christmas approaching, activity increased and work kept me more occupied than had been the case up 'til then. For the first time we erected a huge tent and, twice a night throughout December and to the 6th of January, we put on a Christmas show with dinner for 400 guests. It was a masterpiece of organisation to get the first house cleared in time to welcome the second lot of 400 just forty minutes later.

On Christmas day, after breakfast service, I went home to share lunch with Janet, Emily and Paul. I left a young supervisor in charge of organising all the necessary equipment for the two dinner shows. I returned back at work at 5.00 pm for the 7.00 pm show to find that the young man had done nothing. The tables were not set up and there was nothing ready for the second show at 9.30 pm. I almost blew a gasket. Colleagues from all over the hotels, including some general managers, came to the rescue. With a huge effort from all we had the venue prepared and ready to open the door exactly on time.

My boss Bruce had agreed that I could take a week off right after Christmas. Mario had invited us to spend it with him and his French girlfriend at his home in Rome. Janet had a terrible cold but we all flew to Rome anyway. Mario is the most hospitable person I have ever met. He cooked and washed up for us all week and, on the 29th of December, he loaned us his car and gave us the keys to his apartment in the Apennine mountains. Janet, Emily and Paul are good skiers so for them the venue was paradise. On Hogmanay they were on the ski slopes and had a wonderful time.

That evening we had booked a table in a very rustic restaurant built inside a cave. It proved to be a simply wonderful experience with Italian food at its best, music playing and cheerful people celebrating New Year. What a night it was. By one o'clock, we were all in bed as the three of them wanted to go skiing again in the morning. They did that but, at the top, encountered strong winds and a snow storm. The following day we drove back to Rome very tired. We couldn't have been happier with our few days in the fresh mountain air away from the city, smoke and noise. Back in Paris, it was back to school for Paul, a return to her plethora of social activities for Janet and, unfortunately, a sad goodbye to Emily who had to resume her studies in North Carolina.

THE RECESSION BITES

Paris Fun & Family Resort was now starting to feel the twin pains of lack of revenue and high operating costs. Highly paid executives were either taken to Orlando, Lee Cockerell was one, or let go. Sanjay resigned and was replaced with a French guy. The whole organisation was in a state of disarray and no one was secure in their jobs. Many employees accepted severance package offers. I would have taken that too but I had no prospect of a job elsewhere. Besides which I had by that time been promoted to vice president of food and beverage for the resorts and Restaurant Row. This job came with a car. Janet was not thrilled as that meant I would now work longer hours and she would be left on her own more of the time. While the car, gas, maintenance and insurance were free the parking was at my own expense. Fortunately there was a public parking lot right next door to the apartment.

Having the car meant that I now had to get a French driver's license. It also meant that my peaceful train ride every morning to work and in the evening back home was to be replaced with a 40 mile (64 km) drive each way, the most challenging part of which was to cross the Etoile. This is the circle around the Arc de Triomphe where twelve avenues merge into one place. To negotiate it you have to follow one simple rule ... don't look. That is as in do not look anywhere, not in front, not to the side nor to the back, just go and do not stop. Those who stop never move again - Parisian drivers are not renowned for having a great deal of patience.

The positive aspects to having the car included our new freedom to drive around in the countryside and visit other cities on my days off. We went to Normandy and Paul swam in the English Channel … in November. We went to Dijon, the mustard capital of the world (which I had visited on my travels in my younger days) and to Le Mans where the famous twenty-four hours endurance motor race takes place each year. The fun thing about this place is that you can drive on the circuit with your own car and at any speed you want. Trust me if you are in a car driven by Janet you would know what speed is.

Emily had now returned to spend the summer with us in Paris and, towards the end of the school year, Paul had started to learn Italian. When summer came, my long-time friend Mario agreed to put him up in Rome where he could spend the summer learning Italian. When Paul arrived in Rome he went to the American Embassy and asked if he could work there for the summer. The embassy did give him a job – unpaid of course. Unfortunately, Paul and Mario suffered a clash of personalities which led to fights and disagreements between them on an almost daily basis. But with Paul in Rome, Emily had a room of her own and a bed to sleep in.

In August the three of us made a wonderful drive from Paris to Rome stopping one night in Saint Jean-Cap-Ferrat on the French Cote d'Azur. John, my friend and colleague from Grand Hotel de l'Arc days, was now working as the general manager of the Grand Hotel du Cap there. This is a place in which everyone ought to spend at least one night of their life. The marble from Carrara is king. Passing the magnificently manicured gardens at arrival you enter the white palace and all you see is marble of different tones. Crossing the lobby and looking down to the infinity pool lining up with the sea is as if you have been transported to paradise. The little old fashion crémalière takes you down to the water for a refreshing swim before even checking in.

When you do check in you do so seated on an enormous, over-stuffed armchair with a glass of Dom Perrignon in hand. John had reserved for us what he called regular rooms but it was actually a suite with two connecting rooms. The master bedroom was all white with a floor covered by alternating thick Persian white rugs over marble of the finest quality. The entire wall behind the bed was one huge mirror making the room look twice its actual size. The bed, oh the bed! It had silk sheets such as I had not seen since the Grand Hotel in Rome in the '60s. The finest quality furnishings completed the room. The bathroom was another story again. It had two all marble white sinks and a bathtub large enough to host an orgy. The towels were soft and spongy and the bath robe was so thick and fluffy I couldn't let go of it. The shampoo and all the toiletries were Christian Dior. It seemed almost a shame to use that place as a toilet. Emily's room and bathroom were no less opulent. As every room is different, her bed had a fine cloth wall behind the head board rather than mirroring.

Once installed and showered we were ready to go to dinner with John. We ate with him seated at our dining table on the marble floored terrace overlooking the Mediterranean Sea in one of the most prestigious and beautiful places on earth. The company was stimulating and the food, from a three star Michelin chef, left nothing to the imagination. Janet, Emily and I savoured one of the most remarkable dining experiences of our lives. All too soon it was time to call it a night. John had been the perfect host but he wasn't finished yet. On our return to our rooms we were pleasantly surprised to find a platter of the most exquisite petit fours and a choice of the finest cognacs and liquers had been brought for us. I supposed they were meant to help us to sleep better.

The night was peaceful and we woke up refreshed and ready to leave. Breakfast was served under the huge trees in the garden. Not a buffet but an a la carte offering as elaborate as the dinner menu had been and with the same three star Michelin chef in charge. It proved to be another feast for the eyes as well as for the palate. After a delightful hour, we left and made the short drive to Nice. There we walked the beach and lingered over a café crème in a café on the Promenade des Anglais. We then headed for the Italian border and San Remo passing Monte Carlo en route. It would have been great to have stopped there but time was of the essence as we wanted to make Rome before dark. We arrived there in late afternoon to find that Mario had prepared another dinner, a feast really, just in case there was no food between Paris and Rome. Knowing Mario no surprise there.

Seeing Paul was great and after lots of hugs and kissing we sat down with Mario for dinner. Sadly we soon sensed that Mario and Paul were at odds. Mario is a very strong individual, opinionated at times and Paul is no lamb either. The two characters would clash easily. This was, after all, Mario's house. Paul had been there for a month or so and had managed to stain Mario's piano with hot wax. Mario was, quite naturally, upset about that and the tension could be felt.

One good thing was that we had our car this time. We could move around more easily than always having to rely on public transport. We went to see the places we had missed on our previous visit at Christmas. Paul had found where to get the best ice-cream in Rome so that was our first stop. I also wanted to show them all the places where I had worked as a boy. We went to dinner at the Mediterraneo Hotel. We were served by a waiter who had been an assistant with me in 1959 and who was still there with his flat feet doing the same thing all those years later. I thought how fortunate I had been to leave when I did.

We took the train to the Ostia Lido beach 20 miles (32 km) from Rome and spent a relaxing day on the hot sand and eating lunch in the beach restaurant. As we were all four now together, we went to Florence, Pisa and Siena for four days. Florence with all its works of art is one of, if not, the most beautiful cities on earth. The leaning tower of Pisa couldn't be missed. Neither could Siena, the cradle of the Italian language, especially by Paul as a budding linguist. One early morning we left Paul and Mario, waved goodbye and took off on a different return route via Switzerland.

A ten hour drive at full speed took us to the St.Gottard Pass and in Airolo, in the Italian speaking part of Switzerland, we put the car on the train. We were quickly transported through the 9 mile (14.5 km) long tunnel and drove off a short time later in Goeschenen, in the German speaking part of Switzerland. It was a fun experience, especially for Janet and Emily. Now we were in Switzerland where the roads are just immaculate and everything is clean and functions well - just like their watches. Everything is on time and efficiency is the way of life. I really like Switzerland. Going via Lucerne and Berne we drove to Lausanne where we stopped to admire the beauty of Ouchy. This is the lower part of the town at the shore of Lake Geneva. Curiously enough the Lausannois do not call it that as they do not want to give the lake to the city of Geneva. They call it Lac Leman. No matter what it is called it is indeed a very beautiful place.

Emily had her picture taken holding on to the arm of Charlie Chaplin's life size statue. I couldn't resist taking a look inside the Beau-Rivage Palace Hotel where I had worked twenty-six years previously. It had gone through renovations and was more modern. Yet it still retained the same elegance and glamour that had made it the world class hotel it was so many years before and which it most likely always will be. We had to have a nice, rich and aromatic café crème as the cream served with the coffee in Switzerland is so fresh and so delicious as to die for.

By that time we had been travelling for too many hours. It was time to find a hotel and crash for the night. The next morning we were ready to drive on home. Not before a delicious breakfast, a short drive around Lausanne and a stop off in beautiful Geneva though. Here the most prestigious brands of watches in the world are made. After a brief tour of the city we headed for France, crossing the border at Perly-Certoux and taking the slower, more picturesque route via Beaune, the 'eye of Burgundy'.

Although by that time I was no longer drinking wine I wanted Janet and Emily to see the place where one of my favorite wines, at the time I was drinking, came from. We visited the vineyard at Moulin-a-Vent. From there we headed for Paris and home. We did not stop again. Shortly after that Emily returned to university in North Carolina but she had signed up for a year abroad programme which meant that she came back to France as an exchange student at the University of Montpellier in the South of France.

Fun & Family Resort's financial problems were not going away. A consortium of sixty-two banks held a huge mortgage that couldn't be paid and a rich prince from Saudi Arabia had purchased 24% of the company. Even that would not be sufficient to save it from bankruptcy. The general manager of the Big Apple Hotel was dismissed. I was asked to take over his post in addition to my job as the vice president of food and beverage. I accepted as my choices were non-existent. Had I said no I would have been sent packing too. This meant even longer working hours for me and I soon found that my days didn't have enough hours in them.

Soon Paul returned from Rome, just in time for us to take him to Leamington Spa in England to start history studies at Warwick University. It is one of the finest in the world for that particular subject. His living quarters there were a house shared by five students, three boys and two girls. The university was very open to these kind of arrangements. They supplied the students with a welcome kit that included two condoms! Paul had applied to several universities including Harvard School of Law to which he had been accepted. When he turned Harvard down I asked him why he had applied there if he didn't wish to study law. His reply was, "I wanted to know if I was good enough for Harvard!"

Sometime later Janet and I visited Paul and found just what a house with five students living in it unsupervised looked like. Well, Indian take-away was the staple food and nobody washed dishes. The stink of old curry was so pungent that breathing was a major task. Fortunately, Janet and I were staying in a bed and breakfast.

Emily was now in Montpellier for her six months of studies there. One evening I returned to our apartment to find about twenty young student friends of Emily's from the university of Montpellier 'camped' there.

As I opened the door to enter, a twenty year old redhead wearing the biggest smile imaginable, and little else, greeted me. I thought I was in the wrong apartment. I hadn't known that Emily and her friends were coming. I went to our room and left them to make their own sleeping arrangements on the floor. Emily of course had Paul's bed. This happy group of young people stayed for two nights while visiting Paris and its beautiful sites.

Working conditions at Fun & Family Resort were harder than ever. Each day another member of staff was let go. The insecurity was taking its toll. Nerves were frayed, arguments broke out easily and everyone was intent solely on their own survival with no regard for the well-being of others. It had become a thoroughly unpleasant place to work.

It was not only the interpersonal ambience which was in decline but the physical environment too. Gone was the trademark pristine Fun & Family Resort appearance and in was a shoddy, litter-strewn wasteland awash with discarded food wrappers and cigarette butts and with no orderlies in sight to keep the place clean.

Chapter 19

THE PHARAOHS RISE AGAIN

Over all the time I had been gone from Marriott I had been in touch with Karl Kilburg. He was now the top man in Europe for all of the Marriott hotels in England, continental Europe and the Middle East. He came to Paris often and we made a point of having dinner together. He knew that I was not happy with Fun & Family Resort and would have loved to come back to Marriott.

Marriott had a new hotel under construction in Egypt. Karl was only too aware of how much I had enjoyed Egypt and the work environment there. Marriott was finding the economic conditions in Europe difficult. Like Fun & Family Resorts they were having to cut costs. Their two German hotels in Bremen and Hamburg had been consolidated under one general manager. The redundant manager was transferred to Mina al Janub in Egypt to start the process of pre-opening for that resort. This guy quickly became unhappy in Egypt, found himself a job in Puerto Rico and left the company. Thus it transpired that one day I received a call from Karl's secretary asking me to go to Frankfurt for an interview to explore the possibilities of my return to Marriott.

I couldn't get there quickly enough and soon met up with Karl. He showed me brochures of this beautiful resort village under construction at Mina al Janub about 280 miles (450 km) south of Sakkara. The resort was to have two hundred and eighty-four rooms, two restaurants and an indoor bar which would double as a night club. There would also be a large swimming pool with a snackbar, a man made island with a beach and additional bar. All this right on the beach in a prime seafront location. Behind the resort there were thirty-six apartments with their own swimming pool, tennis court and a full gym with sauna, steam room and an indoor and an outdoor jacuzzi. In addition to the hotel, there was employee housing with three hundred beds to be managed as an additional hotel. The project sounded more than just interesting. The idea of returning to Marriott excited me greatly. After all, I had spent fifteen happy years with the company. In the six years since I had left them, I had been in four jobs and spent seven months in unemployment. I was thinking that I could never work anywhere else but with Marriott.

I also learned that the executive committee which was in place was a team who, with one exception, I had worked with while in Sakkara several years before. They were all young men whose presence pleased me. The executives based in Mina al Janub were housed in a villa in four smart apartments. It all sounded very exciting to me. With all its faults Marriott was still the best company to work for. The prospect of going back to Egypt really appealed to me. So the offer came – and it was a good one. I had no hesitation in saying, "Yes!" Suddenly it felt like I was going back to my family and to my country. There is a saying in Egypt ... "Once you drink of the waters of the Nile you will always return to Egypt." I realised anew just how much I liked that country. With all its problems, confusion, traffic, noise and hypocrisy it was still the best place to live as a foreigner. The people were, in general, very kind and if you had a white face you were considered smart and intelligent.

Now I was ready to return to Paris and the delicate task of informing Janet that she must leave Paris with all its culture, sights, music, theatre and joie de vivre for the heat and dust of the desert and life in an apartment in a hotel. Given my profession, I thought it easier to get to people through their stomachs. I invited Janet to dinner at her favourite restaurant, the Col Vert, not far from the apartment. After ordering Janet's favourite meal I pulled out the brochures and explained to her that I had been made an offer but had only accepted conditional on her acceptance of it too. I said that if she didn't want to leave Paris for Egypt then I would turn down the job and continue in my present position at Fun & Family Resort. Janet's reply was, "When do we leave!"

The very next day I handed in my resignation. I invited my colleagues for a drink after work to break the news to them. Mostly they were happy for me but some expressed a degree of scepticism. They could not imagine that their wives would be agreeable to exchanging Paris for a desert village like Mina al Janub. They were probably right ... but their wives were not Janet.

Two weeks later Karl invited me to attend a regional general managers meeting in Budapest. There I met up with my director of finance, Mohamad Helmi, and all the other general managers in the Europe and Middle East region. With familiar faces all around I quickly felt at home again. It was as if I had never left Marriott. Such was the bonhommerie between us that I resolved to never leave Marriott again of my own volition. I would have to be fired this time. With Emily in North Carolina and Paul in England, making the move was easy. On the 24th of March we finally left Paris and flew to Sakkara. Now I was home. Back to Marriott and back to Egypt.

Janet and I were given an apartment. It was just like the one we had lived in when we were there before at the Zamalek Tower. We soon caught up with all our old friends like Nagla, Juergen's secretary and Jasmine, my former secretary now married and mother of two boys. I was introduced to Abu Bakr, the director of food and beverage and the only member of the executive committee I didn't know. The pre-opening office for Mina al Janub was at the Sakkara Marriott. On my second day after arrival, Juergen took me to meet the owner of the resort. He was a very rich and very fat man with two sons and a veiled wife. I didn't like his limp hand shake nor the fact that he did not look me in the eyes. This concerned me as, if you want to succeed as general manager, you must be liked and be able to work with the owners. My relationship with my executive committee though was good and I generally felt welcome.

The very next day Janet and I flew to Mina al Janub to take a look at the construction and at the village. The location was unbelievably beautiful but it was evident that there was a lot to do.

It was already the end of March and we were supposed to open in May in order to catch the European summer vacation season. The pre-opening work was so far behind schedule that that seemed to be but a remote possibility. Fortunately (from my perspective) the construction work was also behind and the May opening date could not be met. Nonetheless I charged on, ordering equipment and hiring managers for the various positions. All was falling into place.

BACK IN THE OLD ROUTINE

Janet had fallen easily back into the old routine, visiting her old haunts and getting involved in her favourite activities. She was a regular in the gym at the hotel and at the gold and spice shops at Khan-el-Kahlili market. Dr.Moustafa, the hotel doctor, had become our regular doctor again and the Anglican church behind the hotel, our Sunday place of worship. We were also horse riding at the pyramids once more but with less frequency than when we were first in Sakkara. Yes, we were happy.

In June, however, it was time for me to move to Mina al Janub and settle into one of the four heads of departments assigned apartments in the employee housing complex. This housing was built according to the specification Marriott had given the owner. This meant that there were only three line employees per room, two supervisors per room and one head of department per apartment. Each apartment had air conditioning. A games room with table football, table tennis, billiard table and two television sets was at the disposal of the male employees. An additional television room was set aside for the female employees who enjoyed even better accommodation as only two of them were assigned to each room. An air-conditioned bus would run scheduled trips from the housing to the hotel ensuring that employees arrived to work fresh and with their uniforms spotless. When I moved to Mina al Janub Janet stayed on in Sakkara in the comfort of the hotel and the routine she had now set for herself.

Upon arriving in Mina al Janub I made a point of visiting my colleagues at the other five star hotels. My first contact was with the general manager of the Intercontinental Hotel. He warmly welcomed me and offered me a special rate of just 25 dollars per day for double bed and breakfast for whenever Janet would join me from Sakkara. He wanted to be my friend. It was a different story at the Sonesta Hotel. The general manager turned out to be an aggressive American fellow. He resented there being a new kid on the block and accused Marriott of ruining the employment market by offering superior wages, housing, meals and working conditions to our staff. I responded that we were just treating our employees as human beings and following our founder's principle of 'take care of your employees and they will take care of the customers'.

The construction work was still far behind schedule but the owner assured me that everything would be ready to open on the 15th of July. As my team had everything organised and ready, I opened reservations from that date but, when it came around, the building work was still far from completion. We would have been able to open the main restaurant and the bar but only about one hundred and fifty of the rooms. That would have been a start anyway as I didn't expect that we would sell out the entire hotel straight away. Worse than that though, granite slabs were still being laid on the pool deck, the pool and beach bars weren't completed and the gym was bare with no equipment. There was no sauna, no steam room, no jacuzzi and no tennis courts. The electricity was off, the sewage plant didn't work nor did the desalinisation plant. In short - the resort wasn't in any shape to receive guest.

Janet had moved to Mina al Janub at the beginning of July and we were comfortably installed at the Intercontinental. We even got to use the general manager's car which gave Janet the mobility to discover the area and meet new people while I was totally involved working around the clock. The assistant manager's wife at the Intercontinental was a nice young Dutch lady with two school age children. Janet and her got on well. This lady, with some other mothers, was in the process of organising an international school in the new town of El Gouna, some 20 miles (32 km) distant from

Mina al Janub. Janet became very enthusiastic about the project and the idea of working with the children there.

As the 15th of July came round we only had received one booking. It was from a German lady and her ten year old son. With the resort still far from ready, I rebooked her into the Intercontinental. I couldn't get hold of the guest to advise her of the change so I went to the airport to meet her and to explain the situation. But I missed her at the airport and she made her way to our hotel. We found her there on our return some time later, a dejected figure sitting on the steps of a dark and locked hotel with the boy and four large suitcases. I thought she would jump on me and at least scratch my eyes out. To my surprise, she was as cool as a cucumber.

I apologetically explained the situation to her and that we had arranged accommodation for her at another five star resort of international repute until our hotel was ready. I drove her the few miles to the Intercontinental and told her that I would touch base with her every day to keep her up to date with events. I also invited her to come and see the hotel and she did indeed do that. Once we had most of the major items working, I told her that she could move in, so she did. The workers were still building and nailing together the wooden sun shades on the beach. She and her son had great fun trying to talk with the Egyptian construction workers while one of our people held a sun umbrella over their heads.

Eventually the desalinisation plant was producing water and the toilets were flushing. The kitchen was cooking and even the bar had entertainment at night. We were now able to take in other guests even if at a slower pace than normally is done in an opening of a hotel. One of the areas that was not ready to use was our apartment. Construction in the place had stopped so Janet and I moved into one of the suites. The sleeping part was fine but there was no kitchen. All of our meals had to be eaten either in a restaurant or brought to us by room service. For the first two weeks or so that was fine but after that it gets irksome not to be able to make your own meals. That and being at the mercy of the staff every time you want to eat or drink something. It was six months before we could eventually move into the apartment. Janet in the meantime had started, along with several other mothers, to work at the El Gouna school. Every morning she picked up other mothers and children from Mina al Janub for the 20 mile (32 km) drive.

The first chef we hired was a good guy from the Sakkara Marriott. He was a Copt (Egyptian Christian). With a crew of more than 95% Muslims, there was no way they would let him succeed. They undermined him at every turn. One of their nasty tricks was to throw good food away as garbage so as to increase the cost of operation. His boss, Abu Bakr, was in on the act too. He wanted to bring in an Austrian chef he had worked with at the Sonesta Hotel. Accordingly the chef was fired and the Austrian, the dirtiest and laziest chef I ever worked with, was recruited. This waste of space had become a Muslim in order to marry an Egyptian girl. The marriage though didn't go well and he soon ran back to Austria. I also had a Christian secretary but the entire executive committee was Muslim and the poor woman was so pressured that she eventually quit too. Strangely enough I hired an Austrian secretary who was married to an Egyptian fellow and had a daughter. That marriage didn't last either and she and her daughter also ran off to Austria.

The hotel was slowly getting to a manageable point of completion and the gym became ready to open. Considering that our guests were mostly European, with Germans forming the majority, I thought it a good idea to have it open to men and women all day and evening long. This included a mixed gender sauna, jacuzzi and steam bath as, in Europe, I knew that it was considered quite normal for men and women to bathe naked together. The day the sauna opened I joined guests there. I wanted to see first hand the reaction to my liberal idea (I felt it appropriate however to keep my swim trunks on considering the position I held in the hotel). I sat on a lower bench in the sauna with a rather large

Swiss lady above me. As the sauna got hotter she shed both the top and bottom parts of her bikini and flung them over my head. This was the first and the last session of mixed sex use of the gym. From then on I set up a rota of separate times and days for men and women to use it.

We should also have had male masseurs to massage men and female masseuses to massage women as the law specified. There were no local masseuses however and it proved impossible to find a female masseuse to come to Mina al Janub from Sakkara. In the event, a tall, handsome guy was hired. We thought that, because our customers were all foreigners, they would be fine with a male masseur. This worked well enough just as long as the female guests taking a massage were older ladies and of a motherly demeanour. Then one day a twenty year old, blonde California girl booked a massage with him.

Soon afterwards she came to my office in a state of distress and complaining that she had been molested. Her story was rather convoluted and many aspects of the events she recounted seemed improbable to me. The crux of it was that, at some point during the massage, she found herself naked with the masseur massaging her with his tongue between her legs. I was unsure what to do. I called the risk management department at Marriott headquarters to ask for guidance. After consideration of all the facts as best as I could describe them, the risk management officer I spoke to suggested that I offer the young lady a week vacation in the Bahamas as compensation. This on the basis that a week there with food and free lodging was a far less costly outcome than if she sued Marriott in the US, won the case and cashed in to the tune of a few million dollars. I made her the offer, she agreed and the case was settled. I dismissed the young man even though his side of the story was very different from hers.

The water desalinisation plant had been working well and we were able to produce water in enough quantity to support a full hotel. Until one night it stopped. Providing bottled water for five hundred guests at one minute's notice proved to be a severely challenging task. The fact that toilets couldn't be flushed just added to the avalanche of complaints. The crisis lasted for forty-eight hours and the compensation amounts we had to pay back to guests was so great that we could easily have built a back-up desalinisation plant with the money.

The hotel also had a shopping gallery with several shops selling everything from sun cream to the finest jewelry. One of the shops was owned by Tarek Sharif, the son of the famous movie star Omar Sharif. Omar was a frequent visitor to his son and consequently the hotel. He was still then handsome and definitely a seducer but, by that time, penniless. He was poorer than the proverbial church mouse. He came to the hotel for three reasons - One was to visit his son; two was because his son bought him lunch; and three was because he would inevitably find some lonely tourist who would accompany him for the rest of the afternoon, and maybe even the night if the conditions warranted it. While he had enjoyed great fame and earned a fortune, Omar had gambled it all away. He eventually died, poor and lonely at age eighty-three. It is said that he once lost his four and a half million pound home on the island of Lazarote in a game of bridge.

One of the most attractive shops was a jewelry shop selling the world's finest twenty-four karat, hand-made rings, bracelets and necklaces. The young man in charge of the shop was a good looking but pretentious sod who believed that every female client came into the shop to be groped by him rather than to make a purchase. One afternoon a very distressed Swiss lady came into my office with her elderly mother. She blurted out that, just a few minutes before, she (with her mother) had gone into the jewelry shop to try on a necklace she had seen in the window which had particularly attracted her attention. The young man had gone behind her to place the necklace around her neck and that was when she had felt a hard object rubbing against her buttocks. She had immediately grabbed her mother's hand and ran from the store straight to my office just 5 yards (4 m) away.

I immediately called the owner of the business and demanded

that he come to see me straight away. When he arrived and I related to him what had happened, he became very defensive. He tried to convince me that the young man in the shop was a fervent Muslim and, as such, he would never do any such thing. This although he knew as well as I that many young men came from other places to Mina al Janub to release their unfulfilled passions. At that point I realised that there was no need for me to extend the conversation any further. I told him that he had a choice to make; to remove the young man immediately from the shop or I would close the shop down and put him out in the street along with all his merchandise. The young man was gone the next day.

BACK TO BERMUDA

This was also the time that our daughter Emily was to graduate from the university in North Carolina and Janet and I flew to be at the ceremony ... and at the same time celebrate our twenty-fifth wedding anniversary! What better way to do that than for the three of us to take a trip back to Bermuda where it all started? After an emotional and moving graduation ceremony with plenty of tears, we drove to Charlotte and took a flight to this terrestrial paradise. By then the Castle Harbour Resort was a Marriott hotel with my friend from '77 Oldport Beach days, Roger Borsink, as the general manager. He gave us a beautiful suite with a connecting room and treated us like the most important guests in the hotel.

Mike Riby and his wife Rosie were also there. We had worked together in '85 in Mustashat and always remained friends. Mike had transferred from Mustashat to the Castle Harbour when Marriott had taken over that hotel. He was the best engineer in the region and the Castle Harbour the most difficult hotel to manage from the mechanical and construction side of the business. What a beautiful week the three of us had. We rented three mopeds and ran all over the island, revisiting all the places Janet and I had known and enjoyed twenty-five years before. It was fantastic to celebrate together, especially as Emily would be going to Japan shortly after her return to the US.

All too soon we returned to Mina al Janub and the challenges, and fun, that went with it. One night we woke up to the disgusting stench of sewage. Tarek, the director of engineering, did not take long to establish that the sewage plant had stopped working and that the excrement was not breaking down as it should. Now we really had a problem on our hands. Not only was the stench unbearable but the health issue and the danger of contaminated water was a real threat. Some guests insisted on being moved to another hotel, which I had no choice but to do. Others understood the situation and held on. Some, with an engineering background, even offered to help. I learned that it is in circumstances like this that you see the differences in human nature. Most humans are selfish and this is basically down to fear. Yet others don't think of self interest and just help out because it is the right thing to do. Anyway, this nightmare lasted well into the following night before, thank God , it was eventually resolved.

One of the regular features of my Mina al Janub life was the trip I had to make to Sakkara for two nights every month. Many times Janet came with me to visit the many friends she had left behind when we moved to Mina. The reason for my monthly trip was to meet with the general manager of the Sharm el Sheikh Marriott and our director of sales and marketing to plan the following month's activities in each of the hotels. At one of these meetings Juergen informed me that all of the sprinklers installed in the hotel would have to be changed immediately. Shortly after I had a scary encounter with the law.

On this particular day two policemen came to the hotel and told me that I had to accompany them to see the chief of police in Mina al Janub on a very urgent matter. I asked my director of human resources to come with me to translate and went to the police station. I knew I was in for trouble when the chief didn't extend the usual Egyptian hospitality of offering me tea or Turkish coffee.

Instead he threateningly pointed his finger at me and told me that I was to be arrested and deported from the country in the next twenty-four hours for the crime of disrespecting and insulting Islam and all Muslims. This was, and I believe still is, the complaint that would get any foreigner into a lot of trouble in any Muslim country. The charge had been made by some anonymous employee at the hotel. Yet, in all my years in Egypt, I had never once made a single derogatory comment about religion knowing just how sensitive an issue it was.

I suspected that my accuser was the lazy front office manager who I had had occasion to reprimand just a few days earlier for not paying attention to his work. Much as my translating director pleaded with the chief, he would not budge and insisted that I had to leave the country. It did surprise me that a simple police chief in a small town would have such power. Later I learned that he didn't! He was simply trying to show his authority to me – and to everyone else around. In leaving he told me to await his further instructions in the next twenty-four hours.

IT NEVER RAINS

As myself and the human resources director left the police station and set off back to the hotel it started to drizzle. At first it was just a few drops of rain but then the heavens opened and it became a deluge such as I had never seen in all my time in Egypt. Mina al Janub had no drainage system and in less than an hour the whole town was flooded. The little shacks in which the poor people lived were washed away and most people were made homeless in minutes. I got hold of all the managers and a host of volunteers. We loaded a small rowing boat with bottles of drinking water, blankets and food and rowed around doing our part in assisting the people well into the night. By the next morning the changed face of the small town was only too clear to see. Everywhere there was destruction and shocked and desperate people crying for help. We continued for the better part of the day to help out as best we could.

The guests at the hotel however were safe and dry as the hotel escaped the worst of the storm. Critically, the sewage system and the desalinisation plant were unaffected and functioning normally. However, the owner of the hotel had had installed the wrong specification sprinkler system in the hotel and we were about to get our deluge soon enough.

This came about because he had not received approval from Marriott for the specification he had submitted. He wrongly, made the assumption that Marriott must have approved the sprinklers and went ahead and installed them. One Saturday afternoon while Janet and I were having lunch I received an urgent message to call Juergen immediately. Knowing Juergen I figured that it was just another one of his mid-life crises but, when I called him, he was totally out of control. He had received word from Marriott HQ that all the sprinklers installed were not the Marriott approved ones and had to be changed immediately. I was instructed to find the owner and tell him that he had to buy two thousand sprinkler heads and get them installed like now.

Juergen was the one whose responsibility it was, according to company policy, to contact the owner and pass on any such information - and preferably to do so over a pleasant lunch. He knew that the owner would be far from pleased and was of course right on that point. When I informed the owner that he either had to provide the Marriott approved sprinklers or that Marriott would buy them, ship and charge him for them, he went absolutely ballistic. He would have none of the above. He really believed that I personally was the one creating this problem for him.

We got the sprinklers in and Tarek, the director of engineering, started work. He didn't however, have an as-built blueprint. When he started work on the floor above the lobby, a sprinkler with its head removed and which was mistakenly still connected to the water supply, gushed out water which quickly poured down into the lobby. The rugs, furniture and fittings got thoroughly soaked. The guests fled in all directions to avoid a drenching and the owner was right there at the time and saw it all. It later transpired that Tarek's assistant had informed the owner that the work was to be done at that time. This guy, in fact, turned out to be a regular informant of everything that was said and done in the hotel. Anyway, after much confusion, the correct valve was found, closed and the water flow ceased.

Three days after that disaster Tarek and his team continued their work in the part of the building where the front desk was situated. This was where all the computers were installed and where the offices and the leased shops were located. Sure enough, right above the front desk another sprinkler head was missed and the water suddenly gushed down over the desk and the computers while guests were checking in. Plastic bags were quickly put over the computers but no one was willing to unplug them while standing in water. This reminded me of the tragedy that had occurred with the young man many years before in Sakkara. Fortunately nobody repeated that costly mistake and reached for the plugs.

Not unnaturally, when the owner found out about the latest flood, he was less than pleased and called Juergen to complain how stupid Tarek and I were for continuously flooding his hotel through misreading the blueprints. Tarek and I had to fly to Sakkara to show Juergen and the director of engineering that the mechanical plans were wrong. Just after this the owner told Juergen that I was not moving into my apartment, even though it was ready, claiming that I found it easier to live in a nice suite with all my meals catered for. This of course could not have been further from the truth. Once again, I had to fly to Sakkara and show Juergen photos of the bathtub in the middle of the living room and the kitchen with no cooker, refrigerator or sink before he would believe me.

Eventually the apartment did get finished and Janet and I moved in. Janet was busy with helping at the school. She also took scuba diving lessons. The area was a paradise for divers, they came from all over the world. With the love for water which she has and the ability to handle it well it would have been a shame not to take advantage of the diving instructors we had in our diving centre at the hotel. She become an accomplished diver and enjoyed doing it so much that she dived at every opportunity. Paul and Emily also joined us for a holiday and both learned to scuba dive. Paul went on eventually to become a certified instructor and subsequently dived in many places around the world. While there we used to go out on a boat. Janet, Emily and Paul would spend hours diving and exploring the beautiful undersea world. I just enjoyed the ride and chilling out on deck.

At that time Emily had to make the tough decision to either stay in Japan one more year or return to the US where she had finished university. She decided to stay in Japan one year longer. In retrospect it was a bad call as she didn't enjoy it. I mistakenly advised her to go. As she was always an obedient and submissive child willing to please us, she went back and signed up for the extension year. She had also bought a second hand car and that gave her mobility as Nagoya, where she was based, was not a big nor exciting place. Additionally, Japanese culture didn't really sit well with her. Women there were still regarded as second class citizens, a behaviour that she found hard to accept. But her time in Japan did teach her about the Far East, a great attribute in her present work as career advisor in business schools in the US.

BONNY SCOTLAND

Paul also graduated from the university in England. Janet and I went to Leamington Spa for the ceremony and celebration. As a graduation present Paul decided on a trip to Scotland. We drove from Leamington to Glasgow, stopping on the way to see the famous Wedgewood bone china factory. Glasgow is Britain's second city. It was once a thriving port and ship building centre. It is now a cultural centre with art nouveau, Victorian era architecture and home to the prestigious Scottish Opera, Scottish Ballet and National Theatre of Scotland. Museums are everywhere. They are among the most interesting in the world. From Glasgow we drove all the way north to Loch Ness. Paul was determined to swim with the Loch Ness monster. He did swim in the loch but the famous monster, which of course exists, was not entertaining visitors that day. 'Nessie' stayed at home somewhere in a deep and dark cave under the water.

Driving around Scotland was one of the most enjoyable things we've ever done. Everything is green and very fresh. As it rains a lot you breathe in cool and refreshing air. We hiked on Ben Nevis, the highest mountain in the UK standing at 4,411 feet (1345 m) above sea level. Without proper boots it was hard going, more so when descending which was more of a slide on my backside. The views would have been magnificent had it not been for the rain and mist. On our drive to Edinburgh we stopped off at numerous distilleries so that Janet and Paul could sample many of the world's finest whiskies. That was a real treat for them. Even though the drive took us through the most stunning scenery imaginable, pretty towns and picturesque villages, the thing that captivated my attention was the number of sheep grazing peacefully all around. Years later, while visiting New Zealand, I experienced that same feeling of tranquility. Somehow sheep makes me feel that way.

Edinburgh, Scotland's capital, is a beautiful city. With a population of half a million it is neither too big nor too small. The centre is hilly and it's a great town to walk around. There are a multitude of both the historical and more modern sites of interest to visit. We strolled along the magnificent avenues and lanes of the Georgian new town and climbed through the dark alleys and mediaeval cobbles of the old town up to Edinburgh Castle and its sweeping views of the city and its surroundings. For Paul, having just graduated in history at Warwick University, this was one of the highlights of the trip. It has been discovered that the castle site has been occupied by humans since the Iron Age. The castle itself has been besieged at least twenty-six times in its eleven hundred years of existence. This makes it the most besieged place in Great Britain and one of the most often attacked places in the world.

Of great interest within the castle is St.Margaret's Chapel. It boasts a superb stained glass window depicting St.Margaret magnificently clad in a blue gown. The chapel has a checkered history, being originally a place of worship but used during one period as a store room for gun powder. It is the most popular venue in all of Edinburgh for wedding ceremonies. The castle alone could take months to explore, especially for a history aficionado such as Paul. The city hosts its famous festival of the arts in August each year which attracts tens of thousands of visitors from all over the world. There is a vibrant multi-cultural night life all year round and a wide variety of restaurants catering to every taste. Alas, all too soon it was time to take our leave of this gorgeous place.

A short two and a half hour drive to the south took us across the border into England and to Newcastle-upon-Tyne, the birth place of Janet's parents. Crossing the border from Scotland into England it was interesting to see the decline in the standard of general care, cleanliness and maintenance of the surrounds and buildings. This reminded me of crossing from Switzerland into Italy. Scotland looked like Switzerland while England was more like Italy with garbage on the roads, buildings with peeling paintwork and a general appearance of neglect. In Newcastle we visited a cousin of Janet's, Evelyn, whom Janet had not seen since childhood. On arrival we had to tell her who we were. Once she got over the surprise she invited us in and, in typical English fashion, we were offered a cup of tea. It was fascinating to catch up with a family member who Janet had not seen for many years and whom Paul and I had never met. After that pleasant interlude we continued our drive back to Paul's place in Leamington Spa.

Paul had made the decision to become a linguist. Languages had always fascinated him. Particularly so since he had gone to Spain in the summer of '95 where he worked in a variety of odd jobs and attended Spanish language classes. As he was never one to approach any challenge other than head on he had decided that Cambridge was the only place to study languages. There he would learn the skills of phonetic to written translation which he would employ in later life while working for ISL, the International Society of Linguists. This society is at the service of small, indigenous communities around the world who only speak local languages and need help to access literary resources from around the world.

By then he had also developed an interest in political life. He wanted to work for the US government. He studied for a post-graduate degree in economics and international affairs at Johns Hopkins University. This had the additional benefit that the first year of the two year course took place in Bologna, Italy. This gave him the ideal opportunity to perfect his Italian. Then, as he already spoke English, French and Spanish and was qualified in phonetics, he could call himself a true linguist. With Paul now settled in Cambridge for the summer and signed up for Bologna in the fall, Janet and I returned to Mina al Janub.

Janet now decided to stop her voluntary school work and concentrate on her diving and entertaining. The hotel recruited a new executive chef, a tall, good looking New Zealander named Baptiste. Apart from being quite a good chef, he was an efficient administrator and fitted in well. His wife worked in the human resources department at the Sunrise Hotel. At this time Juergen decided to hold the Middle East general manager's conference in Mina al Janub with me as the host. The team was still small in number. There were only two hotels in Saudi, one in Dubai and the three in Egypt. The meetings were conducted in the living room of one of the ten suites which faced the beach and the sea. Juergen only held these meetings because they were a company requirement. They were pretty uninspiring affairs and generally boring.

One afternoon, Cristian Marchese, the general manager at the Marriott in Riyadh, got up from the conference table and went over to the floor to ceiling glass window which overlooked the beach, the pool and the sea. After a few moments of staring down he turned towards the table and, with a discreet wave, motioned for us to join him. Juergen's head was buried in the paper he had himself written but couldn't understand and did not notice us moving one by one to join Cristian at the window. We soon found that the object of Cristian's attention, and now ours, was the many women sunbathing topless at the pool side. It took some time for Jeurgen to realise that he, and his faithful secretary Nagla, were alone at the table. When he did realise, he exploded into laughter.

As I had not heard from the chief of police regarding the deportation issue, I took matters into my own hands and went to the police station to learn my fate. If I was staying I wanted to stay in peace and if I was leaving I needed to inform Juergen. This time I went on my own with no translator. When I entered he was surprised to see me but invited me to sit on the sofa rather than on the hard chair in front of his desk as he had done the last time. He summoned an officer to make tea and Turkish coffee. His whole attitude was altogether extremely cordial and totally different from before. Conversing in my best Arabic and his bad English, I soon learned that his change in attitude was down to the way I and my management team had reacted to the downpour and the ensuing floods. He had seen me in the rowing boat passing out blankets, water and food to anyone, Muslim or Christian or anything else for that matter and knew that the hotel facilities had been made available to all. In the light of all this he had concluded that I was not guilty of discrimination but that actually I was an asset to the town. We then embraced, a sign in Egypt that our total trust for each other was re-established. We were now habibi – friends!

A NIGHT AT THE OPERA

As the summer of '97 drew to an end the opera Aida was performed in Luxor with Giuseppe Giacomini (no relation) in the lead role of Radames. No way could we miss that. Janet, myself, the German housekeeper, her boyfriend and three others rented a mini bus and drove to Luxor to see this once in a life time show. We drove there with a police escort (the reason for that will become apparent). The show was indeed an experience not to be forgotten by any one of the three thousand strong audience in attendance. The sound, the lighting and the whole organisation in the ancient amphitheatre was simply outstanding with even the moon and the stars in the dark desert sky adding to the spectacle. We all agreed that we would most likely never again experience such an event in our lifetimes. In the wee hours of the morning we returned to Mina al Janub, again under police protection.

One month and one day after this most memorable evening, tragedy hit. In the very same place where the performance of the opera Aida took place, the Hatshepsut temple, six men belonging to the Jamaa Islamiyya armed with automatic weapons shot and killed between fifty-six and ninety Swiss, Japanese, German and British tourists. The exact number was never know as every television station gave different accounts. What followed was a mass exodus of tourists from Egypt. When the German government sent planes to take home their nationals who wanted to leave, the hotel was more than half emptied overnight. I had to take quick action in rearranging staffing. Moving out the non-Egyptian managers was the priority.

I made some calls and was able to find a job for the New Zealand executive chef at one of the Marriott Hotels in London. I was happy to pass on this great news to Baptiste and his wife. He was very enthusiastic about the move but, as I made the announcement, I saw his wife's face fall. I felt straight away that she would not go. Sure enough Baptiste came to me the next morning and told me that under no circumstances would his wife leave her job at the Sunrise. The real reason for his wife's refusal to go and which sabotaged his career was never given. I have my own theory regarding that.

Now the owner of the property decided that the drop in business presented a good opportunity to get rid of me. He told Juergen that I had to go. Naturally Marriott loved the general managers ... but loved the owners more. Without them Marriott wouldn't manage any hotels and wouldn't make any money. Juergen told me that I had to leave. Fortunately in those days Marriott still valued its people and would really make every effort to take care of us. I held on hoping for a position to become available. Although unhappy, I continued to work hard and diligently. After all I was working for Marriott and it was the second time I was being technically dismissed, as had happened in Mustashat. Now it was happening again. By February of '98 it was a case of saying goodbye to all the staff. Janet and I left the hotel with just two suitcases each and went to Sakkara for the night. We had dinner in Juergen and Michelle's apartment at the Marriott.

We put all of our belongings into storage in Sakkara. We didn't have any specific place to go but I remembered spending a vacation many years previously in Scottsdale, Arizona. It was a place of desert, cactus, sand and heat - so we went there! I arranged for us to stay for a few days at the then Marriott's Mountain Shadows Resort. Naturally it was too expensive for us so we moved to Fairfield Inn on Scottsdale Road where we were lucky to get a room for 29 US dollars per day. We stayed there for five weeks. In the meantime we bought a three year old Volvo station wagon with only 12,000 miles (19,300 km) on the clock. I was determined to set up a base, a place of our own to which we could return any time. This meant buying a small place which we could always call 'home' and have the keys in our pocket. We found a construction site called Bellasera 18 miles (29 km) from the centre of Scottsdale where the second of three phases was due to start construction. We liked the show home we saw there and just bought it. There I was, out of a job and with no idea what the future might bring yet we had bought a car and a house in Arizona.

On the 20th of March Nagla, Juergen's secretary, left a message for me to be ready to go to Dubai in the next few days. This was the only information we were given other than to make arrangements for the flights and wait for our visas. They duly arrived two days later. Then we were off to Dubai not even knowing what it was all about. Nagla had only said that we would be picked up and taken to the Mystic Horse Hotel. Our faith in Marriott was so strong that we would have gone to the moon blindfolded if they told us to do so.

During the days in Arizona my hair was starting to turn white. Janet had the brilliant idea to colour it in order to make me appear younger. Reluctantly I decided to let her do the colouring for me and together we chose a chestnut colouring product that matched the original colour of my hair. Janet had a lot of fun acting as my coiffeur except that she left the dye on too long and my hair turned bright orange. I wanted to die. It was the first and last time I ever coloured my hair. When I arrived in Dubai I went to meet Juergen as pre-arranged. He looked at me, blinked, blinked again, rubbed his eyes and then opened his mouth - "Fuck Peter, what have you done?" How could he introduce me to the Al Maktoub family, the owners of the hotel where I was hopefully to be working, with such obviously and ridiculously tinted hair?

Al Maktoub, like most United Arab Emirate families, was very wealthy. He had a very large family of three wives, a father and eleven brothers and sisters. Juergen was genuinely worried that I would not be taken seriously by the family. We went to meet the brother who was in charge of the hotels, and now the chairman of the Al Maktoub Group, ABD Al Maktoub. He was a graduate of Cornell University, considered to be one of the finest hospitality management schools in the world. The family owned the Sherodit Hotel too where Juergen had been the general manager many years earlier and knew ABD well. They had mutual respect and trust for each other. Somehow that helped to pass me and my carrot coloured hair through. I was not rejected.

Taking over the Mystic Horse Hotel was one of the most difficult jobs I ever had. My task was to convert it to a Renaissance, a brand Marriott had acquired a few years earlier. The hotel was fairly new but was not in good condition. Marriott had signed a contract with the owners for a twenty year lease subject to certain works and improvements being carried out on the building over the following eighteen months to elevate it to the standards required of a Renaissance hotel. The hotel was supposed to compete with the JW Marriott just about 200 yards (180 m) away. While the JW Marriott was doing well, this hotel wasn't.

Among the flaws, the banquet space was badly designed. A contract had been signed and then rescinded with an Italian entrepreneur of questionable reputation to run the bar and nightclub as a Pizza Peperoni disco. A live Filipino band played there every night. The place was so noisy that no guest in the hotel could sleep until after one in the morning when the band and the DJ stopped playing. The present general manager, Jonas Luge, a young single German, lived in an apartment properly designed for that purpose. As he was still occupying it, he put Janet and I in a suite right above the disco bar. This was done on purpose so we couldn't go to sleep until after the band had stopped playing in the wee hours of the morning. After about a week of this torture of sleep deprivation we moved to a suite on the opposite side of the building. The building is long and only six storeys high. This was far enough away that, while we could still hear the music, it was a very muffled sound.

As Jonas was still occupying the office for the first week after our arrival I had to work in the store room next to it. Then, when he finally moved out of the apartment and of the hotel completely, I took over the office and established a routine. Janet and I moved into the apartment. It was a mess. There was a beautiful, white, fitted carpet. It was filthy. Jonas had been constantly partying with the female flight attendants of the Ethiopian and the Sri Lankan Airlines and the carpet had huge stains of red wine. Along with that the smell of whatever had been smoked by them was so strong that it was hard to breathe. Janet and I moved back to the suite we had just vacated.

By that time we had started to put together the executive committee. Because of the renovations that were going to be carried out, one of the first people to be hired was the director of engineering. He was a single English guy who turned out to be more interested in sports cars, young women, wine and disco music than in doing a lot of work and establishing good relations with the owners. His first assignment was the renovation of my general manager's apartment. This consisted of changing the fitted carpet, taking out the old tiles from the kitchen and replacing them. While this work was in progress Janet decided to go to Arizona to see how our house was coming along. I was concentrating on getting my executive team together and wasn't paying too much attention to the apartment renovation.

When the renovation was supposedly finished and I took a look I was shocked at what a disastrous job he had done. The carpet wasn't laid properly, the kitchen tiles were crooked and uneven and the curtains were hanging over the floor. I was most concerned about how Janet would react. Sure enough, when she saw it, she wasn't happy to say the least.

THE GATHERING STORM

The renovation works that were supposed to start right away were not moving ahead. I informed Juergen. In his usual way, he told me that he would talk to ABD and everything would be alright. We did start to do as much as we could do ourselves but our efforts were but a drop in the ocean compared to what needed to be done. The director of sales and marketing who we had brought in from the Riyadh Marriott was Aadill Aaquib. He had spent sixteen years in Saudi Arabia. He was totally atrophied and cut off from reality. He couldn't sell a room even if the client beat him over the head to get it, and he was arrogant. He told many prospective guests that this hotel was now a Renaissance and if they wanted to stay with us they had to pay Renaissance rates or go elsewhere. They did go elsewhere. Our already low occupancy rate fell overnight from 50% to 30%. He performed the same trick with the restaurant guests. Before I knew it, restaurant sales had plunged to their lowest level ever too.

I organised a daily morning meeting in my office. My team of six sales managers and reps were required to attend and present their plan, agenda and sales target for the day before they went out to visit customers. This included Aadill and the director of sales. At 5.00 pm they had to report back to me with their results for the day. When they reported back I made a practice of phoning, in front of the sales people, the clients they said they had visited. This in order to thank the clients but also to ascertain that the rep had actually visited. It only took two or three days of doing this for them to get the message. Nonetheless I still had to terminate two young women who kept coming back with a different hair do than the one they had left with in the morning.

Scott Sibley, a young American married to Linda and with a baby daughter Claire, joined us as director of food and beverage from the Marriott in Vietnam. We kept on the team the director of human resources, a young single Jordanian and the resident manager, a young and dynamic German married to a Turkish girl.

The only one missing on the team by now was a good director of finance. We did recruit a young assistant from the JW Marriott but the situation with him was complicated and less than perfect. After six months, he was replaced by an Egyptian guy from Sakkara.

At this time we hired Patrick, a nice young and single Indian fellow as our director of restaurants; a front office manager from Sakkara, also a single young man, and we kept the German housekeeping manager. This despite the fact that she struggled to embrace our new Marriott style of participatory management. Eventually I did have to let her go and promoted her assistant who, in spite of also being German, was more willing to embrace the new way of doing business. In fact she was so willing to embrace the new system that she eventually married one of her Indian male housekeepers.

I had inherited a secretary too. She was a married Indian lady of Portuguese decent and, as a consequence, a Christian. She was a loyal and efficient worker from Mumbai. Her name was Bernice D'Saa and she had two small children who she was not happy to have to raise in a Muslim environment. Her name intrigued me. I looked it up and found that it's of Greek origin and appears in the New Testament.

One of the most impressive team members was the Indian purchasing manager. He always wore Italian shoes and silk ties. His Egyptian cotton, hand-made shirts were something more suitable for a chairman of the board than for a simple purchasing manager. The straw that broke the camel's back though was the day he came to work wearing a Hugo Boss suit. I couldn't stand the idea of having him wear such an elegant and expensive suit while I, the general manager, could only afford a 400 dollar suit off the rack at Mark & Spencer – and bought on sale. I fired him. I promoted his secretary and moved the purchasing office into the executive office just two doors away from mine in order to ensure that the next incumbent couldn't afford to wear such expensive designer wear.

The owner's representative, Klaus, was an experienced old hotelier from Baden-Baden in Germany. He was also an alcoholic.

His drink of choice was Johnny Walker Blue label. Our VIP lounge dispensed drink, free of charge, to the guests occupying those specific rooms and suites. Klaus, in keeping with all the previous managers, helped himself to as much booze as he wanted without recording what he took. His wife would also join him in the VIP lounge every evening. They'd get drunk, have loud arguments and leave without paying. Naturally I had to put a stop to that. I informed the owner that I would remove this privilege. He fully understood my intention to stop those abuses and turn the hotel into a serious and respected business.

The youngest member of the ownership family was a twenty-four year old spoiled brat who drove a red Ferrari. He too believed that he was the owner and didn't have to pay for anything. He would go to a disco in town every night. There he would meet some Lebanese, Russian or Asian prostitute and bring them to the hotel. He'd take a suite, a bottle of champagne and then walk out the next morning without paying. Of this I had to inform his older brother ABD who put a stop to it. Now, reluctantly, the brat had to pay for the suite and the champagne.

He pulled the same stunt at the hotel disco, Pizza Peperoni. There he would eat and drink with his gang mates then leave without paying. When I learned that this was happening I asked the disco manager to call me in my apartment the next time that the brat showed up. One night after Janet and I had gone to sleep the call came. I got up, dressed and went down to face him. He was a tall, strong looking fellow, rather menacing. I introduced myself and asked for a quiet word with him in the lobby. There, standing as tall as I could, I simply told him that from that moment on there would no longer be free food and drinks for him and his friends at the expense of the waitresses (who had to pay for all shortages). He would have to pay cash, sign a cheque or be billed monthly from now on. For a moment I thought he was going to whack me but instead he mumbled something in Arabic and went back to his friends. I become the hero that night, at least to the team of the Pizza Peperoni disco.

The hotel had dreams of grandeur from the very beginning as one of their main goals was to compete with and beat the JW Marriott. There was a white Cadillac car that was supposed to be used to pick up VIP guests at the airport. It had been broken down since forever and sat abandoned in the garage. I thought to get it operational but soon found that the engine was blown and the cost of the repair would be so high as to not be worth doing. I traded it in for a smaller, more modest car as the VIPs coming to the hotel were few and far between anyway.

We also had two mini vans for transporting airline crews to and from the airport. I, as general manager, had the perk of a car too. It was a white Jaguar. Janet was provided with a nice Volvo. During the week Janet would drive the Volvo but on Friday, my day off, she would get hold of the Jaguar steering wheel and not let it go all day. I had to keep the car during the week because the owner expected me to be driving it if I was called to go to his office.

It was a common pastime to take a night drive in the desert and enjoy a Bedouin dinner of lamb and rice eaten with our hands while sitting on rugs under a huge tent. These outings could last all night. Dinner was often followed by a camel ride, a game of football or a jeep blast along the dunes. Best of all was just to star gaze as the night skies were very clear and the stars enormous to look at. It was also easy to take trips to Oman and drive through the wadi, the dry river beds that contain water only after heavy rain. This adventure took a whole day in a really strong jeep and was terrific fun.

In order to support Emirate Airlines a rule was implemented whereby all foreigners had to leave the UAE for one day, twice a year in order to qualify for a work visa. This was a round trip to either Doha or Muscat. The first time Janet and I did this the aircraft was full and over 90% of the passengers were women of Eastern European, Asian, African and South American origin. We soon realised that they were all prostitutes. So much for the strict Muslim way of living! Another contradiction is the drinking. Muslims are not supposed to drink alcohol yet our bars were packed full of Muslim men from morning until night. The Sheik had asked them to change from their traditional dress to European clothing while in the bars but none paid attention and they continued to drink and have fun with women at every opportunity.

Summer came and the climate got even more unbearable than springtime with an average August temperature of 106°F (41°C) and high in humidity with it. No foreigner in his or her right mind would come there at that time. In looking at the previous year's accounts for August, I was shocked to find that the hotel had made a loss of 300,000 US dollars in that month alone. I felt that Indians would come at that time of year if the price was low so I made a deal with an Indian tour operator at the (ridiculous) rate of 30 US dollars per room per night. The result was that I reduced the loss for the month of August to just 30,000 US dollars. Even that, instead of making the owner happy, made them even madder with Marriott ... and especially with me.

September had arrived and Janet and I went to Arizona to finalise the purchase of our house which was now completed. With that accomplished I returned to work. Janet remained behind to arrange our furniture which had been in storage, buy things and generally organise the house. Emily, who was now going to Thunderbird and ASU, joined her. She was almost finished with her two Masters. We had decided to spend Christmas and New Year in the house. A few days before Christmas, I flew back to Arizona. Paul came too.

As the house is only a two bedroom one we set Paul up in the den (TV/office room) with a futon for a bed while Emily occupied the second bedroom. We had a great time together. Paul took driving lessons, mostly with me and in our Volvo which we'd bought at the same time as the house. He took his driving test for his first driver's license and passed with flying colours. We cooked Christmas dinner at home and New Year's eve was spent in a Western saloon with lots of would be cowboys. All were dressed in proper cowboy outfits, stetsons and with hand guns in holsters hanging from their waist. Such is Arizona. Provided you get a license you can carry a gun, or two, in public!

BYE BYE DUBAI

Returning to Dubai with Janet after the vacation was hard because the contracted renovation of the hotel was not taking place. The owners expected me to perform miracles with a hotel that was still a mess albeit that it now looked considerably better than it did on the day we took over. They set up three sample rooms according to the best Arab taste. They were so extravagantly colourful that no self-respecting westerner would ever sleep in them. When such things were pointed out to them, they simply ignored and/or rejected whatever Marriott proposed. Marriott became increasingly upset about the lack of progress in the renovation and the owners, for their part, became increasingly upset with the inability of Marriott to make a drastic (upward) change in the income and profit account.

The hotel was a drain on the finances of the owner who continued to labour under the misapprehension that simply changing the name of the hotel and having Marriott manage it would turn it into a magic cash cow overnight. Also there was a lot of discussion about the choice of name. It appeared that the word Renaissance can be pronounced in many different ways in Arabic. Even the spelling of it had different versions. Hours and hours were wastefully devoured at the owner's office by a bunch of Arab speaking individuals trying to find the most likely pronunciation and spelling. They never reached a consensus of course and so the name on the building turned out to be a constant laughable issue.

I was, as you might say, between a rock and a hard place. I made a move that had never been considered before. The hotel rented and paid for outside accommodation for all of the single executives and single department heads. I moved them all out of their subsidised dwellings and into the hotel thus saving a lot of money. This was unprecedented and no other hotel in Dubai did that. The challenge now was to keep in check the partying and control the 'visitors' to the suites of the single executives.

Then I made a mistake. Without consulting with the owner I rented a building to house the rest of the staff. The rent was much lower than the one then being used but had the same capacity. It had all the same facilities and it was a new building with up to date fire protection systems and had never been occupied. Delighted with my initiative I moved all the staff into it. Then the proverbial shit hit the fan! The owner called me over to his office and almost physically assaulted me. What I hadn't known was that the old building belonged to a family member who was charging Marriott, with the owner's tacit approval, an astronomical rent. It was this event and this revelation that suddenly brought home to me the realisation that I could never and would never succeed in that hotel.

Paul had originally joined ISL, the International Society of Linguists, after his summer in Germany where he learned to speak German. He never visited us in Dubai, neither in fact did Emily. It was the only place they never came to. By that time I could also feel that they had grown up and that their lives were their own. I realised that I had to let go of them and just be there for them when they needed me. Although I myself had moved on from my parents at a much younger age, I came to know then just how hard it is for a parent to let go. I am to this day unsure of which is the harder for a child. Growing up in a life like that of Janet and I, constantly on the move around the world or growing up in poverty and living an entire life in the only house you've ever known, like my parents. I shall never know.

Then the regional management team came to visit. There was the regional vice president, Oliver Black, from London, the regional director of food and beverage, the regional director of rooms, the regional director of sales and marketing, the regional director of finance, the regional director of human resources and the director of revenue who was the only female in the team. Naturally Juergen also came. The team locked themselves in a room for three full days and went over every piece of paper our director of finance was asked to produce. It seemed clear to me that the aim was to find something to pin on me for the bad performance of the hotel. Despite their best efforts, they eventually departed without having found there to be any sort of wrong doing or mismanagement on my part. Nor had they found a solution on how to fix that hotel operation. What they had in mind was clear though. I had to go.

While the majority of the team members left together during the day, the director of sales and marketing and the director of revenue chose to leave on a 3.00 am flight the next morning. In my naïve way I offered to drive them to the airport. I took the Jaguar from the parking lot to the front of the hotel to pick them up. When they came out they both got into the back of the car although I had the front passenger side door open and would have expected one of them to sit there. This was a clear indication to me that they looked on me as little more than a private chauffeur, their goffer. I knew then that my days were numbered for sure.

This was in the spring of '99. In those days Marriott kept on file a note of any specific geographical areas in the world managers might want to work. I had noted a preference for the Far East in countries like Thailand, Hong Kong or Singapore or South America. Once before, the regional vice president for South America had asked me if I were interested in going to Maracaibo, Venezuela, where Marriott was managing a hotel owned by an old Neapolitan. The strange thing about this owner was that he had a volatile love hate relationship with Marriott. One day he wanted rid of them the next he wanted them back. The vice president thought that it might be a good idea if an Italian general manager was put in charge. Then maybe, just maybe, the owner would come to his senses. Fortunately for me, the owner decided to throw Marriott out for good before I went there.

By now it was mid July and my meetings with the owner had become no more than a three hour beating for me with never a positive outcome. I was hoping and praying every day that something would happen and I would be transferred. It had already been decided that Atur, another one of the eleven siblings and an incompetent, ruthless brute, would take charge of the hotel.

Then, out of the blue, the call came from Juergen to inform me that the regional vice president for South America was going to call me regarding a Marriott which was under construction in Santiago in Chile. The position of general manager there had not yet been filled. That very afternoon I received the call from the South American vice president. He offered me the post straight away, over the phone. I accepted without the slightest hesitation and we were on our way to South America!

Chapter 20

BY RIGHT OR MIGHT

I went straight to the nearest bookshop and bought a book about Chile. Mentally Janet and I prepared ourselves for the move. On the 23rd of July Janet and I left Dubai on a flight to Paris ... not before shaking the dust off our sandals however. Emily was at that time in Paris working as a volunteer in a home for elderly physically and mentally handicapped men and women. We checked in at the Courtyard in Neuilly-sur-Seine, just outside the city and spent a relaxing weekend with Emily just wandering along the boulevards and stopping for a café crème on a side walk café. It was just so wonderful to be free of the dreadful Al Maktoub family.

Our stay coincided with the last stage of the Tour de France, the most prestigious bicycle race in the world. It was being raced on Sunday 25th July around the Arc de Triomphe and down to Place de la Concorde. The Marriott Hotel on the Champs-Elysees was just the right place to see it. We sat in the lobby near the enormous window and from there viewed the whole event. The American cyclist Lance Armstrong won the tour, and indeed seven of the editions consecutively from '98 to 2005. However, in 2012, he was stripped of all his victories, medals, trophies and honours and banned for life from any race after admitting to doping during all his years of glory. On July the 27th Janet and I left Emily in Paris and flew on Air France to Santiago. Unbeknowns to me, this was to be the final and longest stage of my personal career race.

Business class flying was always the ultimate living for me. The long twelve and a half hour flight from Paris to Santiago was as comfortable as it was exciting. Even if I didn't drink champagne any longer, just the idea of sitting next to Janet and seeing her savour a glass of bubbly and being served paté de fois gras with melba toast was just so stimulating and elegant ... snobbish I know. It was something that would have made my poor parents proud yet cringe at the same time. This kind of cuisine would have seemed totally beyond their reach and understanding. My mother had at least heard about these delicacies and read about them in my grandfather's cook books but, on my father's side of the family, such indulgences would have been beyond their comprehension.

As we disembarked from the flight in Santiago we were offered a Chilean newspaper, printed in Spanish of course. I grabbed it eagerly, anxious to see how much I could understand. I had had my first exposure to Spanish when I was twenty years old while dating Cristina from Buenos Aires. And I had worked with many Spaniards, particularly so in California, albeit that they spoke mostly the Mexican or Puerto Rican versions. I quickly realised that the Spanish spoken in Chile was Castellano and not Spanish. The good news was that I could understand almost everything that I was reading. With that reassurance I was confident that it would be a quick and easy transition into the language when listening to and speaking with the people in Santiago.

We were greeted at the airport by Carlos Labarca, general factotum of the owners. In what was the general manager's (my) middle range Mazda car (a bit of a come down from a Jag plus Volvo) he drove us to the Hyatt Regency where Gordon Fuller was the general manager. It is an impressive building with an atrium open all the way to the top floor and panoramic high speed elevators to whizz you up the seventeen storeys in a matter of seconds. The cone shaped tip to the top of the building had earned it the nickname of 'the condom'!

Upon being escorted to our suite by the resident manager we were impressed to find a welcome gift akin to a full buffet of chilled champagne, goose liver pate, red wild fruits, fillet of fish and Argentinian beef. There was a choice of four red, three white and two rosé Chilean wines. Impressive to say the least. The owners had also left a beautiful arrangement of fresh flowers for Janet. There was a note, written in English, requesting to meet me next day at noon in their office inside the new hotel building which was already well advanced in construction. From the window of our suite we could see it.

We spent the rest of the day exploring the hotel we were in. The VIP lounge on the sixteenth floor was a jewel. At the cocktail hour pisco sour, the typical Chilean cocktail, was served and the bar had a magnificent selection of Chilean wines, champagnes and refreshments to suit every taste. A winding staircase led to the seventeenth floor and a full size billiard table, TV screens in each corner and enormous sofas and armchairs everywhere. The hotel also had a full service spa in a separate building in the middle of the garden with a gym with the most up to date exercise equipment, sauna, jacuzzi and steam room. From the fresh juices pressed in front of your eyes, to the flowers and the aromas in the air and the background music, everything was perfect. The staff uniforms were all black, properly cleaned and starched. A bit dull perhaps but classy nonetheless. To the outside the view of the city was just magnificent. The most spectacular aspect being not towards the city but up to the snow-capped Andes and the Cerro el Plomo peak which tops off at 16,500 feet (5,500 m). It was now time to settle down for the night as Janet and I had had a very long, tiring but exciting day.

It was almost too good to continue without a hitch. During the night Janet got horribly ill with stomach aches, diarrhea and vomiting. The next morning the hotel nurse arrived and diagnosed Janet as suffering from food poisoning. She prescribed teaspoon fulls of Coca Cola. Janet was outraged at that. I wasn't so sure about the food poisoning thing. I insisted that Janet see the hotel doctor but she refused to do that and stayed miserably in bed with her bottle of Coke.

I went to take advantage of what turned out to be a simply fabulous breakfast spread like something out of a fairy tale. There were fresh fruit juices, cereals, charcuterie, cheeses, yogurts, eggs and omelettes cooked to order. To top it all the bread display was comparable to anything I had seen in the finest Paris boulangerie. It was now obvious to me that the owners of my hotel had chosen to house me at the Hyatt so that I would see first hand the competition I was up against and therefore be able to prepare myself to come up with an equally good, or better, offering.

One thing though which I didn't like was the hotel security. I discovered that their director of security was a retired general in the Carabineros de Chile, the uniformed police belonging to the armed forces. He had instituted a military type regime that was more appropriate to a prison than to a five star luxury hotel. Guests were constantly watched. There were three or four security officers in the lobby always looking at everything and everybody and making visitors feel uncomfortable. My aim, the Marriott way, was to have more discreet and friendly staff. This was an important lesson to learn and a mistake to avoid repeating in my hotel.

At 11.45 am I was picked up by Carlos and driven the short distance to meet the owners at the Marriott. The Marriott consisted of a forty storey hotel building in the centre and two office towers, each twenty storeys high on each side. The hotel occupied the floors from the basement to the twenty-fifth level. From the twenty-sixth to the fortieth floor there were to be eighty-nine apartments for sale to private individuals. As I walked in with Carlos I was impressed by the quite different feeling this building had compared to the Hyatt.

A FRIENDLY OWNER

Only one owner, Felipe Amunategui, was available to be with me at our first meeting. He was the one owner with previous hotel experience and a builder too. Felipe and I got on well from the word go. I quickly found him to be a great guy and one I could trust. He was a world-wise Chilean, very cultured and spoke perfect English and French. He loved opera and art and soon we were at a level of friendship whereby we exchanged our complete life stories with ease. What a refreshing experience that was and such a total contrast from my most recent Egyptian and Dubai fiascos. We took a tour of the hotel from top to bottom. At every step we took, the more excited I became to be part of this project. I loved the way the finishing parts of the construction were coming together. The outside was completed in slabs of copper cladding in keeping with the theme of the country as Chile is by far the largest producer of the metal in the world. In the lobby the marble floor had still to be laid and a lot of concrete was still visible.

The basement housed the car parking for both the hotel and the towers, two restaurants, a ballroom, eight meeting rooms and all the kitchens. In the lobby there was the reception desk with all the guest services and, under a beautiful glass dome with wooden beams, there was an impressive lobby bar. The communal gym (both sexes) with a small, open air heated pool was also at lobby level with a private sauna and jacuzzi for men only. The ladies also had a private area with their own jacuzzi but no sauna. All the administrative offices for the hotel were located on the second floor along with a beauty salon. The VIP lounge, situated on the twenty-third floor, was a small and unpretentious facility in comparison to my competitor down the road. The view of the Andes from there was, however, stunning and superior to that from the Hyatt as our building was higher than theirs. All in all I knew that we were going to have a fabulous hotel.

Now we were already at the end of July. I was told by Marriott that we were to open the hotel in October. According to Felipe, we would not be able to open 'til Christmas. Felipe's hotel experience proved to be a real bonus. He knew that it would be an expensive hassle to rent office space outside the hotel to use as our pre-opening centre so saw to it that the first part of the hotel to be completed were the administrative offices. I settled in one of them using construction furniture as normally is the case. The only person already hired was Kiania as the director of sales and marketing. She was a divorced Brazilian lady with a ten year old boy. As was the case with me as general manager, she should have been hired a full year earlier. Notwithstanding that we both just had to get stuck in and make up for lost time. In that respect I quickly realised that nobody had ordered any equipment for the hotel nor had staffing been attended to. This major inconvenience did nothing to quash my enthusiasm.

Myself and Kiania needed to hire a secretary each and I had to conceive and write an action plan. This would detail each step to complete in order for the hotel to be ready to open at the fixed date. I also needed a cash float for out of pocket expenses. Felipe gave me 5 million Chilean pesos which I kept in my briefcase in the office and took back to the Hyatt every evening. I realised that the owners did not have unlimited funds. In order to help them, I booked out of my 150 US dollars per day Hyatt suite and found a 30 dollars per day apartment for Janet and I nearby. Naturally it was less comfortable but it was a smart move as the owner appreciated the fact that I wasn't a prima-donna general manager of the kind they'd experienced before.

Janet was soon back to normal after her alleged food poisoning and out looking for an apartment with a real estate agent the owner had recommended. As with other moves we had done in the past Janet would scout the area and, by a process of elimination, only take me to see apartments in which she was prepared to live. For the next week every evening after work I went around with her and the agent to see what she had visited during the day and one evening we hit the jackpot ... bingo! The apartment she had taken me to see was in Calle Luis Carrera 2600 in the municipality of Vitacura, the most prestigious part of the city and just five minutes from my work.

The building was new in the street. The apartment was only one floor up and in front of the polo club. The view was so great that, from our bed and without even lifting our heads, we could take in the entire view of the Manquehue mountain. We had three parking spaces and a storage area in the basement. The entry hall was so long and wide that it could accommodate a large table and still leave room to dance a Viennese waltz. Off to the right was the large and well-equipped kitchen, behind it was the laundry room and the live-in maid's room. This I promptly commandeered as my office. To the opposite side of the kitchen was the dining room and, off it, a south facing afternoon balcony. Across the hall there was a really big living room attached to an equally big front balcony which was covered by netting to keep birds from flying into the apartment. At the end of the corridor there was a large room in front of the master bedroom which became the TV room and Janet's office. Our bedroom was gigantic with a balcony, an en-suite bathroom and a walk-in closet for Janet. Off in the opposite direction there were two further bedrooms each with a bathroom. Janet decorated and furnished them for Emily and Paul. I regret to this day that I did not take up the purchase opportunity offered to me to buy that apartment for a mere 250,000 dollars.

Things were looking good. We had found an outstanding place to live and the hotel was coming together very nicely. The three owners of the hotel were nice gentlemen. I could see that they were starting to trust my judgement and that I would have an easy ride with them. While I busied myself with the hotel, Janet sought out the many diversions and activities available to an expat wife. There was the British women's club, the American women's club, the Canadian women's club, bible study groups, golf societies, bridge clubs and painting classes. Painting is one of her great passions. There was also the not inconsiderable task of exploring the country. Chile is simply wonderful. It abounds in natural beauty and diverse landscapes. From the driest desert in the world in the north to Antartica in the south and everything in between. It is a veritable paradise ... talking of which, we had also found a good church to attend.

Kiania and I worked on the marketing plan. I had to let her take the lead on that as I had to concentrate on hiring a team and purchasing all the necessary equipment for the hotel. The regional vice president of operations came to help me for a couple of days and we were able to complete the list of equipment needed. With that done, he left and I turned my attention to the hiring of a director of human resources and a director of engineering. As regards the latter position, the decision was made to hire Patricio Urbina then working at the Radisson.

The regional director of human resources, a heavy set American of German descent named Gertrude Eisen, came to interview the candidates for the position of human resources director. It has always surprised me that many people who have no empathy with their fellow beings often make a career in personnel management. Gertrude was one such. After interviewing ten candidates, we settled for an unemployed guy who was handsome, spoke perfect English and had last worked as director of human resources at the Crowne Plaza Hotel in the heart of Santiago. When asked why he wasn't working anymore he told us that there was a new general manager at the hotel with whom he didn't see eye to eye. I had a bad feeling about him but Gertrude was sure that he was the right man for the job.

Soon after he started work I got a call from Eduardo Fahrenkrug the general manager of the Crowne Plaza Hotel to warn me that he had fired this guy for trying to steal a truck load of furniture from the hotel. I was shocked but not really surprised. I called him to my office to ask if what I had heard was true. His answer was that he had been taking the furniture for an orphan's home and not for himself. I had no alternative but to fire him. At that point he reminded me that, under Chilean law, I owed him three month salary. Gritting my teeth, I paid up.

The clock was ticking and the process of hiring had to be accelerated. The resident manager, Ethan White, came from another Marriott in the US. He spoke some Spanish, was married to a Pakistani lady and had two small children. The director of food and beverage, Christoph, was a Swiss guy and came from the Marriott in Aruba. He was married to a Hawaiian lady and had three very young boys. He didn't speak Spanish but spoke Papiamento, the language spoken in Aruba. Because it resembles Spanish and because he was Swiss, I was confident that he would pick up the language in Chile rapidly. The director of finance, Kevin Walker, was an American from the Marriott in Thailand and married with a little girl and boy. But he didn't speak Spanish. This turned out to be a major handicap which eventually led to his dismissal from the company after one year struggling in Santiago.

Now the only position still open was the director of human resources. I reviewed all the resumés of candidates for the position but still couldn't find an applicant who fitted the bill. Then I came up with what I thought was a brilliant idea. We were hiring about three hundred employees to open the hotel. We had received six thousand applications for the positions. I had given Carlos Labarca the task of sifting through all those CVs to categorise them and separate the wheat from the chaff. Carlos had done a good job so why not hire him as director of human resources? He had no human resource management experience but seemed smart enough. I believed that with the proper guidance he could learn the job. Gertrude was against. I was insistant. Carlos came on board.

Paul was in Washington DC doing his second year at Johns Hopkins University. Emily was by now hired as an intern, directly from Thunderbird, by Procter & Gamble Company, to work in Cincinnati.

It was now time to start receiving the equipment ordered for the opening. A large unfinished space at the end of the lobby was designated as the initial storage space for the contents of the many containers arriving. I made a point of personally checking what was actually in every container that arrived and matching that with its bill of lading and with the invoice. I had to sign off the invoices for payment and wanted to see with my own eyes that what I was authorising to be paid was indeed what we received. I supervised the storage too as I knew from my experience of other openings just how important it was for the general manager to know what he would be held accountable for. There was a lot of the owners' money inside those containers. I felt that it was important to ensure that they would get all they were paying for.

Also the rest of the team was coming on board one by one. The executive chef, Kacper Kowal, was a young Pole who had been the executive sous-chef at the Warsaw Marriott. He was married to a lovely Austrian girl who was the pastry chef at the same hotel. My director of restaurants, Martin Contrera, joined us from the Hyatt as did the banquet maître d'hotel, Claudio. Both the front office manager and my director of service, Sandra Stempfle, came from other local hotels and the assistant controller was a local guy recently retired from the Chilean navy.

HIRING AND FIRING

I deviated from the traditional Marriott way of having all staff hired at a kind of recruitment fare in a large hall over a three day period. Instead I had them come to the hotel individually for interview. Applicants were first screened by Carlos and his team. If suitable, they were then sent to either the executive of the department in which they were applying to work or to the executive of the department in which the human resources office felt they would best fit. Then, if they were found to match the characteristics looked for in a Marriott employee, they would be interviewed by the department head who, as the one having to work with and manage the employee, had the final say.

Those applying for the positions of supervisor or assistant manager had to be interviewed by three executives before being sent to the department head. If two executives gave the thumbs up the candidate was sent for the final interview but, when two executives gave the thumbs down then the candidate was rejected. This process, while not without fault, worked well. Soon we had all three hundred employees selected and instructed to report for work on the 3rd of January 2000.

As the team of managers was growing every day we had to hire a company to provide lunch for them. Carlos came up with a list of the best local caterers for the executive committee to choose from. The only available space large enough to act as a lunch room for the team was the corridor between my office and the sales and marketing office. It was on an improvised desk in the last-named office that, on the 6th of October 1999, we set up our first switchboard. Marcela Gonzalez was our first switchboard operator. We required her to speak Castellano, English and any one other language. In retrospect, we realised that we should have insisted on Portuguese as the third language because of the large number of Brazilian guests who came to the hotel and rarely spoke English or Spanish. As regards language, we found that many young

Chileans had either been born or lived abroad because so many families had been exiled during the dictatorial regime of Augusto Pinochet. Thus it was fairly easy to find young people who spoke German, Swedish, Italian, French and we even found one young man who spoke Polish.

We were now approaching the famous scare of the Y2K when it was said that at midnight of the 31st of December 1999 all the computers in the world would cease to function. Of course it never happened. New Year's Eve parties went on around the world with eating, drinking, dancing and fireworks without a hitch. The owners asked me if the hotel could host a roof top party for two hundred of their friends. We were only too eager to oblige. Christopher, the director of food and beverage, and his team, organised a magnificent evening with full bar service, champagne flowing and delicious food and wine which captivated the hearts and minds, not to mention the stomachs, of all. Emily and Paul came. Janet and I were there celebrating with them. I didn't have a thing to worry about, with the operation smoothly controlled and in such capable hands as those of Christopher. Unfortunately I couldn't feel the same when it came to other departments.

January the 3rd was the big day when all three hundred employees started work. At Marriott we always made this a particularly great event for the staff. As they arrived to work, they were surprised to find all the executives lined up and a batucada (a Brazilian band) playing happy music to welcome them. As they passed beyond this point they were each handed a training manual appropriate to their department. Then they were led through to enjoy a breakfast feast such as they had never seen before. After that they were whisked off to start two weeks of intensive training before the opening date of January the 17th when the first guests arrived.

As the day approached I had to take the task force manager, Steve Redkols and put him in charge of housekeeping. Otherwise we would not have been ready to open as the resident manager, Ethan, was not on top of his job and had fallen behind. The director of engineering was weak and didn't speak English. His secretary, Carmen Gloria, had to translate all the technical text manuals coming from headquarters. She had no experience in translating so this became a major problem. And the director of finance didn't speak Castellano. This gave his crooked assistant the opportunity to set up a scheme to defraud the hotel. Fortunately we found out what he was up to and got rid of him.

Then the director of human resources, while a nice enough guy, turned out to be lacking too. The director of sales and marketing was also a problem as she would lose her temper and create chaos in the office every day.

All in all, it became abundantly evident that the choice of executives which either I or the company had made, was not good.

By that time all of us were tired but the show had to go on. I had developed a lip herpes, a sure sign that my body was tired and that my resistance was low. I got Zovirac from the chemist to apply to it. Getting ready for work the next day, I put my eye gel on my lip and the Zovirac in my eyes which started to burn with pain. No matter how much water I splashed on them the pain would not subside. I staggered half blind to work red-eyed and late for my 6.30 am daily team meeting. To be late was unheard of for me. My executives had already nicknamed me Bugs Bunny after a bunny rabbit cartoon character featured in a long life battery, television ad. This rabbit would run around non-stop for days on end and, like me, was in constant motion.

Our first guests, a Californian couple, arrived. They were met at the airport by one of our brilliant hostesses in a chauffeur driven BMW and taken to the hotel. There they were welcomed by myself and the executive committee and led inside to a guard of honour formed of one employee from each department standing there to shake hands. A champagne breakfast had been set up in the lobby and they were presented with a commemorative plaque with their names on it. When they eventually arrived in their room they found two dressing gowns embroidered with their initials and with two matching pillow cases to take home with them.

The regional directorship team was also there for the occasion to support the executive team and to offer guidance. Everyone was smiling, everyone was friendly and it seemed everyone cared. Most of us were also tired beyond belief. As we opened to the public the Café Med restaurant and room service along with the Cordillera Lobby bar also opened. Normally on first day opening a restaurant gets very busy (this is why it's common practice to over-staff) but, in our case, this was not so. The Café Med remained very quiet and the staff in the kitchen and restaurant were standing around doing nothing but waiting for customers who never came. Room service was also quiet as the hotel was next to empty. We took advantage of this to provide staff with more practical training.

The reason for the lack of customers was that January and February are the standard vacation months in Chile. The city is empty with all the people gone on vacation to the seaside, up to the mountains or abroad to Europe or North America. Nonetheless, shortly after opening we started experiencing our first staff losses. Some employees got disenchanted and resigned within the first month. Normally in cases like these it is the good employees who tend to leave as they want to be active and, particularly in the case of waiters, want to make tips.

ROYALTY VISITS

We had set the date of February the 17th for the grand opening of the hotel. I went to the airport in a black Mercedes to meet and greet Mr. and Mrs.Marriott arriving off their private jet. They were accompanied by Ed Fuller, at that time the president of Marriott International and all of the other VIPs. I had taken with me the financial results of the first month of operation as I knew Mr.Marriott would ask me for them in the car before arriving at the hotel. Sure enough he did and, sure enough, he wasn't happy. The fact that it was in the middle of the summer and businesses were either closed or operating at reduced capacity didn't affect him. He, like everyone else at Marriott, was used to opening the doors of a new hotel and having it immediately full to capacity with the restaurants packed with diners and the bars bursting at the seams with customers. I felt a bit of tension as we arrived at the hotel. The standard welcome committee was set up at the main entrance. The resident manager was first in line, then the rest of the executive committee and then the line of staff applauding as we entered the hotel. I was leading the group followed by Mrs.Marriott, Mr.Marriott and Ed Fuller.

At this time a German guest stepped forward from the crowd gathered in the lobby and introduced himself as a Marriott Platinum Member, the highest level a regular guest could achieve in the VIP program. He proudly told Mr.Marriott that he had checked out of the Sheraton to come to the hotel as he loved Marriott the most. More about this guy shortly.

As the introduction of the executive committee concluded I noticed Mr.Marriott lean over to whisper something in Ed Fuller's ear. With the introduction of the rest of the staff completed I escorted Mr. and Mrs.Marriott to the presidential suite. Ed Fuller then pulled me aside to tell me what Mr.Marriott had said in his ear earlier. It was, "Too many white faces!" I knew that this translated as 'too many expensive expat foreign managers' and it sent a shiver down my spine. I immediately got the message that I would have to get rid of some of them sooner than soon and send them back to the US or wherever else they had come from.

Putting that troublesome thought aside I set about reviewing with Ed the agenda I proposed to present to Mr.Marriott. Ed suggested only minor adjustments and found the programme well done. That made me feel a bit better. When I met Mr.Marriott one hour later in the Cordillera Lounge, he didn't make any mention of what he felt was our excessive overload of foreign managers but simply concentrated on the agenda and business at hand. He was pleased to see that the programme had been kept simple and was not the circus-like extravaganza of many Marriott grand openings. I had planned an early morning opening ceremony attended by the equivalent of the minister of tourism followed by a sit down breakfast at a huge rectangular table in the ballroom. A pianist played classical and romantic music.

The only traditional part of a Marriott grand opening which we performed was the cutting of the ribbon and the release into the air, by Mr.Marriott and the minister of tourism, of a giant styrofoam key attached to helium balloons. This signified that the hotel key had been thrown away and that the hotel doors would now forever be open. The breakfast did have one little glitch. Christopher and the chef miscalculated the timing of the egg poaching. This led to a brief but uncomfortable wait for myself, Mr.Marriott seated to my left and Mrs.Marriott seated to my right. Fortunately the moment passed without comment.

Janet was in charge of entertaining Mrs.Marriott for the duration of the visit. She accomplished this with customary aplomb. She had a well planned agenda of visits to typical little markets for souvenirs, churches, museums and stables where beautiful horses were bred, trained and available for riding.

That evening Mr.Marriott wanted to visit the Hyatt for dinner. I made an eight o'clock reservation with Gordon Fuller, the general manager there, for Mr. and Mrs.Marriott, Ed Fuller, Janet and myself. We walked to the Hyatt and Gordon was waiting to meet us at the entrance of the hotel. After a short introduction and some chit chat he showed us to our table in the dining room. He made a very favourable impression on Mr.Marriott who said he'd gladly have Gordon manage one of his hotels. The dinner, luckily for me, turned out to be a disappointment. Mrs.Marriott's fillet of sole was frozen – and still frozen when it was served. She had to return it to the kitchen for more cooking. We walked back to the hotel by 10.00 pm as the Marriotts were leaving early the next day to go to Buenos Aires and their Plaza Hotel there where Haile Aguilar was the general manager.

Now the real business began. The hotel was officially open and there were no more excuses to not have business, happy customers and happy employees. I was left with the great task of making the Marriott brand a household name in Santiago de Chile. I was determined to do so by right or might, as the Chilean national motto states. As business was not picking up, the first thing I had to do was take a serious look at our staffing and decide if I could afford to keep all remaining two hundred and ninety workers on the payroll. I also had to give consideration to Mr.Marriott's 'too many white faces' comment. With the end of February came our first profit and loss statement which showed a staggering loss of 400,000 US dollars since the soft opening on the 17th of January.

After talking to my boss at the regional office (and having kept my job) I decided to see Felipe to apologise for having lost him that kind of money. When I told him he, to my complete surprise, got up from his chair behind the desk and came round to me and gave me a huge hug. He told me that it was a reason to celebrate and took me to the Cordillera Lounge and ordered a glass of champagne for himself and for me a cappuccino.

As I started to relax he told me that by getting the hotel open when I did I had saved him 600,000 US dollars because of the difference between the pre-opening construction loan and the post-opening mortgage loan terms of the bank. He knew that the hotel construction was not near enough completion for the hotel to be opened, yet I had done it and saved him a fortune. For that he was grateful. A memory came back to me of the two previous owners I had worked with in Egypt and Dubai. I thanked the Lord for giving me such a good one now. From the next month on we never lost a cent in the operation of the hotel.

Business was slow but we were able to control the costs and we were turning in a meagre profit each month. The expectation had been that, as the vacation period ends and life returns to normal in Santiago in March, business would pick up. That was not happening and the pressure from my boss was increasing every day.

At this time the 'loyal German platinum guest', who had turned up and spoken to Mr.Marriott on opening day, wasn't paying his bills every Saturday morning as had been agreed that he would do. Following several conversations with him which led us nowhere, I decided to bolt his room and let him sleep on a chair in the lobby until his outstanding account was settled. He had no change of clothes, could only shower in the gym and couldn't eat in the hotel as he had no credit nor cash. Because of his high status I contacted Marriott headquarters and some investigations were made. It was discovered that he had also skipped from paying substantial bills in two hotels in the US and some in other countries too. Eventually he got money from Germany and paid his bill but I didn't let him back into the hotel, the risk was too high.

By June I had to let Carlos go and Anna, the human resources manager too. I took over the running of that department assisted by Vanessa, the human resources secretary. Then Christopher was moved to Texas as the regional director of food and beverage and I assumed his position. Now I had my job, the human resources department and the food and beverage department to run as well. On top of that, occupancy was still low. Gordon, at the Hyatt, was not helping by lowering his rates and all the other hotels were following suit.

At that time I figured that the way to survive was to find other ways to generate income. As the offices in the towers were being rented with our housekeeping staff we started a cleaning service for them and added a laundry and dry cleaning service for the employees of the offices. This generated some revenue but not near enough to meet budget. By September the resident manager was moved back to the US so I took over the room division as well.

OWNING UP

The director of finance, Kevin, was struggling. Due to his lack of knowledge of the law and no support from his assistant he had managed to lose a thousand or so receipts. When I found out about these missing receipts I went to Felipe and asked for his advice.

He advised that the best way to handle a serious problem like that with the tax authority was to go to their office and report it to them voluntarily rather than wait to be audited and found out. This could have led to a fine of several million dollars and a possible prison term for me as the legal representative of the hotel. The idea of a Chilean prison was not an appealing one with the horror stories of the Pinochet dictatorship still fresh in my mind.

I reported the situation to the tax authorities who took a year to pronounce that, because I had reported the situation, they would write off the missing receipts ... but ... should we lose even one more receipt we would be made to pay for the thousand missing ones plus the new losses. In addition I would get a prison sentence of from one to five years. This sentence would depend on whether or not the judge considered me guilty of malicious intent to defraud the taxes. In the meantime Kevin continued to try hard to learn Castellano. His efforts though were fruitless and a short while after this incident he was terminated by the company.

By now I had lost all of the executive committee with the exception of Patricio, the director of engineering. He was also in above his head and could do little more than wander aimlessly around the hotel all day.

The director of finance post was beyond my capability so not one I could add to my portfolio of directorships. The regional director of finance brought in an assistant controller called Matias Contrera, from the Dominican Republic. He was a nice young man, married with two children. Matias had some good knowledge of finance and his first recommendation was to lease the health club to a third party and for us to concentrate on our core business which was the hotel operation.

The word was out in Santiago that we were a soft touch when it came to being billed for banquet events. We had many parties booking events at the hotel in the hope and belief that they would never be billed. To deal with this, my secretary Kathy and I went to the accounts receivable office and started sorting through the banquet cheques, invoices not sent and any other documents that showed that a specific event had not been billed. The task took about three weeks but proved to be a really worthwhile exercise. Soon everyone was being billed and the money owed started rolling in. Then Pedro Perez, an experienced Spanish speaking Puerto Rican director of finance, joined us. With that I now had two Spanish speaking managers in the finance department. I could sleep peacefully in the knowledge that I was now far less likely to be hauled off to prison.

We were now approaching the Christmas holiday and year end festivity. Emily and Paul came to spend the holiday with us. We wanted to explore some of the beauty of Chile together so we booked a week-long cruise to the Laguna San Rafael on the Skorpio 3, the most luxurious boat making that trip. A few days before Christmas we flew to Puerto Montt in the south of the country and slept on board the boat waiting the next morning's departure to the Chilean Patagonia with its fjords, canals and millennial glaciers. What a treat we had in store.

As this was the flagship of the company it was piloted by the owner himself and his wife was the chef. The food was great and the atmosphere on board was very relaxed. The next morning, after all the other passengers joined us, we set off on the cruise. The natural beauty of that magnificent country opened up before our eyes and the unexpected became the norm. The waters were smooth, the vegetation thick, the wind strong, the sky blue. The passengers laughed louder as the consumption of great Chilean wines increased.

On Christmas day the passengers from all the three Skorpio boats navigating in the same direction met for lunch in a large room inside a thermal water spa. It was indeed a big event. Folklore music was played by a live band and a typical mixed grill with an abundance of fish, seafood and fresh vegetables was served. The lunch lasted several hours. Then those of us who could still walk, or even swim, had a reinvigourating thermal bath in the hot natural spa. By the time we all returned to our respective boats it was dark and most of the people didn't make it to dinner that night.

One of the highlights of that trip was definitely the adventure of climbing a glacier. There, once at the top, we received a glass and an ice pick. We chipped away at the millennial ice until we filled our glass and then brought it down the slope to Mr.Kochidis, the owner and pilot. He then poured in a generous measure of whisky for us to enjoy (myself excluded of course). The trip continued with the return stop on the island of Chiloé and from the harbour we took a taxi to the village of Quemchi which is the birth place of Francisco Coloane, one of the most famous Chilean writers. While there aren't many things to do there, it is probably one of the most mystic places on earth. When it came to mysticism the only other place I felt that way about was at the old monastery in Novoburg, Russia. It was now time to return to Santiago on the 29th of December to get ready to welcome the new year in with a party in the courtyard.

I had a standard principle I adhered to regarding the new year celebration. I told my teams that, if by December the 31st the budget hadn't been made, then it was too late. I would allow the party to be held with two conditions. One was that the party had to be done well and make all the guests happy for spending that kind of money so they wouldn't complain to me on the 2nd of January. Two was that no money had to be lost in producing the event. That night we failed on both counts. The set up was terrible with the wind blowing through the courtyard and knocking down even the tall candelabras put on each table. The financial loss was 20,000 US dollars! It was the last New Year's eve party at the Santiago Marriott for many years to come.

Now Laura Barbieri, a human resources manager from the Marriott Plaza in Buenos Aires, was promoted to director of human resources in Santiago. She was twenty-three year old, single and, to say the least, stunning. When she arrived many of the young single guys in the hotel started visiting the human resources office with any excuse just to see her. She broke many hearts. I was so grateful to have a director in that position and, contrary to standard Marriott procedure, I arranged to have the loss prevention department report to her. That department was managed by a young man, Eduardo Saso, who wanted to be a policeman. It had taken some time to convince him that we were not a police department or a prison but a hotel. Being a hotel means being hospitable and I had seen the contrary of that at the Hyatt.

COCAINE WARS

It was now 2001 and we would celebrate our first anniversary with a nice event for our staff. Laura had been on the job about a week when the anniversary party took place on the 19th of January. While the economics were not great we decided to make it a real good party anyway to thank the people for all their efforts, enthusiasm and dedication throughout the year. It was a costume party as would become the custom every year thereafter. This first year it was a beach theme. All the employees came dressed as they would to go to the beach. There were lots of shorts, large hats, bikinis and a wrap arounds. I decided to be conservative and dress like a Bermudian with Bermuda shorts, short sleeve shirt and tie. A band had agreed to play for us for free because we had recommended them for weddings and events all year. The room was set really nice. Prizes to be raffled were bought, others were donated. Awards for each and every good reason we could think of were made to staff with the intention of boosting morale.

All was going well until Eduardo went to the men's locker room and found one of the dishwashers from the La Pintana slum area selling cocaine. His frustrated policeman's instinct took over. He took the seller to his office and summoned me to go there. We had a choice to make. We could have involved the police or we could handle it ourselves. Had we involved the police it would have created a major scandal as the police would have come followed by television cameras and reporters. We would have been on the front page of the Mercurio, South America's leading newspaper, the next morning. In addition to that it was probable that the hotel would be held responsible for the event. In Chile it is not against the law to use drugs, only to sell them. This actually meant that we would have had to send the offenders to detox and foot the bill. Laura also came to the office as a kind of defense lawyer. Eduardo was pressuring the detainee to tell who he had sold the cocaine to. While he was not using any real force he did pressure the guy into giving us a few names. We decided to take all his cocaine off him, poured it down the toilet and terminated his employment on the spot.

Now we had a few names of drug users who were on our payroll but, as the word spread, we found ourselves within a week with a list of sixty-four employees who were buying cocaine. Worse still, several managers were part of the group. The banquet maître d'hotel and the director of restaurants were the two most prominent. Drastic action was required on my part. I informed the regional management team of the problem. I told them on the phone that I had sixty-four known cocaine users in my employ and that I was going to terminate the lot of them. "What!" exclaimed Gertrude Eisen, "Are you asking my permission to fire sixty-four people?" "No," I retorted, "I'm not asking I'm telling you!" This exchange put us in open conflict and made of her my eternal enemy.

The first thing I had to do was to make sure that my executive committee was clean. I arranged for a surprise taking of hair samples. I brought a lab technician from the local clinic and set him up in one of the suites. All of the executives and managers were summoned, one by one, and given the choice of either having a sample of their hair taken and tested or they could refuse to do so. None of them refused. To my delight, all were found to be free of drugs. At this time both the director of restaurants and the banquet maître d'hotel were on vacation. Naturally someone let them know that we were taking hair samples to test for drugs. A few days later they both returned to work with their heads shaved clean! This only made it clear to all that they were guilty as charged.

As we continued to fire people we could see the morale of the hotel staff dropping. I came to realise why Gordon Fuller at the Hyatt was so happy. We had taken over lots of his headaches as many of those people had come from his hotel, not least the managers. The director of restaurants was replaced by a young French fellow and the banquet maître d'hotel was replaced by a Chilean of Italian descent, Paolo Quintiliani. We now had a more solid team and, at least for a while, the drug problem seemed to have disappeared. Business was not picking up however and morale in the hotel was so low that it wasn't fun going to work in the morning. My broken relationship with Gertrude had adversely affected my relationship with the entire regional team, making it difficult for me to work with them. I needed to re-establish those ties.

With the position of director of human resources filled I had more time to dedicate to the operation of the hotel as well as to the sales and marketing department. I initiated special promotions for events in the restaurants every evening of the week with the exception of Sunday and Monday nights. Even with these the income was not increasing significantly.

While in Dubai, I had started a special club with the help of an outside company. It was a dining club that sold memberships to people who then received special benefits such as discounts, free nights in the hotel, parking privileges and the like. An Australian company now approached me to set up such a club so I signed a contract with them. The Hyatt already had a similar club. I was determined to kill their club as sweet revenge for all the scum personnel Gordon had dumped on me. This is how the Marriott Exclusive Club was born.

At first we took over a suite in the hotel as the base for the operation. The Australian company brought in an Argentinian manager to start up the club. His name was Carlos. It became quickly clear that he was not going to succeed. He was a typical 'superior Argentinian'. Argentinians, in general at that time, had this feeling that they were better, smarter and more handsome than any mere Chilean. They looked down on the Chileans and really believed that the locals were incapable of thinking for themselves. The smart Argentinian had to tell them what to do and how to think. It is a bit like the rivalry which exists between Spain and Portugal. There is a popular joke that goes something like this, "Do you know how an Argentinian commits suicide?" Answer, "He jumps from his ego!"

The girls hired for the dining club were bright, young and

dynamic. Once instructed and trained on how to do their jobs they became effective in no time. Carlos was just acting like a bull in a china shop. To try to balance this wave of terror, we asked the company to bring in an assistant manager with a totally different approach. To my surprise and consternation they brought in another Argentinian. Anibal was totally the opposite from what we had seen in Carlos. He was a single guy who had attended military academy in Argentina and he was a born leader. With him things completely changed in that department. Sales improved and soon we surpassed Hyatt's number of dining club members, which was a paltry four hundred.

Now we saw the restaurants start to thrive and become the places in town to see and be seen in. Members would keep their Marriott Exclusive card in a prominent position in their wallet and made sure that every time they opened it their friends would see that they were members of such an elite club. So word of mouth spread the news and the membership rapidly multiplied.

I had learned that there was no such thing as a bad night in food and beverage, there were only bad promotions. The point behind this being that people eat and drink every day but they must have a reason to go to a specific place to get what they want. With this principle in mind we revamped all of the nightly entertainments and the restaurants became alive. We now were the place to go in town. Membership at the Marriott Exclusive Club became the best thing to have if you wanted to be recognized as someone important in the city.

Our club became so prestigious that, before the year end, we had reached the milestone of one thousand members. The club at the Hyatt was left to eat dust. However, as our fearless leader, Mr.Marriott Senior used to say, 'success is never final' so we continued to work hard on the project. By the time I left the management of that hotel, we had reached two thousand two hundred members and the Hyatt had closed its club. It was a small but sweet victory. A few months later Carlos was sent back to Buenos Aires to open another club and Anibal was promoted to manager. The girls loved him and were eager to see him succeed. Besides which, he was a good catch and all the single ones had set their eyes on him. Despite these temptations, he was a true professional and a leader and never dated any of the girls.

TRAVELLING THROUGH HARD TIMES

The year 2001 moved on and, along with every hotel in the country, we continued to struggle as far as the hotel occupancy was concerned. A rate war broke out with every hotel lowering the price of their rooms with the intent of taking business from the competition. This of course is a dog eat dog situation in which no-one wins. Then September 11 came to completely kill the year. With people afraid to fly, video conferencing became the in thing. We got into the business of renting conference rooms fully equipped for large conference calls and seminars. While this initiative brought some results it didn't make up for the lack of 'heads on the beds'.

Soon we were approaching the Christmas and New Year holiday season again and we undertook one of our most memorable family vacation trips ever. Janet, Emily, Paul and I went to the Galapagos Islands. The Galapagos is a volcanic archipelago in the Pacific Ocean and lie about 600 miles (965 km) off the Ecuador coast. They are famous for their abundance of wild life. It is here that Charles Darwin came up with his theory of the evolution of the species. We embarked on a six day cruise around this amazing 'Garden of Eden'.

What makes this place so special is not so much the crystal clear, warm ocean water, the rugged volcanic landscape, the sandy beaches or the blue skies - but the wild life. There is such an endless assortment of animals and wonders of creation to behold. It is not necessary to be an expert in the field to enjoy a swim with gigantic tortoises, penguins and sea lions while watching marine iguanas, blue-footed booby, fur seals, lava lizards and American flamingos. The variety of fish you can encounter while snorkeling is just so magnificent as to take your breath away. You could be swimming alongside a whitetip reef shark while also playing with spotted eagle ray. As you raise your eyes to the sky you will see great blue heron, brown noddy, Galapagos doves and Galapagos hawks flying above with at least another twenty species of birds. There are two hundred species of insects as well. The butterflies are just so beautiful, they come in all shapes, forms and colours. What a sight! To top it all we had to visit the oldest tortoise in the world. His name was George and he was born on Pinta Island at the northern tip of the Galapagos circa 1910. He died on June 24th, 2012. Lonesome George was the very last of his species and, in his last years, the rarest creature in the world.

On New Year's eve we were back at the JW Marriott in Quito and celebrated the arrival of 2002 in the restaurant of the hotel Stefano Piselli. A fellow from Gozzano, the closest town to the village of my birth in Italy, was the general manager at that time. He was married to Galina, an American of Russian descent. They lived in the hotel but they stayed in their apartment that night and never came down to see what was happening at the dinner and celebration party. They were wise to stay away. It was a disaster. The food was mediocre and the service atrocious. We waited so long that by the time the dinner was served we were well into 2002. Stefano and his wife were both heavy set people with poor health. It was for this reason that sometime later he was retired by the company and went to live somewhere near Scottsdale in Arizona. They came to visit us in Santiago once and brought us a wind chimes as a gift. It is now hanging on our lemon tree in the back garden tinkling merrily in the ocean breeze.

Emily and Paul left the day after. Emily was now working full time as a purchasing manager at Procter & Gamble who she had joined as an intern right from post-graduation. Paul was working at ISL in China. Janet and I returned to our normal routine. While business was abysmal to say the least, our social life was positively booming. With copper prices very low many of the expats with whom we had become friends had returned home. The few that were left wanted to make the best of what life in Chile had to offer. That started with the wine, the seafood and the fish which meant that every weekend someone would give a party in their apartment or house. Foreigners loved Chilean wines and never missed the opportunity to have a good share of it. I was no longer a drinker of alcohol and these parties were kind of a routine for me but it was fun anyway. I had learned to enjoy the atmosphere and observe how the evenings would start off and then end.

I noted that, as people arrived at the party, they were generally quiet. Then, with their first glass of wine in hand, they'd wander around greeting people like long lost friends although it was probably only a week and the last party since they'd met. Some advanced to the buffet table where food in abundance to the point of waste was laid out. Some hid away in corners. Others would seek out a person they liked and then stick with him or her all evening. As the evening progressed the level of noise increased. The more wine that was downed the more the volume went up. By the time midnight came many people were no longer in any condition to drive home and taxis were called. As I was one of the few sober individuals and therefore automatically nominated as the driver, Janet at least, was always guaranteed a safe drive home – and no taxi fare.

Janet had taken up skiing again. Within 30 miles (48 km) of Santiago there are four great ski resorts. As the seasons are reversed in the southern hemisphere she would go up to ski in July, August and September. It was on one of those ski trips that she skied into a fence, banged her already injured knee and had to have her leg put in a cast. She was also working as a volunteer with the Helen Keller school for blind children and enjoyed escorting them on their organised ski trips to these resorts. Even after we left Chile she returned once just to do that.

Golf, bridge, mah-jongg and bible study were some of the other activities that kept Janet busy. As she'd become a member at the Balthus Gym, she'd drive me to work each morning before going there for her routine exercise before the day started. She also joined three women's clubs. In one she was the day trip organiser, in another she was the secretary and in the other she was also on the board. All these activities, her ability to keep herself busy and not to have to depend on me to entertain her, are what kept Janet so well over the years of being married to a passionate hotelier. In my business the most common cause of divorce is the work hours of a general manager; that and excessive drinking.

Business was not picking up and it was hard to survive. Meeting were held with the other five star hotel general managers at which agreements to co-operate were reached just to be broken the moment the meetings finished. I had to work long hours as I was covering the department of food and beverage and the department of rooms in addition to my general management role. With the exception of the almost weekly expats party my social life was reduced to lengthy, often boring dinners entertaining potential clients in the hope of attracting business.

We decided to do away with a director of restaurants and have the executive chef cover that position as well. He was supposed to work in the kitchen during the morning to oversee the preparation of the food for the day and then, in the late afternoon, change into a suit and work in the restaurants. This turned out to be a bad experience. It made him think he had become indispensable. With the hotel struggling financially, his ego got even more in the way.

One day he came to my office and demanded, in no uncertain terms, that the hotel provide him with three Bragard chef's jackets with his name embroidered in gold and the Chaîne de Rôtisseurs badge sewed on to the front of them. I thought he was joking and laughingly told him that the economics of the hotel made such a purchase impossible. He became furious and told me he would resign if he didn't get the jackets. I handed him a sheet of paper and my pen for him to write his resignation letter right there and then. He did just that and took it immediately to the notary public, as the law required for the authentication of his signature, and returned it to me and gave me one month's notice.

He then went back to his office and called the regional director of operations to complain that I had made him resign even though, as was the case, his wife was expecting a baby and was due in one and a half month's time. The regional director called me and, shouting down the phone at me in a most un-Marriott like way, insisted that I reinstate the chef. His main point being how could I fire the chef when his wife was due and they would not have any insurance to pay for the clinic and the birth of their new baby. I didn't give in to his order and let the chef work out his month's notice. There are people who it seems, no matter what they do in life, always get lucky. The chef proved to be one of them. On his very last day at work, his wife gave birth to their baby boy. He was covered insurance-wise. The next day he was gone.

Now I had to search for an executive chef. As I couldn't afford to employ an agency, I called all the five star hotels with good reputations for their cuisine to find out who their chefs were. Once I got the name of the chef I asked to speak to him or her, identified myself and explained that the Santiago Marriott Hotel had a vacancy for an executive chef. I never asked them if they were interested in the job. I only asked if they knew someone who would be. Most of the time I would be told that they themselves were interested. This is how Darrel Lauder, an Australian chef working at a five star German run hotel in one of the Emirates, came to join us a month later as executive chef. He was a good chef. His only difficulty was the language. In the two years he stayed with us, and despite having a Chilean live-in girlfriend, he never learned more Castellano than the basic and necessary swear words. We also promoted Victor Parada, a Chilean, to the position of full time director of restaurants.

A TRIP TO REMEMBER

Our Christmas and New Year vacation was now planned and the time came to leave for the crusero de los lagos (crossing of the lakes). Emily, Paul, Janet and I travelled to Puerto Varas, a beautiful small town on the shore of lake Llanquihue, in the south of Chile. From there we crossed Lago Llanquihue on a modern catamaran to the town of Ensenada and from there went by bus to Lago Todos Santos (all saints lake). We made the four hour crossing of that lake on another catamaran and, at the end of the lake, a bus was waiting to take us over the border into Argentina to Lago Nahuel Huapi and the last catamaran trip to San Carlos de Bariloche.

This is one of the most beautiful trips we have ever taken as a family. The scenery of the Cordillera de los Andes provides one of the most magnificent views imaginable. If you believe in God, creation and heaven, here is where you get as close to it as is possible without leaving the earth. The splendour of it all is almost indescribable. It seems that the volcanos, the snow capped peaks, the valleys and the freezing water of the lake are not real but painted by a master. All the colours blend effortlessly. The sky sits on the lakes, the volcanos crown them and the Andes put their arms around it all in a loving embrace. It is so beautiful that emotions are hard to keep under control. It is alright to let a tear or two fall from your eyes in front of God's work.

It was now gone 8.00 pm on Christmas eve. We checked into our little hotel then went to find a restaurant for dinner. After a short walk we found a restaurant called Alto el Fuego Parilla. Just the name convinced me to look no further. Argentina is renowned for its beef and a real Argentinian grill was just the place to relieve us from our tired feet, hungry stomachs and thirsty throats. Bife de Chorizo is a specialty. Although we were more inclined to eat fish after a few years in Chile, we all gave in to this ten ounce steak and really loved every bite of it. Janet and Paul drank Argentinian wine while Emily and I had our usual anaemic glass of water. Boy, what a day.

The next morning, Christmas day, we woke up to thunder and lightening. So much rain fell that it felt as if the sky had pierced a tremendous hole in itself and the water was gushing from it like a giant river in full spate. The breakfast was another feast to enjoy. I wanted to see a special resort that had been there for many years and which is still to this day one of the most luxurious hotel, spa and golf resorts in the entire world. The Llao Llao resort was 15.5 miles (25 km) from our hotel and sits on the shores of Lake Perito Moreno. Still under the heaviest rainfall we've ever experienced we took a taxi up there to have lunch. The resort is everything that it has been described as being ever since it opened. There are stunning views of the Andes and the lakes that even the rain couldn't detract from. It was just as I had imagined and more. The restaurant had the parillas (grills) right in the middle of it and expert parilleros (grill chefs) performed their master work in front of your very eyes. The rain didn't stop all day. Neither did the food coming to our table and the wine being poured into Janet and Paul's glasses. Eventually, when the rain eased and there was no more room in our stomachs, we took a taxi ride back into Bariloche. What another sensational day.

We now had a few days to explore the town which looks like a Swiss village transplanted into Argentina. Naturally the mountains are higher than in Switzerland but the feel is almost the same as walking down the streets in Zermatt. The wooden chalets have the same designs with the geranium plants hanging outside the windows. As this was summer the windows were open and we could hear the sound of tangos coming out of each one of them. Lining the streets were food vendors with their carts selling all kind of delicacies such as hot chocolate and churros dips. This idyllic town is also knows for its winter skiing. Cerro Catedral just 12.5 miles (20 km) from the town is known throughout the world for its pistes surrounded by gigantic evergreen trees. As the resort is only 3,300 feet (1,105 m) above sea level, the vegetation flourishes. We were fortunate to see this God given jewel in its summer dress. The slopes, packed with snow in winter, were now awash with rivers of brightly coloured flowers seemingly flowing down as if to engulf the town.

It was now time to return to Santiago for the New Year's Eve celebration. We made the trip back in a minibus, the four of us and one other couple. The first short coffee stop was at the resort town of Puyehue on the shores of Lake Puyehue. From there we moved on to the city of Osorno and more familiar territory. This is the part of Chile that was settled by the wave of German immigrants, about thirty thousand of them, between 1846 and 1914. They were mostly farmers and brought the skills needed at the time. They built their houses in traditional German style, settled to a climate very similar to what they were used to in Germany and to the cultivation of the same potatoe and root vegetable crops of their homeland.

We then took a detour to the town of Valdivia, another of the lovely German conclaves sitting on the Calle-Calle river and not too far from the Pacific Ocean. While inland there is more abundance of meat here, because of the proximity to the water, fish and seafood are king. Strolling through the fish market on the river's quay is both an educational and an exciting adventure. Educational because I saw here fish which I never even knew existed. They came in all shapes and colours, pretty and ugly, big and small, black, yellow, red, plump and thin. There was also a superb display of fruits and vegetables for sale and a dazzling variety of local cheeses (one of my many weaknesses). These took up so much space under the colourful awnings that it took me a good hour to walk through it.

The most exhilarating sight of Valdivia is the sea lions. They sprawl just yards from you on the quays waiting to be thrown fish scraps from the fishmongers peddling their abundant catch of the day close by. We were advised of course to watch them from a safe distance and not get too close. They are wild animals and can easily snap your hand off if they mistake it for a tasty fish.

Parque Saval on Isla Teja is a birdwatchers' paradise and full of water-lillies with colours to make Monet envious. It's a heavenly park of serenity and calm. We went there with a picnic basket full of cheese from the market, traditional maraqueta flour rolls, water and a bottle of Chilean wine. It felt as if we were in heaven. Afterwards we strolled among the metal and wood sculptures standing in the Parque de Esculturas Guillermo Franco and took a walk to the Castillo de Corral and Fuerte Niebla. This is the strategic point where the rivers Tornagaleones and Valdivia meet the ocean and where pirate ships attacked Valdivia. At the fort the original cannons still point threateningly towards some imaginary enemy ship out in the ocean.

Another place we just had to visit was the Kunstmann museum and brewery. We made sure that we got the real taste of Valdivia by sampling a schop (draft beer) served in a traditional German glass which we got to take home as souvenirs. We stayed overnight in a charming small hotel which just had the feel of being in Bavaria. The next morning, after a German breakfast of cheeses, sausages, dark German bread and strong black coffee we headed off for the final leg of our trip back home to Santiago. Our mid morning coffee stop was in Temuco and we lunched in a rustic restaurant in the ski resort of Chillan. This was our last stop before arriving back home that night. It had been yet again a most memorable trip.

Back at work nothing was changing for the better. The price of copper on January the 1st of 2003 was $ 0.71 a pound. By December the 31st it had only moved to $ 1.04 a pound. The country had stopped working. Keeping people employed had become a serious business. For me it was always painful to have to let people go for the simple reason that there wasn't enough work. Corporations of course don't think like that. Fortunately I worked for a company that saw terminating employment as a last resort.

Yet at times it was unavoidable. In those cases every effort was made to keep in work the older employees, who would have difficulty finding jobs, and people with families to support or with sick family members. The younger and fitter ones were helped to find other positions and moved on. Wherever possible we retrained personnel to work in different areas of the hotel. To keep morale up in times like these is very hard.

The anniversary party was the usual costume ball at which all the staff made great efforts to be creative and have fun. I had my head shaved and had the hotel seamstress make me a Dalai Lama outfit in the same yellow and orange colours as His Holiness wears. What a brilliant evening that turned out to be but, even with such a celebration, morale didn't improve. Food, shelter and clothing are always of foremost importance and being unemployed, or fearing to be soon, the event was of little comfort to people.

Also the enormous mortgage the ownership of the hotel had undertaken with the bank made it stressful for me and the team. Under no circumstances could we afford to lose money. We had to turn in, albeit small, a profit every month. To further save money we started sharing the position of director of sales and marketing with our sister hotel in Buenos Aires. Alex Fiz was that guy. He worked one week in Buenos Aires and in Santiago the next. It wasn't perfect but we made it work. The enthusiasm and the determination of all involved surpassed anything I'd seen before in my life. This went for all the employees, all the way down to the must humble of positions. The employees themselves, maybe unconsciously, had taken on the role of guardian and supervision. If there were any among them who slacked off or behaved contrary to the well-being of the others, the rest would gang up on them, make their life miserable and ensure that they departed sooner rather than later.

On my birthday of that year Janet was back at the house in Arizona. Early in the morning, while still asleep, I received a call from her to wish me a happy birthday. In the same breath she told me to look under the bed for my birthday present. There, wrapped up in colourful paper and with bows all over, there was a package. I quickly ripped it open as I like to open presents by tearing the paper. To my delight I found that Janet, from a photograph, had painted an image of our house in Arizona and produced a most remarkable work of art. For the rest of our years in Chile it always had a prominent place in our bedroom.

It was July the 30th. That evening at the hotel there was a celebration party to mark the Moroccan national day. The ambassador had always been a big supporter of the hotel. His wife was also very charming. She was so involved that she had spent the night working in the kitchen to assist the chef in his preparation of Moroccan dishes. I had never before seen a guest work alongside the chef in the kitchen to prepare food for their own party. This demonstrated the level of relationship which we had established with the embassies in the city.

In September of that year, Chuck Kelly, the regional vice president resigned from his position. Santiago Composto replaced him. Santiago was at the time the general manager at the Nicaragua Marriott. He was a Cuban who, at age sixteen, had to leave Cuba with his family after the Fidel Castro revolution.

PLAYING THE TOURIST

Janet and I continued to take short trips and started to enjoy the coast of Chile much more than we had done in the past. It was not unusual to find us taking Sunday trips out to Viña del Mar, Con-Con, Marbella, Algarrobo, Valparaiso, Santo Domingo, Zapallar, Quintero and even inland to Chimbarongo. There were different things to see and to enjoy in each of these places. All were scenic and each had its own particular attraction. Viña had a real, authentic Italian restaurant called San Marco. It was run by a family from Venice who had immigrated to Viña del Mar many decades back. There was also the Avenida Peru at the edge of the sea where all the gypsies gathered. There you could have your palm read, your future foretold and your wallet stolen all in one place.

Marbella had a very nice golf club. Janet enjoyed golf more than I did but I too had fun walking and hitting a small ball with a stick to try to put it into a hole 500 yards (457 m) away. Algarrobo had the largest colony of Humboldt penguins while Valparaiso had winding streets, colourful art markets and quaint cable cars which, old and noisy, brought back memories of bygone years. It was all so romantic. Santo Domingo is where Bea and Arthur had a beautiful home and we were often invited to spend the weekend. Zapallar is now the top seaside resort in Chile and, naturally, the most exclusive. There is a restaurant there called Chiringuito (a type of fishing boat) where the fish is brought direct from the boats to the chefs, cooked and served to you within twenty minutes of being landed. Quintero was at one time the centre of whaling in the country and there's a museum there now amongst the derelict buildings.

Chimbarongo was a longer trip at 112 miles (180 km) from Santiago. Here the older men and women sit at the side of the road weaving beautiful baskets and wicker work in front of your very eyes. Cauquenes was also a choice destination with its thermal waters and Swiss managed restaurant. The thermal waters have a strong sulphurous smell and taste the same but they are reputedly really good for your health. The particularly enjoyable thing we did there was take a thermal bath in a double occupancy stone sarcophagus, then shower and rest on the terrace for half an hour, before going for a scrumptious lunch prepared to perfection by the owner chef and his daughter.

We never ran out of places to see or things to do in the almost fourteen years we lived in Chile. One of the biggest benefits of our Sunday outings was to escape the Santiago smog and pollution. As the city had prospered and grown so too had the number of cars on the roads. The majority of these cars were diesel fueled and, because Santiago is in a valley, the fumes gathered inside the city. This is particularly the case in winter so a day by the seaside or inland near the Andes was sheer bliss. The wineries, with their top restaurants were also a magnet for Santiago residents. Casa del Bosque, half way to the coast, as well as Viña Morande' and many others are a shorter outing than the seaside but no less a culinary experience to savour.

With Christmas approaching again, we arranged our vacation with Emily and Paul to be at San Pedro de Atacama, a sleepy little town in the middle of the driest and highest desert in the world. We flew to Calama in the north and from there were taken the 62 miles (100 km) to San Pedro by car. The road is paved but the sand from the desert almost entirely covered it. The constant wind reminded me of the Sahara in Egypt. Our hotel was La Casa de Don Tomas which, with the rest of the town, sits on an arid plateau in the Andes. It is in the middle of the driest and highest desert in the world with an elevation of 8,500 feet (2,591 m) and humidity averaging 6% year round. The surrounding were utterly dramatic with desert, salt flats, volcanos, geysers and hot springs. Our days were spent exploring this magnificent landscape both by day and by night.

A French astrologist built an observatory in his back yard. For a few dollars you could look through his powerful telescopes and see the Sea of Tranquility on the moon. The sky is so clear that the stars appear the size of a big man's fist. We visited the Tatio Geysers, a 62 mile (100 km) mini-bus excursion which set off at four in the morning. The four of us were the only people on the bus so we had lots of room to stretch out and sleep for most of the journey.

We arrived at the geyser field just as the sun, big and red, peeped over the horizon. We had been warned that it would be glacially cold so were well equipped with thermal underwear, polar jackets and high altitude survival wear. Straight away a table was laid out and we were served a breakfast of cheese, hams, tea and coffee. The pièce de résistance was the eggs boiled in the steaming geyser water! By the time we finished eating the sun was high enough in the sky for us to shed our winter wear and don swimming costumes for a relaxing dip in the 95°F (35°C) geyser pool which is akin to a whirlpool or jacuzzi at home or in a hotel. There were no barriers around the actual geysers at that time. They shoot out of the ground under pressure and at a temperature twice that of boiling water. We were well advised to stay clear and admire the spectacle from a distance.

The geyser field comprises of eighty geysers at an altitude of 13,800 feet (4,207 m). El Tatio is an enormous plateau of red rock constantly spouting scalding water and steam. The steam from the geysers appears to fight with the sky, first rising as if to become a cloud but then being squashed back into the ground ... a spectacular and never ending cycle. The whole place creates a fairy tale sensation of a land where time has stopped. By 10.00 am we were ready to depart and come down again grateful that the high altitude hadn't had any negative effect on us.

On the way back from El Tatio we found the scenery to be every bit as impressive as being at the top. We passed reflective lagoons with what seemed like floating islands of grass and wild desert flowers and populated with graceful flamingos. All along the side of the dusty, bumpy road there were llamas and wild goats (from which cashmere wool comes) feeding on rare bunches of green shrubs. Then we stopped and another delightful surprise awaited us, Puritama Hot Springs.

This is a natural hot spring formed by the hot water of the Puritama river. The water temperature is around 86°F (30°C) in the naturally created pool and the waters are reputedly excellent for the treatment of rheumatic and muscular diseases. It was a wonderful place to rest. Its basic infrastructure composed of dressing rooms, bathrooms and wooden footbridges, combined with the vegetation that hangs on the edges. Puritama, in native language, means puri (water) and tama (warm). Everything around the area smells of pure and spiritual cleansing. This was where I almost regretted having given up drinking alcohol as we were served canapés of smoked salmon, smoked trout, deviled eggs and macadamia nuts ... along with bottle after bottle of chilled Moet et Chandon champagne.

From there we proceeded on to the fairy tale village of Machuca with its twenty clay brick houses and a small church. A dusty road separates the two short rows of grass thatch roofed houses. Its back drop are the red hills of the Atacama desert. The sky here constantly changes its blues from glaucous, a calm and graceful shade, to medium Persian blue, a soothing shade of blue. Then to sapphire Persian blue which reflects astrological significance, to air superiority blue, a dark shade of blue. I couldn't recognise all of the shades of blue the sky took on in the hour or so we stopped at the village. Life here is definitely very quiet and sleepingly easy paced. The inhabitants make their living from the handicrafts they produce and sell to tourists. From there our slow drive back to San Pedro was, just as the rest of the morning, never to be forgotten. Neither was Valle de la Luna, the place we visited next.

Valle de la Luna (valley of the moon) is a valley in Los Flamencos National Reserve. It is located in the Salt mountain range, just 8 miles (13 km) west of San Pedro. The geological formations, which are located in one of the most barren zones on the planet, are made of stone and sand. It is an incredible landscape to see because of these stone formations, petrified salt and sand, that during millennia, floods and wind have moulded. We also wanted to see for ourselves if the moon is really as big as it appears in the photographs in travel brochures, so we left our hotel at sunset and watched the moon rise. Actually it is bigger in real life.

When the sun sinks it paints pie tones on the edges of the hills while the wind blows among the rocks and the sky passes from a pink hue to purple and finally to black. We took along a bottle of champagne for Janet and Paul, grape juice for Emily and I and sandwiches for all of us. There under the most magnificent moonlight we ate an almost mystic picnic dinner. The Atacama desert is without any doubt one of the most mystic places on earth.

MORE SURPRISES

Before returning we had to take a tour of the salt caverns by the imposing Lincancabur volcano. The valley is absolutely dead. No life of any kind can survive. No vegetation, no animal and certainly no humans. It has the feeling that at any time a spaceship might land nearby and some lunar inhabitant would walk towards us and join us for dinner. A sense of total peace had wrapped me in what felt like the kindest and sweetest of all embraces. I felt so well, happy and almost in a trance. I did not talk much after that for fear of breaking that magic spell. Just 18 miles (30 km) south of San Pedro is the Salar de Atacama salt flats. The salar looks like a remnant of the flood at the time of Noah's ark; the left overs of the salt that the water washed down in the flood that covered all the earth and which only Noah, his family and a pair of each species of animals on earth survived.

Amazingly, smack in the middle of this vast, dead landscape there is a fresh water lake. Its name is Ojos del Salar (eyes of the salar) maybe due to its rounded shape. After spending the morning in the salty air of the salar a dip in fresh water made us feel totally rejuvenated. Yes there was a jump of 9 feet (3 m) before you hit the water but, holding my nose between my thumb and my index finger, I summoned my courage and leaped in. Splash! - What a cool and refreshing feeling that was.

Paul, in his passion for adventure and to see the world in all its magnitude and beauty, took a taxi ride into Bolivia. There were no important Bolivian towns close by for Paul to see but he wanted a Bolivian stamp on his passport to add to his tally of over one hundred and twenty countries visited – and counting.

Now it was time to return to Santiago but on the way back to Calama to catch our flight we stopped at Chuquicamata mine. This is the largest open pit copper mine in the world. It was first exploited by the Chuqui, native American Indians, who took the mineral to make weapons and tools. The 'Copper Man' mummy, dating about 550 AD, was discovered here in 1899 trapped in an ancient mine shaft. Many other legends and historical facts surround this place. The town of Chuqui was home to all the workers and their families. Here is where everyone employed by CODELCO, the government company that manages the mine lived, worked, went to school, worshiped and in general spent his or her entire life. This changed in 2007 when it was decided that the dust produced by the mining as well as the gasses coming from the smelters were a serious hazard to the health of the people and everyone was relocated farther away. The town now is totally abandoned. It is, however, kept in good condition and is a major tourist attraction.

One of the most impressive views of the mine is from the mirador (viewpoint) which is as close as you can get to the actual activity. Looking down into the vast pit you can but marvel at its incredible 2,400 feet (731 m) depth although it's hard to see what's happening down at the bottom because of the heavy cloud of dust that it is generated by the digging into the dry clay. Also the CAEX mining vehicles are a sight that impressed me a lot. These are the heavy machines that run up and down 24/7 to deliver the dirt full of copper to the smelters. Their wheels measure 9 feet (3 m) in diameter, cost 40,000 US dollars each and must be replaced every eight months. What also impressed me was the fact that many of the drivers of these enormous machines were women.

Our tour ended and we drove on to Calama airport for the flight home. It was now time for Emily and Paul to leave us and return to their respective lives, for Janet to resume her busy schedule and for me to go back to work.

At the hotel I had quite a surprise in store. The health club manageress was waiting for me to tell me that, during my absence, she had terminated the employment of the two masseuses. The reason? She had received complaints from guests claiming that our masseuses had been running a separate and very private business! While giving a relaxing massage to male clients they were stimulating them to the point that they were ready to receive a more intimate service and pay the required fee to the girls directly.

No one knew how long this had been going on but it was evident that many men had become regular customers with some visiting two or three times per week. Even colleagues of mine and other general managers with health clubs and massage services in their own hotels had become regular customers of these two girls. It had also transpired that they were drug addicted and alcoholic.

This shocking event did not interfere with our traditional anniversary party which, in January of 2004, was held with an actors and singers theme. I chose to be Elvis Presley. I rented an Elvis outfit and had the beauty salon turn my hair black for the occasion. Bearing in mind my misadventure with hair colouring in Arizona some years earlier, I made sure that whatever was put on my head would wash out the night after the party.

The party was a huge success, lots of fun, no really heavy drinking – and no drugs bust!

Chapter 21

THE GONDOLIERS

In June, Janet and I took a memorable four day trip to see and explore Venice. En route there we stopped off in England to visit Janet's sister's family; in Portugal to see our house and the tenants, who by now were good friends; and in Centonara to visit my parents' graves.

For our visit to Venice we actually stayed in Mestre at the Ramada Hotel, in those days part of Marriott. The frequent bus service took us into Venice early each morning and back when our feet, aching from walking in this most unique place on earth, said 'no more'! Venice is built on more than one hundred small islands on a lagoon in the sea. There are no roads in the city, only canals. To get around you either take a boat or walk ... and walk we did.

Of course it is essential when in Venice to take a trip on a gondola. There is no experience to match it. The gondolier, with his straw hat, blue and white stripe shirt and a tenor voice to make Caruso eat his heart out, took us for a long and romantic punt in and out of wide and narrow canals, under tiny bridges and out into the open water of the sea.

Wherever you are in Venice romance seems to lie in wait. At every corner of every canal, at every café, at every square, at every calle (street). The narrower the calle the more romantic it gets as you now have to walk and hold your loved one even closer.

As in every city there are places in Venice that you just must see. Harry's Bar is definitely one. Since its opening in 1931 this has been the place to see and to be seen in Venice. It was in this bar that the Bellini cocktail was created. Janet paid ten euros for one and sure enjoyed it. I had a virgin Bellini (alcohol free) which only cost me five euros. Carpaccio also originated here. And as well as creating a cocktail and a dish that remain stalwarts of cuisine in any restaurant worth its salt, Harry's Bar is famous for the clientele who, over the years, made it their watering hole. To name a few - Ernest Hemingway, Alfred Hitchcock, Orson Wells, Baron Philippe de Rothschild, Charlie Chaplin, Aristotle Onassis, Woody Allen, Peggy Guggenheim and many more. It was kind of nostalgic to feel the auro of these rich and famous celebrities around us. Maybe I was even sitting on the same chair that they had once sat on. Needless to say that the prices are absolutely astronomical. If you want to rub shoulders with the great and the good then you must be ready to pay the price.

Venice is famous for its carnival but this was June and the carnival had long gone for that year. That minor detail is of no consequence to vendors who easily sell the masks and other paraphernalia of the carnival to the ever eager throng of gullable tourists.

Piazza San Marco - St. Mark's Square – is universally iconic and is the only square in Venice carrying the prestigious name of 'piazza'. All the other squares are mere 'campi' (fields). The life of the city has revolved around this square since the time of the rich and powerful Venetian Republic. On and about this square abounded the life, the market, the politics, the intrigues and the religion. Here was also the place of cruel punishment for those found guilty of theft or adultery. They were either burned at the stake or simply strung up and left there for days to die.

Definitely one of the most beautiful places in the world, this piazza is surrounded on three sides by the arcades of public buildings. On the fourth side is the Basilica di San Marco with its domes, arches and the soaring St.Mark's Campanile (St.Mark's bell tower). Tourists from all over the world, from every religion and belief are found here ... along with the ever present pigeons. The Basilica was the private chapel of the Doges of Venice and, after the remains of St.Mark were returned here from Alexandria, Egypt, in 829 AD, it became the important religious centre which it is today. The Crusaders, the sacking of Constantinople and ship loads of Byzantine art treasures turned Venice into a world of wealth beyond imagination. Its gold mosaics, the golden Byzantine retable known as the Pala d'Oro, its inlaid marble floor, the gold relics and icons are a treasure that must be seen. Hours and hours could be spent writing about this place and not do it justice. You must see it for yourself to truly appreciate its magnificence.

Right next to the Basilica is the equally impressive Palazzo Ducale (the Doge's palace). Take your time to visit this Palace. I had the impression of being brought back in time. The riches of the time of the republic, most of them stolen from other places, had me really wondering how much justice has ever been done for all that robbing of others which made the place so wealthy.

The village of Murano, a short distance from the centre of Venice, was another of the places we had to visit. Occupied since Roman times, Murano consists of seven small islands connected by bridges. Unless you looked at a map you'd never knows that you were going from one island to another. It is home to just five thousand residents – and the most beautiful crystal in the world! Stepping off the vaporetto in Murano felt like entering a different, quieter and more relaxed world than Venice. Yet it still boasts its own Grand Canal. The architecture is varied and pleasing to the eye. Although each passing century has introduced its own style of building, streets and bridges, there are no shocking contradictions. The sidewalks house neat cafés where we took advantage of a morning break to enjoy a real cappuccino and a brioche.

To talk of the souvenir shops loaded with every imaginable kind of glass crafted items would take as long as the endless streets of such establishments and their accompanying glass factories. Since the year 1291 these factories, usually small sweat shops where the owner and a handful of older craftsmen labour in front of burning furnaces, have been producing their famous wares. The glass blowers make the most magnificent vases, birds, statues, glasses, stars and necklaces appear before your eyes. For a small payment they will create your own wish to order as you look on. There is also a fantastic museum with glass pieces dating back to Egyptian times. One day is far too short to take in the churches, palaces, bridges, restaurants and countless other delights which this small hamlet of rich treasures has to offer. It's a place which, like Venice itself, once seen will never be forgotten.

BACK IN THE GROOVE

Vacation over, I returned to Santiago in good spirits. It felt good to be with my people again. Especially so since without me there they had managed to pass the stringent Marriott brand standards. I was so proud of them all. They had worked hard and deserved my admiration.

Just a few days after my return a situation arose which is not uncommon in a hotel. A Colombian guest was brought to my office by Juan, the loss prevention manager. The lady was insisting that the housekeeper had stolen her five rings. She was just so sure that when she took them off her fingers she had left them by the bathroom sink and only the maid had subsequently been there. After taking a reading of the electronic lock we validated that point. We also looked at the records we kept on all of the housekeeping staff. This young Peruvian housekeeper had no previous incident reported of anything ever having gone missing in a room she had serviced. The lady was so sure however of the housekeeper's guilt that she demanded that I terminate her on the spot.

I wasn't about to take any such hasty action. I told her that we would conduct a thorough investigation and inform her of the outcome. I also urged her to look again in all her bags and luggage. At this she became quite belligerent. She felt that we were questioning her integrity and were taking the side of the housekeeper. As she was to leave the next morning, we put the issue aside for twenty-four hours. Her husband was staying on in Santiago and at the hotel for a few more days after she left.

Juan was a stickler for following up on issues and he made a point to call her in Colombia the following day to inquire about the rings. Again she restated that she was sure that the housekeeper had taken them and asked if we had fired her yet. The day following that her husband came to my office. He sheepishly informed me that he'd spoken to his wife and she had told him that she had now found the rings in a pocket of her carry-on bag. These are the times when the temptation to say, "I told you so," is strong. Instead I simply shared with him my joy and relief that all was well.

You see, it's common when something goes missing in a room to first blame the hotel staff. While this can be true, experience had taught me that most of the time it is the guest themselves who have misplaced the item in question ... or ... even arranged to have it stolen in order to collect the insurance. I had one case where the husband had stolen his wife's wedding and engagement rings to subsidise his drug habit. The moral of the story for hoteliers is not to act hastily and fire good employees on the whim of a guest. For guests, it is to look, really look for a missing item before you accuse some individual of being a thief. And, if you share your room with friends, it is even more likely that some of your 'friends' took what was yours.

It also seems that problems never come in ones. Just a few weeks after that the same housekeeper had a guest ask her to deliver some towels to his room. When she entered the room he was wearing only a towel wrapped round his waist. She heard him lock the room door while she was hanging the towels in the bathroom. When she exited from the bathroom he was standing fully exposed, penis erect in front of the door. He had a 50 dollar bill in his hand and asked her to relieve him of his condition. The girl though reacted well. After the initial shock, she pushed him against the closet, opened the door and ran to safety. A few minutes later she and Sandra, the housekeeping manager, were in my office relating the story.

I straight away summoned Juan as witness and together we went to the man's room. I told him that he had fifteen minutes to pack his case and leave the hotel. Failing which we'd call the police to come to take a statement from the housekeeper. In cases like these there is no other solution but to remove the guest from the hotel.

It was now October. On the 18th of that month John Shackley, the new director of sales and marketing, joined us from Brussels. There he had occupied the same position at the Renaissance. John is an Englishman of Irish descent. He was born in Liverpool and had done many jobs before finally finding his vocation in the hotel business. He was married to a Chilean lady who had left Chile for Austria at the age of nine with her family as a political exile. She was really more Austrian than Chilean but Chilean blood, and the fact that her parents had returned after the democratically elected government had taken over, made her want to come back to Chile. She had told John that she only wanted to come to Chile for three years and he had reluctantly agreed. To his dismay, once back she settled in and would never leave Chile again.

My regional vice president, Santiago Composto had, without consulting me, hired an Argentinian director of operations for the hotel called Lautaro Zeus. This came as a shock and it took me several months to work out what had happened. It transpired that Lautaro had been general manager at the Augustus Plaza Hotel in Buenos Aires but resigned from there to fill a position promised him by Santiago. Except that the new job didn't materialise and Santiago was left with the problem of finding him another opening - and one not too far from Buenos Aires as Lautaro was due to marry shortly after that. So he was dumped on me and I had the position in my hotel finally filled after five years of doing all these jobs myself. Santiago had not however done it out of the goodness of his heart or to help me but rather because he was in trouble.

I argued that I didn't need any help, that I had managed for five years and I could do it again until the economics were better. I argued until I was blue in the face but to no avail. Lautaro came - and the chaos started. He was of Turkish descent, young, good looking and tall with black hair. He was a real problem from the word go. Arrogant and self-assured he didn't give himself the time to get to know the people he worked with. He started by upsetting the executive committee members and particularly antagonised Pedro Perez, the director of finance.

In the midst of the Lautaro thing, we were hosting the APEC (Asia Pacific Economic Cooperation) conference in November. This is a conference held by all the countries whose shores are on the Pacific Ocean. We had booked into the hotel the delegation from China and the one from the Philippines with their respective presidents. A third group that was part of the conference were also booked but all their arrangements were done through a separate agency.

The Chilean government had issued an order to all the hotels setting the room rate at a mandatory 165 US dollars. This was not good news for us as this was our first opportunity in almost five years to do some really good business. At least we could charge what we wanted with the other group making the arrangements separately and this group booked many suites.

The hotel has sixty-two suites of three different types and dimensions. Ana, the director of events, had sent the floor plans of each floor to the Chinese forgetting that on some of the floors many of the suites were already assigned to the other group. The Chinese then returned the plan with the names and ranks of their various delegates assigned to particular rooms. It was only then that we realised that we had double sold many of the suites.

One of the central aspect in Chinese culture is to save face. Now I was faced with the task of saving the face, and maybe the career, of the Chinese ambassador as he was responsible to his government for the arrangements. Ana had been taken to hospital for surgery so it was I that met with the ambassador and explained the situation to him. I accepted full responsibility for what had happened. Eventually he accepted my humble apologies. He agreed to resend the plans to Beijing and to inform his government of the mess the Marriott had created. A week later the plans came back and now the problem had disappeared.

Once again we at the Marriott were very fortunate. With the delegation of China taking up one hundred and twenty rooms, the delegation of the Philippines taking up seventy rooms and the other group taking up sixty room, mainly expensive suites, we did rather well financially. The Hyatt didn't. All of their three hundred and ten rooms were taken up by the American delegation at the room rate set by the Chilean government. What a pity for Hyatt but continuing sweet revenge with regard to the drug addicted employees it had offloaded on me.

President Hu Jintao led the Chinese delegation and took his suite just the way it was without any changes to the furniture. This was a surprise to me as, in 2002 we had hosted the then President of China, Jiang Zemin. He was an older president and a real communist in all his ways. We had to dismantle the sled bed in the master bedroom and replace it with a king size bed for him and a queen size bed for his wife. We also had to buy a formica bedside table and a cheap lamp to put on it. Because of fen shui, the dining area had to be transformed into the office and the office made into the dining area. So it was rather a pleasant surprise that President Hu Jintao's only request was for an additional electrical socket.

Amazingly enough in 2004 there were not enough presidential suites in Santiago to accommodate the twenty-one heads of state participating. We had a challenge on our hands. We had two presidents and only one presidential suite. To the displeasure of the Chinese, we had to take the floor above president Hu Jintao and transform half of it into an improvised presidential suite for the President of the Philippines, Gloria Arroyo. We started by building a door at the beginning of the corridor to separate half of the building into one suite with many rooms. Then we knocked down some walls and connected one room on each side of the existing suite and made it look good enough. President Arroyo never complained and we were all set.

Apart from the commotion caused by having two presidents in the hotel, one day was dedicated for the presidents to visit each other in their respective hotels. Every head of state went to visit president Bush at the Hyatt and they all came to visit President Hu Jintao in our hotel too. One of the ballrooms was set with a huge conference table to accommodate the Chinese delegation on one side and the visiting delegation on the other. Those visits were to be quick and productive.

One of the most impressive Presidents to come was Vladimir Putin of the Russian Federation. He was very pleasant and not at all full of himself like many others. The difference between him and President Bush, for example, was absolutely stunning. Putin came to the conference bringing just four vehicles ... his bullet proof Mercedes 600, a car with security to drive ahead, one for the same function to drive behind and a pick-up white van with two mechanics. President Bush, on the other hand, had many times that number of vehicles. A sign of power.

The American entourage consisted of over one thousand delegates and support staff. They had to be put up in hotels as far afield as Viña del Mar, the seaside resort 80 miles (128 km) from the capital. President Bush was scheduled to give a speech at a meeting of the business conference taking place one afternoon at the conference centre in town. I went along. He never was an eloquent speaker but at the end people applauded. Many rushed to shake his hand. I didn't consider a handshake sufficient reason to be trampled under foot by the stampede towards him but I was interested to know if his hands were sweating. I pushed my way to the front and eventually shook his hand. No, it was not wet with sweat.

Finally the closing dinner of the conference was about to start in an old railway station transformed into a very beautiful dining hall. The carabineros (the Chilean uniformed police) were in charge of security. They had a clear order not to allow any bodyguard accompanying any president inside the dining hall. Every one of the heads of state had their security comply with that request. Then President Bush, arriving last for maximum prestige, heard his bodyguard, Nick Trotta, complaining about being denied entry to the hall. Bush, just a few steps ahead, immediately turned, pushed his way through to Nick and grabbed him by the lapels shouting, "He is with me!"

This move left President Ricardo Lagos, the Chilean president and host, somewhat unimpressed. The next evening there was a dinner scheduled at La Moneda, the Chilean government house, for three hundred guests. Because the American Secret Service was insisting that everyone entering the room would have to be searched and go through a metal detector, the dinner was canceled. It was replaced with a working dinner between President Bush and President Lagos in his private dining room. It was sadly quite embarrassing to have these two incidents detract from the lustre of such an important event. Now, with the conference behind us, we were free to concentrate on the business at hand.

Lautaro was becoming a bigger problem every day and this started to affect the operation. The staff were increasingly unhappy and rumours of unionisation were starting to circulate. Then Santiago decided that the executive committee was dysfunctional and that they, not Lautaro, was the source of the problem. He brought in a guru coach from California to lock us up in a meeting room for four days of team building training. It was actually an exercise in futility. By December we were facing increased union pressure so our traditional family Christmas vacation came as a blessed relief.

BLESSED RELIEF

This year our trip was to the Foz do Iguaçu. By comparison these falls on the border between Brazil and Argentina make Niagara Falls look like a hand wash basin. A few days before Christmas the four of us took a flight from Santiago to Asuncion, the capital of Paraguay and checked in at the Hotel Las Margaritas. The name alone (daisy flowers) was a good reason to stay there for the two nights we had given ourselves to explore Asuncion. It was near the Port and the Bay of Asuncion. As we went out to look around the city we soon discovered that, in spite of its name, the hotel was set in the middle of the red light district. Prostitutes paraded on the sidewalks and were not too shy to offer their merchandise to me and my son even if we were in the company of my wife and daughter.

Asuncion is a fairly small capital in a small and poor country with few natural resources in the middle of South America. It borders with Argentina, Brazil and Bolivia. From there to Iguaçu was a local bus ride. The buses in that part of the world reminded me of our days in Egypt and our visits to Tijuana in Mexico. They were always overcrowded with people taking chickens, rabbits and birds to the local markets. No matter how crowded, there was always room for a band to play. When the trip was a long one, a band would get off in a town and another would come on board. It was always fun to ride the public transportation in those countries.

Ciudad del Este was our bus stop. There is a huge flee market in the town which is the main attraction. Right in the heart of the Iguaçu Park is the Sheraton Iguaçu Resort and Spa. It's the best hotel in the area and we stayed there. This hotel is very near the falls and we could easily walk to them, which we did for our entire stay. The view from the resort is breathtaking in spite of not having a clear line to the falls as this is covered by enormous trees. It is also very easy to cross the border to Brazil from where the full view of this immense wonder of creation can be taken in. Only 20% of the falls are in Brazil, so from that side the other 80% can be enjoyed. Walking through the Garganta del Diablo (the Devil's throat) on the elevated wooden walks is an exhilarating experience even for those like me who are nervy around water. I was full of trepidation. The walkway is built on top of supporting columns right in the middle of the cascading water. The sensation I felt was one of being washed away anytime but this (obviously) didn't happen and I would do it all over again.

One of the most interesting spots in the world is where Argentina, Brazil and Paraguay meet. On that very point we could stand with a foot in Argentina and the other foot in Brazil while touching Paraguay with one hand. It was quite fun to do that. The vacation ended at the beginning of January.

Returning to work, an upward boost in the economy just seemed to happen like magic overnight. The price of copper started to rise and, with it, business started to blossom. We were finally seeing the light at the end of the tunnel. It seems always strange that there can't be all things going well, there has to be a fly in the ointment somewhere. In this case it was the discovery that the staff had collected enough signatures to bring in the union at the hotel. On one hand it was better this way as now we knew who we had to deal with. We met with the president of the union while he was still operating 'underground'. Some formalities regarding his position were missing and we could not yet be presented with the official union demands. Our labour lawyer, Laura, the director of human resources, and I sat there most of the time without speaking. We could see that the president had been trained by the unions from the Sheraton hotel. He too didn't talk. The meeting lasted more than three hours and we didn't know any more at the end than when we started. A few days after this meeting I was scheduled for a gallbladder operation and I was out of the hotel for ten days to recuperate.

During this time we were informed that the union had been formalised and that thirty-six members of staff had signed up with them. We now knew the names of the vice president and the secretary of the union and they presented us with a list of sixty demands. Laura and the labour lawyer came to my apartment with this infamous list to discuss what our next step was going to be. The risk of not complying with any of their requests could have been a strike. The risk to comply with some demands was to open the door for more negotiations. After some debate and considering that only thirty-six people out of the entire staff would have been going on strike we made the brave decision to refuse to negotiate. We said no to all of their demands. Now it was a matter of waiting to see the outcome of our bold action. Nothing happened. The strike didn't happen, but now we were officially a union shop. Every time one of the employee broke a rule and was to be disciplined the union president would step in and create chaos.

We called a meeting with all the staff to inform and remind them of the many benefits they already enjoyed. Also to let the union president tell them what the union had achieved from the list of demands they had presented. I informed the staff that, if they wanted to be represented, it was their right to do so. I also told them that if they chose to be represented by the union then all the benefits would have to be negotiated rather than being part of their packages. When they learned that the union had received a negative answer to all of their requests the staff made up their mind that the union had to go. It took about three months after that before the president of the union asked to see me.

By then I knew what he wanted to talk about. I had learned over the years that potentially difficult meetings should always take place outwith your own office. Because of this I conducted all union meeting with the president in the VIP lounge. This meant that I could leave anytime I saw fit to do so. The president of the union came straight to the point. As the union president he couldn't be removed from his job for a minimum of three years but the rest of the employees were putting so much pressure on him, the vice president and the secretary, that they were now ready to resign. How much was I going to pay him if he stepped down and resigned?

I knew I was in the driver's seat and told him that he could stay or go. Either of these two actions on his part would have no effect on the operation of the hotel. But I felt kind of sorry for this idiotic young man and told him that if he resigned there and then I would give him two months of salary. He eagerly accepted and turned in his resignation effective the same day. He got his cheque and left the hotel. Half an hour had not gone by than the vice president asked me for a meeting. Knowing the matter at hand I went to the VIP Lounge with my answer all ready. Less than five minutes later he too was gone. Now only the secretary was left. She was a young cook and she too was anxious to get out. The meeting with her lasted less than two minutes and she was gone - And so was the union destroyed, defeated not by management but by the employees themselves!

The Marriott Exclusive Club was continually growing. We were very strict in the application of our rules, unlike at the Hyatt where they were lax and their club was failing as a result. One of our rules was that only one card per table was to be accepted. One evening I was called into the restaurant to attend to a dentist member causing a problem. He was arguing with the waiter who wouldn't accept his and his friend's cards for the two couples who had dined together. When I approached the table and explained the one card per table rule he became quite officious and verbally attacked me. He asked why we couldn't do as the Hyatt did. Mentioning the Hyatt was the wrong thing to say to me but I went through the explanation again. His response was to suggest that we separate by two inches the two tables that were pushed together thus making it two separate tables. At that point I had to muster all my composure in order not to punch him on the nose.

As calmly as I could I invited him to step away from the table and accompany me to the cashier desk. I didn't want to embarrass him in front of his wife and friends. There I told him to stop playing games. I reminded him that he was a professional man, a respected dentist. I told him, however, that if he didn't want to go along with the rules which he knew full well before purchasing the membership that we would refund him his money and take him out of the club. He saw sense and decided that flashing his membership card at his friends was more important to him than losing it. Yes, the Marriott Exclusive had its share of funny stories.

One of the most stressful was when I had to revoke the membership of a member who visited every Friday night with his nephew. We had an 'all you can eat and drink for one price' menu which he regularly took full advantage of. He would always drink eight cocktails and eat at least the same number of plates of shrimps. With the club benefit of a 50% discount he was paying for one person and eating for eight or more! Had I given him 30 US dollars instead of dinner I would still have come out ahead. I just couldn't win. The best bit was that this gentleman was as skinny as a bean pole and just as tall.

EATEN BY A TIGER

After the turmoil with the union and the excitement with the Marriott Exclusive Club I needed another vacation. Janet and I chose to spend a week in Machu Picchu. The trip there was quite a challenge. We stayed one night at the JW Marriott in Lima, Peru and the following morning took the short but spectacular flight to Cusco. There we checked into a small local hotel. In a corner of the lobby there was a big samovar filled with coca leaves tea. Many guests were taking advantage of the tea as an antidote to altitude sickness. Cusco is at 11,200 feet (3,114 m). I had thought that it was illegal but coca tea is safe to drink as long as you limit yourself to a maximum of three cups per day.

By the next morning we were ready to take the four hour train trip to Agua Caliente, a small village at the bottom of Machu Picchu. This was the most exhilarating train ride we had ever taken as the train had to zig-zag its way up and down the rugged mountain. From Agua Caliente was a bus ride to the entrance of Machu Picchu. There the mystique starts. It can be confusing as you can easily mistake the Roca Sagrada for Machu Picchu which is actually behind you as you look at the Roca. We were fortunate to have the services of an extremely knowledgeable tour guide who spoke perfect English. She could recite Inca history as if she was a history book.

Inside the city and walking through the ruins brought us back to the era of the Inca Empire. It felt as if nothing has changed. It was easy to imagine what it would have looked like during its days of glory. Why the Incas chose such a place for the capital of their empire has never been satisfactorily explained. Maybe it was because it would be too treacherous to reach and conquer; maybe it was because of its natural beauty; maybe it was because of its magical power. No one really knows. What is certain is that they would have been hard pressed to find a more impressive location. Walking around it was just out of this world. From the Royal Tomb to the Carved Avenue; from the Temple of the Tree Windows to the Principal Temple; and finally to the Main Square, it just felt as if you were on a cloud and being carried by invisible angels. What a magic place that is. All too soon it was time to return to reality.

The return bus ride from Mach Picchu to Agua Caliente turned out to be great fun. A small Inca boy dressed in full Inca costume would run down the mountain and appear ahead of the bus at every bend. He made it fun by arriving at the bottom just in time to stand by the bus door to collect his tips and then return to the top on the next bus going up. Only to run down again to entertain the tourists and collect more tips.

Back at work, Lautaro had not learned the lesson. He continued to disrespect the staff. He was just an unmanageable and nasty individual. We, in the meantime, were preparing for our Christmas family vacation, this time to Phuket, Kuala Lumpur and Bangladesh. The flight was a long one. We were travelling business class on Malaysia Airline, one of the best airlines I have ever flown. Janet and I left Santiago and flew to Buenos Aires on Lan Chile airline where we switched to our Malaysia flight. The plane flew to Cape Town for a short stop and then to Johannesburg for one more short stop. Next stop was Kuala Lumpur. On arrival we took a rapid train into the city to the Renaissance Hotel. There, waiting for us were Emily, who had arrived from the US, and Paul, who had made the shorter journey from Dhaka in Bangladesh. The four of us were tired and all enjoyed a blissful night of rest.

The next morning we all flew to Phuket, an island in Thailand. We made our way to the JW Marriott Resort and our suite in what looked and felt like the jungle. The gardens were just fantastic and the resort all that you'd hope for and expect of Asian hospitality. We acclimatised quickly. By the evening we were ready to explore the restaurants, eleven in total. We were all dying to eat good Thai food. The experience turned out to be incredible. What really was most rewarding was to see how eager the staff were to please. Every member of the staff would approach you with a slight bow, hands held together and saying, "Sawatikha," meaning welcome. This was all the more remarkable as the welcome was most sincere and not just a routine platitude.

After a delicious breakfast it was time to head for the beach and the warm ocean. The town itself was like something out of a story book. From the museums to the restaurants to the monuments, there is never a dull moment. By the time we had strolled around the town for a few hours, a good Thai massage was in order. This is so different from what we in the West know as massage. As you enter the house you are welcomed by smiling masseuses and presented with silk pyjamas without any buttons. After you change into these, one of the young ladies washes your feet before you stretch out on the massage bed (with your pyjamas on) and the masseuse joins you on it, straddling you. Here the relaxation starts.

Thai massage is not a stroking massage, it is all about pressure points. After an hour of this bliss, you can hardly tell whether you are still alive or have joined the angels in heaven. My body had become so light that no part of it felt tired or aching. What a wonderful experience that was. For the entire week there we had nothing but the most enjoyable times of swimming in the warm waters of the sea, strolling on the most pristine beaches, savouring the most delicious food and just sharing quality time together.

It was now time to fly to Dhaka and to Paul's apartment for a day, before taking a cruise to the Bay of Bengal and the Sundarbans. At the airport in Dhaka we got a good laugh when Paul handed the immigration officer our passports and greeted him in Bangla. The officer looked at the four white faces on the passports, took a second incredulous look at Paul and then, still hardly believing what he'd heard, answered in Bangla. He couldn't get over the shock of Paul's perfect Bangla.

The formalities over, all was cleared, now we really were in Bangladesh. As we left the airport and into the streets, it felt as if we were transported back in time to Sakkara in 1982. It was now over twenty years since our time there but here before us were the same crowds, noise, people shouting, traffic coming every way which, donkey-drawn carts, filth and the stench of raw sewage at every street corner. This is, after all, one of the most populated cities in the world with, in 2011, over seventeen million inhabitants. The only two differences from Sakkara were the way people were dressed and the transportation, the cycle rickshaws.

Paul's apartment was in a fairly new building, clean and really well kept. He had a young Bangaladeshi girl, Ana, do the cleaning, cooking, washing and ironing. The four of us settled in quickly and the next day left for our cruise to the Bay of Bengal. Here is where we would be seeing a tiger, at least that's what we expected. The bus ride to Khulna took several hours. Paul, always kind, had bought Janet and I the two first class seats at the front above the driver and with the best view in the house; while Emily and he sat at the back with the animals. From there a short private bus ride took us into the Sundarbans National Park and our boat to cross the Bay of Bengal. There, hopefully, to get sight of some of the population of four hundred recorded Bengal tigers still running free in the park.

The boat had twelve people on board most of whom Paul knew well as they were all attached to some kind of NGO. Most of these young people were embracing life while still doing great work to alleviate as much as possible the hardship of the local population. The cabins were clean and comfortable. The food couldn't have been fresher. The fish were caught by the boat chef, cleaned and cooked on the spot. As we sailed closer to our tiger encounter, our bravado ebbed somewhat. After all, tigers do kill people. Every year men going into the Sundarbans to collect honey are attacked and eaten by them. When we nervously disembarked from the boat, two crew members carrying loaded guns accompanied us. Even with this kind of escort we were ... terrified!

As we walked into this wonder of nature the fear subsided. There were no tigers in sight, only foot prints. There was, however, an incredible variety of other beautiful animals to be observed. There were antelopes, monkeys, snakes and even crocodiles are plentiful. A bird watching boat trip is an early morning bliss. There are hundreds, if not thousands, of bird species to be seen flying overhead or simply perched on a mangrove. There were green bee eaters, they are indeed green and white with a long and very fine beaks; black headed cuckoo shrike, all black with white lines on their wings; grey herons, grey and white with a black head; white throated kingfishers, with red beak, white throat and feathers of blue and black.

Considering that this is the largest mangrove forest in the world makes it home to some of the most exotic flowers you would wish to see. The mangrove trees cover everything under their thick canopy. From sunrise to sunset we walked, sailed and cruised in and out of the canals, mangroves and the open bay. We swam in the warm water and did not encounter any crocodiles, reptiles or anything scary. This was contrary to what we had been told and therefore had got unnecessarily tense about. After three days of this dream-like experience it was time to go back to Dhaka.

Although Paul had bought bus tickets, I couldn't face another bus ride. We decided instead to take a boat to Chittagong, stay the night there and then take a short flight back to Dhaka the next day. The small aircraft we flew in had fifty soft and comfortable leather seats, making for a pleasant flight. This made quite a contradiction to the fact that we were in a country struggling to modernize under a stressful financial burden. The greatest asset the country has is definitely its people. Smiling under the harshest conditions of life comes naturally to them, maybe because ignorance is bliss. Not knowing that there are other ways to live makes them content and thankful for what they have.

Back in Dhaka we now had a few days to enjoy life in this fascinating city. Paul took us to the most interesting parts of town, from museums to markets, from luxury to the slums. We saw everything that could be seen. Paul also took us to the American Club, the British Club and the Canadian Club which are each managed by their respective embassies for the benefit of their citizens. They are all equipped with gyms, restaurants, bars, billiard tables, tennis courts, outdoor pools and many other facilities; everything to entertain the expat community in fact. We also enjoyed eating in Bangladeshi restaurants although Janet found the traditional eating by hand method a bit of a challenge. No challenge to her however was visiting Aarong, one of the best shops in Dhaka. Here she had a field day. The prices were quite inexpensive when compared to the west and the quality of the clothing outstanding. Paul had given us vouchers as Christmas presents and we could redeem them there. I bought a nice cotton shirt that I still have, wear and enjoy twelve years later. We spent New Year's eve in an apartment with Paul's friends from work.

On the 2nd of January Emily left to return home to the US. Janet and I left too and flew to Kuala Lumpur for three days of touristic fun. The Renaissance took us in, again in style. Now we had the time to take in the beauty, the rich history and the culture of this great city. The Royal Palace, Istana Negara, was the first place we visited. This is a most impressive palace topped by two large gold domes and immaculately maintained. Certainly different from Buckingham Palace, but no less impressive, its facade conveys both power and a religious sort of sense of peace. The Petronas Twin Towers, at 1,200 feet (365 m), are the tallest buildings in the city and an impressive sight both during the day and when illuminated at night. Set in the middle of a green park complete with lagoons, and built with glass and steel, they shine in the sunlight and shimmer in the rays of the moon.

There are monkeys everywhere in Kuala Lumpur. At Batu Cave they make the long stairway going up to the cave seem effortless to climb as they scamper to the top while people struggle, huff and puff to make it there. It is almost as if they are telling us humans that we are not fit and not deserving to see the caves. In other parts of the city they simply run loose everywhere. I was eating an orange while walking along and one of them simply jumped down from a tree and snatched it from my hand so fast that I could not believe it. They were a sight not to be missed.

The time fairly flew by. All too soon it was time for Janet and I to fly too and return to Santiago.

Chapter 22

BACK IN THE FAST LANE

I always seemed to return to the hotel after the Christmas holiday right on schedule for the anniversary party. This year Laura and the party committee had decided to have a 'back to school days' theme. We were all to dress as we dressed during our school days. As my school years were very few it was quite easy for me. I only ever had one school uniform. It consisted of a black overall with a white collar which buttoned up the back and had a belt of the same material that tied with a bow. The hotel seamstress was very gifted and she made me a beautiful overall which fitted the now enlarged version of myself perfectly and took me back fifty years. I also had a haircut done like the one I had when I was ten years old, forgetting that my hair was now white. With the many nationalities and different age groups it was fun to see how their school days dress had varied. One thing they all had in common however, was that they had all worn some kind of overall. We danced, we ate, we gave awards and the team spirit was tremendous.

I had a routine at these parties to have a chat with everyone during the cocktail hour but I made the point of always sitting for the meal at the table with the dish-washers, the housekeepers and the maintenance people. I ate the starter with the dishwashers, the main course with the housekeepers and the dessert with the maintenance guys. I felt that this showed empathy with them (I had started out as a dishwasher myself) plus I knew that this was a good time to get the real low down on goings-on in the hotel when their tongues were loosened after a few glasses of wine.

Business was doing great. Finally we had no need to be diverted from our core business of running the hotel by side jobs such as cleaning offices and doing laundry. As we came to the end of summer we were all happy and life couldn't have been better.

May was a really good month for the hotel when His Holiness, the Dalai Lama came to Santiago on an official visit. Our hotel had the honour to be chosen as the place where he would stay. While you might dispute the validity and the veracity of Buddhism, what can't be disputed is the feeling of peace, tranquility and love his presence exudes. He proved to be a simple man and he asked for no special treatment of any kind during his visit. The Chinese, who have annexed Tibet, didn't want Chile's president Michelle Bachelet to meet with him so she didn't, claiming a clash of engagements.

In June I attended a meeting in Rio de Janeiro with many of Marriott's top clients. It was a chance to listen to what they had to say about our hotels and what their expectations were. It also presented an opportunity to meet up with all of the South America general managers, director of sales and marketing and regional sales office staff. There was time off too.

Rio is indeed one of the most spectacular places in the world. The sound of samba and bossa nova is everywhere. We were not visiting during the world famous carnival which takes place in February on Mardi Gras (fat Tuesday) each year. I took the cable car ride up Sugarloaf mountain and the funicular to the top of Corcovado and its 115 feet (38 m) high statue of Christ the Redeemer whose outstretched arms seem to embrace the whole city and all its people. I walked the length of Copacabana Beach from the hotel doors and back and got sun burn on my back, so strong was the sun. The jewelry and precious stone shops are a must visit too but, like all big cities, Rio has its shady side. The sprawling favellas are places where poverty, drugs and crime are rife. The police shoot almost indiscriminately at the ninhos da rua (street children) who were born less fortunate than most and are groomed to become thieves and muggers from an early age.

Back at work we had become the 'home away from home' for many of the famous singers coming to Santiago. Luis Miguel, the Sol de Mexico, is an icon in South America. He had become a regular guest. He was easy to please. All he required was a dehumidifier and lots of bottled water to drink in the presidential suite.

There is rarely a day without surprises in the hotel business and routine staff locker inspections sometimes supplied them. On one occasion Vanessa from human resources, Juan the loss prevention manager and Sandra the housekeeping manager found about fifty used condoms in the locker of a night housekeeper lady in her mid forties. Some were dried out but others were still fresh with sperm.

In another inspection a gun was found. This was naturally a more serious situation which required police involvement. As we had established a good relationship with the commander of the nearest police station, he came to the hotel personally making it a courtesy visit rather than turning the hotel into a crime scene. This move avoided television cameras and reporters following the police car to the hotel and it being featured on the news within the next hour.

We had a Chilean guest from the south of the country who looked like a real gangster. His name was Jose Vargas. A short while after he took a room, I noticed a long list of visitors coming to him there. A few were men but most were women who were living in the fast lane. These ladies included two famous sisters, one a successful model and the other a recent Miss Chile winner. One of the sisters became a regular and would stay over with him many nights in a row. We noticed that she had moved some of her clothing into the hotel, among them a red cocktail dress with shoulder straps and a generous low-cut front. One day he got a call from his wife that she was driving to the hotel from the south to see him for a few days. He was panic stricken and had to make a quick move with this cheap whore's clothes or be caught by his wife with all this female stuff in his closet. He decided to send all the clothes to the laundry and instructed them not to deliver them back until he called for them.

A few days later, wife gone, he called to have the valet to bring up all this girl's belongings. All was delivered. Some hours after that this crazy lady stormed into my office carrying the red dress of which the shoulder straps had been cut with scissors. She claimed that our laundry staff had cut the straps of her dress because they were jealous of her being so famous and demanded that I buy her a new dress. It was evident that she was under the influence of, not only alcohol, but some other more powerful substance. Naturally I had to tell her where she could put her dress without being too descriptive for the sake of politeness. It was ridiculous what she was asking.

At first Vargas paid his bills regularly every Friday. Then, after a few weeks, he started missing. At one point he had accumulated a debt of well over 30,000 US dollars. My remedy was to have Juan double lock his room door. This makes it impossible to enter a room with the regular key. I told him that the only way I would give him access would be if his bill was paid in full right there and then. He called his lawyer, who was also the lawyer for the Catholic church and the Democratic Party, and told him to pay me. The lawyer naturally didn't have that kind of cash available so Vargas slept that night in a chair in the lobby. In the meantime I had learned that he was a big drug trafficker and was selling and dispatching cocaine to all these once semi-famous starlets. Also the lawyer was a druggy who depended on him for his many daily fixes.

The following morning the lawyer came with all the money in cash and paid the bill. I asked him where had the cash come from as the day before he didn't have any. He told me, with some hesitation, that another of his clients had given him that money to pay for some purchases and he had instead paid me with it. I decided it was time to get shot of Mr.Vargas. We packed up his possessions, put them on a bellman cart and wheeled it out to the street. Shortly after this incident the lawyer was arrested, tried and jailed for fraud while Jose Vargas kept his flourishing business of drug trafficking. This was one of the most trying events that I had to deal with in my whole hotel life.

Business was really strong. We didn't have to count the paper clips we were using anymore. As a result life generally was more relaxed. I had more time to spend with Janet. In this atmosphere the Christmas holidays came around again. This time our vacation destination was to be Chile's most renowned region of Torres del Paine in Chilean Patagonia. It's a dramatic landscape in one of the most spectacular mountain ranges in the world with peaks of 6,000 to 9,000 feet (1,829 to 2,743 m). There are lakes, waterfalls, fjords and glaciers which majestically honour the Creator. Flora and fauna not found anywhere else explodes here in abundance. This corner of paradise is home to more than forty species of mammal, among them guanacos, pumas and foxes and to a myriad of the most impressive birds. Black vultures, crested cara-cara and the majestic Andean condors soar in peaceful flight overhead. The icing on the cake, so to speak, are the Cuernos del Paine peaks, a sight that sticks in the mind and helps make this national reserve so unique.

As the year 2007 motored on the hotel was doing great and the money was rolling in. There was no pressure from Marriott to cut back on expenses. This made me particularly happy. I could re-establish some of the services we had cut back on during the five years of austerity management. It was also a year when Chile was wrapped up in many corruption scandals. These created much disquiet among the populace but also brought even more business to the hotels. International reporters, flush on company accounts, in need of accommodation and sustenance, flooded into the capital to take advantage of all the juicy stories.

DOING THE HAKA

Janet's brother William and his new fiancée were getting married in New Zealand. Janet and I wanted to attend the wedding. Off we went on another long trip to the other side of the globe. First by Lan Chile from Santiago to Buenos Aires and then by Air New Zealand non-stop to Auckland. As always business class flying had my adrenaline going and gave me enormous pleasure. On arrival, we rented a car to drive south to Bay of Plenty and to Ronnie, William's former wife. She was most welcoming and we stayed with her for two nights. She showed us all over her part of what is one of the nicest, cleanest and well organised countries in the world.

It is so well organised in fact that, even when driving along the completely deserted - other than for sheep, horses and more sheep – road towards Wellington, a police car with flashing light pulled us over. Janet was booked for speeding at 72 mph (116 kmh) in a 60 mph (100 kmh) zone! The fine was a hefty 100 NZ dollars so we had to find a post office in a nearby small town and pay up. In Napier we stopped for the night in a beautiful B&B facing the sea. The last leg of our trip to Wellington passed off with no more fines as Janet kept to the speed limit as if her own life depended on it.

Wellington is a pretty city set on Cook Strait and is the capital of New Zealand. We booked into a very hospitable B&B run by an elderly lady who treated all of her guests as if they were family. There were many things of interest in Wellington for us to enjoy as we walked up and down the many hills of the city. All of the buildings are constructed to the most stringent anti-earthquake standards in the certain knowledge that the city will be hit at some time by a major earth tremor. One of the four parliament buildings is known as the beehive. It's round in shape and does indeed resemble a gigantic beehive. Visiting there was an eye opener. The tour takes you underneath the building and around the foundations where you see that it was built on rollers. It will turn on itself in case of a powerful earthquake rather than just collapse.

We spent three days visiting attractions such as old St.Paul's Cathedral, Sacred Heart Cathedral, Wellington water front and the National War Memorial. Walking on the City to Sea Bridge was the most memorable part of the city. Wellington is affectionately called 'windy Wellington'. Not without good reason. The wind was so powerful that Janet and I had to cling on to the hand rail to avoid being lifted off our feet and flung over it. We had survived Chicago winds but this was even worse and far stronger.

Now it was time to take a ferry from Wellington to Picton in the South Island. It is a three and a half hour trip through some of the most dramatic scenery in the world and always very windy. It is very much like the south of Chile in fact. I was actually a bit apprehensive about this trip as I always get seasick even on calm waters. I had heard that, just the year before, a particular trip had taken eight hours to make the crossing so bad was the weather. Luckily for me though the sea was as flat as a pancake with not even a tiny wave in sight. As if by a miracle, the wind had died completely. It was flat calm. Leaving Wellington behind we entered the open waters of the strait. It was only a short time after departure that we saw a school of maybe ten to fifteen dolphins swimming alongside the boat. They treated us to a show we'd glady have paid a lot to see, jumping happily out of the water, diving and then leaping out again. What a spectacle! There are also whales of different species in these waters but on this trip we didn't see any.

The entrance to the canal on the approach to Picton is like navigating a fjord. It reminded me of an enormous ice-age glacier. The picturesque small town is built around a sheltered harbour. There is a very nice sea front where a stop in a café and the feel of steady ground gave us the reassurance to be on land again. William, Janet's brother, was there waiting for us. After some emotional moments we were ready to take off for the short drive to Blenheim, where William and Jayne lived. Jayne is a lively woman and very much in love with William. This made it all much easier for us to be there. They had a beautiful home which was also used as a B&B. Jayne's sister was also there for the wedding and it was nice to meet more of the new family. After settling in William gave us a tour of Blenheim which, being very small, didn't take long. We saw Seymour Square and Pollard Park but were not able to take advantage of the two most exciting and popular activities - swimming with the dolphins in the Marlborough Sounds or watching the whales in Kaikoura.

Janet was overjoyed to learn that there were twenty wineries within minutes from Blenheim. The very next day we set off in William's Porsche to visit as many of them as possible. The winery are all newer than European and even Chilean ones. Janet did find some of the wines to be of good quality and to her liking but felt they still did not match the Cabernet Sauvignon she had got used to after living many years in Chile. We also found a most interesting honey producing farm unlike anything we'd ever seen before. I bought some and, thinking to outsmart the Chilean customs' canines checking the suitcases on our arrival home, I stashed it among dirty clothes. Only for it to be discovered and taken from me. Not only did we lose the honey but I also got a fine for not declaring it.

We had almost a week before the wedding so Jayne and William gave us the present of a train ride from Blenheim to Christ Church. This is no ordinary train. The line runs along the coast and, in certain places, is so close to the ocean that you have the sensation of falling into the sea. It is indeed panoramic. Untinted giant windows give the impression of travelling outside in the fresh air. There is an actual open wagon too. There, wind in hair, you can breathe in the fresh air while taking in the view of the ocean on one side, where penguins and seals can be spotted, and of the snow capped, rugged Kaikura mountain range on the other. The ride is an eight hour, all-day affair, deliberately slow so that travellers can enjoy the scenery at leisure.

And so we arrived in the most English looking city of Christ Church and its less than four hundred thousand inhabitants. Every street and square has an English name. Its churches and cathedral are built with pure stones of different sizes and perfectly set on top of each other. The most impressive being the Christ Church Cathedral. The botanical garden is a perfect example of English gardening with the variety of trees and the manicured flower beds a sight to behold. In fact, this city is so English, that even the river running through it is called the Avon. As in Stratford-on-Avon in England, the river is populated by magnificent white swans. Taking a flat bottom punt out for an easy afternoon ride is one of the most popular and romantic things to do.

We chose the Heritage Hotel, by far the best hotel in the city, as our base. This very impressive stone and brick building sits right on Cathedral Square. With its main stairways and colourful stained glass windows depicting the royal family shield, it exudes the magnificence of a bygone age of beauty. Yet it is up to date in all its services and facilities. It boasts modern and comfortable beds, large flat-screen televisions, a state-of-the-art gymnasium, spa and massage service to rival any luxury hotel in the world. Even the chefs are top of the class. Delicious breakfast buffet is served every morning with the menu constantly changing. All in all a great hotel stay.

After four days of this bliss it was time to return to Blenheim for the wedding. We decided to rent a car and chose the most scenic route via the area of hot springs. This was a case of leaving behind the world as we know it with its daily worries and concerns and entering heaven. It was all so peaceful. Surrounded by giant trees are fifteen separate thermal pools as well as a lap pool. The water temperature is very pleasant and the sky that day was a cloudless blue so intense as to even appear black at times. As summer with its flood of tourists had not started, we had the entire domain almost completely to ourselves.

We continued from there north on the inland route through forests, mountains and more forests with green foliaged trees and wild flowers covering the ground and creating the sweet aroma of pure, fresh air. What a contrast to polluted Santiago. Our drive took us to Lake Rotoroa and the small village bearing the same name. Very similar to a Swiss Alpine village it is one of the most romantic places I have ever seen on earth. It really is magical. We enjoyed a hand-in-hand walk in the forest there and then made the short drive to Nelson for a coffee stop before returning the car to Picton and being picked up by William.

Back in Blenheim we had still two more days before the wedding. William let Janet have the Porsche and with that we explored all of the northern part of the South Island. Before we headed off to Separation Point at the very top of the island we visited the Omaka Aviation Heritage Centre. While I am not particularly interested in aeroplanes, facts and stories, this museum is among the most educational and inspiring that I've visited. The details of sky battles fought in WW1 and WW2 by the New Zealand forces are so real and captivating that our visit became a surprisingly long one. The time included though a stop at their talk of the town café to savour their specialty pastries and delicious coffees.

Separation Point is at the tip of Adel Tasman National Park. After a good hike through the park we reached the point. Looking south from there, I was amazed to see the horizon line being actually curved and not straight as is normally seen everywhere else in the world. Then I turned my attention to the fur seals, a rare sight. These enormous animals, playing on the rocks and moving with an agility that is almost impossible to believe, are so graceful yet they can be mean, bite each other and are possessively territorial. They're also very proprietorial regarding their females and become very aggressive if another male as much as looks at them.

After an exhausting day of hiking and seeing nature at its best we checked in to the Whariwharangi Hut and settled for the night. We'd lived through a day of such adventure and so different from what life had given us previously as to never be forgotten.

The next morning early, it was time to drive the Porsche back to Blenheim for the best day in William and Jayne's life. At age fifty-nine William was starting a new life and he was so very happy. The house was already all set by then and excitement was growing as fast as the hours were passing. The day came. Early morning we were all up and ready to go. Jayne had prepared a champagne and full English breakfast for all the guests, who were staying in hotels around town, which they were served as they arrived. The wedding ceremony was to be on a cruising boat on Wairau River.

Breakfast consumed, the wedding party and all sixty guests took a short walk to River Park where a little train, decorated with balloons and coloured streamers for the occasion, took them to the River Queen boat. What followed was indeed a pleasant change from the weddings we had been used to in the past. There was no church, no organ music, no priest. Once on board, everyone just continued to party with more food and more champagne.

The boat sailed on for a short distance and came to a stop. It was then that the Justice of the Peace performed the ceremony. All very simple and easy. Very little emotions or tears. In about five minutes William and Jayne become Mr. and Mrs.William Telford! The cruise continued for a few hours more. Eventually all the guests were dropped off at the dock and bussed back to the house where the caterer had put up a banquet comparable to an old Roman feast. It was many hours and many hectolitres of wine later that it all came to an end. The happy couple left for their honeymoon to an undisclosed location and all the guests were taxied back to their respective hotels.

The next morning Janet and I left early for the local airport to catch a flight to Auckland to return to Santiago. What a surprise it was when we ran into Jayne and William also waiting for a flight to their honeymoon destination. They told us then that they were going to an island in the South Pacific but still wouldn't share more information. After two weeks in that beautiful country, having gone from Auckland to Christchurch and having taken in the beauty of it all, I could only summarise the whole experience one way ... New Zealand is the land for lovers!

TAKEN FOR A RIDE

Back at the hotel everything was going well with, of course, the exception of Lautaro Zeus. He had become a total liability. Soon it was Christmas again and Emily and Paul came to Santiago. We had decided that this vacation would be less travelled than previous years. We spent a quiet Christmas in the apartment and around Santiago then left for Mendoza in Argentina for a few days. At a nice hotel in Viña del Mar on New Year's Eve we enjoyed the spectacular midnight firework display after our dinner in the restaurant.

The banqueting area at the hotel was undergoing refurbishment under the experienced eye of my director of engineering, Michael

Chait. He made a wonderful job of modernising the facility with the fitting of new carpeting, the constructing of a new stage and the installation of a new lighting system on a par with even the best rock 'n roll venue. The work was done in time to have the hall host our traditional anniversary party. What else could the theme be but a rockers' night. All the staff, employees and families attending the party dressed up to be like rockers, bikers and rock 'n roll stars. The seamstress, once again, did me proud. She fixed me up with a pair of black, baggy pants to which I added a black shirt, boots, a long hair wig, sun glasses and a chain hanging from my waist almost to the ground. I really looked like a biker ... but without the bike. The best costume competition was won by Juan, the head of the reception, who assumed such a genuine rocker appearance that in his previous life he must definitely have been one.

The very next week Juan was to live his first experience of being taken for a ride. Not on a motorcycle ... but by a guest. It was Friday morning when he received a telephone call from a man asking to rent the Presidential Suite for the weekend for a special celebration with his new wife. As the guest didn't want to guarantee payment on a credit card (first red flag)! he said that he would provide a cheque for 5,000 US dollars when he arrived at the hotel. The mention of the 5,000 US dollars was the second red flag. He proceeded to order wine, champagne, the finest cognac, whiskies and food to be ready in the suite upon arrival. Also two hundred red roses had to be dispersed throughout the suite and scattered as petals on the bed (third red flag)! Juan didn't tell me of the booking as he wanted to surprise me later with news of the great piece of business he had won.

The guest arrived at 5.00 pm, as he had said he would, accompanied by the most stunning looking lady imaginable. He handed over the promised 5,000 US dollars cheque and Juan himself showed the couple to the suite to make sure it was to their liking. The food and drink was impressively laid out in the room as requested and Sandra, the director of services, had created a masterful display of roses. The guest declared himself so pleased with what he saw that he promised he would come back to the hotel often. The couple never left the suite for the entire weekend. Room service delivered their meals, starting with dinner and more champagne that evening. For breakfast the next morning they had everything you could imagine. In spite of that the man did express his disappointment to the room service waiter that we did not serve him Russian caviar and that we might at least have provided Iranian caviar!

Several visitors came to the suite, mainly other couples, all looking clean cut, well dressed and of the Santiago high society. Two female masseuses, also looking very professional, spent all day on Saturday and late into the night in the suite with them and their often changing guests. As they were never spotted outside of the suite for the weekend, they attracted little attention – other than to the room service waiters who were constantly called to bring them food and drinks. Because the hotel had this large cheque no questions were asked and the feast continued until Monday morning at 8.00 am when the two of them checked out. When asked at the reception why they were checking out so early the guest simply said that they were leaving for a trip to Monte Carlo to test their luck at the casino.

When the bank opened at 9.00 am the cheque was deposited. Before the bank had closed that day, we were informed that the cheque had no funds and was bouncing as high as the hotel itself. The total bill amounted to almost the 5,000 US dollars of the rubber cheque and the guests were gone. It was soon established that the passport and the name under which he registered was fake. There was no way to trace either the man or his companion. Juan was mortified. It was a costly lesson to learn but some good did come out of it. From that day on anybody wanting to make a reservation for the weekend had to pay cash. If paying by cheque they had to give us the cheque by Wednesday morning or three full days before their arrival, giving it time to clear beforehand.

Minibars are frequently a problem and a loss of money in many hotels. We were one of the few exceptions. Our minibars were making money, not much, but making money. They were a great service to the guests in the rooms. Shortly after the bouncing cheque incident we had another one that always leaves a doubt in an hotelier's mind ... but you can't do anything about it. It was early one evening when a guest with steam coming out of his ears stormed into my office carrying a miniature minibar bottle. It was half full with a yellowish liquid. With a thundering voice he told me that I would be hearing from his lawyer in the next twenty-four hours if I did not give him substantial cash compensation right there and then. This before even telling me what the problem was.

As threats never went down well with me, I calmed him down and he finally came to the point. He claimed that he had taken the miniature bottle of whisky from the minibar and proceeded to drink it just to realise he was drinking urine. According to him the previous guest had drunk the whisky then peed into the bottle and replaced it on the minibar shelf. He had not noticed the broken seal when he took the bottle out. I had to make an effort to keep a straight face. It sounded very intriguing.

I asked him if whisky was his favourite drink before dinner and he said yes. I asked him how he normally drank his whisky, on the rocks, with soda or straight? "Straight from the bottle," was his answer. That left me even more certain of what had happened but I couldn't prove it so I had to respond to him carefully. The truth of course was that he had drunk the whisky and then peed in the bottle in order to ask for compensation. Fortunately these kind of guests are few and far between but, believe me, they do exist.

There are two particular things that a hotel employee should never say to an irate guest, more so if the guest is already demanding compensation. One is never to admit fault on the part of the hotel for anything and the other is to never mention the word 'insurance'.

WELCOME RELIEF

The year 2008 was presenting itself as a difficult one. The

economy was starting to slow down. It had become clear to me that action was needed on my part before it was demanded of me by the regional vice president. I was also noticing that my secretary, Kathy, would lock herself in Lautaro's office for long periods of time. It is never advisable for any secretary to lock the door of an office when meeting with a director or other manager as this, understandably, creates suspicion. I also noticed that her attitude towards the job and to me had changed. Now, whenever I asked her to do something, I would get a grunt or a moan in return as if I was being a nuisance to her rather than being acknowledged as her manager and one working with her. She also spent countless hours of company time on the phone to her mother and sister in Orlando, Florida.

Taking into account her high annual salary, the bleak economic outlook and her dreadful attitude, I made the decision to let her go. Naturally she called the Marriott hot line complaining that I had dismissed her unfairly. I had to explain my action to a human resource specialist at headquarter whose experience of work in a foreign country probably amounted to a long weekend in Cancun. Suffice to say Kathy stayed gone.

The only person on the executive committee to complain about my action was Lautaro. This was to be expected but all the other members were just thrilled to see her tail walk out of the door. In the eight years she had worked with me she had managed to make a long string of enemies at all levels of the work force. As the saying goes 'problems never come alone' and this time proved to be no exception. In December Lautaro did something that is considered a deadly sin at Marriott and is a reason for instant dismissal, especially if the sinner is a director.

After Kathy was gone I hired a young American lady who was engaged to a Chilean guy. She spoke very good Castillano and naturally her English was perfect. One afternoon she came to my office to express her embarrassment at what she had just seen. She felt, and justly so, that she should report it to me. It transpired that she had collected the guest comment cards for the month, twenty-nine in total. It was her responsibility to mail them to the US to be tabulated. They were in sealed envelopes as the system required. But Lautaro asked her to give the envelopes to him. Reluctantly she did so. She also kept an eye on him though to see what he was going to do with them.

What happened is that he called Camila Polari, the front office manager, into his office and closed the door. Then the two of them opened the envelopes and read the guests comments. He couldn't then reuse the torn envelopes so he had housekeeping send him twenty-nine new envelopes into which he replaced the guest comments forms. Then he returned them to the young American secretary to be mailed out. There was nothing I could do to keep Lautaro on the team, he had to go!

Fortunately, once he was faced with the facts, he turned in his resignation and left the very same day. His protector, Santiago Composto, the regional vice president, was upset but this time he didn't stand up for Lautaro. He just quietly acknowledged the fact that a grave sin had been committed for which there was no pardon. Mauro Barros, who had previously worked at the hotel, was now the director of food and beverage at one of the Marriott properties in Venezuela. He wanted to come back to Chile, so we brought him back in to fill the vacancy.

In March of 2009 Vice-President Joe Biden of the USA visited Chile and stayed at the hotel. Even now the sensitivity surrounding such a high profile guest restricts what can be said but security arrangements were certainly very precise and very detailed. The hotel was total chaos for two days for guests who weren't part of the delegation. Entry to and exit from the hotel was controlled with metal detection and x-ray machines.

Many guests were not slow to voice their displeasure. They couldn't understand why they were not informed when making their reservations that the hotel would not be its normal self and that they should be prepared for some inconvenience. Fortunately, all went smoothly and the Vice-President, his delegation, the hotel and most guests experienced no real problems.

Then in April of 2009 we had a royal visitor to the Santiago Marriott. This time it was His Majesty Mizan Zainal Abidin, XIII King of Malaysia and Her Majesty Nur Zahirah, Queen of Malaysia, accompanied by their two young children, a girl and a boy. This was one of the most impressive personalities I had the pleasure and honour to host in the hotel. They made no fuss, just common courtesy was requested on my part. Upon their arrival I was informed that His Majesty would require my presence at the door anytime the royal couple left or returned to the hotel. This was a simple thing for me to do as every move they made was programmed to the second. Also I was informed that His Majesty would extend his hand for a hand shake but Her Majesty the Queen would not because of religious restrictions. I was already familiar with that after having lived in Muslim countries for several years.

When the family arrived, after the welcome greetings were performed, it was my duty to accompany them to the Presidential Suite. As we entered the elevator His Majesty saw a poster advertising our Italian night in the restaurant. He apologised to me that he couldn't come to eat in the restaurant that evening as he was hosting the President of Chile for dinner at the Malaysian Embassy. He did say however that he would have an Italian meal at the hotel before leaving as Italian food was his favourite. I took that as a compliment and as a possible ice breaker on his part to make me feel relaxed about their presence.

The visit proceeded smoothly until Her Majesty called me to ask if the hotel had a doctor on call. Their little boy was sick and needed attention. Immediately doctor Philips, our house doctor, was called and within minutes I accompanied him to the suite. That was the only crisis and soon the day of their departure from the hotel arrived.

As I was accompanying them to the car which would take them to the airport, His Majesty leaned over to me and said, "Peter, I will finally have my Italian dinner." I was sure that he was just joking until chef David told me that they had asked him to have two plates of angel hair pasta prepared and put on the royal aircraft for him and Her Majesty the queen to eat on board. He was, after all, a man of his word. As a thank you for our services he gave me a Mont Blanc pen which I will always treasure.

The rest of the year was still profitable albeit in a weak market. We were, however, very fortunate. At the Hyatt the renovation of their rooms had been completed. The hotel had been upgraded to Grand Hyatt status. The general manager, Andrea Nauheimer, had the tremendous idea that Hyatt could now increase their room rates based on those two factors, and he did. Soon their clients were leaving en masse and coming over to us; our strategy being that of keeping prices reasonable and to not lose business at a time when there was a financial crisis looming in the USA and the world in general. It was a lesson for all of us that no matter how beautiful the hotel is, how much has been spent on a renovation or what is the category of the hotel you manage - the customer is the one who sets your prices.

While the economics were going well the hotel did experience a very scary moment. Janet and I were in Hawaii to attend the wedding of our Godchild, Regina Stryker, who was getting married in a beach ceremony on the 6th of November. We were staying at the Marriott in Maui. The general manager there was Bill Countryman, with whom I had opened the Anaheim Marriott many years back. At 6.00 am on the 4th I received a frantic call from Claudia, the human resources director in Santiago, telling me that a bomb had exploded in the hotel the day before.

Fortunately the bomb, contrary to what the press said, had not exploded in a hotel bathroom. It had been carried outside by two courageous security agents unaware that a bomb was in the bag they were carrying. The press even reported that, not only had the bomb gone off in the public toilet, but also six people had been injured ('fake news' as President Trump would have rightly said had he been around then).

The team at the hotel, led in my absence by the director of marketing, John Shackley, had done a terrific job in maintaining calm among employees and guests. When I returned to the hotel I submitted the names of the two security agents who had acted with such courage to Marriott head office. They each received a beautiful watch, a hand written thank you letter and a certificate from Mr.Marriott himself.

FRIDAY, FRIDAY

In January of 2010 Mauro Barros was transferred. Once again the hotel was left without a director of operations. Fortunately for us Victor Parada, a young Chilean we had hired at the opening, was just too happy to return home from Costa Rica where he was the director of food and beverage at the Guanacaste Marriott. By mid January we had a complete and strong executive committee again.

Things cannot go without a hitch for too long though. The same week that Victor returned, Michael Chait, our director of engineering, resigned. This did not present a major problem. We had hired an experienced hotel engineer as his assistant and he was ready to take over the position. Michael's last day at work was to be Friday, February the 26th. This was a special day. It seems all good and bad things happen to me on Friday. I was born on a Friday, I met my wife on a Friday and on this particular Friday I was diagnosed as having prostate cancer! I had actually been undergoing some tests for stomach problems and the gastrologist had told his colleague, the urologist, to have me go through a very specific test for prostate cancer.

At the end of work that evening we all went out for a small going away party for Michael. After a few hours of laughter and fun the time came for me to go home and to tell my wife the diagnosis I'd received. This was one time when I wished I had still been drinking. Maybe, just maybe, had I been a bit tipsy it would have been easier to tell her. After dinner I asked Janet to sit with me on the couch. There I told her what the doctor had told me that afternoon. She sat there unable to utter a word, just looking at me as if, in those few seconds, I had grown horns or something equally scary. Finally she recovered from the shock and tears started to roll from her beautiful eyes. It was an emotional time. I have never been known to be a hero. Italians are not supposed to be heroes.

Yes I was scared and most of all I was frightened by the pain that would come with the cancer. When the urologist told me I had cancer and I needed to have an operation, I asked him what the consequences would be of not having one. He was very clear on the subject. He told me that I could live a normal life for maybe six or seven years and then die. To die per se wouldn't have been something that scared me. What did scare me was when he added, "In a lot of pain." That made me think about getting operated on and, hopefully, getting better soon. After holding each other and crying for a while Janet and I went to bed about eleven o'clock.

The next morning at 3.34 am we were awakened by a shaking of the building. We knew what it was. An earthquake of a magnitude of 8.8 on the Richter scale had hit Chile. We had prearranged that, in the event of an earthquake, we would slide off the bed and lie down on the floor each on our side. The china vase near the television in the bedroom came flying down breaking into thousands of pieces. The glasses of water by our bed smashed over us too. In the TV room outside the bedroom, the television flew off its stand and crashed to the floor. Miraculously no dishes or glasses had been sent flying out of the kitchen cabinets but power to the building was cut. The building continued to move for some time as if some kind of evil spirit had entered it and kept tossing it around while groaning and letting out loud screams of agony. It was indeed a scary experience.

As the building stopped moving I knew what I had to do. I had to leave Janet in the smashed up apartment and get to the hotel as quickly as possible. The road was clear, there were no fallen trees. I drove fast, got to the hotel and parked the car in the parking lot. As I drove up I saw that all the hotel guests plus the guests of the Boulevard Suite apartments were outside the hotel ... congregated under all the glass windows!

I went to my office where I always kept the bull horn and a flashlight ready and then proceeded to the front of the hotel. Sandra, the housekeeper, was already there passing out blankets to the guests who had rushed out of their rooms in their pyjamas, a sheet or nothing at all. Here I had to reassure all those fear-stricken guests that all was going to be alright if they followed my instructions.

Sounding my bullhorn to get their attention, I introduced myself and told them to follow my instruction as myself and the staff were trained for such an eventuality. I told them to get away from the windows and that the safest place was in their rooms. For anyone who didn't want to go to their rooms then the ballroom under the building was the safest place to be and we would serve food, coffee and tea to them in there. Nobody wanted to either go back to their room or, worse still, to the ballroom. I knew I had lost that battle. The only thing I could do was to get them as far away from the glass windows as possible. I rounded everyone up at the highest point and away from the windows.

There was only one injured guest. A lady had come down barefoot from the apartments and cut her foot on the stone in the driveway. The executive committee members and the managers who could make it all arrived within the hour. Even Michael Chait, the ex-director of engineering who was no longer an employee, came. He shocked me by his allegiance and I shocked him in return the following month when I called him in to receive an annual bonus cheque. He couldn't believe that I would give him this bonus even after he had left the company. But that night he earned it.

With the earthquake to deal with, the cancer issue had become secondary and I didn't give it any thought. The days ahead had to be totally dedicated to the hotel guests, many of whom were actually traumatized by the event. There were women shrieking, men crying like babies and all looking to me for relief from their anxiety, fear and confusion. Yet none were willing to go back to their rooms and wait there for instructions. The telephones were down, the power was off and the aftershocks kept coming.

Even when the power came back, a few hours later, the elevators had to be brought to the lobby floor and stopped. It was, of course, too potentially dangerous to ride in them. Guests going back to their rooms had to go by the stairs, twenty-five floors for some. Many got angry with me and the loss prevention manager for preventing them from using the elevators!

Sergio, the new director of engineering, and I, now set off to inspect the building from top to bottom. We climbed to the roof and walking down each stairway went from floor to floor walking the length of every corridor. We were amazed to see how little damage the hotel had suffered on the higher floors. On the eighteenth floor only one window was broken. As we arrived at the sixteenth floor the scene changed. The room doors that were closed wouldn't open and the ones that were open wouldn't close. Their frames were twisted like gigantic elastic bands. The ceiling and walls along the corridors and in most rooms had gaping cracks. That floor would remain closed for a long time to come. Fortunately, descending further, things were better. The damage became less and less until we reached the lobby and the cracks were none existent.

Here I found another problem. A lady guest was addressing a large group of fellow guests by the front desk to the effect that she was an architect from California and that the building was about to collapse. She was saying that she had looked up at the outside of the building and had seen that the connections holding the hotel tower and the office towers at each side had detached themselves from one another.

Not knowing if what she was saying was correct, and in order to avoid making the wrong decision, I called the architect who had built the hotel on my mobile phone. When I told this Sergio (yes same name as our new director of engineering) what the lady was saying he was extremely pleased. He told me that the buildings were designed to separate in the case of a strong quake in order to avoid one building pulling the other down and causing a total collapse. He also told me that he was on his way to the hotel at that moment specifically to check the foundation for any movement that might have cracked or moved the building.

When he arrived we went together down all the way to where he could see enough to be sure that the building had reacted to the

8.8 quake in just the way he had designed it to. Nothing had moved. I was totally confident that he was right and the Californian lady architect was wrong. Sergio had studied in Berkley and returned to Chile and assured me that the building codes in Chile were more stringent by far than those in California. Who knows? Maybe California should revise their codes and follow the lead of a small insignificant country – just for a change.

OUT OF THE ASHES

By that time Santiago Composto was not our regional vice president any more but he was the first regional team member to call and ask if any employees or guests had been injured. He didn't ask about the building damage or loss in revenue, his only concern was for the welfare of our people and our guests. This reminded me of the powerful yet human organisation we were all part of.

By the evening of that day we had calculated the quantity of food and bottled water we had at the hotel and concluded that, if the heavily damaged airport couldn't reopen for a week, we would still be able to keep our guests and staff fed. This was a reassuring thought. It wasn't so for our two main competitors. The Hyatt's newly renovated rooms had suffered tremendous damage and the Sheraton had suffered to the point that their general manager called me to ask if we could take all of their guests and airline crews staying with them. Unfortunately, I couldn't help him as we couldn't jeopardise the well-being of our own guests. I was really sad from the humane point of view to have to deny their request but it was the only possible decision at the time.

By the following day it was time to think about our community at large. In the south of Chile some buildings had collapsed, people had died and a tsunami had hit the coast. The reaction of the local people was tremendous. It was as if the world had come to an end and everyone was out there wanting to help others and displaying a solidarity in the face of adversity which was both humbling and inspirational.

The world at large also stepped in sending food, medication, clothing and human aid in the form of fire fighters, paramedics and specialist search and rescue teams. Police too came from all over as, in cases like this, looting is not uncommon. All aspects of the disaster were effectively contained and well controlled by the rapid response of the local authorities and the international community.

We, like all the others who could, did our bit to alleviate the suffering of the less fortunate who had seen their homes demolished by the quake or washed away by the waves. We concentrated, along with our sister hotel the Ritz-Carlton, on the charities the hotels had traditionally supported.

We had, since our inception, been involved with a home for mentally handicapped children and men so we collected and delivered all that we could to them. Our engineering team and lots of volunteers went there the next day to work on repairing the heavy damage the home had sustained. We also organised an expedition to the south of the country with two truck loads of goods and about twenty of our staff armed with shovels and a determination to help.

Slowly but steadily life in Chile returned to normal. The mission to repair the damage proceeded. Eventually Santiago airport was reopened and traffic in and out returned to normal. The airport authorities had done a remarkable job. The airport had been forced to close and the operation of it moved to an enormous tent in the parking lot as the entire ceiling of the terminal building had collapsed.

Sergio, the same architect who had built the hotel, had also worked on the airport building project. While the hotel belonged to his father and he had designed it correctly to withstand earthquakes, the airport was government owned and, to Sergio's frustration, he had been obliged to build it according to the specification given him by the owners. He had the foresight however to have had inserted in his contract a clause exonerating him of responsibility in the event of a catastrophe such as the earthquake because the transport authorities had rejected his plans.

Now, with the earthquake tragedy almost over, it was time for me to concentrate on the cancer operation. The 'jungle drums' in the hotel, often refered to as radio banana or radio corridor, ensure that information, gossip and scandal spread through the hotel like wildfire. Not only that but the information in question is elaborated on and distorted by each person who receives it. They each add their own embroidery or understanding to the story.

Therefore, in order to avoid me being dead before evening came, I had to quickly and almost simultaneously inform first my regional vice president, Andrew Houghton, second the hotel owners, third the executive committee and then the staff; the latter with whom I had called a special afternoon meeting at 3.00 pm. With that all done the urologist gave me the date for the operation.

Once again in my life the coincidence of Fridays and specific dates arose. The operation was scheduled for Saint Joseph's day, Friday, March the 19th 2010. Exactly forty-eight years to the day when I had fallen off the Vespa scooter and broke my right leg! Is this coincidence or was it preordained in my book of life? Each of us can make up our own mind on this subject and all of us would be right.

My belief, however, is that no matter how we try, our life is already written in the book of life and our lives just have to be lived according to it. We also called Emily and Paul that Monday to let them know what was happening and when the operation would take place. Emily and Paul showed little emotion on hearing the news. They were brave and offered only words of encouragement and reassurance that all would turn out well.

Getting myself emotionally and physically ready for the operation was a bit harder. It was starting to dawn on me that this was going to be no walk in the park type of thing. The hardest part for me was to accept that, if I survived, I would be out of work recuperating for two months. The evening before the operation I checked into the Clinica Alemana, a very good private hospital located between the apartment and the hotel. The next morning off I went to be prepared for the operation which would last four hours. I only remember being on the operating bed and feeling very cold. The anesthesiologist came and put me to sleep. From there on I do not know what happened until I was slowly waking up in the late afternoon in a room other than the room I was put in the night before. It was there that I saw Janet standing by me, looking down at me, her eyes were shining and she wore a smile.

This reassured me that everything had gone well and I was still alive. What was not nice is that I had a catheter and a urine bag hanging on the side of the bed. Being moved back into my original room made me feel kind of better. When I awoke from the first of many in and out sleeps and saw Paul there, that was better still. Emily was able to come two days later. I knew the love of my family was strong and would help to pull me through. From the hotel Victor and Claudia came to visit and Eduardo Fahrenkrug, the general manager of the Crowne Plaza came to see me too.

I was let out on the fifth day after the operation but had to keep the urine bag attached to me for several more days afterwards. The urologist, who by then was a good friend, told me that the cancer had encompassed all of the prostate and gone outside of it. This meant he had to take the prostate gland out and carve around it to get all of the cancer. It seems he did a good job. At the time of this writing, eight years have gone by and the PSA reading is only 0.04. Remarkable!

The two months of recuperation passed slowly. I started walking a few steps around the apartment. A week or so later I went out of the apartment and walked along by the river flowing nearby. It was just a short distance but I went quicker and further by the second week. The bag was removed and I had to learn again how to pee. It sounds strange that at the age of sixty-six years I had to learn to do that again. By the first week in May, Janet and I were ready to take a trip to Europe.

We flew business class as usual with a stop in Portugal to see the house and our new tenants. Paul joined us there for one night. The following day the three of us flew to Italy to visit with family who no longer comprised my sister. We stayed at my niece's home where we shared one room. It was, sadly, the last time we stayed there as our relationship with their family is not what I would like it to be.

Here is where, on May the 9th, Janet and I celebrated mothers' day in a restaurant by the side of Lake Orta in the village of Pella. It was a rainy day, blustery and cold. Paul left the following day and we too left for London to visit with Janet's sister and family.

Chapter 23

A NEW HORIZON

My energy had returned and I was now feeling ready to go back to work. Life looked bright again. The staff at the hotel laid on a super celebration party upon my return to work. They were genuinely nice people who wanted a leader with grey hair to lead them down the path of success ... whatever that meant for them. During our visit to Portugal and to our house, Janet and I had decided it was time to start thinking of retirement. Our new tenants were an English couple called Taf (that's fat spelled backwards)! and his lady friend who was twenty years older than him. They seemed to be madly in love with each other so that was probably the most important thing.

While our first tenants, Rita and Brian, who had occupied the house for almost fifteen years had taken care of the house as if it were their own, this couple were sloppy and cheap. We found that, in spite of letting them select the furniture when the five year lease started in 2007, they had installed their own furniture and locked ours up in the third bedroom. There it rotted with the humidity. Praia da Luz is by the sea and, as such, always humid. We had left a dehumidifier for them to use to keep the house dry. They hadn't used it in order to save electricity – and having to pay for it. It was heart breaking for Janet and I to see the deterioration in the condition of our house in only three years.

The end of year holiday season soon came around again. Plans were made and events staged for the Christmas and New Year festivities. 2011 chimed in without any major happenings until Victor was presented with the opportunity for him and his family to move to Kuala Lumpur. He had worked in Dubai with Garrett, who was now the regional vice president of operations for Asia. When the Renaissance in Kuala Lumpur had an opening for a director of operations, Garrett offered Victor the job. Anna, Victor's young wife, didn't really want to move again from Santiago but the opportunity for Victor was too good to pass. They went and I was left to fend for myself once again. However, Victor found himself in a nine hundred room property with a general manager whose methods were much different to mine, a need to speak English all the time, a younger boy who had become very ill and his wife Anna pregnant with their third child. As a result they soon decided to return to Chile. There was no opening at our hotel for Victor so he took the position of vice president of operations for Chile and Peru at Atton Hotels. This is a local hotel group which became a big success story in a very short time.

With January of 2011 our now traditional anniversary theme party took place. It was, yet again, a huge success. The big event of that year arrived with US President Barak Obama's visit to Chile and his stay at the Hyatt Hotel in Santiago. This suited us fine because, to our great pleasure, we had the press instead. The Hyatt always seemed to do us big favours, unintentionally of course, but, by having the President and his delegation there it meant that their guests were subjected to the mess the Secret Service creates for the hotel in the course of their duties.

The press, on the other hand, pay the rates required, spend most of the day and night out of the hotel chasing the President and his delegation and, with the possible exception of a rugby team, are the biggest spending bar customers going. It was a win-win situation. Hyatt got the honour, we got the money. As the mortgage cannot be paid with honour we were happy to take the cash. All the business leaders were invited to go to hear Obama deliver a speech at the convention centre. Eduardo Fahrenkrug and I went along to enjoy the impressive eloquence, if not the content, of what he had to say.

It was shortly after this event that we undertook a total room renovation project. We changed all the carpets, curtains and bedding and updated all the furniture. We replaced every TV with a modern flat screen model. Time was of the essence as the

Presidential Suite had been booked by a famous Mexican singer for three nights at the end of July. He wouldn't come if there was noise or dust. It was a tremendous job done in record time to have, not only the suite, but all the other rooms redecorated and smelling of fresh paint ahead of schedule. It was indeed a masterpiece.

While the remodelling was still in progress I was introduced by other ambassadors at a social event to the latest arrival in the field - Ambassador Abdullah Mohammed Al Mui'ina of the UAE. His Excellency, along with his spouse Madame Aida and their three sons plus a nanny were staying at the Hyatt. This was a formal introduction and people from that part of the world do not discuss business at a social gathering. We exchanged business cards. The next day I received a call from his secretary inquiring as to my availability to receive him at the hotel and show him around. Naturally I became immediately available. An appointment was set and I received him at the front door as protocol would require. After a few minutes of pleasantries and black tea he told me that he was considering moving his family from the Hyatt for a period that could be several months. He needed the Presidential Suite plus three rooms.

Knowing that he was staying in the Presidential Suite at the Hyatt, I was a bit reluctant to even show him ours as it would be considered second class compared to their one. His Excellency quickly told me that he had heard of the difference in grandeur of the product, however, he would still be grateful if I would be so kind as to show it to him anyway. The renovation of the suite was not quite completed at that point but I took him upstairs to see it anyway.

He liked what he saw and we came to an agreement on price right there and then. We arranged that he and his family would move in the very day our famous singer checked out. It all worked out perfectly and they stayed for a full seven months. It was a delight to have them in the hotel. The children were respectful and quiet and Madame Aida his wife, a Tunisian by birth, was a perfect lady. She was soft spoken and very supportive of her children and husband. Every few weeks His Excellency invited me to the suite for tea and a chat and he paid his bill within forty-eight hours of it having been sent to Abu Dhabi. It was a tremendous shot in the arm for us to have this revenue every month without any trouble or interruptions.

Not only did he and his family stay all this time in the hotel, he also arranged for us to host his National Day celebration party. The event proved to be like an Arabian Nights adventure. An original Bedouin tent was set up in the outer courtyard while the ballroom was transformed into the most elegant of the European classics. There was one issue that kept the ambassador awake at night for about a month before the party. When he booked the ballroom I had to inform him that it was already booked until 6.00 pm that day by another group for a meeting of four hundred people. He turned pale because he wasn't convinced that we could turn the room over and be ready for his party by 8.00 pm. It took a lot to convince him to trust me to make it happen but I knew the team that was behind me. They were the ones who would turn my promises into reality and make it all happen. My team was just itching for challenges like that.

The day came. At 6.00 pm our team and I were outside the ballroom waiting for the other group to leave. Lo and behold, who should be standing next to me with a worried look on his face? - His Excellency! still not convinced that we could achieve 'the impossible'.

We were ready, a plan of action in place and each of our team had a task assigned to them. As soon as the other group moved out some team members took away and stacked the four hundred chairs while others folded and carried away the tables. Simultaneous to this we had team members carry in and set up the new tables. The coup de grâce of all this came when His Excellency saw our director of sales and marketing hoovering the ballroom with a gigantic vacuum cleaner. To his amazement the ballroom was emptied, cleaned and reset in forty minutes. Thus giving him another hour and twenty minutes before his party started.

The evening party went off without a hitch and was a roaring success. At my next tea meeting with His Excellency he gave me the biggest box of UAE dates I had ever seen and a Roberto Cavalli wrist watch to show his appreciation and thanks for what we had achieved that night. More importantly, he revealed to me that he had moved himself and family from the Hyatt because he wanted to have a personal relationship with the general manager of the hotel. According to him he had never even met the Hyatt general manager. At the UAE National Day party the following year he honoured me with a plaque and a thank you speech as I was going to retire in two months and move to Portugal.

Prior to that, on August the 30th of 2011, Jenny the singing teacher organised a concert to be given by all her students in the Marriott hotel ballroom. I was to sing two songs - Va Pensiero, the aria from the opera Nabucco in duet with Jenny, and Historia de un Amor as a soloist. I did indeed perform. When I see it on DVD now I realise how poor both songs turned out to be. It was, however, important for me to stand up in front of more than two hundred people and have the courage to sing.

A NOT SO CHILLY DIP

In September of 2011 Janet and I took a trip to visit the Termas Geometricas. We stopped en route at Rari situated at the foot of the Andes in the south of Chile. While unknown to the outside world, the village is famous locally for the magnificent butterflies, earrings, flowers, bracelets, necklaces and brooches which local craftsmen and women lovingly create from horse hair. Be it hair from the tail or the mane, the passion which the villagers put into this dying art is to be admired. I have had the good fortune to see many people in many parts of the world create many beautiful things out of nothing, and mostly out of financial necessity, but here it is done just for the love of what they do. The results are truly remarkable.

It is a more than five hour drive from Rari to the Termas Geometricas which are well hidden in the beauty and the majesty of the Villarrica National Park, near Coñaripe and near the

Argentinian border. These hot springs are unique. The best way to enjoy them is by walking on the redwood walkways to the very top. There, a most magnificent hot water spout shoots steam into the sky creating a perennial rainbow. The way down meant going from pond to pond, seventeen slate covered ponds in total, of hot water. The temperature of the water is between 95 and 102°F (35 and 39°C). All the way down we experienced one of the most spectacular feelings of being at one with nature. The greenery, the dew, the hot steam coming up from the waters and the fresh smell of nature was just overwhelming.

Now imagine this ... You are sitting in water at 95°F (35°C) and the hot steam you just saw rising has gone up high enough into the cold sky to be turned into droplets of cool rain which then drizzle on to your head. Your head is cold and the rest of your body is hot. What a sensation! It is so revitalising as all aches and pain magically depart your body and vanish into the water. Never had we seen any hot water spa which came close to this. What we experienced in these ponds while working our way down cannot be described with words, you must live it to believe it. After a few hours of this sublime bliss we headed back to the hotel in time for an afternoon tea and a well-deserved nap before dinner.

Our tenants in Portugal had difficulty in keeping up to date with their rent. They never told me. I only found out when the bank statement arrived in the mail and I saw that the monthly payment had been skipped. Eventually they were able to bring their payments up to date and asked if we would extend their contract for another five years. We replied that we were planning to retire the following year but that we would honour the life of the present contract which was due to expire on October the 31st of 2012. This made them decide to move out of the house one year earlier than it was contracted for. As they moved out we planned to be there to receive the house back and take an inventory. What a disaster it turned out to be.

Janet and I thought it would be good to sleep in the house to get a feel for it. Well, the sheets on the bed were damp to the point of feeling the wet getting into our bones. After the first night, we couldn't breathe any longer. We had to leave the house and check into a nearby hotel. The walls of the rooms were so thick with fungus and black mould, and the house in such general disrepair, that we decided to completely renovate it. We drew up plans with an architect, recommended by a friendly neighbour called David, to remodel the home and enlarge it by 1,070 square feet (100 sq.m), add a garage, install a swimming pool and a jacuzzi.

Returning to Chile we were getting ever more excited, and nervous at the same time, about our move to Portugal and into retirement. We were after all, on the verge of a complete change of life and taking on a new country, culture and language. So 2011 came to an end and the festivities started again with both our daughter Emily and son Paul coming to visit. It felt so good to spend time with them.

As 2012 started, with it came the hotel anniversary party. We had not told anyone that we would be retiring at the end of this year so in my mind I was sure that this would be the last of the annual parties in which I would participate.

Then, as spring time rolled around, a big project started at the hotel. After two years of debating back and forth with Marriott, owners, architects and decorators, it was finally decided that the great room, which meant the lobby, would be renovated. Katja, the architect, had worked with Marriott to produce the blueprints, the colour boards and sourced all of the materials. Then the general contractor was chosen and the stripping out of the old lobby started. We had to have all this work done in the shortest time possible and a deadline for completion was set so as to minimise inconvenience to our guests and loss of revenue to the hotel. As work progressed the dust, the noise of cutting down the huge marble planters and the demolition of the gift shop were so overwhelming that we were starting to lose guests to other hotels. The contractor was simply not moving fast enough. I had to do something about it.

One afternoon I got so frustrated and annoyed that I went home, got into my old jeans and an old shirt, returned to the hotel and, taking a hammer from the construction man, climbed a ladder and started smashing a wall. I had studied the plans so well that I knew which wall had to come down and which one had to be maintained. What happened next was just amazing.

About ten of my staff, seeing what I was doing, joined in. Before the contractor could react the wall was down and the material removed. The power of leading by example is never to be underestimated. This action not only prompted that reaction from our team but the contractor got a message as well. After sweating tears and a lot of nerve-racking the lobby was completed with very little delay. The end result was outstanding and my last goal at the hotel had been accomplished.

ONE LAST BLAST

About the same time as this was happening the last weird episode with a guest took place. It was by far the most bizarre situation I encountered in all my years in the business. One morning, about 11.00 am, I received a call from reception to tell me that a naked Colombian was standing there and wanted to talk to me. After the first shock and collecting my thoughts, I walked down to see a man with a bath towel wrapped around his waist. He was clearly upset and claiming that he had been robbed. I knew that the first thing I had to do was to remove him from the area. Employing the strategy I had learned and used many times at the Fun & Family Resort, I started walking the man to where two small conference rooms had just been completed nearby and into one of them.

Now he was out of view of the staff and other guests. He continued to remonstrate wildly so I ordered up a coffee for him and let him calm down. Then I asked him to tell me what had happened. His story went something like this ...

"Last night I took a taxi from the street outside the hotel and went to a restaurant for dinner. After dinner I went to Suecia (the red light district in the city). I sat at the bar and ordered a drink. A nice young couple of locals came and sat next to me. We started chatting and after a while the girl invited me to dance. We went to the dance floor and danced for a while. When we returned to the bar I looked at my watch. It was ten to two in the morning. I thought that it was time for me to go to sleep as I had to go to work this morning. I finished my drink in one gulp. The next thing I know after that is that I woke up this morning on my bed in the hotel and all my clothes, my wallet, my computer and even my cigarettes are gone. Those two young people drugged me then came to the room and took everything. What are you going to do about it? I expect the hotel to buy me clothes, a computer and replace all that was taken from my room."

I was stunned by what I had just heard. It was obvious to me that he was totally out of himself. I called Juan Jose, the loss prevention manager, to come up and together we went to the guest's room. It was very clear to us that the young couple had known very well what to do. I told the guest that I needed to understand what had happened inside the hotel. After arranging breakfast for him in his room, Juan Jose and I went to the security room to review the images the cameras had recorded. It was all there to see.

The young couple had come back to the hotel with him in a car. They had walked into the lobby and to the elevator, went up to his room and opened the door with his key. Inside the room there were no cameras but we easily deduced that he passed out on the bed and the young couple then undressed him, took his own bag and put everything inside it.

Then they both walked to the elevator landing. She took the first elevator down and went to the front desk to ask John, the night manager, for a box of matches. While telling John that she'd just been upstairs visiting her boyfriend's uncle, her accomplice came down in the other elevator and slipped out the side door unseen. The girl thanked John for the box of matches and left without raising any suspicion that a crime had been committed.

Now we had more facts we returned to the guest's room and

told him that he had the simple choice to make of either involving the police or not. If we called the police his story would become public. He would feature on TV, in the newspapers and every journalist in Santiago would want to interview him. We warned him that he would become famous (or infamous) all over South America. This would include Colombia where his wife would see him on television naked in a hotel lobby with just a towel wrapped around his waist. He thought a minute about that and decided not to get the police involved.

He persisted to claim, however, that his robbery by these people was the fault of the hotel. At this point, I walked him through the facts. I asked him if the hotel had arranged for the taxi to take him to dinner, the answer was no. I asked him if anyone from the hotel had recommended that he should go to the red light district, the answer was no. I asked him if anyone from the hotel had told him to talk with the young couple and dance with the girl, the answer was again no. I asked him if the hotel had brought the young couple and him back to the hotel and taken them to his room, again the answer was no. I told him that the hotel was not in a position to help him out and couldn't give him anything back. He was furious.

I made the suggestion that he should call his company and ask someone there to go to a store and buy him some clothes, underwear, socks, shoes, trousers, shirt, jacket and watch and have them delivered to him at the hotel. He was not happy to do so but eventually, under threat that I would call the police and let them handle the situation, he agreed. With that accomplished he once more had clothes and could go out in the street again.

Not too long after that I received a call from the manager of his company blustering me for not being flexible about the misfortune that had befallen the guy. My line remained the same – that the hotel was never involved in any of this guy's misadventures. In the evening when he returned to the hotel he once again approached me asking that I pay for the clothes the company had bought for him. Now I decided to put a stop to all this nonsense once and for all. I told him flat out that before I would pay I would call his wife in Colombia and tell her the whole sordid story. This action on my part closed the case and he was never seen or heard from again.

With time moving on, I returned to Portugal to check up on progress at the house. All appeared to be advancing satisfactorily. We had agreed with the architect that the house would be ready on the 1st of May 2013. Back in Santiago the time to inform the regional vice president of my decision to retire was approaching. Normally there was a three month notice period required. As my relationship with Andrew was extremely good, I informed him four months ahead of my intended 31st of December retirement date. I also informed the owners, the executive committee and all the staff. This announcement provoked mixed reactions around the hotel with some people bursting into tears every time they saw me. I believe that most people were genuinely sad to see me go. If anyone was happy at the prospect of my departure then they were very good at hiding it.

The first week of December was time for my PSA test again. The result was 0.09 and the doctor suggested that I should undergo a programme of thirty-six radiation sessions to make sure that, if there were any cancer cells still alive in my body, they would be cooked. Also, in the first week of December, the Marriott general managers' conference took place in Orlando. Andrew organised a going away party for me there. It was a nostalgic but hugely enjoyable event. I received many gifts to treasure, particularly photo albums, from many wonderful friends and colleagues I had known for so many years.

The radiation treatment started on the 19th of December and was scheduled to continue until the 1st of February. I informed Andrew of this delay but it was not a problem for him. He was very understanding of the situation and permitted me to extend my stay as long as I needed to.

Christmas arrived once more and Emily and Paul were coming to Santiago again for our last celebration of the festivities there. I had accepted an invitation to sing at the Christmas Eve watch night service at the church. Paul's flight was scheduled to land at the airport at just about the same time. Janet waited there to pick him up as soon as he arrived and whisk him to the church. Smack on time, just as I was about to sing the Christmas carol, Janet and Paul walked in and joined Emily in front of me in the congregation. What timing. It was so special to have my family there with me at that happy but poignant moment. I sang as I'd never sang before!

There was one last Marriott anniversary party. One more than I had expected but this really was the last. My radiation sessions were completed and the trip into our new life, in every meaning of the expression, was set to begin. With a new horizon set firmly in our sights, I bade my friends and colleagues one fond and final farewell. We didn't know what might lie ahead for us, who does? Whatever it is, and as wonderful as it might be, it would be hard to surpass all the wonder and blessings of life enjoyed thus far.

There is a time for everything and now is my time to say - Goodbye my dearest friends, I shall forever remember you. Just as I remember that my blessed life commenced in the most humble of surroundings but which, fanned by my mother's vision of a grander life for me in the world of luxury hotel restaurants, blossomed into what I believe has been a fitting tribute to her and her dream for me. The same dream that I carried with me into the world all those years ago - in a simple cardboard suitcase.

EPILOGUE

When I returned to my home in Portugal, there on the desk in my study was a stack of photographs of every hotel and restaurant in which I ever worked. Also a staff photo from each one.

And there was a plain card on which the following words had been hand written -

"Hospitality management is one of the most complex and rewarding of leadership careers. You are not only delivering a service, you're fashioning exceptional experiences for guests and helping them to create memories. To do that well takes dedication, determination, supportive colleagues, a loving family and - a touch of inspiration."

Atop the card and the pile of fading nostalgia was perched ... a single white bow tie. And the whole collection was packed inside an old cardboard suitcase.

END

Peter Giacomini

COPYRIGHT AND DISCLAIMER

The Cardboard Suitcase

Adventure, Travel, Romance - A Poor Boy's Dreams Explode Into Reality!

ISBN : 978-1721704002

© Peter Giacomini 2018 all rights reserved